the World Guide to

Whale & Dolphin

Watching

Ben Wilson & Angus Wilson

Colin Baxter Photography, Grantown-on-Spey, Scotland

Contents

Atlantic Spotted Dolphins.

Whale & Dolphin Watching

"Whales should be seen and not hurt" Vassili Papastavrou

Throughout history, whales, dolphins and porpoises have held a unique place in the human imagination. Once the stuff of fishermen's yarns and hefty literary classics, nowadays anyone can experience the unparalleled excitement of an eye-to-eye encounter with a curious whale, enjoy the thrill of cavorting wild dolphins and even savor the fishy stench of a Minke Whale's breath! "Whale watching", as the activity is known, has undergone a meteoric growth since its beginnings in the early 1970s and a new multi-million-dollar industry has grown on this wave of enthusiasm. Opportunities for whale watching are abundant and every day, thousands of people have experiences to rival those of weather-beaten seafarers of old.

This guide is a celebration of whales, dolphins and porpoises and the many different ways that one can see them in the wild. The book is divided into ten chapters and begins by outlining the history of the whale-watching phenomenon, the ways that humans have and continue to exploit whales and how scientists have discovered what we now know about them. Subsequent chapters describe the astonishing lives of these mammals and how the whale watcher can reliably distinguish one from another at sea. The identification section focuses on the species that dedicated whale watchers are likely to encounter. The activity of whale watching itself can take many forms and one chapter is devoted to personal experiences. Guest authors describe their own adventures, reactions and lasting memories. The next two chapters give tips and practical advice for anyone intending to go whale watching. The key points to look for when choosing a trip are described, together with some words on equipment and clothing. The rest of the book is dedicated to a region-by-region guide to the many whale, dolphin and porpoise-watching opportunities available throughout the world. It is in this section that the truly global nature of this wildlife viewing phenomenon becomes apparent. Regions and specific hotspots are covered systematically, along with details of the different types of whale-watch opportunities that are available and the species to expect. This section will be of value to anyone who is planning a whale-watching holiday or wishing to identify the nearest whale-watching locations to where they live. Finally, we finish the book with a directory for finding further information.

There are few people who have been on a whale-watching adventure and not come back with treasured memories. Opportunities to see these animals are everywhere and the diversity of species is astonishing. This world guide will help you identify where, how, whom and what you can experience when out whale watching.

An eye-to-eye encounter with a Gray Whale.

The Whale-Watching Phenomenon

Just two decades ago, if you were to ask the average person or dedicated expert, what opportunities there were for a tourist to go and watch whales, they'd invariably reply with slim odds and a distant location. Much has changed since then.

Put simply, the essential requirement for successful whale watching is getting the whales and watchers (tourists, naturalists, whomever) within viewing distance of one another. Capturing whales and holding them in aquaria is obviously one way of doing it, but raises ethical concerns and loses the unmatched thrill of seeing animals in the wild. So it is the watchers that need to go out in search of their quarry. This idea may immediately conjure up the vision of an intrepid, sou'wester-clad, seasick landlubber clutching a sopping camera on a bucking, spray-tossed vessel with land a distant memory. And in this vision is the key to where whale watching has changed so radically and so recently. Fishermen, ferry drivers and marine biologists knew what this key was, bird watchers and even coastal dog walkers did too; while they were aware, somehow, that, like so much else in life, things didn't happen until the time was right and other factors came into place.

Whale watching isn't just watching whales; the term has a wider meaning. The term should actually be cetacean watching. The cetaceans are a collective group of air-breathing, warm-blooded mammals that contains the whales as well as their close relatives the dolphins and porpoises. But because the earliest cetacean-watching tours were focused on seeing whales, the term "whale watching" has stuck.

What the coastal boat users, bird watchers and dog walkers knew was that potential watchers and cetaceans weren't far apart at all, and that seeing these animals didn't involve slim odds or substantial travel or even a sou'wester hat. Cetaceans, contrary to the popular perception, are surprisingly widespread, common and easy to see. They visit or live along most of the world's coastlines, they come close in-shore, many are not at all shy of boats and most, as we shall describe, are spectacular to watch.

Tourists, naturalists, enthusiasts and local residents alike, the world over, choose their pleasure activities from the opportunities available to them. If no one is offering whale watching as a pursuit then few will ask for it. But if the opportunity is on offer then many will take part. Conversely, without a demand, fishermen, retired ferry drivers and local entrepreneurs won't invest their capital in boats, licenses, safety equipment, guides, merchandise and all the other paraphernalia required to make a living from the activity. This pattern of lack of demand and lack of opportunity forms a vicious circle. In consequence, the vast resource now known

Once the preserve of intrepid mariners, spectacular views of whales are now available to all.

as whale watching remained untapped until very recently. It took just a few adventurous people and a few chance events to get the snowball rolling, and it is still rolling, ever larger, to this day.

Whale watching is now a huge and global activity. It is supported by an industry of professional operators, guides and support staff. Whale-watching companies large and small operate in over 87 countries, from Ireland to New Zealand, Chile to Russia. It is a pursuit that is common to both the developed and the developing world. Whale watchers are to be found in almost any coastal waters from the poles to the tropics. Most watching goes on in coastal areas but enthusiasts now venture far across the great oceans and even deep into the South American rainforests in search of their quarry. Over 10 million people enjoy the pursuit each year. That's equivalent to the populations of Chicago, Los Angeles and Seattle combined. Just imagine how many cherished memories and stories that amounts to. At any moment, over 1000 people are watching whales, dolphins or porpoises somewhere on the globe. Together we spend the equivalent of US$ 1.2 billion each year to watch these magnificent creatures. Of course, most of our knowledge of the whale-watching pursuit comes from fee-charging, organized trips, that either go out specifically to take people to see cetaceans or include them as part of a wider natural history experience. Not included in these figures are the many millions of lucky encounters that people have while sailing or fishing, while riding ferries or beach walking.

A Dusky Dolphin, New Zealand.

The majority of platforms used for commercial whale watching are boats. These range from the tiny to the enormous, the simple to the complex – from kayaks to cruise liners, converted fishing boats to multi-million-dollar multi-hulls. Their size and shape will depend on a plethora of factors: the operating distance from port, the local sea conditions, the maturity of the industry, the behavior of the cetaceans and the nature of the experience desired by the watchers themselves. Needless to say, the type of boat will have a significant bearing on the experience that it's possible to have. Imagine the difference: you leave port on a spacious 100 ft steel boat. The guides spot whales far off on the horizon. Getting closer, you are privileged to get a bird's-eye view of a pod of Killer Whales herding a school of fish towards the shoreline. The guide explains what you are seeing and the comfort of the boat provides shelter from any wind or rain.

Now imagine instead you were out in a kayak and your guided group happens upon the same incident. This time the fish school passes underneath your boat long before you are even aware of anything untoward. You are intently concentrating on your aching arm muscles and the puddle of water sloshing around your seat when you are confronted with a line of whales coming straight towards you. They surface just a paddle's reach in front of you. Moments later their wakes buffet your kayak, you are drizzled by the spray of their breaths and shaken through your seat by their triumphant calls. The platform makes a big difference to the experience!

While the choice of platform does much to define the experience, so too does the duration of the trip. Most common are the focused whale-watch trips of just a few hours. You turn up at the harbor, for example, buy your ticket, board a waiting boat and are taken out to see a local group of whales or dolphins. These trips generally cater to all-comers and the nature of the experience is usually fairly clear before you set out – so much so that many of the companies organizing such trips offer money-back guarantees if nothing is seen. Longer trips have the

Boat size makes a difference to the experience.

potential to be far more adventurous. Live-aboard trips, as the name suggests, offer boat trips that might last days or weeks and cover far wider areas of sea. They may target remote places that are especially good for a particular species or event or may simply offer the chance for wholly unexpected encounters. Live-aboards can range from small motor or sail boats with perhaps a dozen people on board up to the cruise liners that can take passengers rapidly to extreme locations like the Antarctic ice edge or hundreds of miles across the open ocean.

Not all whale watching involves boats. Over a quarter of all commercial whale watching takes place from land. Positioned in sites where cetaceans come predictably close inshore, you can enjoy watching them with binoculars, telescopes or simply the naked eye. Though the experience may be more distant, the contact time can be far longer and more natural. Standing on the beach or on a cliff top, your presence has no direct impact on the animals you are watching and so you can wait and watch for hours without concern.

At the other end of the opportunity spectrum, there are a surprising number of chances to view cetaceans from small airplanes or helicopters. The experiences may be brief and noisy but the views, especially of large whales, can be unparalleled. Of course, many watchers are not simply content with fleeting glimpses as their quarry snatches a breath at the surface. Getting into the water with wild whales or dolphins offers a quite different experience. In doing so, the watcher invites the whales or dolphins to be the master of ceremonies. Most underwater encounters with wild cetaceans involve a small number of "friendly" dolphins, which take up residence in coastal areas. For whatever reason, these lone dolphins tolerate or even seek out human contact. As they have met thousands of flailing wetsuit-clad humans over the years of their tenancies they have created almost as many stories of their antics, skills and sensitivities. Not all swim-with programs focus on these socially mysterious creatures; in a variety of locations swimmers can be literally dropped into the lives of fully wild groups of dolphins or whales. The swimmer may experience a brief sight of these animals from within the splendor of their natural element or they may get a much more intense experience. Dolphins are notoriously curious and playful and it's not unusual for a swimmer to be inspected, teased

Bottlenose Dolphins are often curious.

and then played with. The watcher thus becomes the watched. In so many ways, swimming with cetaceans is an entirely different experience to other forms of whale watching for both parties. It is not without some risks and many are concerned that, unless carefully regulated, these kinds of wildlife adventure can become just a little too intrusive.

"Whale watching" is an all-encompassing term and nothing in it suggests that the whale, dolphin or porpoise being watched needs to be healthy or even alive! There are many millions of individual cetaceans swimming about in the world's oceans and every year a small percentage of them come ashore injured, disorientated or dead. These events are in themselves tragic but invariably draw our interest. Newspapers around the world are littered with descriptions of stranded whales and, for regular beach walkers, finding a beach-cast cetacean is not as uncommon as one might expect. Let's face it, cetaceans are pretty unusual-looking creatures and few would pass up the opportunity for a really good look at one. As a result, when a whale strands within reach of onlookers, crowd control frequently becomes as much an issue for the on-scene authorities as dealing with the animal. Looking at stranded cetaceans is certainly not something marketed by the whale-watch industry but the opportunity of seeing one of these animals, quite literally in the flesh, is not something that should be passed up lightly.

Whale watching in its many forms encompasses an enormous range of natural history experiences. A watcher may happen upon one of these animals while doing something completely different and simply gain a few moments' pleasure. Alternatively, he or she may have spent years planning a single trip and invested the price of a luxury car to make it happen. Most of us, however, encounter whales either as part of a short, organized whale-watching boat trip or from a coastal vantage point. These simple activities now form the backbone of the global whale-watching industry, an economic entity that has experienced meteoric growth in recent years.

History

Modern whale watching began with the Gray Whale. These animals live in the coastal waters of the North Pacific. The best-known population spends its winters breeding in the sheltered waters off Mexico but feeds in the chilly waters of Alaska and the Bering Sea. To get from one place to the other, these whales migrate along the coastline of the western US and Canada, northwards in early spring and south during the fall. Being coastal, and relatively slow swimmers, they were a favorite target for whalers and as a result their numbers were decimated. Motivated by concerns for their survival, students from Scripps Institution of Oceanography in San Diego began a research study. From the mid 1940s, they stood atop tall buildings, headlands and lighthouses and counted the whales as they went by the shore on their annual migrations. It turned out to be a popular pursuit. In 1950, a land-based whale lookout was set up at the Cabrillo National Monument, which commemorates the arrival of the first European in western North America. In its first winter 10,000 people came to see the whales go by. Land-based whale watching was born!

It wasn't long before people were paying a dollar a head for the ride on a boat for a closer look. It's one thing to stand on a headland watching whales pass from stage left to stage right but quite another to go out there, experience the thrill of the hunt and get close enough to see their mottled skin, smell their acrid breath and have them look back up at you. A pioneer whale-watching naturalist, Raymond M. Gilmore, turned these trips into something of a Californian legend. His trips represented whale watching at its best – part science, part education, and full of unpredictable events. So popular were his trips that he continued them for three decades. As the number of people going to see the whales grew, so did the fledgling industry. Boat tours and land-based watching spread slowly northward up the Californian coast to Oregon and Washington. It also spread south, and in 1972 the first long-range commercial whale-watch trip to the Mexican calving lagoons began.

Meanwhile, over in Atlantic Canada, the Zoological Society of Montreal began offering whale-watch tours in the Gulf of St Lawrence. The rationale behind these trips stemmed from conservation objectives. If people could see whales in their natural environment, the thinking went, they would be more interested in protecting them. The excursions that the Society organized passed through some of the world's most accessible concentrations of whales. Passengers were frequently lucky enough to see Fin, Minke and Beluga Whales. The trips were popular and the

Humpback Whales are the mainstay of modern whale watching.

Society ran them for 29 consecutive years until they were superseded by a rapidly growing independent whale-watch industry.

However, it was Humpback Whales that were, and still are, the true celebrities of the whale-watching world. Their magnificent fluffy exhalations, their capacity to leap clear of the water over and over again, their habit of lifting their tail flukes high into the air before dives and their curiosity of boats meant that when watchers encountered these whales, they would really see something to remember. In New England and Hawaii, tours to see Humpbacks began in 1975. The Humpbacks in Hawaii were there to breed and the centrally positioned tourist haven of Maui became the hub of Humpback watching, not only of Hawaii but also of the whole

Pacific. In contrast, the whales off New England were there not to breed, but to feed. They concentrate their efforts over an offshore patch of water called the Stellwagen Bank. Being shallow and muddy, the waters around the bank support a productive ecosystem and the whales cash in on the fish that it produces. In turn, the whale-watch boats are there to cash in on the Humpback Whales as well as Right, Fin, Minke and Pilot Whales – and dolphins and porpoises. In terms of a location, the Stellwagen Bank is positioned well, sitting directly offshore of several major population centers, Gloucester, Provincetown and Boston. The combination of predictable whale sightings, charismatic species and accessibility for watchers meant that within a decade of the New England watching industry starting, it dwarfed the Hawaiian and Californian experiences from which it was born.

From New Zealand to Iceland, whale watching is now a global phenomenon.

In the late 1980s whale watching became a global phenomenon. New whale-watch industries started up in the Canary Islands, the Azores, Central America, the Caribbean, Italy, Madagascar and New Zealand, while existing industries expanded rapidly in Argentina, Australia, South Africa and Canada. In the 1990s, the watching bug spread to Norway and Japan, countries that, ironically, continue to support the killing of whales for their meat. The Norwegian experience drew tourists from throughout Europe to the frigid and wild polar north to see Sperm Whales in summer and Killer Whales in winter, while the Japanese industry got its clientele from Japan itself. A third pro-whaling nation, Iceland, gained the honor in the late 1990s of being the fastest-growing whale-watch destination in Europe. The country hosted over 30,000 whale-watching visitors in 1998, who injected the equivalent of US$ 6 million into the nation's economy.

There is an exclusive club among the whale-watch nations – the "million watchers a year" club. So far the two continental-scale nations of the United States and

Canada are members. The third member is the Canary Islands, a tiny group of Spanish islands off the coast of North Africa. Here the main quarry are Pilot Whales. The predictable presence of these deep-diving, social whales, their interesting behavior, the favorable climate and the seemingly endless supply of European tourists provided fertile soil for an industry seeded in the late 1980s to grow, mature and flourish.

Elsewhere, whale watching is on an entirely different scale. Not far from the Canary Islands, on the African mainland, is the tiny country of The Gambia, which hosts a similarly tiny whale-watch industry. A handful of boats take tourists for daytrips up the estuary to see the sights. On the way home they usually spend some time with the local dolphin population. The operators run small-scale and personal companies, take out comparatively few tourists each year and feature the dolphins as only one part of the trip. At present it's a small local industry but one that suits the setting.

Collectively, the experiences and species available are simply enormous and new technologies and imaginative approaches continue to expand the boundaries. The whale-watching boats, for example, often aid scientists studying whales by directly funding them or by giving them a platform from which to work. In turn, insights gleaned from the research can trickle back to the whale-watchers themselves. No longer are Humpback Whales simply Humpback Whales, but after careful study have become individuals with complex and fascinating personal histories going back decades. A distinctive net scar on a whale's tail, for example, identifies her as a female that feeds in a way unlike any of her associates, or as one that was seen breeding thousands of miles away only weeks before.

Other combinations of skills have also changed the experience. The development of robust, dependable underwater microphones or "hydrophones", for instance, has moved the experience away from simply whale *watching*. Now, while watching we can eavesdrop on their underwater conversations of clicks, whistles, barks, cries and moans. These innovations continually add new facets to the jewels of information that we have about these animals' lives. With each addition comes education and its benefits. Meeting individual whales that may be older than our grandparents, or hearing just how easily motorized vessels drown out their calls, can been powerful illustrations of how our lives and theirs intermesh for better or worse.

Whale watching, it is frequently claimed, is a better "use" of these animals than simply harpooning them and rendering their meat. Seeing whales can be an entertaining and educational experience but also, many hope, one that is ultimately beneficial to the animals themselves. After all, many whale, dolphin and porpoise populations are in peril and the more we know about them and the more personal experiences we have, the more likely we are to fight for their continued survival.

Humpback Whale mother and calf swim in the tranquil waters off Tonga.

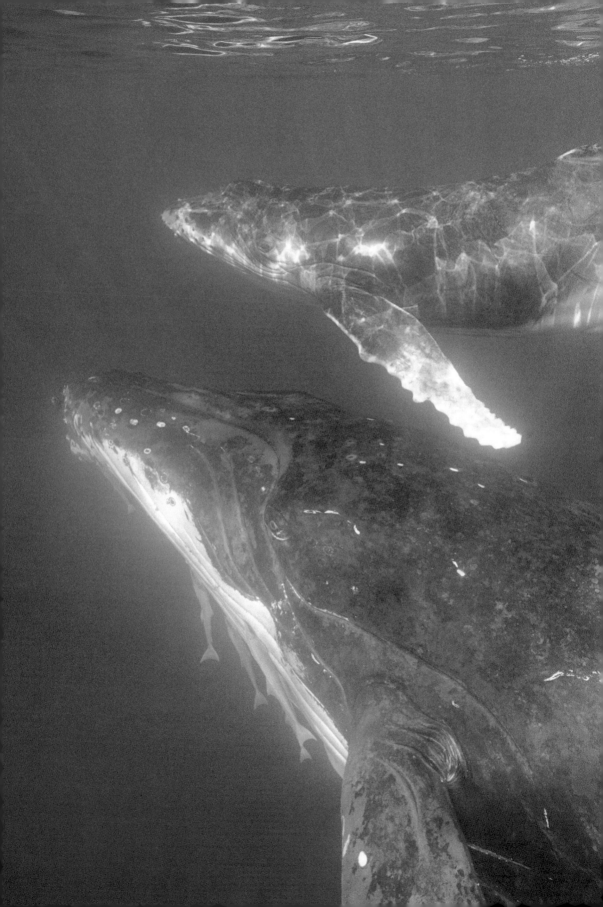

From Whaling To Watching

The lives of whales and humans have been inextricably linked for centuries. The majority of our interactions have been simple: us killing them. The Japanese proudly display prints from the sixteenth century depicting coastal fishermen killing Right and Pilot Whales, while records of Basque hunters taking Right Whales in the north-east Atlantic date from as early as the ninth century.

Commercial whaling on the scale that generated stories like *Moby Dick* began in earnest in the eighteenth century. Whalers would set out onto the high seas in square-rigged sailing ships equipped with huge cauldrons to render the blubber to oil and all the other paraphernalia needed for a sea voyage that might last years. Small catcher boats were carried aboard, ready to be launched when a whale was spotted. The slogging crew would row these boats close enough to the whale for the harpooner to fling his lance – man against whale. Occasionally the whale won but more often it didn't. Once speared (usually multiple times), the whale dragged the little boat until its death, at which point the carcass was hauled alongside the mothership and gradually dissected for its valuable components. The blubber was stripped off like the peel of an orange and boiled down – grease for the cogs of the Industrial Revolution; the baleen plates were cut out – support for the corsets of ladies of wealth; and oddities such as ambergris, a substance from the stomach of the sperm whale, solid and stinking when removed, was used as a critical ingredient in ladies' perfumes. Through the eighteenth, nineteenth and early twentieth centuries dead whales produced money for men, cosmetics for women and light for all.

The problem with exploiting any natural resource is that it has the potential to run out. Living creatures should theoretically be resistant to depletion because they are able to reproduce and so replenish their numbers. But for whales this was impossible. They simply could not produce young fast enough to replace those consumed by the industry's relentless onslaught. North Pacific Right Whales, for example, reached commercial extinction within 14 years of the first one being taken in 1835.

With the advent in the late nineteenth century of steam-powered, followed by diesel-powered vessels, explosive harpoons and spotter planes, the scale and geographical coverage of the slaughter soared. This was no longer a hunt but a highly mechanised business. As whale populations in easy-to-reach areas like the mid and north Atlantic, north-east Pacific and Indian Oceans plummeted, so the wild Antarctic Ocean was turned from a sanctuary to a killing ground. The result was devastating. In 1938 alone, over 38,000 Antarctic whales were killed, over 80 percent of the world catch.

Being slow moving, buoyant and valuable, Right Whales took the brunt of early whaling.

By the late 1930s whale oil was a very valuable commodity. In the earlier years of the century whale oil was used as a raw material for making nitroglycerine for explosives. But after German chemists discovered that whale oil could also be used to make a butter substitute called margarine, demand soared. As a result, whale oil was procured in vast quantities by the ever-expanding British and Norwegian whaling industries. The Antarctic had become a production ground, with sub-Antarctic islands like South Georgia in the South Atlantic hosting factory-scale whale processing and rendering plants. But the industry was beginning to suffer, not because whales were becoming scarce (there were still numerous smaller species

Even the Antarctic was no refuge from hunting for Humpback Whales.

to exploit) but because whale oil was becoming too abundant and other nations were beginning to get a foothold in the industry. Ironically, while driving whale populations downwards, the whalers were also flooding the market with oil and sinking each other's profits. As with crude oil today, the whale-oil industry itself realised that there was a need for carefully controlled oil production and regulation.

Throughout the 1930s the whaling companies forged agreements to suspend prices from further falls and to curb competition between Britain and Norway. The countries carrying out commercial whaling formed an inter-governmental body to regulate the industry. The aim was to set overall catch limits, in an attempt to conserve the resource and manage the flow of whale oil onto the market. In 1946, the major whaling nations signed the International Convention for the Regulation of Whaling, bringing about the birth of the International Whaling Commission (IWC).

Delegates from the member countries of the IWC met annually to agree on the overall catch limits for baleen whales in the Antarctic. The most desired species, on account of its sheer size and oil yields, was the Blue Whale. This whale therefore became the standard measure of whale kills. A country taking, say, 5000 Blue Whale Units could either kill 5000 Blue Whales or make up each Unit by taking several

Blue Whales were the grand prize for whalers and their numbers quickly plummeted.

smaller whales of another species; two Fin, six Sei Whales and so on. This approach continued to supply the industry with whale oil, but caused chaos for those trying to predict how each species was holding up under such ruthless exploitation; it also wreaked havoc on the whales themselves.

Whale numbers plummeted. The all-too-popular Blue Whale nearly vanished. The next-largest species became heavily exploited and began its own rapid decline, followed by the next and then the next species. This major industry, previously turning very healthy profits and supporting thousands of workers, began to feel the strain. Realizing that a crisis was looming, governments decided to act, this time to try to conserve their assets – the whales themselves – rather than focusing on just the profits. By putting stricter limits on the whaling countries they hoped that whale populations would rebound. To guide this process scientists were brought in to estimate the abundances and potential reproductive rates for the whale species, with the intention of coming up with a more rigorous method for estimating catch quotas in tune with the biology of the animals. However, this failed. By the late 1960s whale populations globally were in perilous decline. Some whaling countries (such as the USSR) were exceeding their allocated quotas by thousands of animals and the whales were not recovering in the way that had been predicted. Only the smallest species, those least profitable for the whaling vessels to catch and process on their vast factory ships, remained in any abundance.

Being large, Fin Whales were the next species to be decimated after Blue Whales.

The disaster looming in the whaling industry started to take on significance for those outside the industry as well as those within. At stake was not so much an industry, as the conservation and ultimate continuation of some of the largest and now the most vulnerable species on the planet. The issue became so critical that, in 1972, a resolution was passed at the United Nations Conference on the Human Environment calling for a ten-year moratorium on whaling. It took ten years for the International Whaling Commission (IWC) to act on the UN resolution, followed by another ten years of heavy exploitation in which some countries, seeing the writing on the wall in the form of a whaling ban, maximized their whaling efforts to maximize profits. In other countries, such as Britain and the United States, the whaling companies started to diversify and invest their money elsewhere.

In 1982 the IWC agreed to a moratorium on commercial whaling, which would come into effect in 1986, stopping all commercial whaling, and allowing scientists time to calculate the number of whales still alive, the rates at which they could reproduce, and ultimately, a sustainable level of killing for the industry. Unfortunately the introduction of the moratorium did not bring a stop to whaling. The 1947 Convention included two facets that precluded a complete cessation: the first was the right of any country to object to any decision of the IWC; the second was a rule that any country could issue its own whaling industry a permit to carry out scientific research on whales.

In 1986, following the introduction of the moratorium, the USSR killed over 3000 whales and Japan took 2700 whales because they had each legally filed formal objections. Japan later withdrew this objection and instead embarked upon its own "research whaling". This has continued from 1988 right up to the present day, with regular and sometimes dramatic increases. But Japan is not the only nation still taking whales. Both Iceland and Norway are today carrying out whaling in the North Atlantic. Norway uses its objection to conduct commercial whaling, using modified fishing vessels to hunt Minke Whales around its coasts in the Barents, Norwegian and North Seas. The Norwegian government allocates its industry a quota of over 650 Minke Whales each year, even though these numbers are far greater than the IWC would allow under new rules it has developed for calculating sustainable quotas. Iceland left

Despite being a whaling nation, Iceland has become a center for whale watchers.

the IWC after the moratorium. It has since rejoined and commenced its own "research whaling". A proposal in 2002 by the Icelandic government to kill 500 whales over the following two years was reduced to fewer than 70 whales, a move seen by some as a result of international pressure on Iceland not to resume whaling.

The IWC has never lifted its moratorium. Scientists have developed what they believe to be a reliable method for generating catch quotas for baleen whales. But figuring out the number of whales that can be taken is only half the problem. International exploitation of any resource requires management and this becomes especially difficult when that resource is a living creature and its exploitation is carried out in the middle of a remote ocean far from view. Any future exploitation would require strict observation and enforcement by third parties. This is where issues become political and the IWC is locked in ongoing international wrangles. Whaling countries contend that any management requirements should not be unrealistically extensive or restrictive, while countries interested in promoting whale conservation push for more comprehensive management, in an attempt to avoid the carnage of the past.

Attitudes towards the exploitation of animals have changed significantly since the Whaling Convention was signed in 1946. Whales are no longer regarded simply as resources, but are seen as sentient animals with social systems, large brains and, ultimately, the ability to suffer. Even as the IWC pushes towards a resumption of widespread commercial whaling, with management measures that would prevent extinction of whale species, there are those who believe that whaling should not be carried out because of the pain and suffering it inflicts. The killing method – a barbed explosive harpoon fired from a pursuing boat – has changed little since the heyday of whaling, and is far from perfect. The harpoon head contains a charge that is rigged to explode on impact with the whale, but even this does not assure death. Half of the whales harpooned by the Japanese remain alive after the impact, and around one in five harpooned by the Norwegians is not killed outright. Many people regard this as unacceptable, leading them and others to regard whaling as both unnecessary and cruel.

Ultimately, the only reason for the continuation of commercial whaling is a perceived demand by Japan, and to a lesser extent by a few Scandinavian countries, for whale meat. The blubber that was originally valued by the whaling industry for the oil it yielded is hardly used today, and is tragically often too high in toxic pollutants to be fit for human consumption. Its use in production industries as a lubricant has long since been superseded by petroleum products. Thankfully, in the developed world, whale oil is no longer a component of soaps, candles or margarine.

Though modern whaling is predominantly a mechanised industry, there are still a few places in the world where whaling remains a hunt, and a dangerous one at that. Fishermen from St Vincent and the Grenadines in the Caribbean, are permitted to harpoon about four Humpback Whales a year in their local waters. Inuit huntsmen from Greenland, Canada, Alaska and Russia take small numbers of Bowhead, Minke, Fin, Gray and Killer Whales as well as Belugas and Narwhals. These aboriginal hunts differ from the massive-scale whaling of the past. For a start, there are very real dangers to the people engaged in killing these whales. A swipe of a tail can shatter a small boat while, for the Arctic hunters, freezing water and crushing ice floes pose an ever-present danger. There are other differences too. Instead of the slaughtered whale's products being directly converted to cash, the parts are destined for local consumption and crafts. The hunting and butchering activities also maintain social traditions and family bonds in places where the modern world has shattered so many other time-honored ways of life. Though aboriginal whalers take few whales, there remain justified concerns about the impact this has. Inuit hunters in the eastern Canadian

Arctic are allowed, by the IWC, to take only one Bowhead Whale every other year from the Hudson Bay stock. On the face of it, this seems like a truly trivial catch, but these whales now teeter on the brink of extinction, brought there not by the local hunters, who have pursued these whales for thousands of years, but by the cash-hungry first-world whaling industry which swept through the area before heading off to more lucrative seas elsewhere.

While these aboriginal hunts continue, the shadow of widespread commercial whaling still looms large. Whether or not the massive whaling ships of old will sail again hangs in the balance today. The IWC carries out the wishes of its members and, though the great majority of those members agreed to a moratorium in the 1980s, the players and their views have changed. In recent years many developing countries, with no direct interest in whaling, have joined the IWC. Most of these receive development aid from Japan and vote consistently in favor of commercial whaling. In consequence the membership of the IWC has increased from 14 countries in 1946 to over 50 countries today, yet at the same time, the number of countries actually carrying out commercial or "research" whaling has decreased to only three. If the trend towards new members continues, the balance of power will shift from one of pro-conservation to one of pro-industrial whaling. Manufacturers of explosive harpoons may soon have a lot of new business.

In an attempt to create a new purpose for the IWC, a number of member countries and their scientists have begun to develop the notion of managing whale watching rather than whale killing. The IWC, after all, was formed by nations seeking to maintain whale resources and the financial issues surrounding them. In this regard, some argue, whale watching qualifies. Though it is inconceivable that this new industry could have anything like the impacts of the commercial hunts, there are concerns that the activity could impact the lives of whales in more subtle ways. Who better than an established international body with scientific expertise to oversee this new global industry?

On the face of it, whale watching appears to be an innocuous activity. The pursuit is one of observation and it's difficult to see how simply looking could be a threat. But it is inevitably more than looking. To look, one has to be in proximity. If it's to be a boat that transports the watcher to the whale, then it's the boat that may be the problem.

Just as fast-moving cars pose a risk to children on their way to school, boats often collide with cetaceans. Scan the world's press and you'll see that just about every year a cruise ship comes into one port or another with a hapless and very dead whale wrapped around its bow. It's usually an interesting sight – a large and rapidly rotting whale utterly dwarfed by a multi-million dollar gleaming mass of steel. There are usually a couple of little boats, too, fussing around trying to get the whale off the ship before too many people see what's going on. What's amazing is that the whale is stuck there at all. Imagine the odds of hitting a whale so square on that it remains perfectly balanced in position and all the drag of the passing water does not dislodge it for days or even weeks of cruising. The odds are pretty slim. If you had a ship and a floating whale carcass to play with, you certainly wouldn't manage to get it lodged on the bow on the first or probably even the tenth go! How many whales get just clipped by a passing ship – struck and then left floating, mortally wounded, in the ship's wake? The answer is that nobody knows but it's probably not at all uncommon.

The front of a ship is not the only danger. If a whale or dolphin manages to avoid the bows, it might be swept along and into the propellers or simply surface from a dive right underneath them. Ship or boat propellers are murderous things – knife-sharp blades sweeping around just under the sea surface like mobile food-blenders. Many cetaceans, dead and living, bear the signs of the propeller's kiss. The scars are usually a series of parallel slanting cuts – their spacing and length a tell tale signature of the size and pitch of the blades. The wounds may be just a couple of chops or they may run the length of the animal from head to tail as the turning, angled blades passed their victim from one to the next.

The stinging kiss from a ship's propeller.

Whale-watch boats are only a tiny fraction of the vessels plying our seas so it might seem unfair to single them out in terms of collisions. In many ways, this is true. The impact of commercial shipping – from freighters to ferries – on the world's marine mammal populations is very much underrated. Where investigations have been carried out, the results are usually worrying. The thing about whale watching is that these boats concentrate their maneuvers in areas where cetaceans are most abundant. Coupled with that, they may be around the animals for hours on end, leading to complacency on the part of the whales or dolphins. Perversely, the victims may also intentionally put themselves in the firing line. It's not uncommon for dolphins to seek out the wash immediately behind propellers. The mixture of swirling currents and bubbles must produce sensations not unlike those of a Jacuzzi. It's a dangerous game and not without its victims. In one example, a solitary Bottlenose Dolphin off the UK was enjoying the vibrations just inches behind a boat with two propellers. The skipper had the craft moving forward, and so the twin screws were producing a backward current within which the dolphin could hold position. All was fine, until the skipper, in total innocence, put the boat into reverse. The backward current suddenly became a forward one and the helpless animal was sucked through between the two propellers. The injured animal survived but it was a close call.

Anybody who has put a hydrophone (underwater microphone) into the ocean will be all too aware of the noise produced by boats and ships. The pounding of the pistons; the gurgle and fizz of the exhaust and the swishing of the propellers. Boats are incredibly loud, even tiny ones. Listen underwater on a calm day and if someone were to start a little outboard engine, the type you'd have on a rubber boat for two people, you'd hear it on the other side of the bay. You'd hear the sound of the person tugging on the starter cord and as the motor caught the whole soundscape would be filled with its whine.

And all of this from a little engine that is too far away to see with the naked eye. There are two reasons why this little engine, like most others, is so noisy. The first is because we don't routinely listen underwater. As a result, there's been no incentive for owners or manufacturers to pay attention to how noisy these machines are below the surface. In fact, outboard engines and many others direct their exhaust straight into the water and with it intentionally

Noise pollution from shipping is a major concern.

direct the sound of the pistons. They effectively use the sea as the muffler so that the passengers, above the surface, can enjoy a quiet ride.

The second reason why boats are so audible is because of the sea itself. Sound travels exceedingly well in water, unlike light, which hardly travels at all. A Blue Whale might be unable to see the length of its own body but it will be able to hear the calls of another whale over 1000 miles (1600 km) away. Unsurprisingly, hearing rather than sight has become the primary sense for the cetaceans. They use sound to locate their prey and their predators, to navigate and communicate. We humans construct a visual picture of the world in our heads while these creatures undoubtedly build up an acoustic one. So when a boat and its engines fill the sea with sound they effectively drown out this sense for the animals that are so reliant on it. Sure, the whale or dolphin will know that there is a boat in the area, perhaps right above it or perhaps 20 miles away, but it'll be deaf to all but the loudest other sounds. The visual equivalent for us would be trying to hunt deer in a forest but having a massive belching smoke machine suddenly enter the scene. You wouldn't be able to see anything but the nearest deer as it runs away from you, know whether there was a bear sitting up the tree above you, or find your hunting buddies or perhaps even steer your way out of the forest.

Noise pollution is a truly global problem. There is hardly an inch of seawater anywhere into which you could put a hydrophone and not hear one kind of craft or another. The wrecked *Titanic's* rust-filled ballroom may no longer be graced with the sound of violins but it is certainly still flooded by the sound of ships' engines.

Dall's Porpoises, Alaska.

With all the boat activity in the world, why might whale-watching boats pose a particular problem? Though sound travels a long distance, as it does so it gradually fades in volume. So if boats target whales or dolphins to watch and spend hour after hour, day after day, close to the animals, they will be continually exposing them to this pollution at its highest intensity. In doing so they will mask all the other noises that the cetaceans find so important. Imagine it. It would be like us hunting deer in the forest and instead of the smoke machine being fixed, it follows you about from dawn till dusk.

So how does noise pollution affect whales, dolphins and porpoises? The short answer is that nobody really knows. There are recorded instances of whales leaving a bay where whale watching was particularly intense, and of animals changing their behavior when boats are nearby, perhaps switching from foraging to social activity or apparently resting. But with these kinds of observation, it's rarely clear whether it was the noise of the boat or some other feature that they were responding to. It's also unclear how important these minor changes may be to the lives of the cetaceans. Are they a simple annoyance or do they impact the animal's health status, eventual survival or ability to produce viable offspring? If we know little about the short-term responses, then we know even less about the long-term and important ones. When you're studying animals that can live as long or longer than a research career, these kinds of question are difficult to answer definitively.

One promising approach that has been suggested is to look at how much extra energy the interactions might cost the whales or dolphins. Let's say for a hypothetical group of whales to get from A to B they have to swim around a group of whale-watching boats sitting in front of them. The whales add a dogleg or two to their route simply to avoid the obstructions. This might add 30 percent extra distance to the journey they'd make in any hour. On average the whales are watched for eight hours of any day, so in a 24-hour period the zigging and zagging would add 10 percent to the swimming budget for the whales. If the energy needed to swim costs the whales 40 percent of their total energy, then the swimming deviations would represent 4 percent of the total energy needed to be a fully functional whale in those waters. To compensate, the whales would have to catch and consume 4 percent more fish or squid every day just to be the same whales that they were before the boats came along. This might seem insignificant – if the whales spend half their day feeding then 4 percent would be just less than half an hour. But if the whale population is stable and the number of whales is in balance with the amount of food available, it logically follows that if the whales each have to eat more food every day, then the environment will be able to sustain fewer whales. In our example, simply blocking the path of whales so that they have to swim a little further might mean that over a period of years the population will shrink by four whales in every hundred. Put like this, the new industry of whale-watching may not be so far removed from the old practice of whaling.

While this argument contains many ifs and buts, it gets the point across that seemingly small disruptions in the lives of individual animals can add up to more major changes in their populations. We should not be complacent and many people have argued strongly that we should watch how we watch. As a result, in almost every area where whale watching occurs there have been initiatives to manage how people behave around the animals. In most, these ideas have translated themselves into codes of conduct, which vary depending on the type of cetacean being watched, the sort of watching platform and the host country. The regulations may be legally binding or simply rules of thumb. While there are literally hundreds of them, most contain the same three generalities.

The first aim to limit the disturbance that may be caused by the presence of the whale watchers. The majority of these are formulated with boat-based whale-watching in mind. Typically they limit the distance to which the craft can approach, the time they can spend with the animals and the number of boats present at any one time. They also make recommendations on how the boats should maneuver around the animals – avoiding head-on approaches, cutting through groups, repeatedly leap-frogging steadily moving animals and so on. More occasionally they also single out specific cases where boat behavior should be different – if there is a young calf in the group or if the animals are engaged in a specific activity. They may also suggest times of year or areas where whale watching is discouraged.

The second class aims to minimize the chances of causing direct harm. Rules disallowing people to feed or touch the animals are almost universal. Nobody feeds whales, but dolphins may take morsels that are offered to them, whether they are frozen herring or hamburgers. Not only does this practice encourage them to eat materials that they shouldn't, but it can promote the unfortunate habit of begging with its associated risk of disease transfer and injury to either party. Similarly, guidelines frequently discourage boats from introducing pollutants such as trash and oil into the water.

Third and finally, no matter how hard people try, the proximity of humans to cetaceans inevitably has some form of detrimental impact. But many argue that this negative influence can be offset by the positives of education. The more that people know about these animals, and the marine environment in general, the more they are likely to cherish and fight to save them. Over-fishing, pollution and climate

The more we know about cetaceans the more likely we are to conserve them.

change are far bigger threats to cetaceans than whale watching will ever be, so a public that has personal experiences with cetaceans and a deeper knowledge is one that will have greater drive to deal with these wider issues. Anyone who has gone out on a whale-watching trip with a good tour guide will know that he or she can turn a simple day out on the water into a thought-provoking, even life-changing experience. As a result, codes of conduct frequently recommend that the trips include an educational component, either in the form of written material or through trained guides.

These codes of conduct that aim to minimize disturbance are based to a small extent on observations of how cetaceans respond to boats, but in the most part they come from common sense derived from how people imagine cetaceans might view these interactions. But, many scientists question whether these rules are the right rules. They question whether we are really paying attention to the factors that matter most to the animals. Perhaps whales don't mind boats close by but instead are more bothered by the type of propulsion system they use. A big rumbling fishing boat is far easier to keep out the way of than a dozen quiet kayaks that give few clues as to where they are on the water surface. Equally, rules based on different whale behaviors may be counter-intuitive. Perhaps resting whales are simply killing time and chasing them about will have no undue impact in the long-run, but disturbing feeding whales is more critical. At the moment nobody really knows enough about how cetaceans and boats interact to answer these questions definitively. So in the meantime, the most sensible approach is to formulate and enforce the best rules we can and then put our efforts into improving and refining them as new information comes to light.

Having codes of conduct, even potentially flawed ones, is not a bad thing. These guidelines influence the behavior of people driving boats probably for the better and give boat operators good reasons not to cave in to the, sometimes selfish, demands of their passengers. Above all they encourage people to think about how they might be affecting the lives of the animals they are watching. While the science behind these codes lags way behind their implementation, some argue that this is where the

Resting Killer Whales are easily disturbed.

gathered expertise of the IWC should play a significant role. Cetaceans are complex and mysterious animals and scientific investigations are only beginning to unravel the intricacies of their lives. Meanwhile, whale watching has become a global industry that has encouraged massive investment, that generates substantial revenue and feeds an ever-hungry tourist industry. Cetaceans, and whales in particular, are the resource that underpins this ballooning industry. Whale watching is, in many respects, a modern form of whaling.

Watching To Learn More

Cetaceans are mysterious creatures. It is true to say that we know more about many dinosaurs than we do about some of the whales off our shores today. For us, the oceans are an alien place. To spend time on the water we need boats, and generally the further offshore we want to go the more expensive and complicated they become. The oceans are also huge; 70 percent of the planet, erroneously called Earth, is covered in water, a statistic that is easy enough to state, but much harder to grasp. Take a commercial flight from North America to Europe and after the movies have droned on and the second meal has been served you'll begin to appreciate just how big the Atlantic Ocean is. Flying is one thing but comprehending every swell, wave and ripple is much better considered at eye level. The fastest anybody has managed to row across the Atlantic Ocean is in 42 days. The Pacific Ocean is larger still. In fact it is big enough to swallow up all of the world's continents put together and still have room left over for meteorites and ice sheets. If you then consider that any one species of cetacean may contain fewer individuals than people in a city and that they spend the majority of their time beneath the surface, the problem of studying cetaceans comes into focus.

Of course, we know quite a bit about the more abundant ones living near our shores, but nevertheless many significant parts of their lives remain mysterious. Humpback Whales are the mainstay of the whale-watching industry. They are seen by millions of tourists annually, have been studied by scientists for decades and have even made guest appearances in *Star Trek*. Despite our seeming familiarity with them, we still cannot explain several fundamental aspects of what they do. Take, for example, their spectacular breeding migrations. We do not know for certain why they swim all the way to tropical waters to breed, why non-breeding animals also migrate, and why each male goes to the trouble of singing the same, ever-evolving, song as its neighbors.

While there are substantial gaps in what we know, cetacean research as a field of science has progressed in leaps and bounds in recent decades and continues to expand at a furious pace today. The main meeting for cetacean biologists is run by the US-based Society for Marine Mammalogy. In 1981, the Society had fewer than 800 members, but by 2006 numbers had swelled to over 2300. The age structure of the field is young too, so the future of cetacean science looks bright.

The expanding field has been fuelled by agents that have as much to do with humans as they do with cetaceans. For many of us, cetaceans are charismatic beasts that lead mysterious, interesting lives. Consequently there is never a lack of

Cetaceans flaunt an inviting blend of charisma and mystery.

scientists and enthusiasts willing to embrace any opportunities that become available. Similarly, while these animals are difficult to study, there is no shortage of things to learn about them. Almost any well-conducted research effort will turn up new results. Conservation is also a driving force. The "save the whale" cry is inextricably linked to whaling but ironically today it has more relevance to fishing practices and pollution. No researcher who has come into contact with cetaceans will fail to have increased interest in their conservation. In fact most cetacean research today is targeted, in one way or another, directly towards protecting the animals under study.

With cetacean science being of wide interest and urgent application, researchers have amassed an impressive portfolio of tools to unlock cetacean secrets. This is not to say that cetacean research is now easy, nor that it can answer every relevant question that one might pose, far from it, but the research field, after many decades of slow progress, is now accelerating at quite a pace.

So what tools are there in the scientists' bag? In short they are various and many and just as a carpenter's tools are fashioned for specific jobs so too are those of the science community. They can be broken down into several groups.

The first group requires getting hold of the animal – either its whole body or simply a piece of it. In the early days of cetacean research, these hands-on methods were the primary approach. Researchers would visit whaling stations or go out on the whaling ships and then examine and collect samples from the animals that were caught. Much of what we know about the anatomy, reproductive biology, age, growth, diseases and diet of the large whales came to light in this way – quite literally. Where better to dissect a freshly dead whale than in a factory dedicated to slicing up whales? While some information is still gathered from whales that have been slaughtered, other methods have become more widespread. On coastlines all around the world, cetaceans frequently wash ashore. In many areas, there are teams of people with interests in these animals who will examine and sample the carcasses as they are reported. Dealing with a stranded cetacean can be quite a challenge, especially if it is large or has been dead for a while. The bodies of small animals may be picked up and taken to a lab, but larger animals are more often examined right there on the beach. Whatever the approach, a proper examination and sample collection can be highly revealing. Almost everything we know about the biology of the beaked whales, for example, comes from beach-cast animals. Of course, studying dead, often very dead, animals has its problems. Just like studying humans in the morgue, you might be able to piece together aspects of their lives and what killed them, but there's no getting away from the fact that something caused their death. So, by definition, these individuals are not representative of the live populations from which they originated.

Another approach, therefore, is to collect the samples from the animals while they are still alive. The most obvious way to do this is to go out and capture animals and take samples, just as a vet might from a pet or a farm animal – measurements for growth studies, blood for hormones, swabs for diseases and so on. But opportunities to capture cetaceans without harm are rare or, in many cases, completely impossible. Another way is to grab small pieces of them. For some species this is straightforward. Sperm Whales continually shed large scraps of skin, so if a diver leaps into the water in the wake of one of these animals they can net the fragments. The skin contains DNA and so analysis of the sample can reveal the sex and genetic heritage of that particular whale. Very recently a similar approach was tested on whale feces. This slightly surprising scientific treasure can provide a sample of the whale's DNA with an added bonus: feces can also include the genetic signature of what the whale ate – fish, krill or whatever.

Few cetaceans leave such readily collectable samples in their wake, so many researchers take a more direct approach, most commonly a biopsy dart. As the cetacean surfaces near a boat, a gun, crossbow or pole is used to stick the equivalent of a large needle into the animal. When the projectile is retrieved, a piece of the whale's skin and blubber will be trapped in the hollow tip. Just as with the Sperm Whale's skin sample, the DNA can be extracted

Sperm Whales leave scraps of skin in their wake.

and read, but the underlying blubber may reveal important information as well. There is widespread concern that many pollutants, particularly organochlorines, may reduce the abilities of marine mammals to breed and fight disease. Cetaceans unwittingly store these chemicals in their fat reserves, particularly their blubber, so analysis of the blubber samples taken from biopsies of live individuals can tell us how severe the burdens of these chemicals are in the wild populations, rather than just in the unlucky, diseased or starving animals that wash ashore.

Of course techniques that involve measuring and taking samples from animals cannot tell us everything we might want to know. To find out how many whales there are in an area or where they live and breed or feed, a second group of research tools is required. The simplest of these is to go out and look. This can be as straightforward as standing on a headland and recording what is in view, or as complicated as criss-crossing the ocean in a research ship with trained observers, laser range-finders and statistically formulated route plans. Both approaches provide valuable information but answer different questions.

Records from shoreline observers are useful in determining what species occur in a coastal area. These records are especially useful if they are also documented alongside the effort that went into making them – the number of hours watched, the number of people watching and the climatic conditions. With this extra information it is possible to determine how often animals are seen for a given location and whether there are any patterns with the time of day, tide or year. Are dolphins more common here in summer or winter? Were they more common ten years ago? And so on. Watching cetaceans from shore, or from a boat for that matter, also allows their behavior to be observed. Were the animals hunting prey, interacting with other cetaceans, diving in a particular fashion, avoiding whale-watching boats? Observations of what cetaceans are doing often helps answer questions about what these animals do for a living, how their societies operate and why they are where they are. What observations in single areas can't determine, in most circumstances, is how many animals there are in a population and what is happening in all the other areas not directly being observed.

The most common way to answer these questions is to set up a sightings-survey. In other words, criss-cross a piece of water with a boat, ship or plane and record what's seen along with how much observer effort was needed to see it. A vessel can't cover every inch of water nor the observers spot every whale, so two other parameters are recorded: the distance and angle that each animal is seen from the vessel. With these numbers, the distance from the boat that the animal was seen can be calculated and hence the width of the strip of sea either side of the boat that was searched can be determined. With this information it is possible to work out the density of cetaceans per square mile or kilometer. If the extent of the area used by the population of animals is known then the total population size can be calculated. There are a number of refinements and corrections that make this technique more complicated but the basic approach remains simple and has been used to conduct both local and global cetacean surveys for many years. Multi-million dollar efforts continue to be conducted in the Pacific, Atlantic, Antarctic and Arctic Oceans and there are ships and observers whose careers are dedicated to estimating cetacean abundance in this way.

One benchmark survey was carried out in the North and Baltic Seas off Europe in July 1994. It was called the Small Cetacean Abundance in the North Sea survey (SCANS) and used 9 ships, 2 airplanes and 70 observers. Each vessel covered a different patch of sea and together they surveyed a distance of 16,800 miles (27,000 km) during a one-month period. The numbers that resulted were used to determine how many Minke Whales (8500), White-Beaked Dolphins (8000) and Harbor Porpoises (340,000) were present at that time in the North Sea. A second, follow-up, survey was conducted in the summer of 2005 to see whether the numbers had changed in the intervening years. This second multinational survey cost in excess of €3 million (US$ 4 million), which seems like a huge expense just to establish some numbers. But ultimately, if we are going to conserve these animals and hold them as bellwethers for the state of our oceans, this is money well spent.

Anybody who has tried to see whales, dolphins and particularly porpoises at sea will appreciate the difficulty of actually spotting them, especially if they are small, the sea is rough or the sun is adding glare to the water surface. To get around this, a growing group of researchers are reconstructing the sighting-survey method by replacing the component that required visual sighting with the acoustic detection of their sounds. There are some obvious problems with this approach. The biggest is that the animal has to make a noise to be detected and cetaceans don't make noises all the time, nor do they all produce the same quantities of sound. On the other hand, there are several advantages, most importantly surveys can be carried out day or night and in a wide range of weather conditions. The detection of the animal calls can also be automated, saving on the expense and discomfort of having observers perched for hundreds of hours in ships' crow's nests.

Sighting-surveys work well for species that are broadly distributed and relatively common. For species that occur in scattered patches unsuitable for the sighting-survey approach, there is another method. This relies on getting to know individuals and recognizing them if they are seen again. The method itself is called mark-recapture, and as a numerical tool has been applied not only to studies of animal numbers but has also found uses in factory quality control, estimating numbers of taxicabs, and many other applications. The method works for situations where you are not going to be able to find all of the individuals of whatever it is that you're trying to estimate. In other words, situations where you can't simply count them all. Instead you can see some of them now and again, and once you've seen one, you'll recognize it if it turns up a second time.

The method works like this: imagine you want to know how many coins there are in a cloth bag. Put your hand into the bag and draw out a handful. Count then mark each of those in your hand then put them back into the bag. Give the bag a good shake so that they're well mixed then close your eyes and take a second handful. The ratio of marked to unmarked coins in your hand will tell you approximately how many coins there are in the bag. Ten coins in your hand and only one of them belongs to the 20 from the first handful indicates there were approximately 200 in the bag but if five of them are marked then there were more like 40 in the bag.

The same method can be applied to whales. Go out to sea and spot ten distinctive whales. Wait a week then go out again and see how many sightings are familiar from the first trip. To recognize whales some form of distinctive mark is needed. It is easy to mark a coin or add a little paint to the coat of a seal or clip a patch of fur on a mouse, but physically marking a cetacean is much more difficult.

As a result, most of the times that this method has been used on cetaceans, researchers have exploited natural marks. Probably the most distinctive and widely known individual whale in the popular imagination was Moby Dick. His white skin and deformed jaw meant that whichever whaler was unlucky enough to see him, instantly recognized and feared him. Moby's marks may have been extreme, but look closely enough at almost any cetacean and it'll have physical characteristics that make it distinguishable from its associates: unusual pigmentation, nicks in its fins, or scars, scratches and scrapes. Most cetaceans move too quickly for these features to be clearly visible, so researchers take photographs of the animals then figure out which individual it was later. This practice of using photographs to

Two nicks in this Minke Whale's dorsal fin make it uniquely identifiable.

identify individual cetaceans is known as photo-identification, and has become the backbone of many cetacean research studies. The method was initially pioneered as a way of studying whales without the need to kill them and has gone on to far outdo the information that could possibly be derived from whale slaughter.

Photo-identification and mark-recapture have been used successfully to estimate the numbers of many populations of cetaceans, from Bottlenose Dolphins to Killer and Blue Whales, and the scale of these studies has ranged from the local to the oceanic. Humpback Whales have particularly distinctive and long-lasting marks on the undersides of their tail flukes and as a result lend themselves particularly well to these kinds of studies. Since large-scale killing of North Atlantic Humpbacks ceased, numbers have been steadily increasing. In summer, the population is scattered from the eastern seaboard of the US, right across the temperate and Arctic waters of the north Atlantic as far as northern Norway. In winter almost all of the whales migrate to tropical breeding grounds. The area that they scatter themselves across is simply enormous and consequently far too big for a standard sightings survey. So in 1992 and 1993, a combined multinational team of researchers pooled their efforts under the banner of a project called YoNAH or Years of the North Atlantic Humpback. Their aims were to estimate how many Humpbacks there were, how they moved around in the North Atlantic and quantify their reproductive rates. Each research group went to its prospective study site (Gulf of Maine, US, Canada, Greenland, Iceland and Norway) in summer and photographed and took skin biopsy samples from as many of the whales as they could. They then repeated the exercise on one of the winter breeding grounds (the West Indies) and applied the summer and winter results to the mark-recapture method. Going back to the coins-in-a-bag example, the summer samples were the first handful and the winter samples the second. From this they estimated that there were 10,600 whales in the North Atlantic population.

The study also turned up some other interesting results. For example, prior to this study it was assumed that whales from Norway mated and gave birth in the eastern North Atlantic (the Cape Verde Islands). However, photographic and genetic matches in this study showed that at least some of the whales that summer

Each Humpback Whale has unique fluke markings.

off Norway mingle with whales from the western North Atlantic on the Caribbean winter breeding grounds.

The added advantage of using the photo-identification technique is that repeated sightings of known individual whales, dolphins or porpoises can tell us much more about the animals than just how many there are. If the survey work carries on over a number of years, the frequency with which individuals give birth, their life-expectancy, social networks, residency and migrations can all be pieced together. Photo-identification as a tool is only useful if there are not too many cetaceans in the population to reasonably deal with (tens, hundreds or a few thousand) and if the marks are sufficiently durable that individuals can be adequately followed.

There are of course several cetacean species, particularly beaked whales, which are widespread in offshore waters, are unpredictable in distribution, possess few marks and, worst of all, are shy of boats. For these species, nobody has yet come up with reliable ways to estimate their numbers.

Shore-based watches, sighting-surveys and photo-identification all require someone to be on scene to record the presence and activities of the animals under study. Though we often like to kid ourselves, the sea is not our home and our endurance and capabilities in the cetacean environment remain significant limiting factors. Consequently, many cetacean researchers have explored ways, from the ridiculous to the ingenious, to take the limiting factor – the human observer – out of the equation. Humans have traditionally used the capabilities of other animals to help us – canaries to detect poisonous gases, horses for transport, dogs to sniff out everything from foxes in dens to seal pups on ice floes. So why not use sea lions to film Gray Whales feeding underwater? Yes this has been tried, along with using rats to understand marine mammal dietary problems and plankton to study dolphin swimming efficiency. Though great fun to try, these techniques have not, as yet, led to any major revolutions in cetacean science. The use of micro-electronics, on the other hand, has.

Electronic tags reveal details of whale behavior.

Most obvious has been the development and deployment of a diverse family of tags and transmitters. Just two decades ago these devices were cumbersome, limited in their capabilities and short lived. Today they are the reverse. Tags are now capable of recording the dive depth, location, skin, stomach and water temperature, swim speed and three-dimensional movements of animals and then send all of this information to a satellite overhead. The latest developments include mini-hydrophones that record the sounds that the animal makes and hears and cameras that film its activities. All the researcher has to do is attach the device to the animal and go home. The information will either come to his or her computer across the Internet or the tag can be retrieved and the animal's second-by-second activities directly downloaded. With the human out of the measuring loop, marine mammals that range over thousands of miles of ocean or that dive to inaccessible depths can be studied without disturbance from a shadowing boat, plane, submarine or sea lion! Of course, as always, there's one critical problem: how do you attach these clever devices to these fast-moving, streamlined, slippery animals? There is no ideal solution, but approaches that work include tags surgically bolted through connective tissue on the dorsal fin or back, implanted with mini-harpoons in the skin and blubber or simply stuck to the skin with rubber suckers. In general the less invasive the attachment method, the less pain and suffering will be inflicted but the shorter the time the tag will stay attached. As the electronic revolution continues these devices will keep pushing forward the possibilities of non-human measurement, but their expense and the problems of attachment continue to be significant factors limiting their use.

Another group of tools involves increasing the spatial extent of our existing senses. Just as the SCANS survey used several ships at once to cover the North Sea and the YoNAH project combined the efforts of several research groups at once, so too can the use of scattered receiving equipment be used to investigate the bigger picture of whale biology. During the cold war, the superpowers used submarines to spy on one another and to deliver the threat of nuclear attack. It was therefore imperative that each power knew where the submarines of the opponent were. Going out to find each submarine was impractical, so the navies strategically placed sophisticated listening devices on the seabed to detect the engine and propeller sounds of their adversary's subs. With the thawing of the cold war these microphones have found a new use. They're specially tuned to detect the sounds that travel best underwater – low-frequency sounds. These same frequencies are used by the large baleen whales to communicate and so their sounds are easily detected with this system, and because the sounds travel so well underwater, the hydrophones can track the movements of individual calling whales over entire ocean basins. With this system therefore it's possible to determine where all the calling Blue or Fin or Humpback Whales are in the North Atlantic on any particular day of the year. This is something that would be impossible to find out any other way.

Though the number of researchers working on cetaceans is growing year on year, as is the sophistication of the research tools, cetology (the study of cetaceans) is, compared with say ornithology (birds) or entomology (insects), still in its infancy. One of the factors limiting the field is simply the small amount of time that researchers spend in the presence of the animals they study. Ironically most field-cetologists spend the majority of their time in offices – raising funds, analyzing data, writing up findings, campaigning or simply battling through bureaucracy. For cetologists, getting out in a boat to do what they took up the job to do is a surprisingly rare event. It's not just a matter of time management though. Boats are expensive beasts that seem designed to gobble up research grants as quickly as possible. So time at sea typically has to be well planned and executed. There's very little opportunity to simply watch the animals without an agenda for data collection, or to sit around and wait for something extraordinary to happen. Whale-watch boats, their operators and the tourists that they carry are in precisely the opposite position. These boats and their crews do typically spend large amounts of time in close proximity to wild cetaceans and do have the chance to witness unusual events. The whale-watching industry and science communities therefore have an excellent opportunity to pool expertise and resources. If the boats are large enough they may have the capacity to carry a scientist onboard to collect research data and answer the passengers' questions. Alternatively, if the boats are too cramped for an extra person, the operators can simply inform the researchers of what they've been seeing at sea and in return acquire the latest scientific results for themselves and for their paying guests. Such partnerships are common and in several parts of the world have resulted in some significant scientific discoveries.

You don't have to be on a whale-watching boat to make a contribution. Many significant science projects begin with an interesting observation, report or photograph, so information on cetacean sightings is almost always welcome. To collate such information, researchers in many countries have set up observer schemes to which enthusiasts can send sightings. Similarly, many areas have teams dedicated to examining and retrieving beach-cast cetaceans – live or dead. Obviously these teams can't walk all the beaches and so rely on the general public to call in and help with the retrieval of any carcasses that wash ashore. There are also many opportunities to become involved with cetacean science itself. Funds for the work are almost always in short supply, so helping to secure the underlying finances can be a major contribution; so too is volunteering or becoming a researcher yourself.

Contrary to popular perception, most cetacean scientists are driven to do what they do not by the opportunities of being out in the wild but by the lure of the unknown. We know far more about cetaceans today than we did a couple of decades ago, but with each new discovery there comes a whole new raft of unanswered and often intriguing questions. These may range from the specific (how do Sperm Whales catch their prey?) or the local (when do Scottish Bottlenose Dolphins breed?) to the universal and ultimately important in terms of conservation. We urgently need to deal with several major questions if we are to keep the diversity of cetaceans that we currently have. Probably most important are the impacts of our own activities on them. In the past these were predominantly the result of intentional whaling. But today, tragically, these impacts are almost all by-products of human actions not targeted at cetaceans. We've been aware of the potentially negative effects of chemical pollution on the seas for some time, but still we do not yet know how bad the threat really is to wild populations of cetaceans. Similarly there are indications that sound pollution from ships, military sonar and oil exploration negatively affect marine mammals, but where and when these impacts occur remain little understood, along with the best ways to reduce them. We know that fishing also affects cetaceans, whether directly by catching animals in nets or by removing the prey that they are reliant on. In areas where the problems have been sufficiently studied there is little doubt that they have severe impacts on whole populations of animals and practical ways to reduce these conflicts are urgently needed.

While these questions are undoubtedly difficult to answer, they are relatively specific. Others are more general and require a much deeper understanding of the underlying biology of the cetaceans to answer. We do not yet understand, for instance, why some whale species are recovering well after the cessation of whaling while others are not – Right Whales in the southern hemisphere are doing much better than their cousins in the north. As there is no clear answer to questions of this kind we need to explore all kinds of research paths. Similarly, predicting how cetaceans will respond to climate change will be a massive challenge and requires a fundamental understanding of why cetacean species choose the habitats that they do.

Southern Right Whales are recovering from whaling while their northern cousins are not.

Finally, we must not forget that whale watching itself has the potential to negatively affect the target animals. Collisions between boats and whales do occur, while the proximity of noisy engines and alien objects have the capacity to frighten the animals or disrupt their normal channels of communication. There have been several studies of these impacts in which short-term disruptions to cetacean behavior have been observed. What remains unknown, however, is how these short-term changes translate to long-term impacts on individuals and the survival of their populations. Though the threats from whale watching necessarily occur on a more local scale than the those described above, whale watching is rapidly spreading to become a global phenomenon, so its potential for harm must not be ignored.

Just Whom Are We Looking At?

Whale watching as an activity targets more than just the true "whales". Most whale watchers hope to also include dolphins and porpoises as part or all of their experience. Together these animals form a distinct biological group known as the cetaceans – a collection of biologically related, warm-blooded, air-breathing, milk-producing mammals that live their entire lives in the sea. Indeed "cetacean watching" might be a more accurate depiction of the hobby. Simple enough, you might think? Unfortunately, the picture is complicated by one critical mistake that is forever lodged in our common language. When the original fishermen, whalers and biologists named the species we are now familiar with, they broke them up, quite logically at the time, by size. Whales were the large ones, porpoises the small ones and dolphins the intermediates. Fair enough, but evolution didn't work that way. If we look at how these animals are actually related to one another then we discover the absurdity that some of the so-called "whales" are more closely related to porpoises than they are to other whales. Is this really an issue? Well if we want to go further than talking simply about the "big", "medium" and "small" cetaceans and actually understand these animals a bit better, appreciate their ways of life, patterns of feeding and so on, then we need to understand how these species are actually divided and related.

In the broadest terms we can divide the cetaceans straight away into two groups or, to use the correct term, suborders. One suborder has teeth and the other does not. Look into the mouth of most cetaceans and you can tell instantly to which group they belong. The toothless ones are called the mysticetes – literally moustached cetaceans – and instead of teeth they have mouths crammed with plates made from a material called baleen. These plates are flattened pieces of keratin, the same tough material that makes our fingernails, except that in these animals they range in length from the span of your hand to the height of a fully grown person. A mysticete may have hundreds of these plates dangling down from each side of the upper jaw. Together they form an intricate structure used to sieve food from the water. Because big filters often work better than small ones at engulfing swarms of food, these animals tend to be large and hence all 13 or so species fall into the group most commonly referred to as "whales". For obvious reasons, these animals are also called the baleen whales. Without a doubt, the grandest is the Blue Whale at 110 feet (33 m), forever famed for being the largest animal ever to have lived on this planet. The smallest baleen whale is the, still substantial, Pygmy Right Whale at a length of 21 feet (6.4 m). Most baleen whales feed by dropping their lower jaws to engulf entire schools of small fish or crustaceans. Closing their mouths, they ram

Blue Whales may be the heaviest animal alive but they are also remarkably sleek.

their tongues up against the baleen, squeezing out the water, leaving the food behind, which is then swallowed. Sometimes baleen whales simply lunge at schools of prey or alternatively actively corral the prey into convenient gulp-sized aggregations. Humpback Whales are masters at this kind of feeding. In many areas they hunt small fish by corralling them with intricate nets of rising underwater bubbles and loud, blood-curdling underwater screams. Gray Whales also gulp, but instead of focusing on swarms of prey in the water, they stoke their bulk by biting out chunks of the seabed and filtering out the invertebrates that were sheltering

Humpback Whales can engulf entire swarms of prey with their enormous gape.

there. Right Whales take a different approach by skim-feeding, that is swimming through the water with their mouths slightly agape and continuously filtering out the food items from the water through which they pass.

The other suborder contains the majority of cetacean species and these belong to the evolutionary subdivision called the odontocetes or "toothed" cetaceans. This diverse group of around 70 species includes the remaining whales as well as all of the dolphins and porpoises. At one end of the size spectrum is the Sperm Whale – a 60 ft (18 m) leviathan whose weight alone would easily squash a bus. At the other is the Vaquita, an animal tiny enough (at 5 ft / 1.5 m in length) to tuck behind the Sperm Whale's front flipper. But let's not forget that even though the Vaquita is dwarfed by the Sperm Whale it is still a big animal. It is longer and heavier than a large overfed dog and in fact its name comes from the Spanish for "little cow". The odontocetes, even the smallest of them, are sizable creatures.

Although all odontocete species have teeth in one form or another, they vary substantially in shape, size and number. Most have peg-like teeth, two rows in the lower jaw and two rows in the upper. Common Dolphins may have as many as 240 tightly interlocking teeth while others, particularly those that feed on squid, have far fewer. Sperm Whales and Risso's Dolphins, for instance, only have teeth in their

A living yo-yo; Sperm Whales combine breathing at the surface with feeding at great depth.

lower jaws while beaked whales have lost most of theirs. In several species, it's only the males that have teeth and in these cases they have kept only two. These are not used for feeding but instead have been developed into tusks that are used in combat with one another. Narwhals are also odontocetes and have few if any teeth. When males (and occasionally females) do develop them, they are unusual indeed. One tooth emerges from the upper jaw and grows straight out in front of the animal, forming an impressive sword-like tusk that may be 8 ft (2.5 m) long. It is this tusk that most probably led to the myth of the unicorn. While most Narwhals have only one tusk, occasionally whales will develop two.

While feeding structures are the most obvious physical characteristic used to separate the mysticetes from the odontocetes, there are many others: from the details of their blood chemistry to major differences in their physical appearance. The mysticetes, for example, have two large nostrils ("blowholes") on the top of their heads while the odontocetes have only one. Also, their behavior patterns, ways of life, communication and intellectual capabilities differ substantially. These differences stem from the distinct evolutionary paths that these suborders have taken, and while they help us separate the species we should not forget that they have many features in common. They all swim by beating their tails up and down, rather than from side to side like fish and aquatic reptiles, and they all suckle their young. They share these features because they have a common evolutionary history, having arisen from the same ancestors.

Stepping Away from the Land

Before looking back to their origins, perhaps we should appreciate just for a moment what complex works of functional beauty modern cetaceans are. We know that these animals evolved from land-based mammals, but they are not simply their descendants with enough modifications to survive at sea; they have far surpassed this. Dry land now means nothing more than death. They are the marine élite and hold their own against the swiftest and smartest of the fish. They have among their ranks the top predators of the oceans and in generating them they have brought to the sea capabilities possessed by no other marine organism. What is more, we should not look at these animals as a strange evolutionary offshoot of the mammal lineage to which ourselves and everything from cats to camels belong. The cetaceans can rightly call three-quarters of the earth their home while we, and all the other mammals, remain shackled to the smattering of islands called land.

Tracing the evolutionary history of any animal group is a challenging task. It must be reconstructed from a mishmash of anatomical and behavioral characteristics drawn from living animals and combined with scant geological clues from the ground. These geological morsels come to us in the form of fossilized bones, sometimes complete skeletons but most often isolated fragments. Fortunately, animals that die in marine or estuarine environments are more likely to be preserved than those that die on land, and the bigger the animal the more chance that its bones will survive the mineralization process and be found. Consequently, cetaceans and their predecessors are better represented in the fossil record than many other mammalian groups. That said, much of the evolutionary past of the animals that we now call whales, dolphins and porpoises is a mystery that remains to be, literally, unearthed.

If you are trying to understand the biology of an animal and have only one fragment of it, the most useful piece to find is the skull. The shape will indicate what the animal ate, its features will tell you which group of animals it belonged to and the size will help determine how big the animal was. It is no surprise then that the discovery of fossilized skulls, and in particular their teeth, have provided the keys to unlock the mysterious background of the cetaceans. And these clues have been found in places that would be worthy of any Indiana Jones movie – arid parts of Egypt, Pakistan and India. These locations were once the bed of an ancient ocean – the Tethys Ocean – a waterway that covered very much the same area we would consider as the Mediterranean Sea, but which was joined to the Atlantic and the Indian Oceans. It had large areas of shallow water and may have been the venue that ancient land mammals first placed their hoofed feet into the water.

The earliest whale-ancestors that have been discovered are called the Pakicetids. They lived around 50 million years ago in areas that are now Pakistan and India. These animals were between the size of a fox and a wolf but looked like a dog crossed with a rat. They probably weren't particularly brilliant swimmers but lived around shallow waters eating fish and carrion and had ear bones with the beginnings of features we find in modern cetaceans. Their later relatives, the Ambulocetids, lived in similar areas and would look to us alarmingly like furry crocodiles, with broad, flattened, bodies with massive heads and long jaws crammed with teeth. These 9 ft (3 m), 400 lb (360 kg) predatory creatures had squat back legs that were better adapted for swimming than walking and probably moved by undulating their backs much like modern whales. If they looked a little like crocodiles they probably also behaved like them, lurking in the shallows waiting to grab unsuspecting prey. These animals probably spent much of their time resting their heavy heads on the sand and this is where modern whale hearing might have got its start. Low-frequency sounds travel well through the ground and the Ambulocetids might have used the vibrations from their prey's foot-falls to hunt. The rhythmic thumps of any animal walking nearby would conduct through the ground and up into the heavy jaw bone as it rested on the sand; from there the vibrations would be conducted up to the ears. This hearing feature would later prove advantageous to the future cetaceans as they honed hearing suited to picking up vibrations in the open water.

Later species, living around 45 million years ago, had developed tail flukes and accordingly must have been more accomplished swimmers. Nevertheless, since they kept well-developed hind legs they probably retained their abilities to climb back onto land. By 38 million years ago, the wider seas were inhabited by marine mammals resembling the cetaceans that we have come to recognize. Bones of the monstrous Basilosaurus were first found in North America in 1840 and when pieced together, revealed an impressive 50 ft (16 m) long, fully aquatic serpent. Though clearly precursors of modern whales, these leviathans still had stumpy little back legs. These limbs were not, however, simply redundant organs that hadn't yet disappeared but were muscular and had a joint that allowed them to be tucked in or extended straight out to the sides. There's been much discussion about what these little legs might have been used for. They were clearly useless for walking but as these animals had long, snake-like bodies, it's possible that they had a role in reproduction. To mate, the bodies would have to line up precisely and perhaps these little legs allowed the animals an embrace? The Basilosaurids also shared their home waters with a similar but dolphin-sized group of animals called the Dorudontids.

The original Pakicetids and their subsequent relatives, including all modern cetaceans, had some interesting characteristics that hint at who their nearest other relatives might have been. Their fossilized teeth, as well as the DNA and blood chemistry of modern whales, all have links to modern ungulates – sheep, pigs and hippopotami and so on. And this suggests that cetaceans and modern terrestrial ungulates share a common ancestor. Interestingly, features of the behavior of these two groups of animals also point in the same direction. Many ungulates fight by clashing heads; think of deer and their antlers, or the charge of a bull. Most other land mammals don't do this; they bite, scratch or punch. However, in the sea, cetaceans for the most part also fight by clashing heads. It's lovely to think that while the body form of these animals has changed beyond recognition over tens of millions of years, evolution has chosen to keep the way these animals battle.

Cetaceans: Winners within the Waves

The ecological success of any group of animals is often assessed in terms of their distribution and abundance – how widely they are spread and how many there are. If we use these measures to gauge the cetaceans then it is clear that they beat the other marine mammals fair and square. Cetaceans range from the poles to the tropics and populate the open oceans, coastal waters, several major river systems and even poke their noses into the ocean depths. Furthermore, as a group they are more abundant than all the other marine mammals put together. Of the others, the sirenians (manatees and dugongs) are limited to tropical coastal waters. Though they spend their whole lives in water, like cetaceans, the vegetarian diet of the sirenians limits them to sheltered coastal waters where marine plants grow in sufficient abundance. Otters are also limited to water near land as they have to breed and rest ashore and have only a moderate diving capacity. Seals come closest to contending with cetaceans. They are most abundant in temperate and polar waters and, being accomplished divers, can range far out into the open sea. But they are still tied to safe places on land to breed and molt their fur. Cetaceans have no such restrictions. They can feed and breed in the water and in doing so have dispensed with the need for land entirely. Their success is augmented by their superb body form which allows movement in the water with as much efficiency and maneuverability as the best of the fish.

Their bodies are supremely streamlined to the point of being the envy of any submarine designer. The thrust comes from the up-and-down motion of the tail flukes. These are gristly structures that extend laterally from each side of the tip of the backbone. There's much variation in the size and shape of cetacean tail flukes and just from looking at them it's possible to predict the speed at which the owner tends to swim. Slower-swimming species (such as Northern and Southern Right and Sperm Whales) tend to have large, broad flukes, while faster species (Fin and Minke Whales for example) have narrow, sickle-shaped tail fins which they beat rapidly over a narrow arc. The pectoral flippers are the ancestral arms and provide stability and steerage. Many species also have a cartilagenous dorsal fin on top of their back. The dorsal fin's primary function is, like that of the keel on a boat, to stop unwanted rolling. Of the species without dorsal fins, most live in polar waters or rivers where they'd frequently bump any upward-pointing fins on floating ice or branches. Like the tail, the body shape of a cetacean is a very good giveaway to its swimming prowess. Bowhead Whales are slow swimmers that feed on slow-moving (planktonic) prey and migrate over relatively short distances. As well as having broad tails, they also have dumpy bodies which are ideal for retaining body heat in cold Arctic water. Faster species, like Blue Whales, tend to be long and sleek. Species with large pectoral

The streamlined form of a Minke Whale.

flippers, like the Humpback Whale, are highly maneuverable, adopting actions that on land might be regarded as pure ballet if performed by, say, an elephant!

Except for a few sensory bristles around the snout, cetaceans have lost all traces of external hair, presumably as an adaptation to becoming more streamlined. Likewise, the genitals and nipples are tucked away inside folds in the skin, again presumably to reduce drag in the water. Even the strange nodules on the leading edges of Humpback Whale pectoral flippers have recently been discovered to aid the efficiency of water flow. Below the skin is a thick organ, called the blubber layer. Being made of fibrous tissues and oils it acts as a heat insulator and fat store and also streamlines the body by smoothing out any lumps or bumps.

Being mammals, cetaceans breathe air, which they do with impressive economy of motion. A whale, dolphin or porpoise need only brush the surface for a moment and it will have exchanged around 80 percent of the volume of its lungs with the atmosphere. Look closely at a surfacing cetacean and you will see that it begins to

Humpback Whale exhalations or "blows" hang in the air.

exhale moments before reaching the surface. The rising air bursts explosively through the surface forming the "blow" that whalers and now whale watchers are so keen to spot. The blow itself is made up of exhaled warm air and a fine mist of seawater, mucus and oils. In bigger species, the blow may hang visibly in the air for several seconds and the distinctive shape and height of the plume can often help indicate the species that produced it. As the surfacing continues, the head and back break the surface and then, without pause, there is a rapid, usually audible, inhalation before the animal disappears beneath the surface once more.

To make a living in the open seas, cetaceans have become magnificent divers. Being able to swim at speed and with energetic efficiency, they are able to reach phenomenal depths on the oxygen reserves they can store in their bodies. Sperm Whales and many of the beaked whales are amazingly accomplished divers which can penetrate to depths of a mile (1500 m) or more below the surface. And yet they are not simply going down and then returning; this is where they find their food and so they must actively hunt at these depths. Consequently, they must hold their breath for up to an hour on each of these dives. We tend to think of these animals as superb divers but in many respects we are looking at it the wrong way around. Instead, we should call them "surfacers", because they live at huge depths but make brief forays to the surface every now and again to obtain oxygen – much to the benefit of whale watchers.

Cetaceans have several adaptations that allow them to spend such extraordinary lengths of time underwater. Most important is their ability to carry large reserves of oxygen. Though they have efficient lungs, they are not terribly large in comparison to the body, and in any case, the air that a whale or dolphin carries in its lungs will be quickly squeezed to nearly nothing by the pressure of the depths. Instead, cetaceans store most of the oxygen they need in the large volume of haemoglobin-rich blood and the high concentrations of myoglobin in their muscles. Cut into a dead whale and this volume of blood and dark color of the myoglobin in the muscle are immediately obvious. As well as storing large oxygen reserves, they are also frugal in how they use it. Species that routinely dive to great depths typically cut back on the blood flow to non-essential organs – their skin, intestines and blubber. That way these tissues can simply tick over in suspended animation until the next surfacing.

Though human breath-holding divers have nothing like the diving capacity of cetaceans, the invention of an aqualung has done much to increase the depths that we can reach. However, diving with a canister of gas strapped to our backs brings with it huge dangers in the form of "the bends". This is a crippling ailment that arises when nitrogen that dissolved into the blood at depth comes bubbling out of solution if the scuba-diver returns to the surface too quickly. It was long thought that cetaceans didn't have this problem because they only breathe their air at the surface. However, this conventional wisdom has been turned on its head by recent events. On various coastlines around the world, groups of cetaceans, mostly beaked whales but also baleen whales and some dolphins, have come ashore alive but clearly very sick. These events remained unexplained for years until it was noticed that they coincided with nearby naval exercises. Examinations of the bodies of these animals suggest that many may have died from something very like the bends that we know so well from humans. The exact cause is still unknown but it's very possible that the loud underwater noises made by these ships frighten the whales at depth and cause them to surface much too fast. The tissues in the bodies of these animals then begin to fizz just like a bottle of soda water when the cap is removed too quickly. The whales must die an agonizing death, effectively boiling from the inside. Unsurprisingly, these findings have prompted new research and as a result it's been discovered that deep-diving beaked whales normally surface much more slowly than was previously thought and follow very deep dives with a curious sequence of increasingly shallow dives. So not only are diving whales managing their oxygen stores with great care, they also have to pay close attention to the nitrogen in their bodies.

Predators on land have to have keen senses to find and outwit their prey and of course the same is true underwater, but the complement of senses must be very different. Water, suspended sediment and plankton all absorb light very quickly so vision plays a secondary role to other senses. Sound, in comparison, travels extremely well underwater and as a result marine mammals, particularly the cetaceans, have honed their hearing abilities to extraordinary levels. We know that they use a wide variety of sounds to communicate and in doing so can coordinate hunting. But odontocetes, and perhaps some mysticetes, have taken the use of sound to much higher levels. Like bats, odontocetes echolocate, that is, produce loud sounds and then listen to the echoes that return. The strength and direction of the echoes then tell the hunting animal what is out in front of it. They produce their sounds by shunting air back and forth in their nasal cavities and focus the resulting clicks using a bulbous fatty structure called the melon on the front of the head. If you swim with odontocetes, whether they are Sperm Whales or dolphins, you will no doubt be able to feel these high-intensity sounds literally banging off your body. They may be a series of rhythmic clicks like a slow-turning bicycle wheel or come as an intense buzzing or whine. The information that odontocetes can glean from these sounds is extraordinary, whether it's detecting an object the size of an orange at the distance of a football pitch or determining whether there is a fishing net ahead. And of course all of this can be carried out in total darkness. Firing sound off your prey is a great way to hunt so long as the prey can't hear the sounds and know that you're coming. Seals have excellent hearing and can easily hear echolocation sounds, consequently Killer Whales echolocate only sparingly when trying to sneak up on their prey. Most fish can't hear high-frequency sounds and so remain oblivious to the predators as they bear down on them in the darkness. However, a small number of fish have evolved very sensitive hearing and it is thought that they have done so to detect echolocating cetacean predators.

While we know that cetaceans can hear and see well, we also know that they have an acute sense of touch. You only have to watch a school of dolphins to notice how often they brush up against one another as they move around. River Dolphins often grub around in the bottom sediment for prey items and are clearly using tactile senses to guide them. Accordingly they retain bristles on their snouts into adulthood that are normally used by suckling calves to feel their mother's side. It's not known how much cetaceans taste or smell, though it is clear that the areas of the brain devoted to these senses are very much diminished. We also know very little about what other senses they possess. Being able to detect pressure, and as a result depth, would clearly be very useful, as would an ability to perceive the earth's magnetic field, but at present we don't have enough information to determine if these are cetacean senses. But as they are both abilities possessed by other creatures, it remains possible. Clearly many important discoveries await us!

For animals that never come to land it's interesting to know how they rest or even sleep. Studies by neurobiologists suggest that they do indeed sleep and they

Life under water for these Common Dolphins requires a refined complement of senses.

do this by adopting an interesting trick; they can allow half of the brain to sleep while keeping the other half awake. So if you see a pod of Killer Whales swimming for a prolonged period in perfect synchrony, side by side, this may be because they are actually sleeping.

Reproduction – Mammals in the Slow Lane

Take a look at the capacity of different animals to reproduce and it becomes immediately apparent that there is an enormous range across the kingdom. Many species, especially fish, can produce literally millions of offspring in a lifetime while others, including ourselves, only produce a few. Yet the highly fecund haven't taken over the world. Reproduction clearly isn't only a numbers game, it is also a balancing act. Successful parents should, on the one side, produce as many young as possible and on the other, give each enough resources to stand a fighting chance of becoming successful themselves. Since no animal has limitless resources, prospective parents make a trade-off between these two opposites. Offspring that are produced in their hundreds or millions typically receive hardly any help to mature and the risks of failure for any individual are high. Progeny that are produced in much smaller numbers receive more help from their parents, so that once they are

Humpback Whales migrate huge distances to give birth in the ideal habitat.

independent, their chances of survival are good. Parents can make this investment in different ways. Bestowing an embryo with a large egg is good but, better still, giving it a long gestation inside the body of the mother allows young to be born larger and with more acute senses, abilities to detect and avoid predators and find food. Care subsequent to birth can have the same outcome but parental care can go further still. Parents can directly provide food for their offspring and teach them how to make a living before they need to do so alone.

So where do the cetaceans sit on this reproductive spectrum? They have plonked themselves firmly at one end of it – at the few and well-cared-for offspring end. Cetaceans hold among their ranks the animal record holders for lowest lifetime reproductive output and the most covetously nurtured offspring. Being mammals, cetaceans gestate their young, and being large, have accordingly long pregnancies. Female porpoises carry their young for about eight months while Sperm Whales are pregnant for 16 months. But even this marathon pregnancy is short when you consider that the offspring are usually 8 to 10 percent of the mother's weight at birth and yet have developed from the union of just a single sperm and an egg cell.

Accordingly the fetal growth rates of cetaceans are among the fastest in the animal kingdom.

The young are born fully formed and able to see, hear and swim from the start. They have to, as they are born underwater but breathe air. They are also born alone. No living twin cetaceans have ever been recorded. Though fully able to swim, young cetaceans don't need to catch prey immediately; they are nursed by their mothers just like other mammals. But female cetaceans don't produce milk like the cow's milk that we put into our tea, but milk that is much richer in fat. In fact, odontocete milk is 10 to 30 percent fat and in some mysticetes it can be as much as 50 percent fat – literally half and half! The milk

Where Killer Whale mothers go, the calf goes too.

is produced from two teats either side of the genital opening. Cetaceans don't have pursing lips so the young can't form a seal with which to suck; instead, the mother squirts the milk out under pressure. Baleen whale and porpoise calves may be suckled for 6 to 12 months after birth and delphinids (ocean dolphins) may suckle their young for much longer before weaning. Bottlenose Dolphins, for example, suckle their young for two to three years, while elderly female Pilot Whales continue to produce milk even when they may have stopped producing calves of their own. It's thought that they continue to lactate to improve the survival chances of their relatives, especially the offspring of their own offspring.

Finding out how long cetaceans live has proved to be an interesting pursuit and has turned up some surprising results. But how do you determine the lifespan of a whale or dolphin? The ages of odontocetes are hidden in their teeth. If you take a Harbor Porpoise tooth, for example, and cut it neatly from top to bottom you will see that inside it is ringed much like the trunk of a tree. Count the rings and you have the age of the animal in years – simple! It turns out that a good lifespan for a Harbor Porpoise is around 15 years and a really old one might live into its twenties. Larger odontocetes live longer. Bottlenose Dolphins can live into their fifties and Killer Whales may reach 80 or more. Aging baleen whales is harder because they don't have teeth, but it's been found that many species have a waxy plug that fills the ear canal. If the plug is removed and carefully sectioned, it too has bands that indicate years. From these we know, for example, that Blue and Fin Whales can live to over 100. This method does not work for Bowhead Whales so their age has remained a mystery until very recently. Inuit hunters in Alaska kill a number of Bowheads each year. The meat is eaten and during the process of cutting animals up, the remains of several ancient harpoon tips have recently been discovered. These ivory and stone tips had clearly been lodged in the flesh of the whales for well over a century, as metal harpoons have been used ever since. Further investigations of the levels of aspartic acid (an amino acid) in the eye lenses of these animals confirmed that they were very old indeed. In fact the oldest whale was around 211 years old at the time of its death. That whale, alive during the term of President Clinton, was also gliding slowly and gracefully through the Arctic Seas when Thomas Jefferson was president.

So cetaceans live life in the biological slow lane, produce few offspring, mature slowly and live long. This is clearly a strategy that works and has allowed them to compete with other species in the battle for evolutionary survival. However, it has one major drawback and it is one that has become ever more significant in recent centuries. Slow breeders have a low capacity to bounce back when their numbers are knocked down. The hunting of Blue Whales, for example, may have ended in the Southern Ocean in 1965 but we are still waiting for them to recover to anything like their former numbers.

The investment in offspring is not divided evenly among the sexes. Males devote most of their energies to the events before fertilization rather than afterwards. In other words, male reproductive strategies are primarily concerned with improving their chances of mating and, if this occurs, maximizing the chances that they will be the father of any resulting offspring. The way that cetaceans do this varies from species to species. Male mammals on land often hold territories but this would be impractical at sea; there is no way for a male to mark a territory or keep the resources that might make a good territory in any one piece of water. Instead they resort to other methods. Males of many species set out to impress females and intimidate other males with their skills or sheer bulk. Male Sperm Whales are a third larger than females and use their enormous mass to fight one another. Beaked Whales joust by charging at one another and use their teeth as weapons to scar the body of their rival as they crash past each other. Males with the most scars, it is thought, have survived the most fights and so must be the most attractive to females. As well as fighting, male Humpback Whales also sing the most famous underwater songs in existence. Males can hang motionless underwater on the breeding grounds and sing hugely

Bottlenose Dolphins lead intensely complex social lives filled with politics and rivalry.

complex yet precisely repeated songs that last for hours. The exact rules underlying these songs remain mysterious despite years of scientific study. The whales sing an ever-changing song but at any one time all the males in an area will sing the same song. Male Bottlenose Dolphins take a more direct approach. In many parts of their range the males form alliances with other males. These long-term pairs or trios swim in synchrony searching for a receptive female. When they find one, they shadow her movements and mate with her frequently, chasing off any other males that approach.

Observations in Western Australia have added an interesting twist to this story. Previously warring male alliances will temporarily gang up with each other to displace another alliance from a female. These complex actions of manipulation and implementation amount to what could quite logically be considered to be dolphin politics. To do this requires sophisticated communication, intent and an ability to form context-dependent partnerships – all characteristics that require and benefit from having an intelligent mind.

Even after mating, competition between males might not be over entirely. During the breeding season female Right Whales mate with many males in succession. So for an individual male, it is not him but his sperm that end up doing the competing to ensure he fathers the offspring. Male Right Whales therefore produce vast

Cetaceans are social animals – Killer Whales live in the same social groups for life.

quantities of sperm to dilute that of the other males and increase the odds of their sperm getting to the egg first. Accordingly, male Right Whales can boast the largest testes on the planet, weighing in at around a ton each.

While most male cetaceans invest all their reproductive efforts before fertilization, some play a slightly different game. Fish-eating Killer Whales live in a maternally dominated society. Maturing males and females don't leave their mother's side and accordingly end up living in a close family group. If a male wants to ensure his genes are passed on to the next generation, he can breed with females from other groups of whales and, crucially, also help his own family survive. After all, he will share at least a quarter of his genes with his brothers and sisters so their survival and reproduction will promote his own genetic inheritance.

Cetaceans, by and large, are social creatures. When you see one at sea, you will most often see several and sometimes hundreds. These groupings come under a variety of names: aggregations, groups, schools, bands, pods, herds, shoals, packs and so on. To most people these terms are interchangeable and basically refer to several animals appearing in the same view and perhaps behaving in a similar manner as one another. But just as the names for these groups vary from place to place, whale watcher to whale watcher, so do the reasons why these animals seek out each others' company.

Most basic to cetacean societies are the bonds between mothers and their calves. Because calves are dependent on the milk of their mothers, protection from predators and, to varying extents, the opportunity to be taught, the mother-calf association is the strongest social bond among all cetacean species. If a calf loses contact with its mother, the sea quickly becomes a very big place and for a young calf this means almost certain death. As a result, mothers and calves usually swim in close contact.

Unlike the baleen whales, all odontocetes have calves that are nutritionally dependent for longer than the mother can abstain from eating. Consequently, the females have a problem; they need to keep in contact with their offspring but they also need to feed. Their food, however, can be deep below the surface and the calf can't necessarily hold its breath long enough or swim fast enough to follow the mother on her submarine hunting trips. Sperm Whales are the perfect example. Their food is thousands of feet below them in the deep sea and a female will embark on dives lasting 40 minutes to an hour in length. The calf can't possibly follow her down on these dives and so the risk of it being separated or attacked by predators is significant. Fortunately, because all breeding females have this problem, there is an opportunity to share the load by babysitting. Consequently, female-female bonds are the second building blocks of cetacean, particularly odontocete, societies.

Once a calf is weaned it need not necessarily disperse right away. There's value to be gained by sticking with its mother's group. The group, as a whole, may be better able to locate their prey; once detected they may be able to round it up or ambush it together. They will also be better able to identify and fend off predators and there will be many more opportunities to learn the social mannerisms of their societies. As mentioned already, Killer and Pilot Whales have taken this system to an extreme. Young males and females stay with their mothers' group for life. Other odontocetes are less faithful, female Bottlenose Dolphins may associate with their mothers' group for decades but males disperse after three to five years. Young Harbor Porpoises disperse shortly after weaning. Baleen whales are similar; calves stay with their mothers for the first 6 to 12 months then go their separate ways.

As described earlier, males associate with other animals to enhance their chances of breeding, but they may also be social for other reasons. Catching prey is a difficult thing and to be successful, cetaceans have to compete with many other types of predators. One of the key characteristics that give cetaceans their competitive edge is their ability to cooperate and coordinate. Groups of Humpback Whales spin elaborate bubble nets to catch entire schools of fish, mammal-eating Killer Whales set up ambushes for seals and groups of Dusky Dolphins take turns to round up schools of fish deep below the surface. In these cases, the gains of working together outweigh the costs of sharing out the prize.

Of course group hunting can be an anonymous affair – each animal simply responding to the behavior of its neighbors and the state of the prey. However, there's more to be gained if the hunters can improve their tactics from one hunt to the next by developing roles for specific individuals. Cetaceans do exactly this. For example, it is usually a particular Humpback Whale in a group that blows the bubbles that form the net and it is usually a specific Killer Whale that carries out the herding while others form the trap. To act in this more sophisticated manner, individual cetaceans need to recognize one another. In many situations they may not be able to see their accomplices but instead use sound to convey information. Bottlenose Dolphins are best known for this. Each individual appears to have a specific whistle of its own and by broadcasting this sound, the individuals in close proximity will know who is where.

We tend to think that if we can see animals coordinating their behaviors together they are a distinct grouping or herd. But it is becoming increasingly clear that we have historically been seeing the lives of these animals a little bit too much through our own eyes. Most cetaceans are vocal and produce sounds almost continuously. The reasons why they do this are in many respects mysterious. But it is likely that some of these sounds are for communication over ranges far longer than it is possible for us to see in the air. Before modern shipping added its noise pollution, a Fin Whale's call was loud enough to travel from one side of the Atlantic to the other. The valid question has therefore been asked; why would an animal make such a loud sound, unless it was of some value to other animals in the far distance? If Fin Whales and other cetaceans are communicating over such large ranges then our idea of what actually represents a group of these animals needs to be reconsidered.

Mysterious Migrations

The world is anything but a stable place and the annual wobble of the earth on its axis does much to shift the opportunities for any animals with the option to move. We are all familiar with the annual migrations of a wide range of species; the arrival of a new complement of birds in the spring, the spectacular herds of grazing-moving-grazing mammals in Africa, the mysterious red crabs on Christmas Island and so on. Yet it took man many hundreds of years to figure out that cetaceans also migrate.

Seafarers and whale hunters knew that whales appeared off their coasts at certain times of year, but they had no way of knowing where the whales went between times. Though we now know more, many well-known species keep their movements secret. For example, Minke Whales appear off the coast of north-west Europe each summer, then simply disappear. Even now, nobody is sure where they go in the winter. Of the migrations that we do know about, the movements are nothing if not spectacular. The annual migrations of eastern Pacific Gray Whales are perhaps the most easily observed. These animals spend their entire lives within a few miles

Female Gray Whales swim the length of a continent to give birth, and then return with their young.

of shore and yet their annual migrations of 10,000 nautical miles (18,500 km) take them from the lagoons of Baja California to the northern side of Alaska. Their progressions along the shorelines of this phenomenal path are as predictable as the migrations of swallows. Humpback Whale populations in every ocean in the world (except one) go through similar seasonal changes in latitude. They spend the summers feeding in high-latitude, food-rich temperate waters then migrate to the nutritionally barren but warm tropical breeding grounds to give birth and mate. To achieve this, the migrating animals must endure a phenomenal period without food – up to eight months in every year. To do this, the whales have to store massive fat reserves and to do that they have to be large – perhaps this is why they are so large! But, at the bottom of it all, the reasons why the whales make these migrations at all are intriguingly controversial. Conventional wisdom ran along the lines that the young newborn calves had much more chance of survival in the calm, warm waters of the tropics. The energy that they would save by not having to keep warm in the cold feeding grounds could be put directly into growth. It's a neat idea but unfortunately doesn't really fit the facts. Because newborn whales are as large and well insulated as they are, staying warm is not likely to be a huge problem for them. As a result, other explanations have been sought. One is that these migrations are simply an evolutionary tradition carried on by the whales from times when the continents were much closer together. More recently, a new idea came to light that is perhaps more convincing. The proponents suggested that these whales migrate as a result of seals! Cold, high-latitude waters are productive places. They support the whales during their four-month summer feeding frenzy and they also support large numbers of seals. The seals, in turn, support populations of mammal-eating Killer Whales. So while the food-rich waters might be a good place to feed for self-sufficient whales, they are not a good place for the newborn calves, which are especially vulnerable to Killer Whale attack. So the pregnant whales give birth in the tropics, a region devoid of seals for the most part and at distances too far for the predators to follow. Because females come into estrus just after they give birth, then the males have to follow them on these massive migrations. It's a long way for these animals to travel but a considerable benefit to whale-watching communities the world over.

It is not just the large whales that migrate, many small cetaceans make seasonal movements as well. Throughout many temperate areas, the complement of dolphins seen in coastal waters changes through the year. This is particularly evident off the coasts of the eastern US. Each summer, Bottlenose Dolphins move northwards. They are not going through the same kinds of migrations as the baleen whales but instead following the advance of warmer water. The same occurs on the western seaboard of the US, but as well as annual shifts in water temperature the Pacific experiences temperature variations that extend over several years. In these El Niño events dolphins tend to move much further north than usual. When the water returns to normal temperature, some of the dolphins hang on in their new home before eventually dying off or moving back south.

As we find out more and more about cetaceans, it's becoming increasingly clear just how much their behavior is tuned to the conditions of the sea and that these relationships, as the interactions between whales and seals showed, may be anything but immediately obvious to us. As global climate change takes hold and sea temperatures, currents and weather patterns shift, we should be prepared for some unexpected changes in the places cetaceans choose to live and, if we are lucky, survive.

Having hunted all night, Spinner Dolphins rest during the day.

Identifying Whales, Dolphins & Porpoises

Correctly identifying cetaceans in the wild is enormous fun but can also be a challenge even for the expert. Accurate identification usually relies on a combination of characteristics and it is helpful to have a mental checklist of things to look for. Larger whales are often first spotted by their blow or spout, a fine mist of water droplets forced skyward by their exhaled breath. On calm days, the sound of this exhalation can be heard for up to a mile and the shape and height of the vapor cloud are useful clues to the identity of the animal below. Blows of smaller whales, most dolphins and porpoises are less clearly visible but can be heard at close range.

A glimpse of the body will give an idea of the animal's bulk. Remember that judging distance at sea is notoriously difficult so use birds or other boats to help gauge the scale. As the cetacean breaks the surface, note the shape of the head. Is there a distinct beak or a smooth transition from the top of the head to the tip of the snout? If a melon is visible, what shape is it? What colors do you see on the head and flanks? As the animal goes through its surfacing routine, pay attention to the order of features as they appear. Do you see the whole back at once or does the animal appear to roll at the surface with the snout appearing before the back and dorsal fin? Note the shape and location of the dorsal fin; is it mid-way along the back or is it nearer the tail? Is it triangular or sickle-shaped (falcate)? Finally, as the cetacean dives, note whether the tail is visible and also its shape and any color patterns.

Behavior is helpful too. Different species surface to breathe in characteristic ways and jumping, bow-riding and other behaviors give clues. The degree of social affiliation varies greatly between species so try to count the numbers. Did you see a solitary individual or a group of a dozen or several dozen? The way that they surface relative to each other also gives identification clues. If they are diving in synchrony and heading in the same direction they are much more likely to be associated and so belong to the more social species. If they are in the same spot but diving out of sequence and pointing in different directions, they may simply be there because of a common food resource rather than any social affiliation. Consider the habitat (river estuary, inshore or deep offshore) and the geographical region that you are in.

Of course, you may see something really unusual or hard to identify, perhaps an animal outside of its normal range or one of the many species for which little is known. In these cases, pictures or video will give you, and others, a second chance for a correct identification.

The following section describes the different species of whales, dolphins and porpoises known to live in our oceans, seas and rivers. The pages illustrate the diversity of cetaceans and ways to identify them. To help clarify the situation, particular attention has been paid to those cetaceans you are most likely to encounter while whale watching.

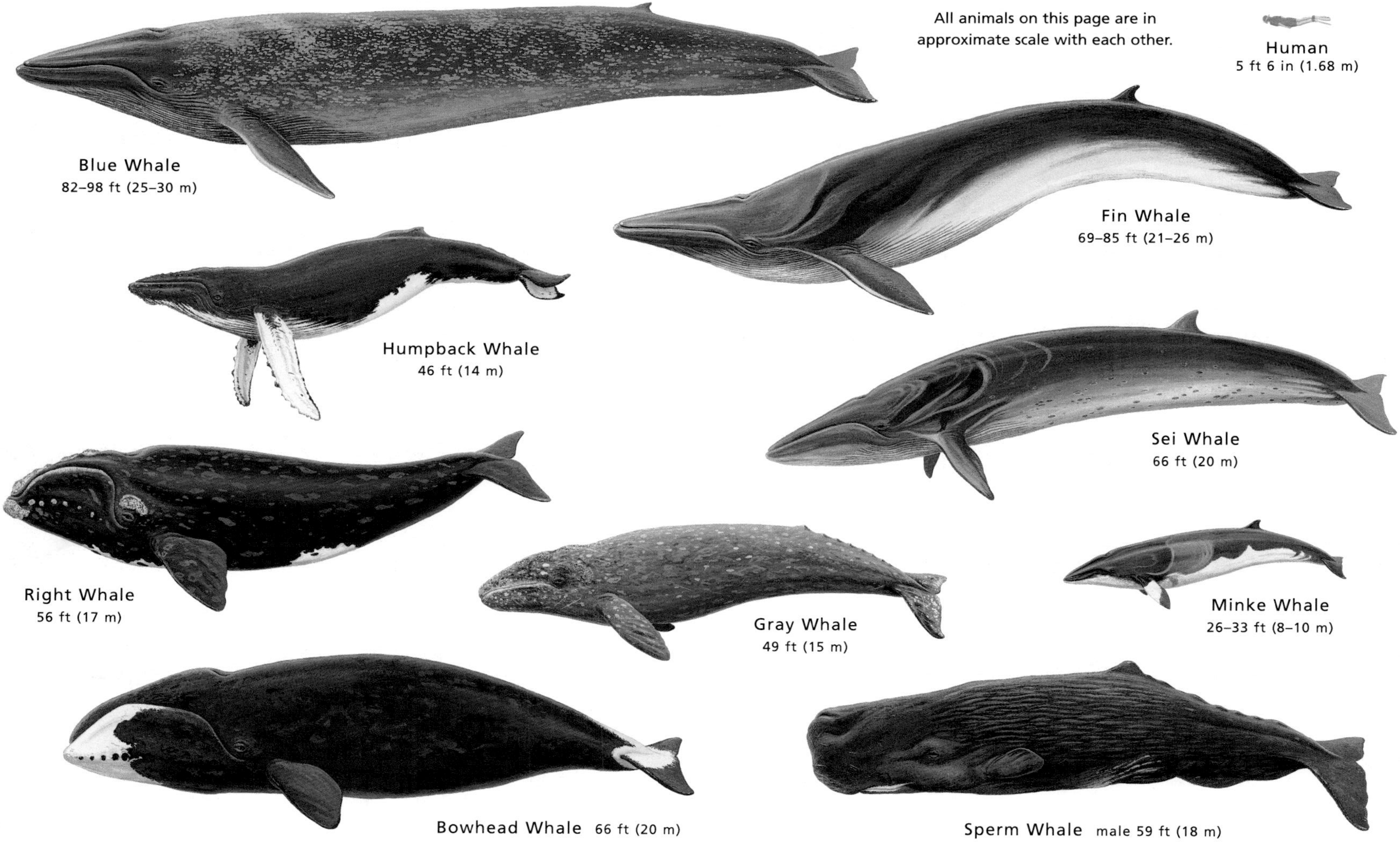

All animals on this page are in approximate scale with each other.

Human
5 ft 6 in (1.68 m)

Fin Whale
69–85 ft (21–26 m)

Sei Whale
66 ft (20 m)

Minke Whale
26–33 ft (8–10 m)

Sperm Whale   male 59 ft (18 m)

Gray Whale
49 ft (15 m)

Blue Whale
82–98 ft (25–30 m)

Humpback Whale
46 ft (14 m)

Right Whale
56 ft (17 m)

Bowhead Whale   66 ft (20 m)

IDENTIFYING WHALES, DOLPHINS & PORPOISES

All animals on this page are in
approximate scale with each other.

Northern Bottlenose Whale
20–30 ft (6–9 m)

Beluga Whale   13–16 ft (4–5 m)

Narwhal   13–16 ft (4–5 m), tusk: 5–8 ft (1.5–2.5 m)

Cuvier's Beaked Whale   20–23 ft (6–7 m)

Killer Whale
male 23–30 ft (7–9 m)

Long-Finned Pilot Whale
20 ft (6 m)

Human
5 ft 6 in (1.68 m)

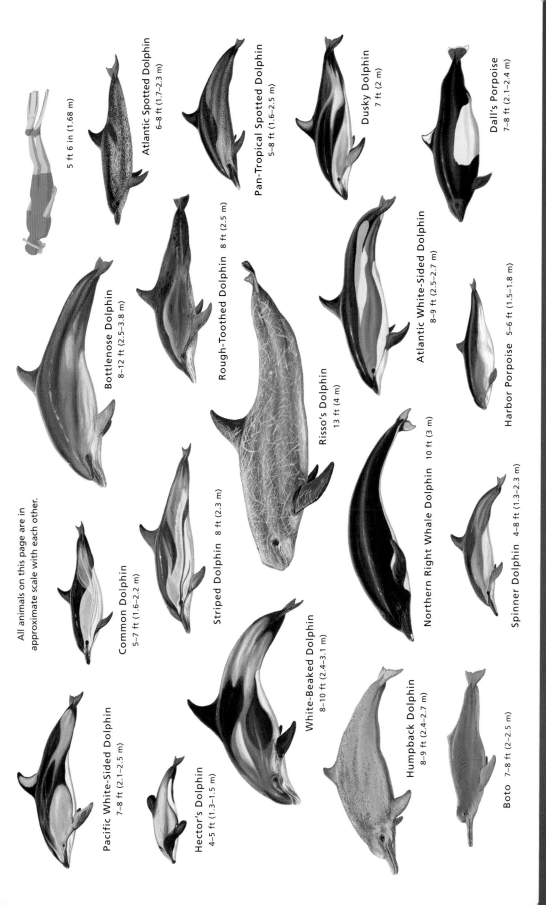

All animals on this page are in approximate scale with each other.

5 ft 6 in (1.68 m)

Atlantic Spotted Dolphin
6–8 ft (1.7–2.3 m)

Pan-Tropical Spotted Dolphin
5–8 ft (1.6–2.5 m)

Dusky Dolphin
7 ft (2 m)

Dall's Porpoise
7–8 ft (2.1–2.4 m)

Bottlenose Dolphin
8–12 ft (2.5–3.8 m)

Rough-Toothed Dolphin 8 ft (2.5 m)

Atlantic White-Sided Dolphin
8–9 ft (2.5–2.7 m)

Harbor Porpoise 5–6 ft (1.5–1.8 m)

Risso's Dolphin
13 ft (4 m)

Northern Right Whale Dolphin 10 ft (3 m)

Spinner Dolphin 4–8 ft (1.3–2.3 m)

Common Dolphin
5–7 ft (1.6–2.2 m)

Striped Dolphin 8 ft (2.3 m)

Pacific White-Sided Dolphin
7–8 ft (2.1–2.5 m)

Hector's Dolphin
4–5 ft (1.3–1.5 m)

White-Beaked Dolphin
8–10 ft (2.4–3.1 m)

Humpback Dolphin
8–9 ft (2.4–2.7 m)

Boto 7–8 ft (2–2.5 m)

IDENTIFYING WHALES, DOLPHINS & PORPOISES

BOWHEAD WHALE *Balaena mysticetus*

Inhabitants of the extreme north, Bowheads are rarely found far from ice. Their thick blubber and battering ram of a head allow them to withstand this harsh ice-choked environment.

Their rotund bulk, hump in front of the blowholes and depression behind, white lower jaw and lack of dorsal fin or callosities make these whales distinctive.

The curved jaw houses the longest baleen of any whale (up to 14 ft / 4.3 m long). There are no longitudinal grooves on the throat or belly.

Like that of the Right Whales, the blow is bushy, vertical, up to 20 ft (6 m) high and V-shaped. Unlike Right Whales, there are no callosities and the white tip of the lower jaw may be visible.

The tail is broad, triangular with a deep central notch and often raised when diving. Many individuals have a light area on the tail stock.

Also known as **Great Polar Whale, Arctic Whale, Arctic Right Whale,**
Greenland Right Whale or **Greenland Whale.**

Identification: Dark blue-black overall with a distinctive white patch on the lower jaw.
Close views may reveal a horizontal row of irregular black spots within the white patch.
Living year-round at high latitudes, this robust whale is protected from the icy water by
an exceptionally thick layer of blubber up to 2 ft (0.75 m) thick. The immense head makes
up nearly one-third of the 15 to 65 ft (5 to 20 m) total body length. Females are larger
than males. The paired blowholes, at the highest point of the head, create a bushy,
V-shaped blow. As animals age, the pale band just ahead of the tail fluke (peduncle
patch) turns whiter and larger and very old animals may develop all-white tails. Ancient
harpoon tips collected from recently killed Bowheads suggest that they may live for well
over a century and are possibly the longest-lived of any mammals. Usually found alone or
in small groups but larger congregations may occur in areas of exceptional feeding. They
can lift their tails clear of the surface when diving, and breaches and lob tails are often
observed. At southern edge of range might be mistaken for Northern Right Whale, but
lacks distinctive callosities and has a hump in front of blowhole, or Humpback Whale,
which has a visible dorsal fin and much longer flippers, and possibly Sperm Whale,
which has distinctive wrinkled skin and a square rather than bowed head shape.

Where and When: Found only in Arctic and sub-Arctic waters (between 54-75° N).
Frequenting the southern edges of the sea ice during the winter and moving along
leads and into areas of broken ice during the summer. Bowhead Whales spend a great
deal of time under the ice, using their massive heads to break through several inches of
solid ice to create a breathing hole. Most of the world population occurs in the Bering,
Chukchi and Beaufort Seas with smaller numbers in the Sea of Okhotsk, Davis Strait,
Baffin Bay, Hudson Bay and a relict population in the Greenland and Barents Seas.

Best Chances: In spring (mid May to June), solid pack ice may funnel migrants within
sight of shore off Point Barrow, Alaska, as they migrate eastwards into the Beaufort Sea.
Some expedition cruises visit Isabella Bay on the east coast of Baffin Island, Canada.

Key Facts

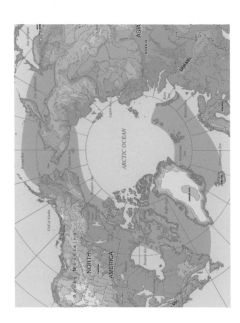

Average Length: 66 ft (20 m)

Length at Birth: 13 ft (4 m)

Adult Weight: 90 tons

Life Span: Possibly 200 yrs

Distribution: Arctic and sub-Arctic waters.

Status: Decimated by whaling, numbers off
Alaska are recovering but other populations
near extinction.

Grouping: Usually solitary but may gather in
mating areas or form echelon formations to feed.

Main ID Features: Large, rotund whales
without dorsal fin. Black with prominent
white around snout.

BOWHEAD WHALE

RIGHT WHALES

Southern Right Whale
Eubalaena australis

North Atlantic Right Whale
Eubalaena glacialis

North Pacific Right Whale
Eubalaena japonica

Distinctive horny skin growths, called callosities, encrust the jaws, chin, around the blowhole and above the eye. Populated by whale lice and sometimes barnacles, their function remains mysterious.

Right Whales are stocky, slow swimming, range from blue-black to brown in color and have no dorsal fin. Their blubber, baleen and ease of capture ensured their value to early whalers.

Like that of the Bowhead Whale, the blow is bushy, vertical and V-shaped. However only Right Whales have callosities. The head is narrow on the top and the curved jaw line is often visible.

Head is large comprising a quarter to a third of the body length. The jaw line is strongly curved and the flippers broad. Unlike the rorqual whales, there are no longitudinal grooves on the throat or belly.

Tail flukes are black, broad, deeply notched in the middle and with smoothly tapering tips. They are often raised during a dive.

Also known as **Black Right Whale**, **Biscayan Right Whale** or **Japanese Right Whale**.

Identification: All three species are readily identified by the combination of rotund, barrel-shaped body, gray-black, black or dark brown body, knobbly whitish patches (callosities) on the head and absence of both dorsal fin and ventral grooves. Broad black tail and flippers. Body 15 to 60 ft (4 to 18 m) long. Two blowholes produce characteristic V-shaped blow, up to 16 ft (5 m) high. Tail often raised above surface as animal dives. They are slow swimmers and feed by swimming with mouth agape and filtering prey. Black baleen plates may be visible. Breaches, lobtailing and other aerial activities common. The shapes and extent of the callosities are sufficiently variable to distinguish individuals. They swim singly or in small groups. Larger aggregations occur in areas of rich feeding or around fertile females in the breeding season. The courtship groups may involve animals packed very densely with much touching and rolling. The three species are distinguished by their distributions. Only other large dark whale in the northern hemisphere without a dorsal fin or hump and a vertical blow is the Bowhead.

Where and When: Southern Right Whales: Circumpolar within temperate and subpolar waters of the southern hemisphere. In the winter, adults move to inshore waters to mate and calve. In the summer, many migrate to Antarctic waters to feed. **North Atlantic Right Whales:** Severely depleted by whaling. Once found on both sides of the North Atlantic. Now very rare in European waters. Main population off the Canadian and eastern US coast. Follows a seasonal migration over shelf waters, often close to land. **North Pacific Right Whales:** Waters off southern Japan, Sea of Okhotsk, Kuril Islands and up into the Bering Sea or Gulf of Alaska. Occasionally off the west coast of the US and Mexico.

Best Chances: Southern: Hermanus, South Africa and Valdez Peninsula, Argentina. **North Atlantic:** Gulf of Maine in summer or New England coast south to Florida and Gulf of Mexico. **North Pacific:** now extremely rare. The **Pygmy Right Whale** (*Caperea marginata*): Small, rare and little known. Grows to 21 ft (6.4 m) and easily confused with Minke Whale but arched jaw and plain gray pectoral flippers are distinctive. Occurs in temperate southern hemisphere waters.

Average Length: 57 ft (17 m)

Length at Birth: 15 ft (4.5 m)

Adult Weight: 90 tons

Life Span: 70 yrs +

Distribution: Temperate and polar waters in both hemispheres. Migrate between coastal breeding sites in warm inshore waters and feed in more temperate habitats.

Status: The focus of early whaling, which decimated numbers. Both Northern species at or near collapse. Southern species recovering well.

Grouping: Usually alone or in pairs but aggregate in areas of good feeding or for breeding.

Main ID Features: Rotund whales without dorsal fin. Black body with creamy white callosities on head, V-shaped blow, may raise flukes on dives.

RIGHT WHALES

GRAY WHALE *Eschrichtius robustus*

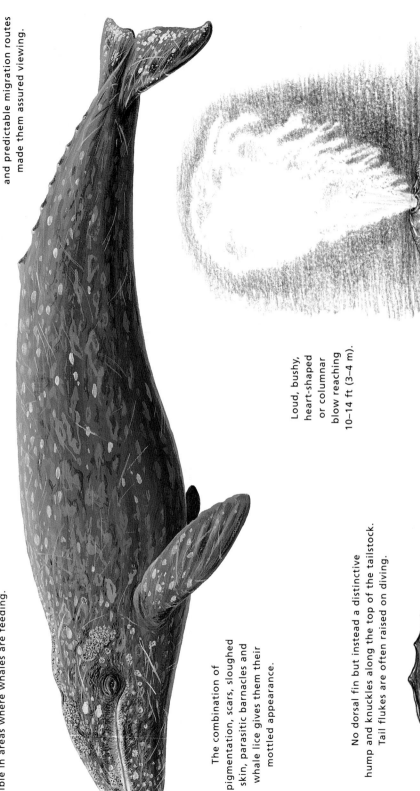

Often feed by straining invertebrates from the bottom sediments. Clouds of disturbed mud may be visible in areas where whales are feeding.

Modern whale watching began with the Gray Whales off western North America. Their coastal range and predictable migration routes made them assured viewing.

The combination of pigmentation, scars, sloughed skin, parasitic barnacles and whale lice gives them their mottled appearance.

Loud, bushy, heart-shaped or columnar blow reaching 10–14 ft (3–4 m).

No dorsal fin but instead a distinctive hump and knuckles along the top of the tailstock. Tail flukes are often raised on diving.

Also known as **California Gray Whale**, **Devilfish**, **Mussel-digger** or **Scrag Whale**.

Identification: A large whale growing from 16 to 50 ft (5 to 15 m). General body shape and degree of arching of the jaw-line is intermediate between Right Whales and Rorquals. Head triangular in cross section with top jaw narrower than lower jaw. Baleen plates yellowish white. No dorsal fin but instead a series of bumps ("knuckles") extend along the rear third of the back. Flippers and tail flukes broad. Body mottled gray with white or orange patches of encrusting barnacles and whale lice. Surfacings low and unspectacular but frequently approach boats, breach, lift tails, flippers or head into the air. Blow is vertical, rising 10 to 15 ft (3 to 5 m), loud and has a characteristic heart shape when seen from in front or behind. During the summer feeds in bottom sediments and may surface with plumes of mud spilling from jaws. Often seen alone or in pairs, though on the breeding grounds or in areas of productive feeding, much larger groups may form. The body color, head shape, vertical blow and lack of dorsal fin distinguish Gray Whales from other species.

Where and When: Occurs in shallow coastal waters of the North Pacific. Two stocks recognized. Eastern Pacific stock breeds in lagoons off Baja California peninsula, Mexico, in winter then migrates northward in spring to feed off British Columbia, Alaska and the Bering, Chukchi and western Beaufort Seas. The western Pacific stock is neither abundant nor well known. It breeds somewhere off southern China and feeds off north-eastern Sakhalin Island in the Russian far east.

Best Chances: The coastal nature, abundance and predictable migrations off the North American seaboard make them reliable targets for whale watchers. Spectacular views of breeding whales are possible in the lagoons off western Mexico. Migrating whales are visible from coastal headlands from California to Alaska, especially during northward spring migration. Timing varies by latitude: California (February to April), British Columbia (March to May). Chances to see western stock animals are far fewer. Summer sightings possible off Sakhalin Island, Russia.

GRAY WHALE

Key Facts

Average Length: 50 ft (15 m)

Length at Birth: 16 ft (5 m)

Adult Weight: 35 tons

Life Span: Up to 40 yrs

Distribution: Coastally in the North Pacific. From Baja California, northwards to northern Alaska. From the Sea of Okhotsk to southern Korea.

Status: > 20,000 in the eastern Pacific but < 200 in the western Pacific.

Grouping: Usually alone or in pairs but aggregate in feeding areas or for breeding.

Main ID Features: Bushy blow, mottled gray color, "knuckles" between indistinct dorsal fin and tail.

BLUE WHALE *Balaenoptera musculus*

Famed as the largest animal to have graced our planet, the Blue Whale can reach a colossal 100 ft (30 m) in length and weigh in excess of 200 tons.

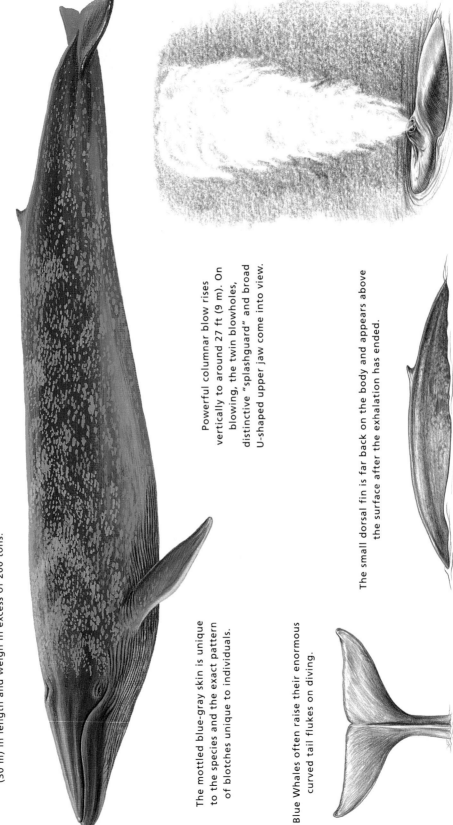

Powerful columnar blow rises vertically to around 27 ft (9 m). On blowing, the twin blowholes, distinctive "splashguard" and broad U-shaped upper jaw come into view.

The mottled blue-gray skin is unique to the species and the exact pattern of blotches unique to individuals.

Blue Whales often raise their enormous curved tail flukes on diving.

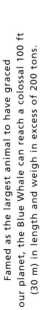

The small dorsal fin is far back on the body and appears above the surface after the exhalation has ended.

Also known as **Sulfur-bottom, Sibbald's Rorqual** or **Great Northern Rorqual.**

Identification: Identified by its huge size, growing from 23 to a massive 100 ft long (7 to 30 m), tall blows (up to 30 ft / 9 m high), blue-gray mottled skin color, and typically falcate (concave rear edge) but tiny dorsal fin set far back on the body. The head is broad and flat with a prominent ridge from the tip of the jaw to the bump ("splashguard") in front of the blowholes. Each animal's skin pigment patterns vary slightly along the dorsal ridge, near the dorsal fin. This feature is exploited by scientists to distinguish individual whales. The tips of the tail flukes are rather pointed, and the trailing edge is usually smooth and straight with a median notch. There are 60 to 88 parallel grooves that run along the underside of the animal from the tip of the lower jaw to the navel. These allow the mouth and throat to distend massively when feeding. Closely related to Fin Whales, but the body of a Blue Whale is mottled and lighter in color and its dorsal fin is not as tall and pronounced as that of a Fin. Also, the right lip and the baleen plates of Fin Whales are pale and the underside of the body is white. A number of hybrids between Blue and Fin Whales have been recorded, testifying to their close relatedness. Blue Whales in polar waters may be tinged yellow-green or brown and this yellowing led to the "sulfur-bottom" name used by whalers.

Where and When: Found in all oceans from coastal waters to the open ocean, the tropics to the ice edge. Particularly abundant in the eastern North Pacific. The winter breeding and calving grounds of the north-eastern Pacific population are not known with certainty but might lie in an area 500 miles (800 km) off the coast of Costa Rica.

Best Chances: Regularly encountered by whale-watching trips off central California, USA, during the summer and early autumn where there is a population of some 2000 to 3000 animals. Blue Whales are often sighted in the Santa Barbara Channel, Monterey Bay, Gulf of the Farallones and Bodega Bay. Elsewhere, other reliable localities include Baja California Sur, Mexico, the waters surrounding the Snaefellsnes Peninsula in Iceland, the St Lawrence River estuary in Canada, and Sri Lanka.

Key Facts

Average Length: 82–100 ft (25–30 m)

Length at Birth: 23 ft (7 m)

Adult Weight: 80–150 tons

Life Span: 80–90 yrs

Distribution: All oceans and seas, except Mediterranean. Usually offshore but may approach shore in areas of especially high productivity.

Status: Drastically depleted by whaling, rare in the Atlantic, Antarctic and most of the Pacific.

Grouping: Usually seen alone or in small groups, may aggregate around areas of high food abundance.

Main ID Features: Large sleek body, prominent mound in front of blowhole, turquoise mottled coloration, tiny dorsal fin, tall blow, often raises flukes on dives.

BLUE WHALE

FIN WHALE *Balaenoptera physalus*

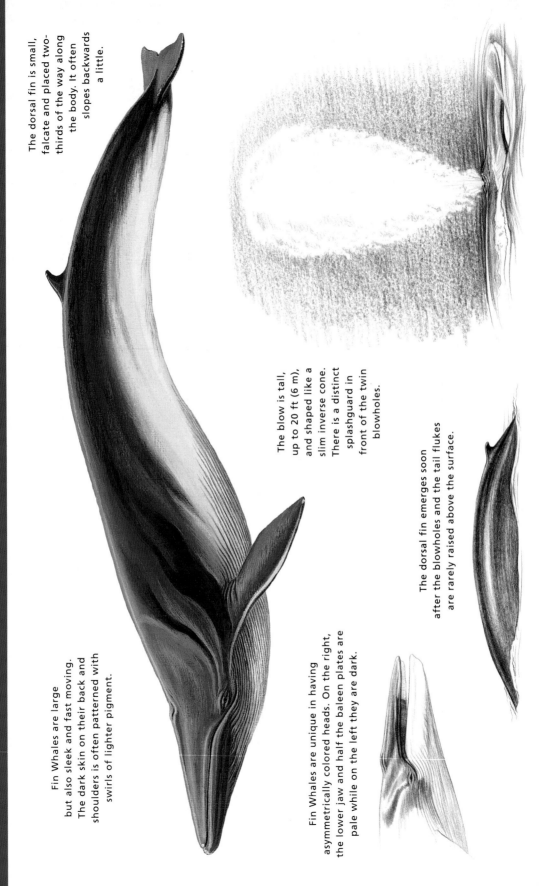

The dorsal fin is small, falcate and placed two-thirds of the way along the body. It often slopes backwards a little.

The blow is tall, up to 20 ft (6 m), and shaped like a slim inverse cone. There is a distinct splashguard in front of the twin blowholes.

The dorsal fin emerges soon after the blowholes and the tail flukes are rarely raised above the surface.

Fin Whales are large but also sleek and fast moving. The dark skin on their back and shoulders is often patterned with swirls of lighter pigment.

Fin Whales are unique in having asymmetrically colored heads. On the right, the lower jaw and half the baleen plates are pale while on the left they are dark.

Also known as **Finback, Finner, Common Rorqual, Razorback** or **Herring Whale.**

Identification: A sleek, fast-swimming whale, second only in size (20 to 90 ft, 6 to 27 m) to the Blue Whale. Dark back with a prominent, slightly falcate (concave rear edge) dorsal fin positioned two-thirds of the way along the animal. Fin shape varies between individuals and appears several seconds after the blow as the animal, on surfacing, rolls forward, thus the blowholes and dorsal fin are not seen at the same time. Robust spout rises 20 ft (6 m) into the air and often they blow repeatedly in a short period. As with all baleen whales, there are twin blowholes. Fin Whales typically do not lift their tail flukes clear of the water when diving. These are fast-swimming whales that cruise at 5–8 knots (10–15 km per hour) and can increase speed to 15 knots (30 km per hour) for short bursts. While they surface with a smooth, purposeful roll, behaviors such as breaching or other acrobatic activities are rare. These whales most often capture their prey by gulp feeding, where they rapidly engulf then strain large quantities of water containing schooling fish, squid or krill and other planktonic crustaceans. Close views reveal the highly distinctive asymmetric coloring on the head, with a whitish patch on the upper and lower lips and along the baleen plates of the animal's right side. This pale blaze continues up across the side of the face to near the blowhole. In contrast, the left side of the head is dark slate-gray. In many individuals, two angular stripes called chevrons originate behind the blowhole and above the flipper. This asymmetric arrangement of pale pigmentation is unique to Fin Whales. The dorsal fin is higher than that of Blue Whales but lower than in Sei or Bryde's Whales.

Where and When: Occurs in all temperate and polar waters (except the Black Sea) and occasionally in the tropics. Occurs in the open ocean, however, most sightings are from coastal or shelf waters.

Best Chances: One of the most frequently encountered large whales off the east coast of the US and Canada. Peak abundance occurs during the summer (April to October). The north-western Mediterranean, in particular the Ligurian Sea, can also be excellent for this species.

Key Facts

Average Length: 70–85 ft (21–26 m)

Length at Birth: 20–23 ft (6–7 m)

Adult Weight: 120 tons

Life Span: 80–90 yrs

Distribution: All oceans, primarily oceanic but can encounter near exposed coasts.

Status: Numbers devastated by whaling, now abundant in the North Pacific and Atlantic but recovery slow in Antarctic.

Grouping: Usually seen alone or in small groups, may aggregate in areas of abundant prey.

Main ID Features: Long streamlined body, chevron on back, dorsal fin falcate with straight leading edge. Raised flukes rare. Asymmetric coloration on lower jaws, left dark, right pale.

FIN WHALE

SEI WHALE *Balaenoptera borealis*

Sei Whales are large, fast and streamlined whales. Despite a near-global range, their unpredictable occurrence makes them an exciting find for the whale watcher. They feed on a wide variety of schooling or swarming organisms from fish to plankton.

The flukes usually remain below the surface when diving.

The twin blowholes produce a moderately tall columnar blow with the dorsal fin appearing at the same time.

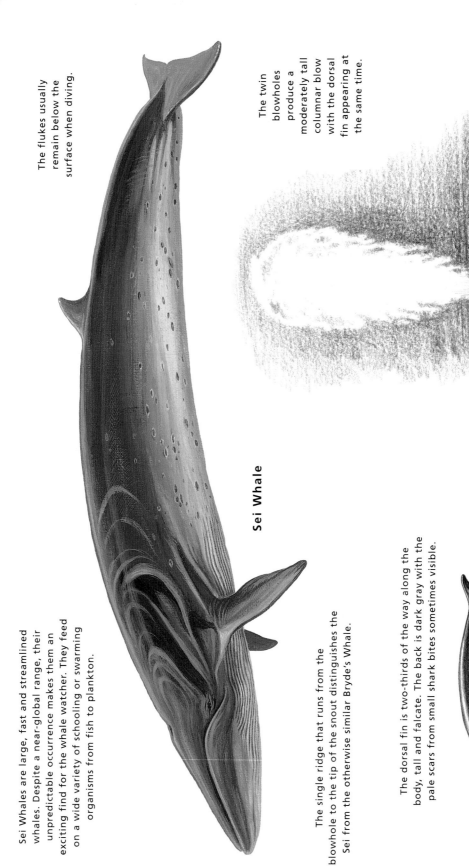

Sei Whale

The single ridge that runs from the blowhole to the tip of the snout distinguishes the Sei from the otherwise similar Bryde's Whale.

The dorsal fin is two-thirds of the way along the body, tall and falcate. The back is dark gray with the pale scars from small shark bites sometimes visible.

Pronounced "sigh" whale. Also known as **Pollack Whale, Japan Finner** or **Rudolphi's Rorqual.**

Identification: A large whale growing from 15 to 65 ft (4.5 to 20 m). Similar appearance to the Fin Whale and a difficult species to positively identify. Both sides of the jaw are the same color, the pectoral flippers are dark. The dorsal fin is tall, falcate and two-thirds of the way along the body. The blow is bushy and up to 10 ft (3 m) high and so lower than those of Blue or Fin Whales. Sei Whales don't always show the tip of the snout but the blowholes and dorsal fin are simultaneously visible. Dives at a shallow angle and the tail is typically kept below the surface. Sei Whales rarely breach.

Where and When: All oceans, over continental shelf and deeper water, and the western Mediterranean. Typically some further offshore than Fin Whales. Southern hemisphere: restricted mainly north of the Antarctic Convergence in summer; Indian Ocean: January–March northern limit is 35–40° S. Spend winter north of 30° S.

Best Chances: Regularly seen on George's Bank off New England, USA, in spring.

Bryde's Whale *Balaenoptera edeni*

Pronounced "broo-does". **Identification:** Similar to Sei Whales but has three parallel ridges on the head rather than two or one. The blow is tall, thin and hazy and the tail remains below the surface on dives. **Where and When:** Warm or tropical oceans, between 30° N and 30° S. A "dwarf" version occurs around the Solomon Islands. Probably less migratory than other baleen whales, feeding year round in the same area **Best Chances:** From boats out of Ogata, Japan and Simon's Town, South Africa.

Key Facts: **Average Length:** 43 to 53 ft (13-16 m). **Length at Birth:** 13 ft (4 m). **Adult Weight:** 20 tons. **Life Span:** 50 yrs. **Distribution:** World-wide tropical and warm temperate, coastal and offshore. **Status:** Subject to whaling in the N Pacific but not at risk of extinction. **Grouping:** as Sei Whale. **Main ID Features:** Sleek body with three parallel rostral ridges, very falcate dorsal fin, body frequently arched when diving but tail remains below surface.

Key Facts

Average Length: 65 ft (20 m)

Length at Birth: 15 ft (4.5 m)

Adult Weight: 45 tons

Life Span: 50 yrs

Distribution: All oceans and most seas, coastal and offshore waters.

Status: Impacted by whaling, locally abundant in north Pacific and Atlantic, still rare in the Antarctic.

Grouping: Usually seen alone or in small groups, may aggregate around areas of high food abundance.

Main ID Features: Long sleek body, single rostral ridge, steely blue-gray color, tall falcate dorsal fin, blowholes and dorsal fin visible simultaneously on surfacing.

SEI WHALE & BRYDE'S WHALE

HUMPBACK WHALE *Megaptera novaeangliae*

Humpback Whales are the mainstay of modern whale watching. Their coastal distribution, spectacular behavior, slow swimming and curiosity towards boats make them impressive viewing.

The trailing edges of Humpback tail flukes are serrated. The undersides range from all white to all black but more usually feature unique patterns of both. The very long pectoral flippers are also distinctive.

The "humpback" in the species name refers to the whale's habit of sharply arching its back before a dive, emphasizing the fatty hump upon which the stubby dorsal fin is set.

As these whales surface, the tubercles on the snout may be visible. The blow is tall and bushy and the dorsal fin is visible at the same time. Humpbacks usually lift their tail flukes clear of the surface before long dives.

Also known as **Hunchback Whale, Hump Whale** and **Bunch Whale.**

Identification: For many, this is the first whale they will ever see. Large robust body, growing from 13 to 56 ft (4 to 17m) in length. Large head with small distinctive bumps ("tubercles") on both upper and lower jaws, reminiscent of rivets on old steel ships. Mostly black baleen plates and deep grooves in the lower jaw and belly. Extremely long pectoral fins with bumps running along the leading edges. Small dorsal fin is variable in shape, often tattered, and sits on its own hump on top of the back. The tail flukes are large and have a lumpy trailing edge. The body is mostly black with areas of white on the belly. The undersides of the tail flukes have variable, individually distinctive, patches of black and white. Pectoral flippers are either entirely white (most areas) or white on the undersides (North Pacific). Tend to blow as they break the surface, pectoral flippers often clearly visible when surfacing, blow rises 10 ft (3 m), usually bushy but can be V-shaped. The rest of body appears and back arches into typical humped shape before dive. The sequence usually culminates in the tail flukes being lifted clear of the surface. Humpbacks frequently breach, wave pectoral flippers in the air or slap them or their tail flukes down onto the surface. Can be confused with Sperm Whales, which have a similar sized and shaped body and habit of lifting the flukes above the surface. However, the Humpback's white pectoral fins, white undersides of the flukes and vertical blow are distinctive.

Where and when: A widely distributed species, occurring in all oceans from Arctic to Antarctic and occasionally in the western Mediterranean. Usually feed in coastal or shelf waters in temperate or polar waters. All populations but one, migrate from these cold-water feeding grounds to warm-water breeding areas in winter, especially near islands and reefs. Because of the difference in seasons, northern and southern hemisphere populations breed and feed out of phase from each other.

Best Chances: New England, USA (summer), Silver Bank, Caribbean (winter). British Columbia, Canada and SE Alaska, USA (summer). Ogasawara Islands, Japan (winter). Hawaii (winter), and in the South Pacific: Cook Islands (winter), Tonga and Niue (winter), New Caledonia (winter), east and west coast of Australia (winter), Antarctica (summer).

Key Facts

Average length: 46 ft (14 m)

Length at birth: 13 ft (4 m)

Adult weight: 40 tons

Life span: 40–50 yrs

Distribution: Breed and feed near land in all major oceans, most populations migrate towards tropics in winter.

Status: Heavily impacted by whaling, most populations recovered or recovering well.

Grouping: Most often single or in pairs but larger aggregations can occur in feeding or in breeding areas.

Main ID features: Bushy blow, long pectoral flippers, distinctive dorsal fin, serrated trailing edge to tail flukes.

HUMPBACK WHALE

MINKE WHALES

Minke Whale
Balaenoptera acutorostrata

Antarctic Minke Whale
Balaenoptera bonaerensis

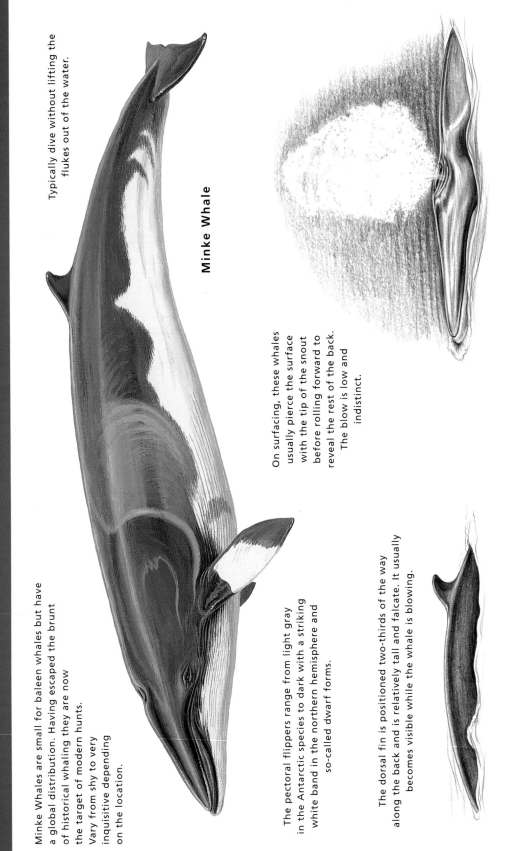

Minke Whale

Typically dive without lifting the flukes out of the water.

On surfacing, these whales usually pierce the surface with the tip of the snout before rolling forward to reveal the rest of the back. The blow is low and indistinct.

Minke Whales are small for baleen whales but have a global distribution. Having escaped the brunt of historical whaling they are now the target of modern hunts. Vary from shy to very inquisitive depending on the location.

The pectoral flippers range from light gray in the Antarctic species to dark with a striking white band in the northern hemisphere and so-called dwarf forms.

The dorsal fin is positioned two-thirds of the way along the back and is relatively tall and falcate. It usually becomes visible while the whale is blowing.

Pronounced "minky". Also known as **Pikehead, Little Piked Whale, Little Finner, Sharp-Headed Finner, Lesser Finback** or **Lesser Rorqual.**

Identification: One of the smallest baleen whales, 7 to 32 ft (2 to 10 m) in length. Typically sleek rorqual body shape but with noticeably pointed snout. The baleen plates are creamy white (gray towards rear in Antarctic species) and there is a single ridge running along the top of the upper jaw. Dorsal fin is tall, falcate and two-thirds of the way along the body. Fifty to 70 longitudinal grooves run along the underside of the lower jaw and belly. Coloration black or dark gray on back, paling to white on the belly. Northern hemisphere whales have bright white band on the pectoral flippers, while a dwarf form that occurs in the southern hemisphere has more white on the flippers that may extend onto the shoulder. The pectoral fins of Antarctic Minke Whale are light gray. The blow is indistinct and on surfacing the dorsal fin comes into view just before the blowholes disappear. Generally don't lift tails into the air when diving. Whales often seen alone but often in association with dolphins, seals or feeding seabirds. Can be curious of boats and may breach, particularly in rough weather. Most often confused with Sei and Fin Whales, but have smaller and less visible blow, and white flipper patches.

Where and When: Found worldwide, in oceanic and coastal waters, sometimes very close to shore. As with other rorquals, most populations of Minke Whales migrate between cold-water feeding grounds and warmer-water breeding grounds, but are less predictable in their timing and routes than the larger species. Some populations (e.g. in North Pacific) may not migrate at all. The Dwarf form Minke Whale lives in the southern hemisphere with the Antarctic Minke Whale but does not venture as close to the ice edge.

Best Chances: Minke Whales are frequently seen off western Scotland and Ireland, the St Lawrence estuary, Canada, and Bay of Fundy in the summer months. Dwarf Minke Whales come into shallow waters of the northern section of the Great Barrier Reef in Australia during the winter and can be seen from dive charters. Antarctic cruises near the ice edge offer chances to see the Antarctic species, sometimes very up-close.

Key Facts

Average Length: 26–32 ft (8–10 m)

Length at Birth: 7–10 ft (2–3 m)

Adult Weight: 6–9 tons

Life Span: Up to 50 yrs

Distribution: All oceans and most seas, both inshore and offshore.

Status: Only targeted for whaling recently, abundant in many areas.

Grouping: Usually alone or in pairs but aggregate in areas of good feeding and breeding.

Main ID Features: Small size but typically sleek rorqual form. Pointed rostrum, small blow, falcate dorsal fin, white patch or band on pectoral fins. Flukes rarely seen.

MINKE WHALES

SPERM WHALE *Physeter macrocephalus*

Made infamous by Melville's *Moby Dick*, Sperm Whales are found throughout the world's deep oceans. Supreme divers, they can stay submerged for 40 minutes or more while hunting deep-sea fish and squid.

Broad, often tattered, flukes raised aloft signal the start of a deep dive

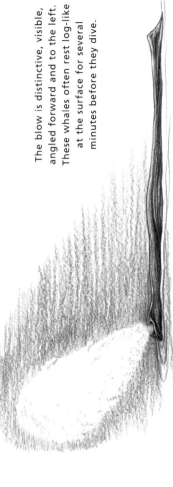

The blow is distinctive, visible, angled forward and to the left. These whales often rest log-like at the surface for several minutes before they dive.

The head is huge, particularly in adult males, and contains the spermaceti oil used to focus their echolocation sounds. This valuable oil led both to the species' name and to sustained slaughter by whalers.

Sperm Whales have a hump rather than a dorsal fin and distinctive knuckles along the tail stock.

Also known as **Cachelot**, **Spermacet Whale** or **Pot Whale**.

Identification: Largest of the toothed whales, reaching lengths of 54 ft (18 m). Adult males are a third longer than females and double the weight. Head is massive, around a third of the total length, skin dark brown or gray in color, with distinctive wrinkles reminiscent of a prune! The single blowhole is at the tip of the snout and placed asymmetrically on the left side of the head. Consequently, the distinctive bushy blow projects forward.

Sperm Whales often lie log-like at the surface, blowing repeatedly, before finally raising tail flukes high into the air and diving for 40 minutes or longer. Tail flukes are broad and triangular, often with a tattered trailing edge. Pectoral flippers are rounded and the lower jaw is long, thin and under-slung. Teeth are only present in the lower jaw. Highly vocal, consistently producing regular loud clicks when diving. This allows animals to be located even when submerged on long dives. Females associate in groups of a dozen or more including immatures and calves. Maturing males may associate with one another but become more solitary as they age. Can be confused with several species of baleen whale but wrinkled skin, logging behavior and forward-pointing blow are distinctive.

Where and When: Found worldwide, almost invariably in deep water (600 ft / 200 m or greater) off the continental shelf or over submarine canyons. Females and immatures favor the tropics or sub-tropics whereas adult males migrate to colder temperate or polar waters to feed. Periodically they migrate back towards the equator to mate.

Best Chances: Two of the best spots for seeing Sperm Whales are Andenes, Norway and Kaikoura, New Zealand, where bulls gather to feed over deep submarine canyons. Female groups can be seen throughout the tropics including Dominica in the Caribbean and the Azores in the eastern Atlantic. For some reason, as yet unknown, Sperm Whales occasionally mass strand on beaches, affording tragic but unparalleled views.

Key Facts

Average Length: 36 ft (11 m) F–59 ft (18 m) M

Length at Birth: 13 ft (4 m)

Adult Weight: 22 tons (F)–58 tons (M)

Life Span: 60 yrs +

Distribution: Shelf break and beyond, most oceans and seas.

Status: Abundant across most of range, some local populations may be threatened by human activities.

Grouping: Adult females form groups of a dozen or so animals including calves and immatures. Adult males are less social and often seen alone.

Main ID Features: Bushy blow angled forward from snout tip, dark gray, wrinkled skin, rounded dorsal fin, often remain stationary at surface, raises broad flukes before long dives.

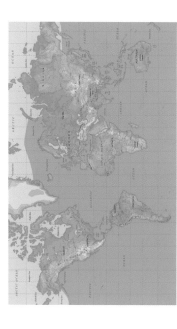

SPERM WHALE

SMALL SPERM WHALES

Dwarf Sperm Whale
Kogia sima

Pygmy Sperm Whale
Kogia breviceps

Also known as **Owen's Pygmy Sperm Whale, Lesser Sperm Whale, Short-Headed Sperm Whale** or **Lesser Cachalot.**

Identification: These are small, mysterious and rarely seen whales. They grow to between 8 ft (2.5 m) (Dwarf) and 12 ft (3.8 m) long (Pygmy) and have robust dolphin-like bodies but with a square head and no beak. The dorsal fin is falcate, midway along the back and tall in the Dwarf Sperm Whale and smaller and further back in the Pygmy Sperm Whale. The skin is bluish-gray to blackish-brown on the back, paling to cream on the belly.

A unique feature of these whales is the pale vertical crescent between the eye and the flipper. This gill slit-like pigmentation, along with the underslung jaw and sharp pointed teeth, are features reminiscent of sharks. Why these whales appear to mimic sharks is unclear. Another unique feature is their squid-like ability to vent a dark inky fluid when alarmed.

As with their larger cousin, the Sperm Whale, the blowhole is typically positioned slightly to the left of center. They rise to the surface slowly and produce an inconspicuous blow. They then may lie motionless, log-like, at the surface with the head and dorsal fin exposed and tail flukes hanging down. They swim slowly on the surface and rarely breach. When they dive, they simply drop below the water surface and vanish.

Both species are typically seen alone or in small groups of up to 10. The shy nature of these animals rarely affords prolonged views so they can be confused with a variety of other small cetacean species. Key characteristics are the size, dorsal fin, coloration, underslung jaw, logging and sinking behavior. Their similarity of features meant that the Dwarf and Pygmy forms were only recognized as separate species in 1966. This similarity also renders them effectively indistinguishable at sea unless the views are exceptional.

Where and When: Found in deep waters throughout the world's oceans except for polar or sub-polar seas but most commonly in temperate and tropical waters.

Dwarf Sperm Whales appear to be the more abundant of the two, especially at the point where the continental shelf drops off into much deeper waters (shelf break and slope). Stomach contents of stranded Pygmy Sperm Whales suggest that they may favor even deeper waters than the Dwarf species.

They are not known to make strong seasonal movements, and overall little is known about their status and potential changes in abundance. Some animals are taken in harpoon fisheries in the Caribbean and Indian Oceans but of greater concern are the (probably widespread) deaths caused by accidental ingestion of plastic bags and collisions with shipping while they "log" at the surface.

These are shy, unobtrusive animals and the best views are possible from boats shortly after they have returned from a deep dive. Very little is known about any sounds that they might produce.

Best Chances: Regularly encountered in the Tañon Strait separating the islands of Cebu and Negros in the Philippines.

Sightings also comparatively frequent in the Caribbean and strandings are often recorded off the south-eastern United States and South Africa, suggesting that they may be not infrequent off these shores also.

There are over 20 species of beaked whale and collectively they represent the most mysterious yet utterly fascinating group within the cetaceans. While our entire knowledge of some species comes only from a scattering of remains found on beaches, others are slightly better studied. Northern Bottlenose Whales and Baird's Beaked Whales were targeted by whalers in the North Atlantic and Pacific, and in the process details of their lives, distribution and behavior have been uncovered. In recent years, hotspots for other species have been found and researchers have begun to investigate their lives.

Beaked whales are well adapted to living in the deep sea and are most often encountered where water depths exceed 980 ft (300 m). While many also consume fish, they appear to be specialists at eating squid and have long tube-like jaws with a tongue that acts like a piston to suck in their prey. To allow the throat to expand during this sucking maneuver, there are two longitudinal grooves or pleats in the skin of the throat. Because they suck rather than bite their prey, there is less need for teeth and so most species have almost entirely lost them. Instead, it's only the males that develop teeth and use them as tusks for combat with other males.

Other characteristics of this group include: small indentations in their sides, allowing the flippers to lie flush with the flanks, reducing friction with the water. Similarly, their tails characteristically lack a central notch. Feeding in the deep sea means that these animals must be deep-diving specialists and so are capable of spending prolonged periods underwater. This, coupled with their shy behavior, means that it is only the lucky or persistent whale watcher that gets to see them.

There are at least 14 species of Mesoplodon beaked whales, and all are poorly known. Species include the Sowerby's, Andrews', Hubbs', Blainville's, Gervais', Ginko-toothed, Gray's, Hector's, Strap-toothed, True's, Longman's, Pygmy, Stejneger's and Shepherd's Beaked Whales. They range from 12 to over 19 ft (3.7 to over 6 m) long and vary in color from slate gray to olive brown. Their bodies are spindle-shaped with a small triangular or falcate dorsal fin located approximately two-thirds of the way back on the body. The head is small and tapered and the melon blends without a crease into the beak. The length of the beak varies from short to very long depending on the species. As a rule, they are extremely difficult to distinguish at sea and usually a photograph of the head of an adult male is needed for firm identification.

Location is key to a correct identification: both the geographic location of the sighting and the anatomical location of the erupted teeth of the male. The teeth in the lower jaw of the different species range from a single pair at the tip to a single pair near the corner of the mouth. For some species the jaw line is straight and for others it is humped and the teeth may be peg-like, triangular or curved. These teeth are used for jousting and the bodies of adult males are frequently marked with pale scars from past encounters.

Mesoplodon whales are widespread and members of the group can be found in almost any oceanic area of sufficient depth. Several hotspots for finding Mesoplodons are now well known to whale watchers. These include deep waters directly off ocean pinnacles such as the Bahamas, Hawaii and the Azores, as well as along continental slopes such as the Bay of Biscay and outer banks of North Carolina.

Bottlenose Whales

Northern Bottlenose Whale
Hyperoodon ampullatus

Southern Bottlenose Whale
Hyperoodon planifrons

Also known as **Flathead**, **Bottlehead** or **Steephead Whales**.

Key Facts

Average Length: 20–30 ft (6–9 m)

Length at Birth: 11 ft (3.5 m)

Adult Weight: 6–10 tons

Life Span: Up to 37 yrs

Distribution: Northern: North Atlantic only, shelf edge and slope. Southern: from 30° S to the Antarctic ice edge.

Status: Northern: heavily exploited by whalers. Southern: probably stable.

Grouping: 4 to 10 most common but 25 or more do occur. Sometimes approach boats.

Main ID Features: Bulbous melon with steep forehead (often pale), dolphin-like beak, falcate dorsal fin.

Identification: Relatively large beaked whales, reaching 20 to 30 ft (6 to 9 m) long. Most obvious feature is the bulbous melon (forehead) and dolphin-like beak. Mature males develop larger melons than females, the front steep and flattened. Immatures and females usually toothless; males develop two conical teeth from the tip of the lower jaw, not always visible. A moderate-size dorsal fin, two-thirds of the way along the back, is falcate to triangular and may have a pointed tip. The small flippers taper to a point. Broad flukes, with no central notch, and concave trailing edges. Coloration: chocolate brown to yellow and lighter on the flanks and belly. Rarely raise their flukes when submerging and dive for an hour or more to the seabed. The bulbous, flat-ended forehead is unique to Bottlenose Whales.

Where and When: Northern Bottlenose Whales are confined to the northern Atlantic Ocean, in cold temperate to Arctic waters. From Davis Strait south to New York on the US east coast, usually over very deep water, 2500 ft + (750 m +). Also common in southern Davis Strait off northern Labrador and between Iceland and the Faroe Islands. Southern species has a circumpolar range from 30° S to the Antarctic ice edge.

Best Chances: Northern species: "The Gully", 100 miles (160 km) east of Nova Scotia, Canada. **Southern species:** southern Africa to the Antarctic pack ice, usually south of 60° S.

Baird's Beaked Whale
Berardius bairdii

Arnoux's Beaked Whale
Berardius arnuxii

Giant beaked whales also known as **North Pacific** and **Southern Four-Toothed Whale**.

Identification: Largest of the beaked whales, growing to 28 to 36 ft (8.5 to 11 m) long. The two species are closely related and are very similar in appearance. The body is slender and the head comparatively small. The rounded, bulbous forehead is separated from the back by a distinct crease that is evident as animals break the surface. The head often comes out of the water at a steep angle, allowing the bulging forehead and long dolphin-like beak to be seen. Two pairs of teeth erupt from the tip of the lower jaws in both males and females and the lower pair is sufficiently large that they show even when the mouth is closed. The low falcate dorsal fin is positioned two-thirds of the way along the body and normally breaks the surface after the head has submerged. Depending on the light, skin looks blue, dark gray or brown and adult males may be heavily scarred with long narrow scratches on the back and flanks. Color is palest towards the belly and may have irregular patches of white.

The blow is low and indistinct. These whales may swim alone but are more often found in groups of 2 to 9 and more occasionally up to 30 individuals. Entire groups will often surface and blow in unison and may raft at the surface, resting after a deep dive. With the dorsal fin hidden below the surface these resting groups can resemble a group of Sperm Whales. Spyhopping, lobtailing and logging have all been observed. Baird's and probably Arnoux's Beaked Whales appear to have an unusual social system. Males can live to about 84 years while females live to less than 55 years. This is the converse of most

other cetaceans. Why males live longer is a mystery. Adults might be confused with Minke Whales if the head and scratches are not seen, or with Southern Bottlenose Whales if the melon is not visible. Immatures can be readily mistaken for other beaked whale species.

Where and When: Baird's Beaked Whales are limited to the North Pacific, where they range in offshore waters, especially over the continental slope. They occur from Korea and Japan northward to the Aleutians and Bering Sea and then south-east to Baja California. Arnoux's Beaked Whales have a circumpolar distribution in deep cold temperate or sub-polar waters of the southern hemisphere that extends north to northern New Zealand, São Paulo and southern Africa. Arnoux's Beaked Whales are probably still at or near their historical level of abundance but Baird's Beaked Whales have been culled by whalers since the 17th century. That said, the numbers taken have been small compared to the baleen whales.

Best Chances: Baird's Beaked Whales are particularly abundant around the Aleutian Islands in the North Pacific, in the Sea of Okhotsk and off northern California. They are occasionally encountered by whale-watching and birding trips off the west coast of North America (British Columbia to central California), most commonly between April and October, with the peak in August. Also sighted off north-east Japan, including Choshi peninsula and north-east Hokkaido. Most records of Arnoux's Beaked Whales are from the south-east coast of South America, near the Antarctic Peninsula, South Africa, and in the Tasman Sea.

CUVIER'S BEAKED WHALE *ziphius cavirostris*

Though elusive, one of the most widespread of the beaked whales. Usually seen over deep waters or where the continental margin comes close to shore. Generally avoid boats but may approach on occasion.

The skin varies from chocolate brown through creamy white to purple-blue or gray. As with many other beaked whales, adults are frequently crisscrossed with pale scars from combat with other whales and pocked by small shark bites.

The head shape is distinctive with a smooth convex then concave transition from the melon to the tip of the beak. In adult males, two teeth protrude from the tip of the lower jaw and may be colonized by stalked barnacles.

Blow is low and inconspicuous and may be angled slightly forward. The head is often visible, especially in fast-moving animals, and the dorsal fin is positioned two-thirds of the way along the body. The fin is small and varies in shape from falcate to triangular.

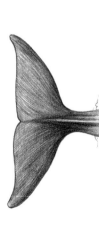

The tail flukes are large and slender with a concave rear margin which has only a small or no central notch. Flukes may be lifted before long dives.

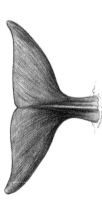

Also known as **Goose-Beaked Whale**.

Identification: A robust cigar-shaped body with a blunt head and melon (forehead) that curves gently (without a crease) into a short, thick beak. Two teeth erupt from the tip of the beak in adult males and protrude even when the mouth is closed.

These teeth may become colonized by tassel-like barnacles. The dorsal fin is relatively small and set two-thirds of the way along the back. It varies from falcate to triangular. The flippers are small and narrow while the tail flukes are large and lack a distinct notch in the middle.

The blow is weak and bushy and may be angled slightly forward. Body color is typically dark slate-gray or olive- or red-brown with a distinctively pale head and upper back, particularly in adult males. This whiteness may be accentuated in older animals, especially adult males, by heavy linear scars from battles with other males and circular wounds from parasitic sharks. Newborns are dark black or bluish-black above and lighter below. They are often seen alone or in groups of up to seven animals. They only occasionally breach and dive for half an hour or longer. Unless a close-up view is obtained, these animals can easily be confused with other beaked whales, but the melon sloping to the end of the beak and teeth at the tip of the lower jaw in adult males are distinctive.

Where and When: Probably the most common and widespread of all the beaked whales but their shyness has meant that they have been little studied. Strandings suggest that they occur in all oceans and most seas except high polar waters. Appear to favor waters more than 3300 ft (1 km) deep with a steeply sloping bottom.

Best Chances: Regularly encountered in the Gulf Stream of North Carolina, in the southern section of the Bay of Biscay and deep areas of the Mediterranean.

CUVIER'S BEAKED WHALE

Key Facts

Average Length: 20–23 ft (6–7 m)

Length at Birth: 9 ft (2.7 m)

Adult Weight: 2–3 tons

Life Span: 40 yrs +

Distribution: All oceans and most seas except high polar waters.

Status: Not well known due to shy nature but probably more common than number of sightings suggests.

Grouping: Lone or in small groups

Main ID Features: Cigar-shaped body, sloping melon, brownish coloration, dorsal fin position and teeth at the tip of the lower jaw in males.

Beluga Whale   *Delphinapterus leucas*

Also known as Qilalugaq qaqortaq (Greenland), **Belukha**, **Sea Canary** or **White Whale**.

Key Facts

Average Length: 13–16 ft (4–5 m)

Length at Birth: 5 ft (1.5 m)

Adult Weight: 0.7–1.6 tonnes

Life Span: 25 yrs +

Distribution: Estuarine, coastal and offshore, Arctic and sub-Arctic northern hemisphere.

Status: Abundant in some parts of their range, but several populations at risk of extinction from human activities and climate change.

Grouping: Social, often forming large groups, frequently found in same-sex or age groups.

Main ID Features: Uniform gray or white skin, absence of dorsal fin.

Identification: Unique white coloration makes adults virtually unmistakable. The thick layer of blubber gives them a fat, wrinkled appearance with a relatively small rounded head, distinguished from the back by a flexible neck. Dorsal fin is reduced to a tiny ridge, only visible at close range and no doubt an adaptation to ice-bound seas. The lumpy body narrows before the spatulate and slightly upturned tail. Calves are slate-gray or pinkish brown, becoming darker and bluer during their first year. Females are smaller than males. Can be confused with Narwhal, but lack the tusk and mottled skin.

Where and When: Confined to the Arctic with isolated population in the St Lawrence River, Quebec, Canada and in the Cook Inlet near Anchorage, Alaska, USA. Almost invariably encountered in groups, sometimes herds of hundreds or thousands concentrated at river mouths (e.g. Mackenzie and Churchill Rivers) or ice fronts. They venture deep into the Arctic pack ice, moving between openings and leads that are miles apart. Occasionally travel considerable distances up freshwater rivers feeding on salmon smolt. On the edges of the ice shelf, Belugas often associate with Bowhead Whales.

Best Chances: In July and August several thousand Belugas gather at the mouth of the Churchill River, Manitoba, Canada. A more accessible but smaller population (~650) can be seen in the St Lawrence and Saguenay Rivers near Tadoussac, Quebec, Canada, within easy reach of Montreal and Quebec City. Although numbers have declined, Belugas can be seen from the shore along Cook Inlet near Anchorage, Alaska.

Also known as **Narwhale**, **Unicorn Whale** or **Sea Unicorn**.

Identification: A more torpedo-like shape than the Beluga and only a very slight hint of a beak. The blow is weak and inconspicuous. The head is barely separated from the body, which is smooth and finless. Body color changes with age. Adults have white underparts with dense gray spotting on the upper surface. The spotting is strongest in females, making them look relatively dark, whereas elderly males can appear almost completely white at a distance. The dorsal fin is almost absent but remains as a dark line along the middle of the back in older and whiter animals. Juveniles are much darker, appearing gray with a limited amount of white spotting on the underparts. Males are easily distinguished by the unique unicorn-like tusk – a tooth from the left upper jaw which erupts through the lip, and is ridged in a left-handed spiral. Rarely the right tooth also erupts, giving two tusks. Females are slightly smaller than males and rarely exhibit an external tusk. Although the ranges of Narwhal and Beluga overlap broadly, they generally do not form mixed herds.

Where and When: Only in the high Arctic, separated into two populations by the Greenland landmass and permanent polar ice. In summer months, Narwhals concentrate along the receding edge of the pack ice, following cracks and isolated openings reaching into deep bays and fjords. They move offshore in winter and are found in broken ice and between floes. In winter, darkness and poor weather make them difficult to find and study.

Best Chances: Organized viewing trips from Pond Inlet, Baffin Island, Nunavut, Canada. Also possible from cruises to Canadian Arctic and Greenland.

Key Facts

Average Length: 13–16 ft (4–5 m). Tusk 5–10 ft (1.5–3 m)

Length at Birth: 5 ft (160 cm)

Adult Weight: 1–1.6 tons

Life Span: 25 yrs +

Distribution: Coastal and oceanic waters of the high Arctic.

Status: Hunting and climate change threaten several populations.

Grouping: Highly social, often forming large groups, often found in same-sex or age groups.

Main ID Features: Mottled skin, absence of dorsal fin, unique tusk in males.

Narwhal

KILLER WHALE *Orcinus orca*

The blow is low, bushy and most easily seen against the sunlight. The dorsal fin is tall and falcate except in adult males, where it grows very tall with a straight, rather than curved, trailing edge.

Though called whales, these are actually large dolphins. Their large size and power give them a sedate majesty but they are capable of rapid turns of speed and can hunt down and consume the fastest of the other whales and dolphins.

Killer Whales routinely display a wide variety of behaviors including spyhopping (as here), tail slapping, and breaching.

The black-and-white coloration, large dorsal fin, paddle-like pectoral flippers and blunt head make Killer Whales among the easiest cetaceans to identify.

Also known as **Orca**.

Identification: Largest of the ocean dolphins, with a robust body and conical head. The melon reaches almost to the tip of the upper jaw so there is no obvious beak. Dorsal fin positioned mid-back, tall and falcate. Fin in males develops disproportionately and may be 7 ft (2 m) tall. Pectoral flippers are large and rounded and tail flukes are broad with tips down-turned in males. Coloration, black with well-defined white patches on the lower jaw, above the eye and on the belly to lower flank and underside of the tail. There is also a variable smokey white or gray patch (called the "saddle"), immediately behind the dorsal fin. The white patches in newborn calves may instead be orangey yellow.

Killer Whales are highly social, living in close-knit family groups for their entire lives. As such they are rarely seen alone. They consume a wide variety of prey from fish to marine mammals and birds, but any one group may have highly specialized foraging behaviors. Best known are the two coastal populations of whales in the northeast Pacific which forage on entirely different sources of prey (fish or marine mammals). The bold coloration and erect dorsal fin render Killer Whales practically unmistakable.

Where and When: Killer Whales are cosmopolitan, being found in all oceans and most seas. They range from the polar ice edges to the tropics and from the shore-line to the open oceans. Their abundance is thought to be highest in temperate and polar waters.

Best Chances: There are several places where Killer Whale sightings are predictable and spectacular. Most famous are the waters around Washington State in the US and British Columbia, Canada, specifically the San Juan Islands at the south end of Vancouver Island and Johnstone Strait at the north end. Sightings are best between spring and autumn. Conversely, spectacular winter views of Killer Whales are possible in northern Norway in the sheltered fjords inshore of the Lofoten Islands, particularly Tysfjord.

Key Facts

Average Length: 23 ft (7 m) F – 30 ft (9 m) M

Length at Birth: 7–8 ft (2–2.5 m)

Adult Weight: 3–6 tons

Life Span: 29–90 yrs

Distribution: World-wide, all oceans and most seas, from the polar ice edge to the tropics and coastline to open ocean.

Status: Abundance patchy. Slow reproduction coupled with human hunts and pollution led to heavy impacts in some areas.

Grouping: Highly social, lives in extremely close-knit family groups from 3 to 50 individuals.

Main ID Features: Black-and-white coloration, tall dorsal fin.

KILLER WHALE

PILOT WHALES

Long-Finned Pilot Whale
Globicephala melas

Short-Finned Pilot Whale
Globicephala macrorhynchus

The head is bulbous and the melon characteristically overhangs the jaw. The pectoral flippers are slender and long with a distinct angle on the leading edge. Pectoral fins differ in length between the two species but difficult to judge in field.

The skin is jet black or dark gray with variable patches of gray or white on the belly, behind the dorsal fin and in a thin band running from the eye towards the dorsal fin.

Long-Finned Pilot Whale

The blow is strong and may be 3 ft (1 m) or so high. In calm conditions it can be audible and visible when seen against the sun. The dorsal fin is noticeably forward of the mid-back, has a broad base and is often strongly falcate.

In areas where they overlap, the two Pilot Whale species are challenging to distinguish. They are medium-size cetaceans with stout bodies and deep-diving abilities. They can lie motionless at the surface and often tolerate boat approaches.

The tail flukes are black and slender. They have a concave trailing edge with a distinct notch in the middle. Tail may be lifted clear of the surface before long dives.

Also known as **Pothead Whale** or **Blackfish**.

Identification: These animals have robust long bodies with males larger than females. The head is distinctive, with a rounded, bulbous melon that may overhang the lower jaw. The dorsal fin is variable in shape but always low, falcate (sometimes hooked), broad based and forward of the center of the back. Pilot Whales are mostly black to dark gray, can appear brown in strong sunlight with a grayish band sweeping up and backward from the eye, they also have a gray saddle patch behind the dorsal fin and pale underparts. Long-Finned Pilot Whales have flippers that are around a quarter of the body length. The two species are distinguished by the length of their pectoral flippers. Long-Finned Pilot Whales have flippers that are around a quarter of the body length, with a distinct angle to the flipper around a quarter of the way along. The flippers of Short-Finned Pilot Whales are a sixth of the body length or less.

Where and When: Pilot Whales occur throughout most of the world's oceans and seas. They are offshore species feeding on squid and fish in deep water. The two species overlap in distribution over part of their range but the Long-Finned Pilot Whale appears to prefer cooler waters from 30° S southwards in the southern hemisphere and from 25° N northwards in the North Atlantic. They are not present in the North Pacific. Short-Finned Pilot Whales prefer warmer water and occur world-wide in a band from around 40° N and S towards the equator. Their distribution in the North Pacific extends further north to the Aleutian Islands.

Best Chances: Being deep-water specialists, Pilot Whales are most easily seen in areas where the coast and deep water are in close proximity. The waters around the Canary Islands in the North Atlantic are particularly reliable for sightings of Short-Finned Pilot Whales.

Distribution Map: The distribution of the Short-Finned Pilot Whale slightly overlaps that of the Long-Finned species. These areas are indicated in the darkest shade of blue on the map (right).

PILOT WHALES

Key Facts

Average Length: 20 ft (6 m)

Length at Birth: 5–7 ft (1.5–2 m)

Adult Weight: 1.3–2.3 tons

Life Span: 35–60 yrs

Distribution: Long-Finned: southern hemisphere and North Atlantic temperate to sub-polar waters. Short-Finned: all oceans, temperate and tropical waters.

Status: Abundant world-wide, have been taken in coastal drive fisheries.

Grouping: Highly social species, living in tight-knit family groups of between 20 and 90 individuals.

Main ID Features: Black body, white saddle, bulbous head without beak, hooked dorsal fin forward of mid-back.

Melon-Headed Whale

Peponocephala electra

Also known as **Melonhead Whale, Many-Toothed Blackfish** or **Electra Dolphin.**

Identification: Relatively small (9 ft / 2.7 m), dark-colored whales. Body tapers front and rear with sloping forehead and no beak, falcate dorsal fin set in mid back. Is mostly dark in color with a slightly darker gray back cape that broadens down on the flanks parallel with the dorsal fin.

The face is also darker than the gray sides but the lips are characteristically white. In the field, it is easily confused with Pygmy Killer Whale but has a more triangular head when seen from above and more pointed flippers. It is much smaller than the False Killer Whale.

Generally travel in large, fast-moving herds, sometimes numbering in the hundreds. Behaves rather like a dolphin, leaping clear of the water as it travels and occasionally bow-riding, may also be shy of vessels. Thought to feed on fish and squid at considerable depths.

Where and When: Worldwide in tropical and sub-tropical water (77° F / 25° C or greater), especially the western tropical Pacific. Often associate with Fraser's and Rough-Toothed Dolphins.

Best Chances: Regularly encountered in the Philippines, notably the Tañon Strait. Also fairly common in the Caribbean (e.g. Dominican Republic) and off eastern Australia.

Pygmy Killer Whale

Feresa attenuata

Also known as **Slender Blackfish** or **Slender Pilot Whale.**

Identification: Has a moderately robust body (7 ft 6 in / 2.3 m long) that appears heavier forward of the dorsal fin than behind. The head is rounded and blunt and the large melon extends to and slightly beyond the tip of the jaw. The moderately long flippers are rounded at their tips. The dorsal fin is mid-set, tall and falcate. The skin is almost entirely gray or black, and like the Melon-Headed Whale there is a darker cape on the back that widens at the dorsal fin. The belly has irregular patches of white and the lips are frosted with white. Pygmy Killer Whales are most often seen in groups of 12 to 50 animals although groups of 100 or more have been recorded. This species may bow-ride boats, make spectacular leaps and spyhop. Little else is known about their behavior but it is suspected that as well as fish and squid they may include smaller dolphins in their diet. Pygmy Killer Whales are difficult to distinguish from Melon-Headed and False Killer Whales, which share their range. Certain identification will probably require a good view when bow-riding. Pygmies lack the distinctive bump on the leading edge of the pectoral fins typical of False Killer Whales and have a more rounded head than the Melon-Headed Whale.

Where and When: Worldwide in tropical and sub-tropical water, generally well offshore.

Best Chances: Regularly encountered in waters off the Dominican Republic, Hawaii, Sri Lanka and southern Japan.

Also known as **False Pilot Whale** or **Pseudorca**.

Identification: Relatively large (16–20 ft / 5–6 m) dolphins with a body shape rather like a stretched Killer Whale. They are predominantly black with a lighter patch between the flippers. The dorsal fin is upright and falcate, set on the mid back and not particularly large. Their most distinctive features are the angled pectoral flippers which have a bulge on the leading edge and the very rounded melon that considerably overhangs the lower jaw. These are social animals, swimming in groups of 20 to 100 individuals, and consume large fish, squid and other cetaceans. They have various interactions with humans that range from regularly bow-riding boats to stealing fish from fishing lines. As well as bow-riding this species is fast-swimming and often jumps clear of the water. False Killer Whales frequently come ashore alive and in entire social groups. These events often lead to the deaths of all the individuals but the reasons why they occur remain mysterious. The centrally placed dorsal fin, overall size, overhanging melon and bulged pectoral flippers distinguish these animals from Pilot, Melon-Headed and Pygmy Killer Whales.

Where and When: Worldwide in tropical and sub-tropical waters, occasionally into temperate waters as far north as Maryland, USA, Scotland, southern Japan, Hawaii and British Columbia, Canada, and south to Argentina, Cape Province, Tasmania, South Island of New Zealand and Chile.

Best Chances: Regularly encountered during whale- and dolphin-watching trips around Hawaii.

False Killer Whale

Also known as **Sarawak Dolphin, Shortsnout Dolphin, Bornean Dolphin, White-Bellied Dolphin** or **Fraser's Porpoise**.

Identification: A relatively stocky dolphin with a short but distinct beak. Adults about 7–8 ft (2–2.5 m) in length with a distinctive black stripe across the face and along the body. This is broadest in adult males, more variable in adult females and absent or faint in juveniles. A less visible cream strip borders the black band. The back, dorsal fin and flukes are gray or brownish-blue while the pectoral flippers are dark gray or black and appear joined to the black body stripe by a dark band running from the base of the flippers to the angle of the jaw. The belly is white or pink. The dorsal fin is comparatively small and triangular in shape. The pectoral fins are also relatively small. Often form large schools numbering in the hundreds or thousands. Their synchronous diving behavior can be particularly spectacular. Often mixes with other cetaceans such as Melon-Headed Whales, Short-Finned Pilot Whales, Risso's Dolphins, Spinner Dolphins, Bottlenose Dolphins and even Sperm Whales.

Where and When: Tropical regions of all three major oceans, mainly along the continental shelf or in deep oceanic waters. Most common near the equator in the eastern tropical Pacific and at the southern end of the Bohol Strait in the Philippines. In light of this wide tropical distribution, it is remarkable that prior to 1971, Fraser's Dolphin was only known to the world from a single skull from a beach in Sarawak.

Best Chances: Oceanic islands in the tropics with narrow continental shelf, such as the Maldives, Sri Lanka, the Philippines and Fiji.

Fraser's Dolphin

100

Bottlenose Dolphin
Tursiops truncatus

Bottlenose Dolphins

Indo-Pacific Bottlenose Dolphin   100
Tursiops aduncus

Also known as **Gray Porpoise, Black Porpoise, Bottle-Nosed Dolphin** or **Cowfish.**

Key Facts

Average Length: 8–12 ft (2.5–3.8 m)

Length at Birth: 3–5 ft (80–140 cm)

Adult Weight: 397–1102 lb (180–500 kg)

Life Span: 50 yrs

Distribution: Temperate and tropical seas world-wide. From estuaries to the open ocean.

Status: Abundant but some populations heavily impacted by man.

Grouping: Highly social in groups from a few individuals to hundreds.

Main ID Features: Gray coloration, tall falcate dorsal fin in mid back, distinct bottle-shaped beak, lively behavior.

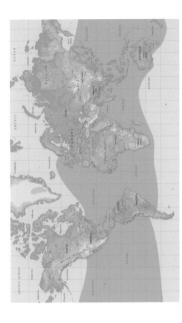

Identification: Though two species are listed here, these animals are highly variable in almost all aspects of their lives including their anatomy. There may thus be more than two species. Bottlenose Dolphins are the archetypal dolphin: they are medium-sized with males only slightly (if at all) larger than females. The dorsal fin is tall and falcate or triangular and placed mid-way along the body. The melon is clearly visible and distinct from the blunt, robust beak. The pectoral flippers and tail flukes are medium-sized. Body color is mainly gray with a gun-metal back paling to a cream or pink belly. The two species are hard to tell apart, but the Indo-Pacific form often has belly pigmentation spots. Social and energetic, they often leap, splash and bow-ride boats. They are also aggressive and often display scratches from the teeth of their associates. Harbor Porpoises are attacked and killed in areas where the two overlap. Bottlenose Dolphins are typically found in groups of 2 to 50 but sometimes in larger groups. They are the species that often "befriends" humans.

Where and When: A wide variety of temperate and tropical habitats from shallow coastal waters and estuaries to deep offshore waters.

Best Chances: Coastal waters of Florida, California, Scotland, Ireland, western and eastern Australia, Japan and New Zealand.

Sousa teuszii

Sousa chinensis

Key Facts

Average Length: 8–9 ft (2.4–2.7 m)

Length at Birth: 35–45 in (90–115 cm)

Adult Weight: 375 lb (170 kg+)

Life Span: 30–40 yrs

Distribution: Inshore coastal, tropics from western Africa to China and Australia.

Status: Unknown but likely impacted by many human activities.

Grouping: Usually in small groups of 15 or fewer.

Main ID Features: Gray or pink coloration, small falcate or triangular dorsal fin on its own hump, long narrow jaws.

Indo-Pacific also known as **Pink Sousa** or **Chinese White Dolphin,** Atlantic Humpback also known as: **Cameroon Dolphin.**

Indo-Pacific Humpback Dolphin

Identification: Body shape is broadly like the Bottlenose Dolphin's but the beak is noticeably longer and more slender, the dorsal fin is smaller, triangular or falcate and on a distinct hump. Coloration varies regionally. In many areas they have a dark gray back and light gray belly (west and south Africa), in others they are a uniform gray (northern Indian Ocean), while in Hong Kong, they are white or pink. May also have speckling. Calves are usually born dark gray. They form small fluid groups and are often seen alone.

Where and When: Both species favor coastal, estuarine, occasionally riverine habitats, especially areas with relatively shallow water. The Atlantic species occurs in waters off west Africa from Morocco to Southern Guinea. The Indo-Pacific species has a much wider distribution, including the rim of the Indian Ocean, from southern Africa to India, and south-east to Asia and Australia. Also in the Red Sea, Persian Gulf and western Pacific as far north as China.

Best Chances: Hong Kong and Macau: organized tours to see the famous "pink" dolphins. Queensland, Australia: resident in Moreton Bay, and adjacent offshore waters, also in Tin Can Inlet, Great Sandy Strait.

Tucuxi
Sotalia fluviatilis

Pronounced "toó-koo-shee" Also known as **Estuarine Dolphin**.

Identification: A small dolphin, 5–7 ft (1.5–2.1 m), similar to the Bottlenose Dolphin but smaller and more delicate with a longer, slender beak. Light gray to bluish gray on the back, pinkish to light gray from the belly up to the shoulders. A distinct band of darker gray extends from the eyes to the pectoral flippers. Flippers, dorsal fin and tail flukes are gray. The large eyes have black pigmentation around their rims. The dorsal fin is triangular and may be slightly hooked at the tip. In rivers, live in small groups (2 to 10) in freshwater habitats, with the Boto, but the upright triangular dorsal fin and smaller, more compact body form of the Tucuxi are distinctive. In coastal marine habitats off southern Brazil, may be hard to distinguish from Franciscana but the Tucuxi has a shorter beak and more pointed dorsal fin. The small body and triangular dorsal fin make them distinguishable from other coastal delphinids.

Where and When: Found in the extensive river systems of the Amazon and the Orinoco, as well as along the coasts from Brazil to Nicaragua. The smaller freshwater subspecies, *fluviatilis*, inhabits only freshwater and is found as much as 155 miles (250 km) up the Orinoco River system and as much as 1550 miles (2500 km) up the Amazon River system. The larger marine subspecies, *guianensis*, is found in the coastal estuaries and bays of the east coast of South America as far south as the Brazilian city of Florianópolis. Wary in areas with lots of human activity, more approachable elsewhere.

Best Chances: Locally abundant in some parts of its range, including the Pacaya-Samiria National Reserve in northern Peru.

Irrawaddy Dolphin
Orcaella brevirostris

Identification: These dolphins look like small Belugas but genetically belong to the dolphins, in fact the Killer Whale is probably their closest relative. The head is rounded with no hint of a beak, and like the Beluga they have sufficient neck mobility to move their heads to the sides. The dorsal fin is two-thirds of the way along the body, small and triangular or only slightly falcate. The color pattern varies regionally, from dark gray to light gray with a paler belly. They are small, reaching around 7 ft (2.1 m) in length and males are slightly larger than females. When surfacing, the head appears first and then disappears before the back emerges; the tail is rarely seen. They travel in small groups, often around 6 animals but occasionally up to 15. Usually keep a low profile in the water but will on occasion spyhop, breach or make low-angle leaps. New studies of the anatomy and genetics of animals from Asia and Australia suggest that the Irrawaddy Dolphins off Australia and Papua New Guinea could possibly be renamed Snubfin Dolphins (*Orcaella heinsohni*).

Where and When: Widely distributed in tropical coastal, estuarine and riverine waters from the Madras coast of India to the northern coast of Australia. Inhabited countries include Bangladesh, Myanmar, Thailand, Malaysia, Indonesia and the Philippines. Also penetrate deep into several river systems including the Mekong River in Laos and Cambodia, the Mahakam River in Indonesia and the Ayeyarwady River (formerly Irrawaddy) in Myanmar (formerly Burma).

Best Chances: These are little-known animals living in areas where whale watching is still gaining momentum. The most reliable places to see Irrawaddy Dolphins include the Mekong River in Cambodia, northern Sarawak (Borneo) and northern Australia.

Also known as **Lag, Pacific Striped Dolphin, White-Striped Dolphin** or **Hook-Finned Porpoise**.

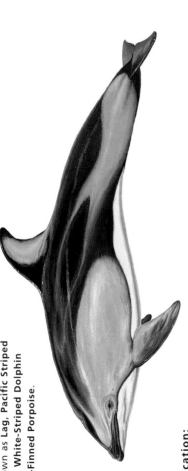

Identification:

Medium-sized but powerful oceanic dolphin. The black body is offset by striking light-gray flank patches and pearl-white belly. Two gray stripes, easily seen when the dolphin surfaces, run along the latter half of the body and tail stock. The beak is short, forming a smooth curve with the head. The black and gray dorsal fin is tall and strongly falcate. Generally found in large groups, often hundreds and sometimes thousands of individuals. An energetic dolphin, often harassing other marine wildlife and bow-riding. Can form mixed herds with Northern Right Whale Dolphins and Risso's Dolphins.

Where and When: Temperate waters of the North Pacific. Generally in deep water with a surface temperature of 34–63° F (6–17° C) though frequently visit coastal waters.

Best Chances: One of the most abundant species of dolphin in the North Pacific, can be encountered in deeper water almost anywhere on the arc from Japan to Baja, Mexico. Large groups sometimes visit the sheltered water of the Johnstone and Queen Charlotte Straits off north-eastern Vancouver Island, British Columbia, Canada and often seen on Killer Whale-watching trips. Sightings also common in Monterey Bay, California, USA, typically in association with other small cetaceans.

Key Facts

Average Length: 7–8 ft (2.1–2.5 m)

Length at Birth: 35 in (90 cm)

Adult Weight: 198–330 lb (90–150 kg)

Life Span: 40 yrs

Distribution: Cold temperate waters of the North Pacific. Mostly offshore but approaches coasts.

Status: Net fisheries and hunts may have local impacts but populations in N Pacific remain large.

Grouping: Highly gregarious.

Main ID Features: Medium-sized, no beak, falcate black and gray dorsal fin, large gray side patch.

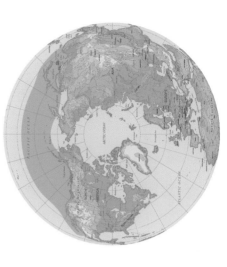

Pacific White-Sided Dolphin

Dusky Dolphin   *Lagenorhynchus obscurus*

Also known as **Fitzroy's Dolphin**.

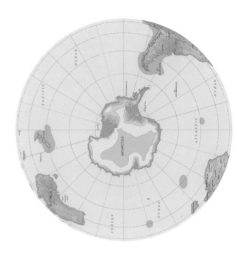

Key Facts

Average Length: 7 ft (2 m)

Length at Birth: 35 in (90 cm)

Adult Weight: 220 lb (100 kg)

Life Span: 35 yrs or more.

Distribution: Discontinuous range in southern hemisphere coastal waters.

Status: Abundant but suffered significant catches in southern South America.

Grouping: Highly gregarious.

Main ID Features: Medium-sized dolphin, no beak, falcate black and gray dorsal fin, large gray patches on side.

Identification: Similar shape and size to the Pacific White-Sided Dolphin but the pale bands on the tail stock do not extend as far up the body and the face region is paler. The difference in hemispheres means that there is no chance of confusing the two, but Duskys can be confused with the darker Peale's Dolphins. Dusky Dolphins are highly social and can be seen in groups of tens to hundreds and occasionally thousands. They show considerable plasticity of behavior across their range. Off Argentina they form hunting packs during the day to search for small schooling fish, then aggregate around their prey, while in coastal New Zealand they may rest inshore during the day and hunt offshore at night. They are energetic and acrobatic.

Where and When: Mostly occurs in temperate and sub-Antarctic waters of the southern hemisphere including southern South America, western South Africa, southern Australia, New Zealand and oceanic islands of the southern Atlantic Ocean and Indian Ocean. Primarily an inshore species but also ventures into the open ocean.

Best Chances: Abundant in waters off New Zealand, Chile, Argentina and South Africa. Commonly seen in popular whale-watching spots such as Peninsula Valdez (Nuevo Gulf), Argentina; Table Bay, Cape Town, South Africa and Kaikoura, New Zealand.

Also known as **Wilson's Dolphin** or **Southern White-Sided Dolphin**.

Identification: A stocky but beautifully patterned dolphin. Relatively small at 5 to 6 ft (1.4 to 1.9 m) in length with a rounded melon and short but distinct beak. Overall the body color is black with a white belly, white or gray throat and two white patches on the flanks. The first extends along the tail stock from near the tail to below the dorsal fin. The second runs backwards from the junction of the melon and beak, over the top of the eye to below the dorsal fin. These two flank patches are joined below the dorsal fin by a thin line that gives the dolphin its distinctive egg-timer or hourglass color pattern. The beak, eye and upper portion of the melon, pectoral flippers, dorsal fin and tail flukes are all black. The centrally placed dorsal fin is large, falcate or broad and bent sharply backwards at about mid-height. Usually seen in small groups but herds of 100 animals have been reported. They may also swim in association with other whale and dolphin species. They will bow ride and occasionally leap from the water, although more typically they swim at high speed, barely breaking the surface when breathing.

Where and When: Circumpolar in pelagic waters of the sub-Antarctic and Antarctic zones, generally south of the Subtropical Convergence; most sightings occur between 45° S and 65° S in relatively cold waters (0–12° C) but not closely associated with pack ice. Also found in the cold northward-flowing Falkland Current.

Best Chances: Regularly encountered by ships visiting Antarctica, South Georgia or Macquarie Island in the Australian sub-Antarctic.

Hourglass Dolphin

Also known as **Blackchin Dolphin**, **Peale's Black-Chinned Dolphin** or **Southern Dolphin**

Identification: A stocky dolphin with a rounded head and short beak. They are dark gray or black on the back with two lighter areas on the flanks. The rear light patch is white to gray and runs from the tail stock to below the dorsal fin, then narrows to a thin line that curves over the shoulder then down to the eye. The second broad gray patch extends from the flank below the dorsal fin forwards to the eye. A distinct dark line separates this patch from the pale belly. The dark back coloration extends over the melon all the way to the beak. The tail flukes and leading edge of the pectoral flippers and dorsal fin are dark, while their trailing edges are pale. Young dolphins are lighter, the pale patches on their flanks less clearly defined. Similar to the Dusky Dolphin but Peale's Dolphins have only one pale line running forward from the rear flank patch, they are somewhat darker overall and the forward pale flank patch does not extend onto the melon. Found in smaller groups than Dusky Dolphins.

Where and When: Widespread throughout the Patagonian shelf waters off southern Argentina and the Falkland Islands. Found in bays, estuaries, harbors and shallow fjords often within a few miles of land and hunts within kelp beds. Occasionally reported far offshore. They will often approach boats closely and bow-ride.

Best Chances: Punta Deseado, in southern Argentina and Chilean fjords near Puerto Monte.

Peale's Dolphin

White-Beaked Dolphin · *Lagenorhynchus albirostris*

Also known as **White-Nosed Dolphin, Squidhound** or **White-Beaked Porpoise**.

Key Facts

Average Length: 8–10 ft (2.4–3.1 m)

Length at Birth: 4 ft (1.2 m)

Adult Weight: 770 lb (350 kg)

Life Span: Unknown

Distribution: Temperate and sub-Arctic North Atlantic. Mostly between the coast and continental shelf margin.

Status: Poorly known but not in immediate danger.

Grouping: Highly social and usually in groups of 30 or fewer but sometimes more.

Main ID Features: Tall, falcate dorsal fin, short thick white beak, pale patch behind dorsal fin and on flanks.

Identification: A very stout dolphin with a short but distinct beak. The dorsal fin is large, mid-set and falcate. Dark bodied with a whitish saddle behind the dorsal fin and variable white-gray bands on the flanks. The tail flukes, dorsal fin and pectoral fins are all black, the beak is white or ash-colored. Fast, powerful swimmers that frequently leap and occasionally bow-ride. Can be confused with the Atlantic White-Sided Dolphin but have less clearly defined color patches and a gray-white flank patch between the dorsal fin and tail flukes that extends all the way up to the upper edge of the tail stock. This feature is clearly visible when these dolphins surface.

Where and When: Restricted to cold sub-Arctic waters of the North Atlantic. Found widely over the continental shelf, but tend to concentrate along the shelf edge in the western Atlantic and across the shelf and into coastal waters in the eastern Atlantic.

Best Chances: Off south-west coast of Iceland, off Newfoundland and surrounding areas of eastern Canada, southern Greenland, the Faroes, Ireland, northern Scotland and Norway.

Also known as Jumper, Springer, Lag or **Atlantic White-Sided Porpoise.**

Key Facts

Average Length: 8–9 ft (2.5–2.7 m)

Length at Birth: 4 ft (120 cm)

Adult Weight: 375–500 lb (170–230 kg)

Life Span: 20 yrs or more

Distribution: Temperate and sub-Arctic North Atlantic, particularly around continental shelf break.

Status: Not in immediate danger of extinction.

Grouping: Gregarious, tens to hundreds.

Main ID Features: Bold colors, particularly white and tan patches on flanks, black along entire back, tall falcate dorsal fin.

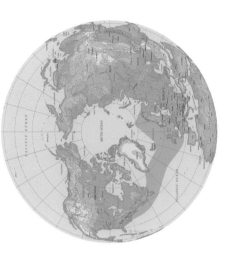

Identification:

Robust and beautifully colored dolphins. Smoothly sloping head and melon with distinct juncture to the beak. Dorsal fin tall and falcate. The back is black. There is a white patch on the flank below the dorsal fin and a tan-yellow patch above this, extending to near the tail. The flanks are otherwise gray and the belly white. The dorsal fin, tail flukes and pectoral flippers are black and the eye is surrounded by black pigment with a narrow black line running from the eye forward to the beak-melon junction. Often form large groups, between 100 and 1000 animals, but groups of around 40 are most common. They are rapid swimmers, take short dives and often swim alongside other cetaceans.

Where and When:

Temperate and sub-Arctic waters of the North Atlantic. Range as far south as New England and Brittany and north to Greenland, Iceland and Svalbard. Particularly abundant around and past the continental shelf break (> 600 ft / 200 m). More often seen in coastal waters in the western rather than eastern Atlantic.

Best Chances:

Can be seen on whale-watching tours off Ireland, Iceland and in cooler waters of New England and the Canadian Maritimes.

Rough-Toothed Dolphin   *Steno bredanensis*

Also known as Slopehead.

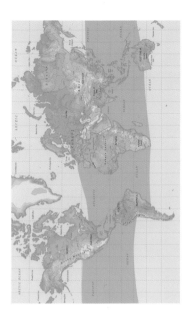

Key Facts

Average Length: 8 ft (2.5 m)

Length at Birth: 3 ft 3 in (1 m)

Adult Weight: 330 lb (150 kg)

Life Span: 30 yrs +

Distribution: Tropical to warm-temperate, deep and offshore waters.

Status: Nowhere particularly common.

Grouping: 10 to 20 individuals, occasionally more.

Main ID Features: The only long-beaked dolphin with smoothly sloping melon. Large mid-set dorsal fin, between triangular and falcate.

Identification:

Similar to the Bottlenose Dolphin, but its long narrow beak blends smoothly into the forehead, giving an oddly reptilian look. The skin is dark gray or blue-gray on the back, paling toward the belly, with a distinct transition between the dark back and paler flanks. Often has spots on the underparts and scars on the head and flanks. The flesh around the mouth is white or pinkish white, which extends underneath onto the throat. The eyes are comparatively large and surrounded by darkly pigmented skin. The dorsal fin has a wide base and curves only slightly backwards. The body and tail stock taper markedly behind the dorsal fin. The flippers are large and set relatively far back. The flukes have pointed tips and a central notch. Can occur in groups of up to several hundred individuals but usual group size is 10 to 20. Often with other cetacean species, and may occasionally bow-ride. They get their name from the tiny vertical ridges or wrinkles found on their teeth.

Where and When:

Generally encountered in tropical to warm temperate waters and so occur in low latitudes of the Atlantic, Indian and Pacific Oceans. Usually seen in the open ocean over deep water. Probably feed at considerable depths, capturing relatively large fish which may be torn into pieces before being swallowed.

Best Chances:

Deep waters off Hawaii, Northern Gulf of Mexico, Lesser Antilles. Also found in Mediterranean and Gulf of Mexico.

Also known as **Grampus**
or **Gray Dolphin**.

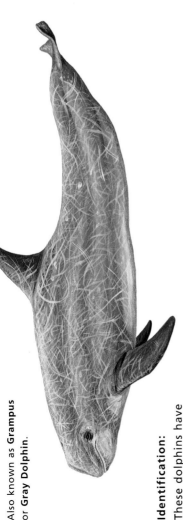

Identification:

These dolphins have
a robust body but a narrow tail stock. They are quite large, reaching around 13 ft (4 m)
long, males and females growing to the same size. The head is made bulbous by a large
melon and no beak. The melon has a cleft at the front running from top to bottom.
The mid-set falcate dorsal fin is extremely tall, leading to occasional confusion with Killer
Whales. Infants are born with a gray to brown back, white or cream belly and a white
anchor-shaped patch between the pectoral flippers. Calves darken to nearly black, while
keeping the anchor patch. As they age further most of the back and flanks become
covered in pale scratches and scars such that older animals can appear almost completely
white. The dorsal fin, however, remains dark. Risso's Dolphins are gregarious, living
in groups of 10 to 50 or more occasionally several hundred but may also be seen alone.

Where and When: Widespread in tropical, sub-tropical, temperate and sub-Antarctic
waters. They favor areas where water temperatures range between 15 and 20° C.
May occur along the edge of the continental slope and in coastal waters.

Best Chances: Monterey Bay, California, USA, eastern Taiwan and the coastal waters
of western Scotland, particularly the Isle of Lewis.

Key Facts

Average Length: 13 ft (4 m)

Length at Birth: 3–5 ft (1–1.5 m)

Adult Weight: up to 882 lb (400 kg)

Life Span: 30 yrs or more

Distribution: World-wide in temperate and
tropical oceans, mostly offshore but coastally
in some areas.

Status: These are little-known animals
and their global status is unclear.

Grouping: Social dolphins, living in groups
from a few tens to occasionally hundreds.

Main ID Features: Bulbous head,
profuse scarring and tall dorsal fin.

Common Dolphins

Also known as **Saddleback Dolphin, White-Bellied Dolphin, Criss-Cross Dolphin** or **Cape Dolphin.**

Key Facts

Average Length: 5–7 ft (1.6–2.2 m)

Length at Birth: 35 in (90 cm)

Adult Weight: 440–518 lb (200–235 kg)

Life Span: Possibly 40 yrs

Distribution: Warm temperate and tropical waters worldwide. Nearshore and offshore.

Status: Abundant in many parts of their range but heavily impacted by many fisheries.

Grouping: Tens to hundreds.

Main ID Features: Solid, streamlined appearance, delicate beak, criss-cross color pattern and energetic behavior.

Short-Beaked Common Dolphin

Identification:

Common Dolphins have a solid but highly streamlined appearance. They have a long, moderately stout beak that is well demarcated from the melon, and a well proportioned, moderately falcate dorsal fin, set mid-back. The color pattern is distinctive with a dark gray or black back and pale cream or white belly, a broad yellow or ocher flank patch between the dorsal fin and the eye and a broad pale gray patch below the dorsal fin to the tail stock. This latter gray pigmentation continues as a thin stripe to the eye. Together the two flank patches are hourglass-shaped. The dorsal fin, flukes and pectoral flippers are dark and there is a dark stripe from the base of the flippers to the lower jaw. The two species have only recently been classed as separate and are difficult to distinguish at sea. A possible third species, the Indian Ocean Common Dolphin (*D. tropicalis*), occurs in the northern Indian Ocean including the Persian Gulf and tropical western Pacific. These are highly social and energetic dolphins, often seen in groups of tens to hundreds. They are avid bow-riders.

Where and When: Live in temperate and tropical seas worldwide. The Short-Beaked species is the more abundant and seems to prefer deeper, cooler water. May make seasonal migrations into higher latitudes in summer and autumn.

Best Chances: Many places, including the West of Ireland, Canary Islands, Azores, Straits of Gibraltar, Gulf of Maine, California, Red Sea, Japan, South Africa & New Zealand.

Right Whale Dolphins

Key Facts

Average Length: 10 ft (3 m)

Length at Birth: 3 ft 3 in (1 m)

Adult Weight: 243 lb (110 kg)

Life Span: 40 yrs

Distribution: Northern species: Cool temperate and sub-Arctic waters of the North Pacific. Southern Species: Circumpolar sub-Antarctic and cool temperate southern oceans.

Status: Little known but probably not threatened.

Grouping: Gregarious, forming groups of hundreds or thousands.

Main ID Features: Monochromatic upperpart coloration, long bodies, no dorsal fins, tiny tail flukes, low-arching leaps when on the move.

Northern Right Whale Dolphin

Also known as
Pacific Right Whale Porpoise (Northern),
Mealy-Mouthed Porpoise (Southern).

Identification: These dolphins may be long but are sinuous, with an extremely narrow and tapering body. They have a distinct, but not particularly long beak and most obviously the total absence of a dorsal fin. The pectoral flippers and tail flukes are tiny. Both species are black and white only but the extent of the white differs between them. Northern Right Whale Dolphins are mainly black with a white patch that runs along the belly from the flukes to the throat. There are also white patches on the tip of the snout and undersides of the flippers. Southern Right Whale Dolphins have more white, with the belly patch rising mid-way along the body and covering most of the head and beak. The pectoral flippers are also predominantly white. These gregarious animals are fast and energetic, often associating with other cetaceans and frequently leap and bow-ride.

Where and When: Northern species occurs in cool temperate and sub-Arctic waters only in the north Pacific. Southern species has a circumpolar range also including cool temperate waters. Typically in the open ocean, occasionally close to exposed coasts.

Best Chances: A spectacular marine mammal, keenly sought-after by seasoned whale watchers. Northern Right Whale Dolphins can be seen in inshore waters off California in winter and cooler waters off Japan. Southern Right Whale Dolphins are rarely seen with the best chances off the coasts of Namibia, New Zealand (Kaikoura) and Chile.

Atlantic Spotted Dolphin *Stenella frontalis*

Key Facts

Average Length: 6–8 ft (1.7–2.3 m)

Length at Birth: 3 ft (1 m)

Adult Weight: 310 lb (140 kg)

Life Span: Unknown

Distribution: Restricted to tropical and warm-temperate Atlantic, coastal and oceanic waters.

Status: Overall abundance unknown but probably not threatened, accidentally caught in fishing nets.

Grouping: Gregarious and inquisitive, often interacts with other cetaceans and humans.

Main ID Features: Medium size, falcate dorsal fin, flurry of spots, white beak tip and lateral blaze.

Also known as **Spotted Porpoise, Spotter,** or **Bridled Dolphin, Gulf Stream Spotted Dolphin** or **Long-Snouted Dolphin.**

Identification: Midway between a Spinner Dolphin and Bottlenose Dolphin in shape and size. A well-proportioned body, mid-set falcate dorsal fin, small melon and stout but long and clearly differentiated beak. The coloration varies considerably, but one constant is the "spinal blaze", a pale band that sweeps up from the shoulder towards the rear of the dorsal fin. The general coloration is a gray back, light gray sides and pale cream or pink belly, overlaid with variable intensities of spots. Calves are born without spots and they become more profuse with age. In some animals the snow-storm of light and dark spots is sufficient to obscure the underlying coloration. Beak tips are often white. These dolphins are most easily confused with Bottlenose Dolphins and Pan-Tropical Spotted Dolphins, which overlap in range. The combination of numerous spots, white beak tip and lateral blaze are however distinctive.

Where and When: Restricted to tropical and warm-temperate Atlantic, from around 50° N to around 25° S. Primarily oceanic but also inhabit shallow waters where they are near steep drop offs and feed primarily over deep oceanic water at night.

Best Chances: Relatively common in the Caribbean, including Bahamas, Florida Keys and in Gulf Stream. Spotted Dolphins are best known from their curious interactions with swimmers off the Bahamas (e.g. Little Bahama Bank).

Also known as **Spotted Dolphin,
White-Spotted Dolphin, Bridled Dolphin,
Spotter, Spotted Porpoise**
or **Slender-Beaked Dolphin.**

Identification:

A slender-bodied dolphin, with a long, narrow snout that is tipped with white. Lacks a shoulder blaze and the solid dark cape is narrow on the head, becoming broad below the dorsal fin. Light gray flanks and belly with fine spotting that becomes darker and more extensive with age. Dark line extends from base of snout to flipper. Can be difficult to differentiate in the field from Atlantic Spotted Dolphin. Gregarious, forming groups of 100 to 1000 animals, typically composed of distinct subgroups such as cow-calf pairs, adult males, or juveniles. Offshore pods are usually larger than coastal ones. Very acrobatic and leaps high in the air, also rides bow waves. Feeds near the surface and is often seen in feeding aggregations with other species of dolphin, including Spinners, tuna and seabirds.

Where and When: Widespread in warm-temperate and tropical oceans. Generally found beyond the shelf edge or around oceanic islands. They maintain a large home range of several hundred miles and groups may move 18 to 30 miles (30 to 50 km) per day. One of the most abundant dolphins in the Gulf of Mexico and Gulf Stream waters off Florida.

Best Chances: Common throughout the Hawaiian Island archipelago, especially the inter-island channels, fishing banks and on the leeward side of the islands.

Key Facts

Average Length: 5–8 ft (1.6–2.5 m)

Length at Birth: 3 ft (85 cm)

Adult Weight: 220–265lb (100–120 kg)

Life Span: 40–50 yrs

Distribution: Tropical and warm temperate seas, usually offshore.

Status: Abundant offshore but heavily impacted by tuna fishing in some areas.

Grouping: Highly gregarious.

Main ID Features: Small fast-moving dolphins with dark back extending low onto flank, body peppered with spots.

Pantropical Spotted Dolphin

Striped Dolphin   *Stenella coeruleoalba*

Also known as **Euphrosyne, Whitebelly, Blue-White** or **Streaker Dolphins.**

Key Facts

Average Length: 8 ft (2.3 m)

Length at Birth: 35 in (90 cm)

Adult Weight: 330 lb (150 kg)

Life Span: 50 yrs +

Distribution: Warm temperate to tropical waters, world-wide. Usually offshore.

Status: Globally abundant but hunts in the western Pacific and disease outbreaks in the Mediterranean killed significant numbers.

Grouping: Groups of 10–30, or more.

Main ID Features: Light stripe from behind eye up towards dorsal fin. Bold black stripes from eye to anus and eye to pectoral flipper.

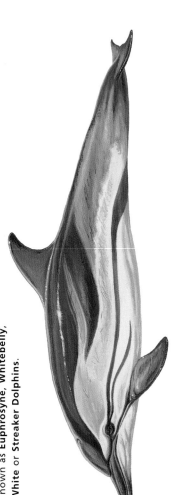

Identification: Delicate small, sleek dolphin reaching a maximum body size of 8 ft 6 in (2.6 m). Comparatively long, narrow beak, falcate dorsal fin in mid-back and striking coloration. Background color is dark gray to black, particularly on the back, with lighter gray flanks and a diagnostic well-defined black stripe (often known as the "bilge stripe") running from the eye to the anus. The pectoral flipper and angle of the jaw are joined by a dark line. There is also a bold pale blaze extending from above the eye to the base of the dorsal fin. Beak, dorsal fin, pectoral flippers and tail flukes are dark. The pale belly varies from white to pinkish. The combination of bluish-gray flanks and white belly gives the alternative name Blue-White Dolphin. These Dolphins are gregarious and sometimes found in large groups. They also frequently associate with other species, especially Common Dolphins. Energetic and when fast moving frequently leap clear of the surface.

Where and When: Worldwide in temperate to tropical oceans, predominantly found in deep pelagic waters beyond the continental shelf. Often follows warm-water currents and eddies and so often reaching higher latitudes in summer and fall.

Best Chances: Often seen on offshore trips in the Mediterranean and Bay of Biscay, tropical Pacific, Gulf Stream off Florida, Carolinas and Caribbean.

Spinner Dolphin *Stenella longirostris*

Also known as **Longsnout, Spinner, Long-Beaked Dolphin** or **Rollover**.

Identification:

Highly variable in shape and coloration. Generally slender with a long narrow beak, flattened melon, mid-set falcate dorsal fin and medium-sized flippers and tail flukes. The classic patterning is a dark back, pale gray flanks and white, cream or pink belly; the transition between them may be distinct or diffuse. Flippers, dorsal fin and tail are dark gray. There may be a stripe from the flippers to the eye and the lower jaw is typically pale. The most dramatic color variant occurs in the eastern Pacific with entirely gun-metal gray animals. The shape also varies with the eastern Pacific animals again taking an extreme, the males having a prominent bulge under the tail stock and a forward-canted dorsal fin that appears to have been placed on backwards. Spinner Dolphins are highly gregarious and well known for clearing the water and dramatically spinning on their long axis. In the central and eastern Pacific they were heavily affected by tuna fisheries in the 1960s and 70s and their numbers were massively reduced.

Where and When: All tropical and sub-tropical waters worldwide from 30° N to 30° S. Typically open ocean residents but in many areas enter coastal waters abutting ocean depths to rest during the day before heading offshore to feed at night.

Best Chances: Offshore cruises in the tropics but most easily seen coastally off oceanic islands such as Hawaii, Fiji, Japan, the Caribbean and the Maldives.

Key Facts

Average Length: 4–8 ft (1.3–2.3 m)

Length at Birth: 29 in (75 cm)

Adult Weight: 154 lb (70 kg)

Life Span: 20 yrs +

Distribution: All tropical and sub-tropical waters worldwide. Typically open ocean but coastal populations also occur.

Status: Widespread and numerous but catches in fishing activities (notably for tuna) have threatened several populations.

Grouping: Highly gregarious and often swim with other species.

Main ID Features: Long slender dolphins, long beak, spinning leaps.

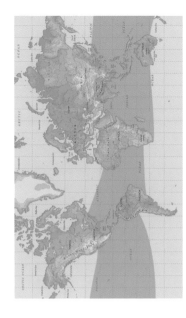

Clymene Dolphin
Stenella clymene

Also known as **Short-Snouted Spinner Dolphin, Helmet Dolphin** or **Senegal Dolphin.**

Identification: Until the 1980s, thought to be an Atlantic variant of the Spinner Dolphin, now considered a distinct species. A small stocky dolphin, up to 7 ft (2 m) long, with a moderately long beak. The back is dark-gray, the flanks pale gray and the belly white or pink. The dark gray back or "cape" runs from the tip of the melon to the tail and, unlike the Spinner Dolphin, its lower margin dips noticeably towards the belly below the dorsal fin. Close-up views reveal black pigmentation around the edge of the jaws and the tip of the snout. A dark stripe runs along the top of the beak. The melon is streamlined with a distinct crease at the junction with the upper jaw. The dorsal fin is triangular or falcate and gray, and flukes are gray. These are gregarious dolphins that form schools of tens of individuals and occasionally hundreds. They are energetic swimmers and may leap and spin in a way similar to Spinner Dolphins. Also approach boats to bow-ride. Most easily confused with Spinner Dolphins but the dip in the margin of the cape along with the dark band on the top of the beak are distinctive.

Where and When: Restricted to warm temperate and tropical waters of both the North and South Atlantic Oceans, including the Gulf of Mexico. Generally found in deep water beyond the continental shelf or around oceanic islands. Hard to identify at sea, thus not much known of its range and movements.

Best Chances: Most likely on deep-water trips in the Gulf of Mexico or south of the Florida Keys that extend beyond the continental shelf edge. Also follows Gulf Stream up to the Carolinas.

Chilean Dolphin
Cephalorhynchus eutropia

Also known as **White-Bellied Dolphin, Black Dolphin** or **Chilean Black Dolphin.**

Identification: A small stocky dolphin, 5 ft (1.6 m), in the *Cephalorhynchus* genus and not dissimilar to the Hector's Dolphin in appearance. The melon is moderately rounded and extends to the end of the snout. The body is essentially lead gray, with the dorsal fin and rear portion being darker than the flanks, shoulders and melon. The flippers, dorsal fin and tail flukes are dark gray and a dark band runs from the flippers to the eye. Like the Hector's Dolphin, there is also a dark crescent from the blowhole down and forward to outline the lower perimeter of the melon. The belly and throat area are white and a small backward-pointing finger of white also extends onto each lower flank on the tailstock. The dorsal fin is set just behind the mid-back, upright and very rounded at its tip. The flippers are also rounded on their leading edge and tips. Shares its range with the Burmeister's Porpoise, Commerson's Dolphin and Spectacled Porpoise but is distinguishable by the combination of gray coloration and upright dorsal fin with a profile so rounded that no tip is obvious.

Where and When: Restricted to cold, shallow coastal waters of middle and southern Chile, approximately from Valparaiso in the north to Tierra del Fuego in the south. Favors rapid tidal flows and rips, known to enter Rio Valdivia and other rivers. Unfortunately, these dolphins are still hunted in Chile and used as bait for the king crab fishery, they are consequently wary of boats.

Best Chances: Locally common off Playa Frailes, Valdivia, Golfo de Arauco, and near Isla de Chiloé.

Also known as **Skunk Dolphin, Piebald Dolphin, Black-and-White Dolphin, Jacobite** or **Puffing Pig.**

Identification: In common with the other members of the *Cephalorhynchus* dolphins, Commerson's have a small (5–6 ft / 1.5–1.7 m) porpoise-like appearance with chunky body and rounded fins. The color pattern is highly distinctive. The head, as far back as the blowhole and pectoral flippers, is black. The flippers are also black. The dorsal fin and its base back to the rear tail stock and tail flukes, are similarly black. The rest of the body is pure white, including the trunk, belly and the throat area. The head is rounded and the beak just a little forward of the melon but it is not clearly demarcated. These small dolphins are most often seen alone or in small groups of a few individuals. These groups sometimes aggregate into larger assemblages. Commerson's Dolphins are agile swimmers and frequently approach moving boats to bow-ride. They can also be seen surfing waves out in the open water and close inshore and, on occasion, swimming upside down.

Where and When: Has an unusual distribution. Main stronghold is in the South Atlantic, particularly in the inshore waters of Argentina, the Strait of Magellan and around the Falkland Islands, but it also has an isolated population on the other side of the world at the Kerguelen Islands in the Indian Ocean. The animals in this population have subtle differences, including being slightly larger, and were probably founded by a small group arriving after the last ice age.

Best Chances: Punta Deseado, in southern Argentina.

Also known as **South African, Benguela** or **Heaviside's Dolphin.**

Identification: Porpoise-like shape with a small body (6 ft / 1.7 m), blunt head and chunky appearance. Pectoral flippers are rounded and almost paddle-shaped. The dorsal fin is proportionally large, tall and triangular. The front half of the body is uniformly gray, with the dorsal cape, dorsal fin, flanks and tail stock all dark blue-black. A similarly colored stripe runs along the back from the blowhole to the cape. The flippers and eye patch are the same color. The underside is white, with white "armpits" behind the flippers and a rhombus shape on the chest. A finger-shaped patch extends from the belly up along each flank towards the tail. Haviside's dolphins are most often found in small groups of between two and ten but may assemble into larger groupings from time to time. These are energetic small dolphins which can perform a variety of leaps, from long low jumps when fast-moving to vertical leaps that appear to be intended to maximize the splash. They may approach boats and have been known to bow- or wake-ride. The small size, porpoise-like body shape, triangular fin and finger of white on the flanks, coupled with the restricted range of this species, makes it relatively straightforward to distinguish them from other species.

Where and When: Restricted to inshore waters of south-western Africa, from northern Namibia (17°09' S) south to Cape Point in Cape Province (34°21' S). Mostly seen in coastal waters, within 5–6 miles (8–10 km) of shore and in water less than 330 ft (100 m) deep.

Best Chances: Lambert's Bay, South Africa and Lüderitz, Namibia.

Hector's Dolphin *Cephalorhynchus hectori*

Also known as **Little Pied Dolphin, New Zealand Dolphin** or **New Zealand White-Front Dolphin.**

Key Facts

Average Length: 4–5 ft (1.3–1.5 m)

Length at Birth: 25 in (65 cm)

Adult Weight: 121 lb (55 kg)

Life Span: 20 yrs

Distribution: The coastal waters around New Zealand.

Status: Heavy tolls from entanglement in fishing gear has impacted already small populations.

Grouping: Gregarious, forming small but fluid groups of 2 to 10 individuals.

Main ID Features: Small rotund shape, rounded dorsal fin, no beak.

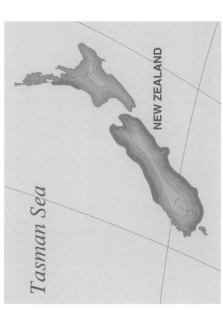

Tasman Sea

NEW ZEALAND

Identification: A small, chunky dolphin with a shape more reminiscent of a porpoise. The head is tapered without a distinct beak. The dorsal fin is set just rear of center and is unusual in being rounded with an overhanging rear margin rather than being falcate or triangular. The color pattern is a complex mix of black, gray and white. The belly is white with a lobe that extends onto the lower flank. The bulk of the sides and back are light gray but the snout tip, face, rear back, dorsal fin, flippers and tail flukes are black. When seen from above, there is a dark crescent running from the blowhole to the snout tip. These are social dolphins, forming small groups that rapidly join and split. Submarine and aerial acrobatics are common. The species is considered threatened because of the restricted range, small localized populations and habit of becoming entangled in fishing nets.

Where and When: Endemic to the inshore waters around the main islands of New Zealand. The North Island and South Island populations are distinct and it has recently been proposed that the North Island population be renamed the Maui Dolphin.

Best Chances: There are many opportunities to see Hector's Dolphins along the northern and eastern coast of the South Island of New Zealand. Particularly the Banks Peninsula near Christchurch, off Kaikoura and Greymouth.

Dall's Porpoise *Phocoenoides dalli*

Also known as **True's Porpoise** or **Whitesided Porpoise**.

Identification:

Robust, stocky bodies. Although lacking a defined beak, their small heads are less blunt than other porpoises'. Body black with white patch extending along the sides and belly. Also white on the dorsal fin, flippers and flukes, particularly in older individuals. The mid-back dorsal fin is wide-based and triangular with a sharp tip. Males are larger than females and develop a hump on the lower tail stock, their dorsal fins are broader and the trailing edges of their tail flukes are convex rather than straight as in adult females. Energetic swimmers, typically producing walls of spray either side of their bodies as they surface. Can be confused with Pacific White-Sided Dolphins, but the dolphins' taller and more falcate dorsal fin and complex color pattern aid identification. There are two forms of Dall's Porpoise. In the *truei*-type of the NW Pacific, the white flank patch extends forward to just in front of the pectoral flipper; in the *dalli*-type it is short of the flipper.

Where and When: Endemic to the cool temperate North Pacific from northern Mexico to central Japan, northwards to the Okhotsk and Bering Seas. The *dalli*-type occurs throughout the species' range but the *truei*-type is restricted to the western Pacific, east and North of Japan. Found over deep water and close to shore.

Best Chances: Along the coasts of Washington State, British Columbia and Alaska.

Key Facts

Average Length: 7–8 ft (2.1–2.4 m)

Length at Birth: 3 ft 3 in (1 m)

Adult Weight: 386 lb (180 kg)

Life Span: 15 yrs

Distribution: Coastal & oceanic North Pacific.

Status: Abundant throughout much of range but catches in western Pacific probably unsustainable.

Grouping: Usually lives in small, fluid groups.

Main ID Features: Small & robust, defined coloration, rapid swimming & distinctive surface splash.

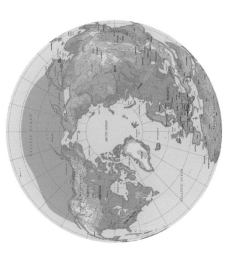

Spectacled Porpoise
Phocoena dioptrica

Also known as **Marsopa de Anteojos** (Chile and Argentina).

Identification: Small robust body 3 to 8 ft (0.9 to 2.3 m) long, rounded head with no distinct beak. The dorsal fin is roughly triangular with rounded tip, long base and straight or convex front and rear edges. Coloration is highly distinctive with a jet-black back that is clearly defined from the white lower flanks and belly. There is a black eye patch, usually outlined with white, and the lips are black. These animals are not well known but when seen, were traveling in groups of two or three animals. They share parts of their range, and can thus be confused with Burmeister's Porpoises, Commerson's and Chilean Dolphins. However, Burmeister's Porpoises appear completely dark and have more pointed dorsal fins set further back on the body; Commerson's Dolphins are more social and acrobatic and have a white coloration that extends onto the back in front of the dorsal fin. The Chilean Dolphin has a more rounded dorsal fin and is colored with shades of gray on the back and sides rather than the two phase, black or white, of the Spectacled Porpoise.

Where and When: Coastal and offshore waters of the cold temperate southern hemisphere including south-eastern South America (southern Brazil to Tierra del Fuego); the Falkland Islands; South Georgia; Îles Kerguelen; Heard Island; Tasmania; Macquarie Island; Auckland Islands and Antipodes Islands.

Best Chances: Likely requires extensive time in suitable waters. A long-shot possibility from cruise or expedition ships traveling between Ushuaia and the Falkland Islands or to Antarctic from Ushuaia, Tasmania or New Zealand.

Burmeister's Porpoise
Phocoena spinipinnis

Also known as **Marsopa Espinosa** (Chile, Argentina) and **Chancho Marino** (Peru).

Identification: Typical robust porpoise body shape 2.5 to 6.5 ft (86–190 cm) long. Rounded head and no beak. Dorsal fin distinctive, set two-thirds of the way down the body, rather than mid-way, small with a rounded tip and convex rear edge. Entire fin swept back so that tip points backward rather than upward. Coloration: charcoal gray lightening slightly, if at all, towards the belly. Usually seen alone or in small groups. Like most other porpoises, they are hard to spot and show little of the body or wake when surfacing. They can be confused with the Franciscana but lack the upward-pointing dorsal fin and the prominent beak. The fin shape and all-over dark coloration distinguishes it from the Spectacled Porpoise while the dorsal fin of the Chilean Dolphin has a more rounded tip and upright appearance.

Where and When: Restricted to the southern half of South America, ranging from central Brazil (28° S) on the Atlantic side down to Tierra del Fuego, the Beagle Channel, and Cape Horn. On the Pacific coast, extends much of the length of the cool Humboldt Current reaching northern Peru (5° S). Usually seen in or around inshore kelp beds but also offshore and in coastal river mouths and estuaries.

Best Chances: A very shy and easily overlooked porpoise favoring the edges of kelp beds along the coastline or in large rivermouths, channels and fjords. There are few reliable locations, however, careful watching from shore in suitable habitat (e.g. near Valdivia, Chile and in the Beagle Channel, Argentina/Chile) may be rewarding.

Also known as **Shushuk** (Pakistan), **Limbur** (Java), **Sunameri** (Japan) and **Jiang zhu** (China).

Identification: These animals are difficult to spot, being small, shy, colored like the silty water they live in and, above all, having a low ridge instead of a dorsal fin. Their heads are rounded without a beak and their slim 2.5 to 6 ft long (75 to 190 cm) bodies are uniform grays (ranging from cream to charcoal depending on age and region). They are usually encountered in small groups but occasionally up to 50 animals in areas of rich feeding. Breathing at the surface usually consists of an inconspicuous roll, leaps are rare. These porpoises do not bow-ride and are generally shy of motorized vessels. Though difficult to see in the first place, there are no other similar cetaceans within their range with which they can be confused.

Where and When: Coastal waters including estuaries and mangroves in warm temperate and tropical waters from the Persian Gulf in the east to Japan (38° N) in the west and southwards as far as the northern coast of Java. These animals favor areas with soft or sandy bottoms less than 160 ft (50 m) deep, and in some areas range up estuaries, rivers, and shallow channels. A small population (<2000 animals) is resident in the Yangtze River and several large lakes in China.

Best Chances: Because of their inconspicuous nature, locals may be unaware of the presence of this species, even in areas where they are relatively common. However, Kyushu and the Inland Sea, Japan and waters around Hong Kong offer good possibilities for sightings.

Also known as **Cochito** (Mexico) or **Gulf of California Porpoise**.

Identification: Typical porpoise body shape with rounded head and no beak. The body is small, ranging from 2 to 5 ft (70 to 150 cm) long. Dorsal fin is tall and triangular or falcate (concave along the trailing edge). Dark gray on the back, becoming gradually paler on the sides and belly. The eye, chin and lips are rimmed with black, there is also a dark line running from the pectoral flippers to the lower jaw. Dorsal fin, flippers and tail flukes are all dark gray. These porpoises typically swim alone or in small groups up to a maximum of around seven. They are wary of boats and surface briefly and with little splash. Bottlenose and Common Dolphins also occur in the upper Gulf of California but can be distinguished by their larger body size, beaks, more energetic swimming motion and larger group sizes.

Where and When: This species has the smallest range of any cetacean, being restricted to shallow lagoons and muddy waters near the Colorado River delta in the upper quarter of the Gulf of California in Mexico.

Best Chances: Sadly this inconspicuous but interesting porpoise is very difficult to see due to the small population size, tendency to avoid boats and highly restricted range. Furthermore, the signs are that numbers have dwindled to an all-time low as a result of fishing for mackerel, shrimps, sharks and rays and especially a large sea bass called the totoaba. It may not be much longer before this species is impossible to see alive.

Harbor Porpoise *Phocoena phocoena*

Also known as **Puffing Pig** or **Common Porpoise**.

Key Facts

Average Length: 5–6 ft (1.5–1.8 m)

Length at Birth: 2 ft (70 cm)

Adult Weight: 132–176 lb (60–80 kg)

Life Span: 15–24 yrs

Distribution: Northern hemisphere temperate and sub-Arctic coastal waters

Status: Abundant throughout much of their range but accidental capture in fishing nets threatens many populations.

Grouping: Typically alone or in small groups.

Main ID Features: Small size, black or dark-brown back, triangular fin, unobtrusive behavior.

Identification: Distinctive features include their small size, dumpy body shape, rounded head (without distinct beak), triangular, black dorsal fin and splash-less rolling motion when surfacing. Their charcoal back gradually pales to a cream or white belly. They are shy and rarely approach boats. Jumping is rare but when moving rapidly their heads and upper bodies may clear the water surface. In most of their range, there are few other species with which they can be confused. In the North Pacific, Dall's Porpoises may appear similar but have white on the dorsal fin and are more energetic swimmers.

Where and When: Restricted to cold or temperate coastal waters of the northern hemisphere. In the Pacific, range coastally from Japan to the Aleutians and Alaskan mainland to central California. In the western and mid-Atlantic, range from New England to Baffin Island and along the southern coast of Greenland to Iceland and the Faroe Islands. Common off northern Europe, including the North and Barents Seas and as far south as northern Africa. An isolated population occurs in the Black Sea and numbers in the Baltic Sea are now severely depleted.

Best Chances: Best sightings occur in areas of high porpoise density. In the Atlantic, these include the Bay of Fundy off the North American eastern seaboard. European coasts especially the North Sea, particularly off northern England, Wales, Scotland, Ireland, Denmark and western Germany. In the Pacific: coastal waters of Oregon, Washington, British Columbia and Alaska. Most often seen in calm water.

The so-called River Dolphins are not closely related but share similar habitats and appearances. Three of the four species live in the large rivers of South America and Asia, while one lives in the shallow coastal waters of South America. They all have quite sinuous bodies, mobile necks, large paddle-like pectoral fins, tiny eyes and long pincer-like jaws full of teeth. Their dorsal fins vary in size and shape but all are small and rounded. Together these features are well suited to the spatially complex, murky habitats in which these animals live. The flexible bodies and broad, rounded fins allow them to turn in tight spaces and currents; the long jaws are used for foraging among underwater vegetation and soft mud. As the suspended sediment inhibits their eyesight, they use their sensitive beaks to feel out their prey and echolocation to detect objects in front of them.

Most of the habitats occupied by the River Dolphins are also adjacent to extensive human populations, leading to accidental captures with fishing nets and hooks, intentional catches for dolphin oil, pollution, damming, water removal, prey depletion, boat strikes and other disturbances have all taken their toll, and the River Dolphins are among the most threatened of any of the cetaceans. It is widely believed that the River Dolphin that lives in the Yangtze River in China (the Baiji) will be the first to become extinct. Some believe that the few remaining animals should be caught and kept in semi-natural reserves for breeding and eventual release; others believe that the risk of captive breeding is too big and removing animals from the wild will take away any incentive to save the natural habitats. Doing nothing will result in these animals soon becoming extinct. The future for other species looks brighter.

Also known as **Yangtze River Dolphin, Beiji, Pei C'hi, Whitefin Dolphin, Whiteflag Dolphin or Chinese River Dolphin.**

Identification: Robust 2.5 to 8.5 ft (75 to 250 cm) long body with a small head and long, narrow, slightly upturned beak. The eyes are small and dorsal fin is low and triangular with a rounded tip. Blue-gray back with a pale belly. Found singly or in small groups. Groups larger than 10 are extremely unlikely due to the critically small number of individuals remaining. Co-occurs with the Finless Porpoise but can easily be distinguished by presence of a fin. However, the Baiji may share the lower reaches of the river with Humpback Dolphins, which appear in many ways similar but have the distinctive hump and a more falcate dorsal fin.

Where and When: Lives only in the middle to lower reaches of the Yangtze River's main channel. They appear to favor areas where the river flow is disturbed, especially at the joins of side branches or downstream of islands.

Best Chances: Baiji are one of the most critically endangered marine mammals and are very difficult to see alive. Intrepid whale watchers may consider going to China and visiting appropriate areas for a last chance to see. Importantly, your visit will help bring the plight of this species to the attention of local and national authorities. There are several nature reserves associated with the Yangtze River System including the Shishou City National Baiji Reserve, Tian-e-Zhou Oxbow "Semi Natural Reserve", The Xinluo National Baiji Reserve, Zhengjiang Provincial Baiji Reserve, Poyang and Dongting Lakes.

Boto   *Inia geoffrensis*

Also known as **Amazon River Dolphin, Bufeo** or **Pink Dolphin**.

Key Facts

Average Length: 7–8 ft (2–2.5 m)

Length at Birth: 2 ft (76 cm)

Adult Weight: 264–396 lb (120–180 kg)

Life Span: 30 yrs+

Distribution: River basins of the Amazon, Madeira and Orinoco Rivers in South America.

Status: Face many threats but still occupy much of their original range.

Grouping: Usually single or in small groups.

Main ID Features: Restricted range, dorsal ridge, long beak, pink or gray coloration.

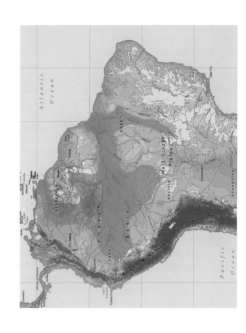

Identification: Color varies from bright pink to deep gray, depending upon age and geographical area. In the Amazon, adults are relatively pink but tend to be shy and inconspicuous in behavior, whilst in the Orinoco River system, they are grayer but more surface active. In the Arauca River of Colombia many adults are very pink and very active at the surface. Often heard before they are seen, making loud snorts or chuffs as they exhale. Instead of having a dorsal fin, Botos have a broad-based dorsal ridge which runs along their back. The 2 to 8 ft (76 to 250 cm) body itself is highly flexible. Head has an extremely long narrow beak and the eyes are tiny. Solitary or in small groups. Occasionally gather in larger numbers when prey is concentrated. Share range with Tucuxi and Bottlenose Dolphins but long beak and absence of a tall, falcate dorsal fin makes them readily distinguishable.

Where and When: Found in the drainage basins of the Amazon, Madeira and Orinoco Rivers in South America (Brazil, Bolivia, Peru, Colombia, Venezuela). Frequent a variety of riverine habitats, from the actual river mouth to far upstream reaches until blocked by impassable rapids. The junctions between rivers appear to be a preferred habitat, presumably because of rich food source. Distribution is influenced by seasonal changes in river height. In floods (December–June) leave river channels to enter surrounded flooded land and occasionally become trapped in ponds during the dry season.

Best Chances: River cruises on the Amazon and Orinoco.

Also known as **La Plata Dolphin, Cachimbo** and **Tininha** (Brazil).

Identification: One of the world's smallest cetaceans at 2.5 to 6 ft in length (80 to 175 cm), with a long narrow beak and small melon. Body color is brown or gray, with paler undersides. Dorsal fin is small and triangular, with a rounded tip, and continues as a ridge down the tail stock. The flippers are broad and almost triangular in shape. Typically found in small groups but occasional groupings of up to 20 animals at rich food sources. Shares its range with Burmeister's Porpoises which are larger, darker, have a more pointed dorsal fin and no beak. Overlaps along the coast of Brazil with the Tucuxi, which has a shorter beak and more falcate dorsal fin. Franciscana are regularly drowned in gillnets and the expansion of inshore fisheries within their range is a cause for concern.

Where and When: Restricted to nearshore waters of Atlantic coasts of Brazil, Uruguay and Argentina. The northern limit: Itaúnas, Espírito Santo State, Brazil and southern limit: north coast of Golfo San Matias, Chubut Province, Argentina. The specie's range is more or less continuous along the coast, with the exception of two gaps in the Brazilian states of Rio de Janeiro and Espírito Santo. Most animals occur in waters less than 100 ft (30 m) deep, but they may occur in deeper waters.

Best Chances: Bay of San Blas (Buenos Aires Province, Argentina).

Also known as **Susu** (Ganges), **Bhulan** (Indus), **Gangetic Dolphin, Blind River Dolphin** or **Side-Swimming Dolphin.**

Identification: Small dolphins 2 to 8 ft (70 to 250 cm) long with extremely long and slender beaks. Teeth remain visible even when the jaw is closed. Eyes tiny. Dorsal fin little more than a triangular ridge. Body a uniform, dark gray, sometimes with a pinkish belly. Frequently swim on their sides and may occasionally jump above the surface in low leaps if fast moving. Their long beaks are often visible during surfacing. Groups usually of a dozen or fewer. May be confused with Irrawaddy Dolphins that are also found in the confluence of the Ganges and Brahmaputra Rivers but can be distinguished by the dorsal fin shape and long slender beak.

Where and When: Found in the main channel of the Indus River (Pakistan) downstream of the Chashma Barrage. Ganges, Brahmaputra, Meghna, Karnaphuli, Sangu, Karnali River systems (India, Bangladesh, Nepal). Generally concentrated in counter-current pools below channel convergences and sharp meanders and above and below mid-channel islands, bridge pilings, and other engineering structures that cause scouring.

Best Chances: Indus: Highest densities in Sind Province, between the Guddu and Sukkur Barrages and Punjab Province between Taunsa and Guddu Barrages. Ganges: Vikramshila Gangetic Dolphin Sanctuary (India) and lower Sangu River (Bangladesh).

An exciting moment! Heading out from an Azorean harbor in search of whales.

The Whale-Watching Experience

As the media will often tell us, cetaceans – whales, dolphins and porpoises – hold a special place in our collective consciousness. But, pinpointing exactly what distinguishes them in our minds from most other organisms is a challenge. The key qualities are probably different for each of us and range from the factual to the emotional.

In terms of sheer majesty, whales are in a league of their own and most are sufficiently enormous to relegate us to dwarf status. They also inhabit an environment that is alien to us and with this comes a strong element of mystery. But being mammals they also retain features that we find familiar; complex social lives and tenderness towards their young. Cetaceans are famed for their large brains and complicated behaviors which together hint at a rare intelligence. And to swell this popular idea of 'a mind in the ocean', cetaceans can be just as curious of us as we are of them. Not many people who have had an eye-to-eye encounter will fail to mention the heart-stopping gaze. And if it's not the eye, it's the jaw. The endearing dolphin grin effortlessly wipes away the sinister, maleficent airs that other marine predators (think sharks) exude. While this fixed smirk is an artifice, the extraordinary rarity of aggressive encounters directed at humans by cetaceans remains a defining feature. Along with all of these attributes, these animals have also received their fair share of hype. Cetaceans have had a rough time at the hands of man and yet have assumed an emblematic role. They have become a symbol of both the struggling environment and individual freedom. One thing is for sure, these animals are undeniably and unashamedly beautiful to watch.

As a result of these factors, most people can remember when and where they saw their very first whale or dolphin. In comparison, how many of us can remember, exactly where and when we saw our first monkey puzzle tree? Exotic plants may be unmistakable, biologically curious and rare but somehow they don't have sufficient pizzazz to burn themselves into our memories.

Just as people are different, the thoughts, feelings and memories that individuals draw from what may appear to be the same whale-watch experience diverge substantially. In this chapter we attempt to capture some of this diversity of experiences, emotions and thoughts, as well as a taste of what individual whale-watch opportunities are actually like. To do this we invited colleagues, friends and family to think back through their own whale-watch experiences and describe their private thoughts from a particular trip.

Torchlight Torpedoes

Bioluminescence and Common Dolphins, Azores

It had been hours since the sun had sunk below the horizon. I was alone on deck, with only the steering wheel and compass for company. The loadstone sitting in a tiny pool of light hemmed in by a world of darkness. The only clue that there was any kind of ocean out there was the abrupt horizontal end to the bustle of stars that loomed overhead. I got up from the damp seat to scan the inky horizon. We were far offshore so there was no risk of collision with rocks or fishing boats. There were ships out there though, container ships, oil tankers and military ships plying their way between distant shores. To them our sailing boat was the minutest of blips on the radar screen, easily missed and just as easily crushed. These ships move fast, so every few minutes I nervously scanned the blackness for their navigation lights. As had been the case all night – nothing. I was about to return to the steering console when something caught my eye, a faint glow in the water several hundred meters to starboard. My eyes were tuned to the dark, but still I couldn't make out what it was. It was blurred and moving. In fact it was moving fast towards the boat. As a wave passed, the boat settled into a trough and the lights disappeared. A second later they crested it, not one light now, but several. Five sparkling green comets tearing along just below the surface on a direct collision course with the boat's hull. Impact was imminent.

This sight is not uncommon at night in the open seas. In times of war it has had ships scrambling into battle stations as the night-watch calls the torpedo attack alarm. The sight had me transfixed. Yet the submarine fireballs were not malicious weapons but a curious meeting of marine creatures – a clash between the magnificent and the minute.

Food chains in the oceans are driven by plankton, tiny creatures that make a living while floating at the mercy of the currents. They give seawater its distinctive color. Blue if they're absent, green if they're teeming and occasionally red-brown. Some of them have an unexplained habit; if disturbed they emit a pulse of light, a tiny spark of green, so faint as to be invisible in all but the dark of night. If the night-time sea is quiet then they remain dark but if suddenly bumped they release their light.

As I stood on the deck, frozen in horror waiting for the imminent impact, the burning balls of light veered at the last moment, in a graceful arc that took them to the bows. There they caught the boat's motion and began to twist and turn just inches from the ploughing hull. Dolphins! Or rather their ghosts, black shapes in inky water made visible by millions of tiny planktonic sparks streaming off their bodies. I flicked on the autopilot, clipped on my safety harness and scrambled up to the bows for a better look.

I've no notion of how long the dolphins rode our boat's bow wave, perhaps five minutes or ten. I was too riveted to mark time. I lay on the deck with my nose barely a yard above the water and them the same distance below. Their bodies were utterly invisible and yet their every curve, their every edge was turned into

Common Dolphins by day, torpedoes by night.

a fluorescent, streaming trail. A three-dimensional rendition of their underwater trajectories – their sparkling wakes an echo of time. At one moment there was a splash of light up ahead. A school of fish had been lurking under the surface but their flight produced an explosion of light like a firework going off. The dolphins took chase and disappeared into the night. I was left staring into blackness for a moment before they returned in a repeat fake torpedo run for another session of submarine chicken. And then, as quickly as they had come, they took off, dragging their brilliant wakes behind them.

Charles Reid

Maldives Magic

Dolphins and Whales, Dhaalu Atoll, Maldives

Just after dawn, the skipper moved our vessel, *Isis*, about a mile closer to
Faandhoo, a small, uninhabited island with terns flying around it. Although
the birds are protected by law, we noticed a local boat and four men collecting
eggs. Charles 'Chas' Anderson, the expedition leader, took the boat's registration
number and promised to report them later to the authorities. We had time for
a brief snorkel before breakfast and then sailed west, back out to the open sea.
The conditions were close to flat calm and the visibility in terms of spotting
cetaceans, was stunning.
A few distant Spinner
Dolphins started the day
and a lone large shearwater
flew by laboriously, on our
starboard side. A few
distant noddies and terns
could be seen, and fish
jumped out of the sea in
all directions. Chas went
up on top of the bridge
to look out and quickly
returned saying he could
see animals on the horizon
and we would head

Gregarious False Killer Whales.

towards them. Little did we know what the next few hours were going to bring.
As we sailed towards the horizon two or three Dwarf Sperm Whales appeared on
our port side, rather more distant than the one we saw a couple of days earlier.
Our attention turned to the bow again and it was clear a number of other
cetaceans had appeared ahead of us. Blackish animals with tall dorsals with some
dolphins in amongst them, Pilot Whales perhaps? As we finally got closer we
realised we were looking at False Killer Whales and were quickly surrounded
by small groups, some coming from the stern and swimming down the sides of
Isis. Long and sleek, with a very distinctive high dorsal fin, hooked back at the top
and slightly rounded. We could even hear them whistling to each other. A group
of about 70 Bottlenose Dolphins lay to the north. Chas finally admitted the
group of animals he had spotted in the first place were possibly another goodie.

We turned towards them and were about halfway when we saw another set of fins in the water ahead. Chas thought they may be Rough-Toothed Dolphins and indeed their 'pink lips' confirmed this. They swam down the side of the vessel, giving superb views as they raised their heads to breathe. Gently sloping foreheads led to the longish snout and pinkish lower jaw line. Some of them looked as if it was the first time they had put lipstick on, smearing it clumsily in the process. One animal seemed very pale, almost leucistic. These dolphins look somehow prehistoric, almost reptilian. The dorsal fins seem somewhat shark-like, with ragged trailing edges. Normally seen only once a year, we were very lucky. False Killers continued to be scattered over the sea, in groups of four to six, we estimated 75+ in total. We finally headed for the line of animals that started it all. They stayed in a tight line formation, creating great quantities of white water on the tranquil seas. Stout, stocky, with no real beak, we were closing in on another Maldives speciality, Fraser's Dolphins. We slowly approached; there were about 200 animals and some of them turned and started bow-riding, shutters soon clicked away. We could hear their high-pitched whistles as they communicated with

Fraser's Dolphins: energetic and enigmatic.

each other. We spent about half an hour with them, occasionally seeing their pink bellies as they came up to breathe. While all of this had been going on a few beaked whales had appeared and vanished and several of the group saw what may have been a Sperm Whale blow in the distance. Time for lunch, what a morning!

After lunch another single Dwarf Sperm Whale appeared near us and then characteristically disappeared. We also came across the pod of Rough-Toothed Dolphins again. This time there was some tail-lobbing and some of the animals rose halfway out of the sea and splashed back down again (headslapping). We left them in peace, headed back north and into the atoll towards Vommuli, where a few distant Spinners could be seen. This would be our anchorage for the night.

John Brodie-Good

Kaikoura Encounters

Sperm Whales and Dusky Dolphins in New Zealand

I was amazingly lucky enough to enjoy two of the most incredible and moving experiences of my life on the same day – seeing wild Sperm Whales and swimming with countless wild Dusky Dolphins. It was a perfect first day on a whistle-stop two-week backpacking holiday around the South Island of New Zealand.

My first adventure began at the Whale Watch Kaikoura visitor center where we listened to a short safety briefing before boarding a coach that transported us to the Whale Watch boat. We sped out to sea, the boat crashing up and over the waves. Our guide told us about the whales we all desperately hoped we

The flukes of a diving Sperm Whale.

would be privileged enough to see and what to expect from the trip. It wasn't long before the boat slowed down and began circling a smaller area. The engine was switched off and we were asked to go out onto the viewing deck.

As soon as I stepped outside I saw it – a huge dark gray mass bobbing in and out of the water, just meters away from me. A Sperm Whale! It stayed still for about 10 minutes until disappearing beneath the surface. Then, just as I thought it had gone, the whale's huge tail appeared above the water as it began its dramatic dive back into the deep. All of the 30 or so people on board were silent as the huge animal slowly sank into the water – all that could be heard was the click and whirr of cameras and the sound of the waves lapping against the side of the boat. And then – as suddenly as it had appeared, it was gone. We were lucky enough to see another two whales during our few hours at sea, before returning to the shore.

Later, we checked in at Dolphin Encounter for our next adventure. Our first task was to struggle into wet suits and listen to our second safety talk of the day. I was concerned about whether the welfare of the dolphins was compromised by tourist activities like these. But it was made very clear that these are wild dolphins and it is their choice to swim with you. We were given strict instructions not to try and touch them. We were told that to encourage dolphins to get close to us we should swim in small circles and make groaning noises through our snorkels! We then clambered aboard a small motorboat accompanied by several guides. I had some very last-minute snorkeling tuition (it was the first time I'd done any) before nervously heading towards the back of the boat for my first dive with wild dolphins.

After lowering myself into the water I quickly got to grips with breathing through the snorkel and was soon ducking down below the surface hoping for a glimpse of even just a single dolphin. I saw a few dolphins flash by and was so excited I forgot to breathe for a while. Reluctantly I came up for air and adjusted my snorkel before trying again. This time I was able to stay beneath the surface for longer and put the techniques I'd been taught into practice, swimming in ungraceful circles and honking loudly through my snorkel. Dolphin after dolphin swam by me, some even brushing up against me. I couldn't believe they were coming so close and it was all the more magical as I knew that these were wild animals that were choosing to come close.

Dusky Dolphins.

All too soon the siren sounded again, calling everyone back to the boat. It was chaos as everyone struggled to climb back on board, but we all had huge grins on our faces. What an experience! Four or five similar dives followed and during each one I got very close to hundreds of these fabulous creatures. They made me feel ungainly and comical under the water as they slid effortlessly past. It was only later that I learned I had been snorkeling for the first time in waters that reach depths of up to 1000 ft! A wildlife tour followed, and we were treated to a spectacular display of dolphins jumping out of the water and reaching such amazing heights they looked like they were flying.

Before we set out on both trips we were warned that we may not see either a single whale or a dolphin, so I prepared myself for disappointment as I was fully aware that these were wild animals and there are never any guarantees where they will be on a given day. But thanks to the expert knowledge of our guides and quite a lot of luck I saw everything I had hoped for and more. It was an experience I will never forget.

Helen Briggs

Tearing around in Tenerife

Short-Finned Pilot Whales, Canary Islands

I hadn't planned to go whale watching whilst in Tenerife but my enthusiastic friend persuaded me. We made our way down to the harbor where there were loads of trips to choose from, all lasting about 2.5 hours. We chose a relatively small boat and set out. The day was warm even though it was overcast, but it was quite windy and this was whipping up the sea into little peaks. Our guide said that this might make spotting the whales difficult, but we would still try.

The aim of the trip was to see Short-Finned Pilot Whales which, we were told, dived down to over 1000 ft to find their major food, squid. The whales are really large dolphins, so we weren't expecting to see giant plumes of breath when they surfaced, making it difficult to spot them.

The stocky profiles of Short-Finned Pilot Whales.

As it turns out, it wasn't! I was surprised at how close in to shore we were when, about half an hour after leaving the jetty, the shout went up that Pilot Whales had been spotted. Any concerns I'd had about being able to spot them were immediately dispelled – they seemed to be everywhere! A flotilla of black fins was cutting through the water about 500 yards away, awesome numbers, invoking images of sharks for some bizarre reason – I'd never seen such big, black fins on what I was expecting to be a dolphin. They were all at a distance, but it felt as though we were surrounded!

In the distance the architecture of holiday-resort Tenerife (we had taken a trip out from Los Cristianos, a highly developed tourist area) set a backdrop of white cuboids against a gray sea in which it seemed a hundred black fins were scything past us. I'm sure I was so bowled over to see the Pilot Whales that their numbers were hugely inflated in my mind's eye, but the impression they made was both strong and exciting.

The boat somehow selected a group of Pilot Whales and moved in on it. Ours wasn't the only boat out and we were soon joined by a far larger whale-watching boat, carrying over 100 people, when we were a cosy group of only about 15. The little sleek, black whales came in close and a few of them took to bow-riding for a while – it was so exciting and we had wonderful views from the upper deck on our boat. The animals stayed with us for about 15 minutes, after which it was clear they wanted to move off. I was not impressed with the other whale-watch boat accompanying us – it was driving very close up behind the Pilot Whales, even though they weren't bow-riding and looked as though it was pursuing them. Our guide explained that the larger boat had a glass-bottom bubble in which passengers could view under the water. This meant that the boat was trying to get "on top of" the whales so that people could see them. I wasn't impressed.

As our pod decided to head away it was wonderful to watch. Clearly a family group, with a calf and at least one larger youngster. At one point I saw this smaller animal turn back as the group passed by a floating white plastic bag. (I'd heard that marine wildlife mistake plastic bags for jellyfish and swallow them, so I was a little

Pilot Whales have short pectoral flippers.

worried.) The young Pilot Whale swam up to the bag and, if a whale can examine an object, it examined it. It then turned and, with a flick of its tail chased back to the rest of the group. An adult, possibly its mother, seemed to check out the arrival of the youngster back in the group. What a view! It really brought the animals alive for me, seeing them exploring the environment and interacting with each other rather than simply swimming ahead of the boat. A two and a half hours well spent.

Laila Sadler

A New England Tour

Right Whales and Humpbacks

One of the great things about whale watching, and nature overall, is never really knowing what to expect each time you leave the dock. Oh, sure, we often say this with some expectation of what may be coming based on the morning's trip, or the whales that we had been seeing in the prior week, but you never really do know when the unexpected will take place. It can be the whales, or the people riding along with you.

Take a day in the early spring of May, 1995. It had been a tough spring – not many whales around, elusive behavior from the whales we had seen, and even a few trips where no whales were seen. On the particular Sunday I am thinking of, the day was gray and the sea choppy. The morning trip, where we went far up Jeffreys Ledge to find only two elusive Fin Whales, did nothing to brighten our spirits for the afternoon trip. The foggy mist that started falling during lunchtime didn't add any to our spirits. Yet there were the whale watchers, eager to go out. Since the morning's sightings had been less than promising, we changed our destination and angled to Stellwagen Bank, which was closer, and at least would get us home more quickly if the trip was disappointing.

Then, about 7 miles offshore, we saw a pile of birds hovering near a fishing boat, and a blow nearby. Looking again, we saw the blow had a faint V-shape, indicative of a North Atlantic Right Whale, one of the rarest whales in the world. As we approached, we could see the gaping maw of this whale at the surface – clearly it was skimming plankton at the surface of the water, and not diving. As we got there, we saw another blow nearby – a second Right Whale! Soon a third showed up, and within minutes, we and a minimum of five feeding Right Whales around us (almost 2 percent of the entire population).

As of 1999, it has become illegal to approach Right Whales closer than 500 meters because of their endangered status, but no such restriction existed at the time. Our captain, Jeff Egan, maneuvered us to get great views of the feeding whales, without disturbing them. Then, without warning, one turned and approached our boat. Skimming so high in the water that its tongue was visible, it approached us to about 10 ft away, stopped, lifted its head, turned, and continued to feed. Heart stopping. As of today, in 25 years, I've never had a better look at a feeding Right Whale.

There have been other sightings like that. I remember as a novice naturalist in my first year seeing a huge Fin Whale far east of Stellwagen. In my mind, that whale was far bigger than any other Fin Whale I had seen (and they are common around here). It wasn't until almost 20 years later, when I looked back at the photos of that whale, that I realized it was the first sighting of a Blue Whale in New England waters! Ah, if those passengers only knew.

The toughest questions we get are always from small children. My favorite was when a little boy came over, gathering up all his courage to talk, and shyly mumbled, "Do whales sneeze?" OK – do they? How would you know? Or the little girl who wriggled her way up and said, legs wrapping each other, "How big is a whale's bladder"? It's times like those that can make the job of a naturalist worthwhile.

We also have to remember our perspective can be so different, because we are out there every day.

One day we had a trip which was fair – we saw six different Humpback Whales, but they were elusive and staying down for a long time. We eventually left the area with reasonably happy passengers but an unsatisfied feeling among the crew. As I went around and talked to people, I came

A Humpback Whale waves its enormous pectoral flipper.

upon a family with a 10-year-old daughter. They told me that she was having a very risky heart surgery the next day, and that she had only a 50-50 chance of surviving. The Make-A-Wish Foundation had arranged for her to meet her life's dream – seeing a whale. She was beyond thrilled at what we had seen, and felt her greatest desire fulfilled, regardless of what happened the next day. Needless to say, we treated her like royalty for the rest of the day – she drove the boat home, had a whale gift package waiting for her at the dock, etc. We were never told how things went the next day for her, but it was certainly humbling and moving to know that a day that couldn't satisfy us could make another person's life.

So every time we drop those lines and head out, you never know when the day will live in your mind forever – even if you've done it hundreds, or thousands, of times before.

Maison Weinrich (Whale-Watching Tour Guide)

Eye to Eye with a Fin Whale

A Snorkeling Experience near Corsica

It was a typically hot and breathless summer's day in the Mediterranean. The yacht I was crewing on languished in the calm, crystal-clear water with the sails hanging limply from the masts. We were heading towards Corsica away from the stifling crowds of the Riviera and in absolutely no rush. This was already turning into a fantastic summer, my first time at sea and we had been lucky enough to visit some exotic places and see some amazing sights. We had seen leaping sailfish, schools of tuna, and earlier that day we had been passed by an underwater squadron of manta rays flying elegantly and lazily past our bow.

The chat and excitement of seeing the mantas had begun to ebb but as we headed back across the deck towards the cockpit we heard an eerie whooshing sound nearby. Richard, the skipper, said he had heard that sound once before and thought it was a whale blowing. It sounded as if the noise was coming from astern so we rushed to the aft deck and began eagerly scanning the water.

We held our breath and after a few moments of anticipation the sea nearby exploded into a 15 ft tower of shimmering water vapor. Wow, what a sight, the massive blow looked like a fire hydrant exploding and the cloud hung in the air as the hulking back of a Fin Whale broke the surface. The sea was so clear that we could easily make out the immense size of the beast through the water and we watched in fascination as it slid back down into the blue depths. Over the next few minutes the whale continued to surface and we soon realized that it was actually checking out the boat as it circled us. As the minutes passed and the whale stayed around the boat, Gordon, the first mate, had the idea to get into the water with a diving mask in hope of seeing the animal underwater.

We couldn't resist giving it a go. We decided to trail the yacht's dinghy on a long rope so we could use it as a snorkeling platform. The two of us quickly grabbed our masks and hopped into the dinghy and slowly began to drift the rope's length away from the stern of the yacht. We didn't want to disturb or scare the whale so we planned to stay by the dinghy as we snorkeled. Slipping into the bath-warm water, we began to look down into the endless depths. Nothing for a while, but then I became aware of a ghostly shape emerging from the deep. As the whale came closer I could make out the whole of the animal's immense body. Wow, this magnificent animal was within a few yards of us and began to gracefully swim by. It was an incredible sight, the whale looked so elegant and peaceful as it slipped past. The water was so clear it looked as though the whale was suspended in air and I could see the sunlight dancing on its skin. Strangely, it reminded me of the patterns of light you often see playing on the tiles in swimming pools and it was odd to see something so strangely alien seem so familiar. The whale continued upwards and we saw it break the surface as it breathed. I popped my head out of the water to watch in amazement as the deafening blow filled my senses. The whale inhaled with a whoosh and I saw the gaping blowholes clamp shut as its giant back continued to roll endlessly past. The whale slowly dropped away from the surface and I ducked back under to watch the animal dive. The whale

continued to circle us and gradually got closer as its curiosity grew. It eventually approached our dinghy and swam slowly right past us. I looked directly into the whale's eye and felt a sense of long lost connection between us and imagined what was going through the whale's mind. We must have looked like two tiny insects clinging to a piece of flotsam! Eventually the whale passed us and we felt the gentle rush of water as it slowly beat its tail and retreated back into the blue.

That was the most amazing swim of my life and a truly moving experience. The whale repeatedly revisited me in my dreams over the next few months and the image of the giant leviathan remains forever etched into my memory. I can see it now, looking at me with that ancient, peaceful eye. *Simon Ingram*

An Arctic Adventure

In Search of the Elusive Narwhal

Our Arctic adventure began off Greenland in mid August, aboard the expedition cruise ship *Academic Ioffe*. What a way to spend a holiday, above the Arctic Circle in search of wildlife. The main purpose of our trip was to see the mysterious Narwhal. The males carry a long extended tooth that gave rise to the legend of the unicorn. Imagine seeing a whale with such a tusk! This was all I could think of as we crossed the Davis Strait to Baffin Island.

For hour upon hour, I scanned the sea alongside my equally anxious companions, coming to the realization that Narwhals are as mysterious in revealing themselves as they are in appearance. Narwhals, as it turns out, almost never raise their tusks out of the water when traveling through the open sea. We had come all this way, clearly we had to try harder.

Hunting cetaceans has always been a part of the local Inuit way of life, and over the centuries, the Narwhals have developed a healthy wariness of humans and the boats that carry them. No doubt they were out there, swimming secretly away from any approaching boat, not waiting to find out if the passengers are Inuit hunters or anxious wildlife enthusiasts.

Just as I was losing all hope of ever seeing a Narwhal, there was a commotion on the top deck. Someone had spotted what appeared to be a distant group of Narwhals on the other side of the inlet. Following the crowd across the slippery deck, I immediately rushed towards the stern. Did someone say they saw a tusk? Is that possible? Is this the real thing at last? Adjusting my binoculars, I could clearly see the finless back of a cetacean. Maybe more than one. Narwhals at last! Then, they disappeared as quickly as they had appeared, but it was enough to get the adrenaline pumping. I might have seen it, or I might have imagined it, but this unforgettable experience left me wanting for more. Seeing a glimpse of such an elusive whale, real or imaginary, was by itself well worth the trip to the magnificent waters of the Arctic.

Naoko Tanese

Baja Encounters

Meeting Gray Whale Families

Our vessel gingerly headed through the narrow entrance to the lagoon from the Pacific Ocean. Once into the calmer waters we quickly dropped anchor as three small pangas with their Mexican fisherman drivers headed towards us. These small boats fitted with an outboard engine were to be used within the lagoon. In every direction we could see Gray Whales breaching, lob-tailing, spyhopping, and just breaking the surface to breathe every few minutes: we were about to experience one of the wonders of the natural world. As we moved away from

our vessel in the pangas, cow/calf pairs were already coming towards us. The boatman cut the engine and we drifted. It's very hard to describe such an experience, the mother Gray Whales were bringing their young to meet us, and they wanted to get very close indeed. Before we knew it, our first baby whale had thrust its head out of water, resting against the side of the little boat, and it wanted physical contact. We took it in turns to pet, rub, scratch and even kiss the little whales. The more we did it, the more they seemed to like it. I suddenly realized that mum had positioned herself directly under our boat. A 40 ft whale inches beneath a 15 ft boat was a very sobering thought. There was no doubt who was in charge of this situation and it was not us. The mother just stayed there, not once touching the boat. If she wanted to, she could have launched us into low earth orbit with a single flick of her tail. The baby whale was now amusing itself, and us, by suddenly blowing air and water from its blowhole straight into our faces. Looking a whale directly in the eye is a humbling experience; 'life-changing' say some. Why did the mother approach us with their young? Theories abound but I can only think it is to warn the youngsters. "This is the creature that used to hunt us, when you grow up, stay well away from them". The old whalers used to call Gray Whales 'devilfish'. They were one of the few species that would fight back when harpooned and certainly took a few unwitting whalers into the depths with them. *John Brodie-Good*

Kayaking with Killers

Killer Whales in Johnstone Strait, British Columbia

I'd said I wanted to have an adventure, one with plenty of exercise and fresh air. And, given that I was going to British Columbia in Canada, I also wanted to see the Killer Whales. My boyfriend found the ideal solution – a week's sea kayaking trip in Johnstone Strait, where sightings of resident Killer Whales were common. I had been on a few whale-watching trips from large vessels but had never been in a kayak, let alone down near the water when a whale was around. I was told that we would obey the same whale-watching codes as the commercial vessels –

not getting too close, not pursuing the whales (slim chance in a kayak!), keeping quiet. Also, I was told, as we were so low on the water the view may not actually be as good. So what. The experience had to be a good one.

We chose to go in September; we were camping for the week, which allowed us to stay out on islands, surrounded by forest wilderness behind and the local channels and straits frequented by the Killer Whales just off the beach.

On the very first day we set off in bright sunshine, paddling along close to the island edges where harbor seals poked up their heads and watched us go by. Within an hour or so we heard distant growling roars coming from a little island. "Elephant seal? Here?" said my friend, slightly perplexed. "Steller sea lion?" I suggested. We set off, paddling out into the channel, and, sure enough, as we approached through a rippling tide race we could see the vast recumbent figures of golden brown Steller sea lions basking in the sun. They seemed oblivious to our presence as we bobbed silently in the lee of the island, watching from a respectable distance.

Setting off once more into the face of the incoming tidal currents I found myself in a remarkably flat area of water – upwelling current bouncing off some obstruction far below. As I paddled quietly along a small dorsal fin popped out of the water. I looked at the little triangular fin, lighter grey skin on its trailing edge, and heard the "pfft!" as a Dall's Porpoise surfaced, rolled and dived again, turning within a very small area as it hunted for fish, oblivious to my presence.

Next day was grey, but we could see the commercial whale-watching boats out in the Strait and they were clearly onto a group of Killer Whales. We set out, no chance of catching up with or following the large vessels, but it was great to know that there were Killer Whales nearby. As we headed for the shore of the neighboring island, a tall, black fin suddenly appeared about 400 yards away. A Killer Whale! Within minutes another few animals were heading our way, among them an adult male, his huge dorsal fin rising into the air like a great pointed monolith. Even from our distance of a few hundred yards I could see the water running off as the fin, much to my surprise, wobbled as it came upright. Living tissue on a living, breathing whale. It was amazing.

A few hours later we had rounded the island and moved away from the area where two whale-watching boats were following a small group. It included a calf and the young whale was visible, slapping its tail against the water as the boats came closer, perhaps to show it was upset. We steered clear. Ahead of us, unseen by the boats, was a disturbance in the water, black shapes appearing and disappearing, spray flying up. We paddled slowly towards it, stopping when it became clear that it was indeed a group of Killer Whales – playing! There's no other word for it. They were tumbling and writhing over one another, pushing up into the air, white bellies flashing, flukes appearing, disappearing; heads popping up here and there, dorsal fins out then gone – it was like a Killer Whale soup! The whole group disappeared beneath the water at once – had they spotted us? – then rose again at the same spot, still engaged in their marine wrestling. Eventually the group disentangled itself and set off slowly in the direction taken by the other groups of Killer Whales we had seen that morning. We sat there, bobbing on the calm water, stunned.

The other truly memorable moment was sitting beside our campfire on the beach one night, darkness all around, when suddenly, unseen in the engulfing blackness, we heard the blow of a whale. Then another. The air was still and the breaths so loud they seemed to be within meters of us, but we couldn't see a thing. Just hear the chorus of about six animals, faint splashes and loud blows in the night, as they swam past. This must be what their world beneath the water is like – shapes made from sound, not a thing to see. Amazing. *Laila Sadler*

Swimming with Dolphins

Indo-Pacific Bottlenose Dolphins in Japan

The powerful engine roared as the *Dancing Whale* struggled to keep position
in the strong current that hurtled through a gap in the jagged rocks. Lookouts,
scattered on all four points of the small diving boat, stood on tiptoes straining
to catch sight of the dolphins in the choppy water. At the stern, I sat on a
narrow ledge shoulder-to-shoulder with several other nervous passengers. Our
facemasks were in place and finned feet held up out of the water, mindful of the
whirring propellers just inches away. Suddenly the engine cut. "Go, go, go!"
commanded Tomoko Takahashi, the lead guide, and like hapless lemmings we
leaped into the churning water. A moment of chaos and disorientation followed.
Where should we swim? Where are the dolphins? Looking up at the boat, which
was drifting away with alarming rapidity, I could see Tomoko gesticulating
furiously with her hands. Huh? The signal looked like "Downwards!
Downwards!" but was this another of those peculiar Japanese hand signals
so unfamiliar to westerners?

Confused, I glanced down into the water and was both shocked to see six
Indo-Pacific Bottlenose Dolphins lolling just a few feet below us. They were so
close that I somehow assumed they were members of our own group! By now
another of our guides, Hou Kyonsun, who is an expert free-diver, was in the
water with us and with a few lithe undulations of her body dropped downwards,
joining the dolphins in a graceful aquatic ballet. Presumably, a familiar sight,
the dolphins immediately accepted her presence and for a moment she was one
of their group, not ours. One individual rolled over as if in greeting, revealing
its white belly delicately suffused with pink. The group and guest sank slowly
towards the sandy seabed 30 or 40 feet below. Floating at the surface, arms
and legs outstretched, we simply watched transfixed by the scene. As fast as
the encounter had begun it was over. Hou Kyonsun rose towards the surface and
the dolphins drifted off into the darkness. Finally the spell was broken and we
all began to thrash and splutter in the turbulent chop on the surface. Having
carefully kept its distance, the boat motored over to pick us up and we scrabbled
onto the ledge and back into the real world again. A welcoming cup of steaming
hot tea was thrust into our trembling hands and everyone babbled excitedly in
Japanese and English. The words were unimportant because we were united by
this remarkable shared experience.

This scene took place off Chichi-jima, the main island of the Ogasawara or

Bonin group, a cluster of volcanic rocks that emerge from the Pacific some 600 miles south of Tokyo. For half of the year, these warm waters are home to several hundred Humpback Whales that use the protection of the islands to mate and raise their calves. Dolphins are more or less resident, including the Indo-Pacific Bottlenose Dolphins we swam with and several groups of smaller Spinner Dolphins. It is not an overstatement to describe the Ogasawara Islanders as whale crazy. The coastline is studded with whale-watching lookouts and visitors arriving by ferry to Chichi-jima and nearby Haha-jima are greeted by dramatic full-sized

Whether you speak Japanese or English, this sight is a thrill.

Humpback Whale sculptures. Whale illustrations adorn many of the buildings and shops. The main town has a smart whale-watching center, offering a lecture on whale watching the evening the ferry arrives from Tokyo and provides a booking service with copious information on viewing opportunities, including a chalkboard listing of recent sightings. This wonderful celebration of whales is proof that the hardline stance on commercial whaling expounded by the Japanese government is really not a true reflection of the feelings of the Japanese people.

Charles Reid

In Search of Northern Right Whales

Whale Watching in the Bay of Fundy

Our flight arrived at Saint John, New Brunswick and an hour's drive brought us to Black Harbour and the Grand Manan ferry. Calm conditions over to the island gave views of hundreds of Harbour Porpoises as well as distant Humpback and Fin Whales – a promising start!

The next afternoon we boarded our first whale-watching trip from Seal Cove towards the south end of the island. We asked the skipper about our chances of

seeing Northern Right Whales; his response was not encouraging. Very few had been seen so far that year and they were generally keeping over towards Nova Scotia. Numbers in recent years had been much fewer than previously, and it seemed this year was no different.

The sea was still calm and we encountered several groups of Humpback Whales, including one huge animal being bow-ridden by a group of Atlantic White-Sided Dolphins. No Northern Right Whales were seen but it had still been an excellent trip. On the way back to harbor some encouraging news came over the boat's radio – another operator had found some Northern Right Whales – and best of all, it was the operator we were going out with tomorrow! The GPS position was carefully noted down in my notebook for "the next day". A terrific sunset followed later in the evening; would the weather hold for tomorrow in this notoriously fog-prone part of the world?

The following day dawned bright, clear and dead calm again – perfect! We made our way up to North Head for our trip and soon boarded our sailing vessel. We headed out past Swallowtail Lighthouse in a northeast direction. The boat was very full and looking ahead through a mass of people was not feasible. After more than an hour, with nothing more than a few Harbor Porpoises in the calm sea, a shout came about distant splashing. This sounded like more Humpback Whales so, without too much excitement, I managed to find a small spot through which I could see ahead. Indeed there was a lot of splashing a long way ahead in the increasingly calm water. When I looked through my binoculars I was electrified to see a paddle-shaped pectoral fin, rather than the expected long thin pectoral fin of a Humpback. Northern Righties! Yes! and Wow! were the only printable comments that followed!

The splashing subsided as we got closer but a few "blows" could still be seen, indicating that they were still there. After what seemed an age we arrived in the area and soon afterwards were entertained by two Northern Right Whales surfacing near the boat, allowing prolonged, detailed observation. The callosities were clearly visible as well as the jaw-line. After a few short surfacings the animals dived, both showing fantastic tail flukes as they went under. I checked my GPS – they were in exactly the same position as the day before. The two animals, together with a third, then gave more great views over the next half hour or so, surfacing every 4-8 minutes, sitting at the surface for a half-minute or so, before diving again. Being under sail too gave us the advantage of being able to very clearly hear the animals' blows without any engine-noise. It would be difficult to imagine a better encounter than this. That was until I discussed the species enthusiastically with the skipper and a researcher who was studying Northern Right Whales for her PhD. Both told stories of encounters with 60-80 animals around the boat in previous years, with lots of courting activity to boot!

Although this sounded utterly amazing, I wasn't too worried, having thoroughly enjoyed our own great encounter. Chatting to the researcher I also learned of the very interesting work they are doing, including DNA studies of old whale specimens, as well as tales of whale feces, mitochondrial DNA and dogs with life-jackets, but that's another story to be published in academic circles once the work is complete. What was also interesting was that there doesn't seem to have been a recent crash in the species' numbers, it just seems that fewer animals are feeding in the Bay of Fundy nowadays and more are elsewhere, perhaps a reflection of a change in ocean currents or temperatures?   *Mike Scott-Ham*

Dolphins at the End of the Road

Bottlenose Dolphins in the Scottish Highlands

For our family, going on holiday involves setting out to experience something extraordinary without having any particular "something" in mind. And that's how we got involved in whale watching – by accident.

We, like many other families, view the car as our magic carpet to adventure. The ride begins with nothing more than extricating ourselves from the hotel or campsite and into the family chariot. We then consult the road map in a random kind of way and set off. If there's an interesting-looking road or a place with

A Scottish Bottlenose Dolphin and her calf.

an exotic name then that's our destination. This particular morning we chose Rosemarkie and a route that would link up Claggan, Loch Knockie, and Culbokie. Could there be a better way to explore the Scottish Highlands? As a bonus we'd also get a chance to scrutinize the waters of the infamous Loch Ness for the monster. Having arrived at Rosemarkie, we kept

on driving. The road took us down past a golf course out to a lonely little lighthouse. Then having reached the end of the road, we parked. Sitting at the very end of the peninsula with water on three sides we broke out the coffee and sandwiches. Of course, the windows immediately steamed up and as I leant forward to wipe away the condensation something extraordinary happened.

As my hand brushed aside the steam, a black blob appeared in the clear bit of window. I was dumbstruck. My mind was still full of thoughts of our Loch Ness search a couple of hours before. I couldn't work out what I'd just seen and began crazily wiping the rest of the window and shouting "look, look" at a volume totally out of proportion to the size of the car. Everybody looked, but the glass was already steaming up again. I began re-wiping but the kids were already bailing out of the car. By the time I had managed to extricate myself too they were whooping and yelping with excitement and pointing like they were possessed. I couldn't see anything, just the gray water as it swirled around the headland and the occasional breaking wave. Then I saw them. Two puffs of mist followed by gray sickle-shaped fins and then tails lifted high into the air. We were watching dolphins! Three more surfaced and then one leapt clear out of the water; its creamy gray sides glistening in the afternoon light and then "whoompff", it hit the water.

As we stood at the water's edge the dolphins were barely 10 yards from us.

Urban aquanauts, Bottlenose Dolphins at home off eastern Scotland.

The tide was tearing round the spit of land now and the dolphins battling to hold position in the current. We could hear their snorts and see every detail as they broke the surface. It was pure magic.

It was at that moment that we swapped our nomadic holiday for a resident one. That night we pitched our tent in the local campsite and there it stayed for the rest of our holiday. On each incoming tide we'd make our way down to the point. We'd simply stand awestruck and watch what we discovered were the Bottlenose Dolphins that live off the coast of north-eastern Scotland. *Ade Helipson*

Preparing to Watch Whales

As hobbies go, whale-watching is one of the more straightforward and relatively little is required in terms of equipment and preparation. Put simply, the key is getting yourself into suitable habitat, usually the open ocean or an appropriate coastal vantage point, where you can look for whales and dolphins. Of course, there are a number of things you can do to ensure the experience is pleasurable and maximize your chances of seeing the animals well. The following two chapters provide practical advice about the basic equipment you should bring with you, getting to whale or dolphin habitat whether on a boat or from land, and finally some tips on locating and viewing animals to the best advantage.

BASIC PREPARATIONS

Dressing Appropriately

On the water it is often windier than on land and consequently it can be much colder. Even on a hot summer's day, it can turn unpleasantly chilly as soon as the boat rounds the breakwater and catches the full force of the breeze. The T-shirt you were wearing comfortably on the harbor wharf suddenly won't seem such a good idea! The best advice is to always bring plenty of warm clothing regardless of the time of year, preferably in the form of multiple layers that you can add or remove as needed. It's true that larger boats often have a cabin that offers shelter from the wind, but it is difficult to spot whales through glass or plastic windows and the stagnant air increases the risks of seasickness (see below). In addition to an adequate supply of clothing, it is sensible to bring sunscreen (or sunblock) because the strong reflection of the sun off the water (or ice) can give you a nasty sunburn and ruin the experience. Even if you are only going out for a few hours, take the time to apply sunscreen to all areas of exposed skin. Sunglasses with polarized lenses can be helpful to shield your eyes from bright light and from the wind. Many outdoor activity stores offer brands that have been designed for sport fishermen or sailors but work just as well for whale watchers.

The decks of ocean-going vessels often get wet and slippery from salt spray or rain. Rubber-soled shoes or sneakers offer the best traction and should be comfortable because you are likely to spend hours on your feet. Don't wear your finest dress shoes as your feet are almost guaranteed to get wet. In wet weather or if you are in a small boat where spray is a problem, waterproof over-trousers are great for keeping your legs dry and warm. Commercial fishermen often wear thick polyester bib-style over-trousers but "stormpants" made for sailing and hiking do

Photographing whales at sea is challenging, and requires good preparation.

just as well. Don't forget a rain jacket to keep the top half of your body dry, preferably something that won't flap around in the wind, with a hood to keep your head dry if it rains heavily. Gloves can be a blessing, even in the warmer months. Many commercial whale-watching vessels advertise heated handrails but these really don't make much of a difference in cold weather.

If temperatures are likely to be near freezing or lower, such as in the polar regions, additional clothing is required. Multiple layers of thermal underwear trap warm air close to the body without being too bulky. Silk is particularly effective at trapping heat without accumulating sweat. These layers should be worn below a water- and wind-resistant shell. Though expensive, navy or coast-guard survival suits or good winter outdoorsman's suits, which envelop the whole body, are also a good choice for keeping your core warm and dry. In fact, operators in particularly cold or wet climates often provide these to their passengers. Down-filled jackets are warm but are much less effective if they get wet. Bring multiple pairs of thick gloves or mittens, something to wrap around your neck and a warm hat. Well-designed Gore-Tex jackets have a tall neck collar that can be fastened comfortably to protect this vulnerable area. A balaclava helmet or combination of scarf and woolly hat can achieve the same effect. If you're wearing a hat with a brim or peak, it's a good idea to tie it onto your coat somehow. Good sailing jackets often come with a strap specifically for this purpose but a piece of cord will do the job. After all it's unlikely that a whale-watch boat of any size will divert its course to retrieve your much-loved hat from the waves.

Optics

Besides a camera, one of the most useful items to bring along is a good pair of binoculars. These are essential if watching from land but can also work well from boats. Unless the seas are rough, using binoculars will enable you to scan the mid- to-far-distance, watching for spouts or glimpses of surfacing animals. Binoculars will also allow you to get better views of any whales or dolphins that choose not to approach the boat, which is often the case with exotic beaked whales, porpoises and some of the more shy species of dolphin. All binoculars are given two sets of numbers (e.g. 7x42) which describe their optical properties. The first figure indicates the magnification or number of times the image is enlarged. This is usually 7x, 8x, 9x or 10x, but there are binoculars of 12x and 16x as well; traditionally the latter are carried by retired ships' captains and racehorse enthusiasts and are not useful for whale watching. The second figure indicates the diameter in millimeters of the "objective lens" – the lens furthest from your eye. The larger this lens, the more light reaches your eye and the brighter the image. In terms of magnification, seven or eight power (7-8x) is ideal for scanning the water from a boat or a headland. This will give you a sufficiently large image and a relatively broad field of view. With this magnification you also get a good depth of field, meaning that you can see clearly at a range of distances without having to refocus. This helps in scanning the large swaths of ocean in which a cetacean could pop up almost anywhere. Avoid using those tiny "pocket" binoculars with a very narrow field of view. These are almost useless at sea, having much the same effect as looking through a keyhole.

While larger boats are usually more stable than small boats, they are also more prone to engine vibration. What may feel like a gentle motion when you're sitting gazing at the horizon can become an earthquake when you're looking through binoculars. One way to deaden these jitters is to hold your binoculars loosely. Squeezing them lightly at each side between your palms, rather than gripping them with the whole hands, may do the trick.

With all optics it's important to keep saltwater spray off them both to maintain the clarity of the lenses and prevent corrosion. Gently wiping them with a soft cloth, if possible dampened with fresh water, will clear the view once again. The same applies to glasses, sunglasses and camera lenses.

Photography

The best type of camera to use for whale and dolphin photography is an SLR (single lens reflex) camera, one that allows you to look directly at the subject through the lens. This should to be paired with a telephoto or zoom lens because the animals will usually be some distance away. An 80-300 mm zoom lens is probably the best compromise. Longer lenses (400 mm and upwards), like those used by bird or land-based wildlife photographers, have a relatively small field of view and it can become prohibitively difficult to find a surfacing animal in that split second required. If animals approach the boat it may be a good idea to switch to a standard 50 mm lens or even a wide-angle lens. A polarizing filter attached to the end of the lens cuts down the glare off the water and in doing so will help capture more of the animal below the surface. But beware, this comes at the cost of reduced shutter speed or depth of field.

The advent of digital SLRs is set to revolutionize wildlife photography, especially for the non-professionals with limited budgets. With digital media, image quality has improved markedly in recent years and is approaching the quality obtained with slide film. A huge benefit is that you can get instant feedback on your photos by viewing the images on a small color screen on the back of the camera and, more importantly perhaps, it allows you to evaluate the exposure using the camera's histogram function. Better still, if you have time between sightings, you can review the photos on a laptop computer to better evaluate exposure, sharpness and composition. Once you have paid for the memory cards, digital images are essentially free and so you can fire off as many shots as you wish during a wildlife encounter, then simply discard the unwanted images during a lull period or some later time.

A variety of memory cards are available and the choice depends on the brand of camera you buy. Compact flash cards are extremely reliable and tolerant of moisture or even of being dropped. In most cases, the card supplied with the camera has a laughably small capacity (8 Mb) and you are well advised to buy several cards of 256 Mb or greater. Once you fill a card, it only takes a couple of seconds to swap it for a fresh one, far less time than changing a roll of film. Many photographers store their memory cards in convenient "wallets", habitually placing used cards in one orientation and unused ones in the other to avoid confusion.

It's usually good practice to use as fast a shutter speed as you can. For whales aim for a 250th of a second or faster and for rapidly moving dolphins or porpoises, shoot at a 500th of a second or faster. This helps to freeze the motion of the animal

Photographing leaping whales requires quick reactions and fast shutter speeds.

and compensate for the movement of the boat. At these speeds, the water looks as if it has a wonderful smooth texture and drops of spray become frozen beads, adding to the appeal of the photograph. Fast shutter speeds mean that you need plenty of light and this can be difficult on overcast days or at dawn or dusk. Digital cameras are now as sensitive as conventional film and offer a variety of "film speeds" (ISOs). Under sunny conditions set the camera to an ISO equivalent of 100 or 200. In poorer light you can switch to higher ISO values (400 or 800) but be aware that the images will become progressively grainy, so don't forget to switch back to 200 when the light improves.

Once you get ashore, your images can be downloaded, processed or printed. Don't underestimate the value of careful image processing. With thought, some manipulation of the image, especially a digital image, can help transform an everyday shot into something wonderful. For example, images can be sharpened, straightened and cropped in imaginative ways to complement the shape or movement of the animals. For distant animals you can "throw away" much of the image by cropping it so that the eye zooms in on the action. Remember to leave a little more space in front of the animal than behind.

Video cameras offer a great alternative to still photography. It is much easier to capture good views of the animals by training the camera on the area you expect them to surface. With still photography you must release the shutter at exactly the right moment, but with video you can simply begin recording and wait for the animals to pop into view. Often the excited shouts and squeals of your companions will add an amusing and memorable soundtrack, bringing back the thrill of the encounter. Nowadays most video cameras have very good optical zoom lenses and are remarkably effective in low light conditions. Despite manufacturers' claims, the extra "digital zoom" power that comes with many video cameras is of little use. Images can become horribly pixilated and we recommend setting your camera to use the optical zoom only. Even then, be careful with the zoom. At high magnifications, movies that seemed fine at the time can lurch dreadfully back home in the living room. If you're in doubt, pan back a little. Your whale might look a bit smaller but at least you won't feel seasick on the living room couch! Again, excellent software is available for home editing movies, allowing you to splice together the best shots into an interesting but not overly long sequence.

Do not forget to protect your expensive camera gear from getting wet. Some experienced wildlife photographers like to wrap their camera body in plastic kitchen wrap. It won't look pretty but kitchen wrap keeps salt and moisture away from the delicate electronics. Splash-proof bags, which attach to the lens hood and the camera base, are also available and are easily opened or closed with Velcro or a zipper. Even simpler, unzip your coat to about breast height and tuck your camera in there till the moment it is required. The key is being able to get to your camera quickly should a whale or dolphin suddenly surface near the boat. If you are carrying long lenses or multiple cameras, consider buying a water- and shock-proof case that you can keep on deck beside you. Add a piece of cord to the handle so that you can tie it to something solid. That way, if the boat lurches, your camera case won't go skidding away across the deck. Also put a small square of towel into your case and keep it near the top. This will shield the contents from spray while you're rummaging about in it and can be used to quickly wipe away any splashes before they soak into the electronics.

There can be no doubt, capturing impressive photographs of cetaceans is not particularly easy. Skill and practice are important but so is luck. That said, there are many ways to increase your chances of getting satisfying pictures. Having the reflexes and aim of Clint Eastwood helps but more important is being prepared. Encounters with whales, dolphins and porpoises at sea usually follow one of two patterns. Most often somebody sees something in the distance – a blow, a leap or splashing. This information trickles down the chain of command and the skipper adjusts the heading to close the distance. There's usually a period of confusion at this point because distances are hard to judge on the water and the initial sighting may have been too brief to establish the number of animals, exactly what they were and their heading. In terms of photography, this is the time to get yourself sorted out. Many of the other passengers may still be oblivious to the sighting and will be munching sandwiches or applying sunscreen, so this is a good time to stake your claim to a good vantage point. Be ready for the animals to pop up unexpectedly close to the boat but if they surface in the medium to long distance, hold your fire. Your opportunities are very likely to get better. Instead, use this time to simply

A Humpback Whale checks out the boat.

watch the animals and observe how they behave, while keeping your camera primed in case one should choose to leap.

As the boat gets closer, or better still the animals approach, your photographic chances will increase. Cetaceans spend the majority of their time underwater. In most situations when they descend below the surface, they are invisible, but if you watch them closely when they are at the surface you can glean clues as to when and where they are likely to return from their dives. Most cetaceans dive with a rhythm – several short dives in succession then a long one. Or to look at it from the photographer's point of view – a run of surfacings before they vanish for a while. This diving pattern is usually repeated over and over so that during any one encounter there will be about the same number of surfacings in each bout, the display of surface behaviors are likely to be similar and the long dive will be about the same length. Whales, especially Humpback and Sperm Whales, frequently end their last surfacing before a long dive by lifting their flukes high into the air. The maneuver helps them head vertically downwards, and means almost invariably that they'll be out of sight for a while, but also offers an excellent photographic opportunity as the huge tail is majestically lifted skywards.

If the animals have disappeared below the surface on a longer dive, you'll have a chance to organize yourself again. For dolphins, you might have a couple of minutes while for Sperm Whales you may have 40 minutes or more! This is a good time to wipe spray from lenses and review the status of your batteries, film or memory card. If you've a few pictures left in your camera, this is also the time to fire them off with pictures of your companions, the boat or scenery, and reload. Forgetting to do this guarantees that the moment you get yourself into the perfect position, with excellent lighting and animals finally behaving in a spectacular manner, your camera will decide to rewind the film or give you the "memory full" symbol.

Photographs of cetaceans leaping are particularly spectacular. There are some people who always seem to get these shots and there are those that greet them with surprise, curses and fumbling. Having your camera pointed in the right direction seems like an obvious thing to do, but when there may be animals all around or if the boat keeps repositioning, it can be less than simple. Having the camera ready is important but being aware of the bigger picture is even more so. It's easy to focus your attention on the shiny backs right in front of you and most whale watchers do exactly that. But having an inkling about whom you are looking at and what is actually going on, gives you an important edge. How many groupings are there? Are more animals coming to join? Is there a fight breaking out between any of them? And so on. One way to help with this is to take a look around,

Pre-focussing your lens can make a difference.

every now and again. There may be other animals behind you or coming in quickly from elsewhere. When they join the group that everybody else is watching you won't be surprised. Recognizing individuals also helps and comes from registering the little details – the mother and calf you want to photograph always surface just after the animal with the white blotch on its fin, and so on. Another aid is to give the camera some warning about what you are about to do. In other words, if you suspect that something spectacular is just about to happen, prefocus the camera on that spot and so if it does happen all that you will have to worry about is composition before squeezing the shutter release.

Experienced cetacean photographers vary in their attitudes to auto-focus or manual lenses. Good manual focusing takes practice and a sharp eye while auto-focusing can be quick and can produce pin-sharp results. That said, on calm days or in foggy conditions, auto-focus lenses can really struggle and end up hunting about for a focus point without letting you take a picture. Inevitably, this will be the moment when your quarry is gyrating in mid air. In these conditions, being comfortable switching between auto-focus and manual gives you the best of both worlds. Similarly, using zoom lenses allows flexibility in framing options and latitude if animals are popping up at unpredictable distances. It's worth practicing zooming in and out with your lens so that you know instinctively whether it's towards you or away for more or less magnification.

When looking through a camera lens, people usually close one eye and use the other to squint through the viewfinder. However, there's much to be gained if you learn to keep both eyes open so that you are aware of what's going on outside of the camera's limited view. After all, you may be looking down the camera at a breaking wave when there's a whale joyfully leaping just out of the frame.

It may not seem like it at the time but there's plenty of scope for creative composition out there on the waves. Be inventive! If the animals are close, you don't necessarily need to include the whole animal. Pictures of the eye or emerging snout can be particularly spectacular but of course this requires good timing on your part. Many digital cameras introduce an annoying delay between pressing the shutter release and actually taking the picture. For cetacean photography, particularly for dolphins or porpoises, this will be disastrous. Switching the camera into a mode where the digital viewing screen is off can help. If the animal appears too small in your frame, take a step back and include the animal along with the context: the bow of the boat, other watchers craning for a better look or the coastline behind. With much of the frame then filled, the black dot in the middle won't seem so minuscule. Viewers usually find pictures where the animals are entering the frame more visually pleasing than if they are exiting and if you have any choice in the matter try and get the point of best focus at the animal's eye. It's instinctive to take pictures in landscape format – that is, holding the camera the normal way up – but, if care is taken in focusing, portrait pictures at sea can introduce interesting perspectives of distance. When concentrating on your subject and bracing your stance, it's easy to forget to keep the camera held straight, but there's nothing more annoying than a wonky horizon in an otherwise perfect whale picture.

In all whale-watching locations (except the tropics at midday) you'll have the position of the sun to contend with when taking pictures. Essentially, it'll either be in the sky behind them or behind you. You are certainly not in charge of the animals, so unless you're in charge of the boat, you'll have to take whatever lighting conditions you can get. Both orientations end up providing good but very different photographic opportunities. Light coming from behind will tend to throw the cetaceans into silhouette. As a result, your photographs will lose all the detail of the animals' color and markings but gain the creative opportunities with pin-sharp outlines, the simplicity of their shapes and magnified effects if there are any splashes or blows in the air. Backlit scenes can play havoc with camera metering so it's worth paying particular attention to the exposure settings. Light coming from behind you will have the opposite effect, flattening the image but bringing out all the details of their skin, particularly the color. You're also much more likely to be able to see something of your target while it is underwater.

While encounters with cetaceans most frequently begin with sightings near the horizon, cetaceans, especially dolphins and some porpoises, can sneak up on boats totally undetected. The first anybody knows about it is when there's a puff of spray straight in front of the bow. While even large whales sometimes ride the bow-waves

Common Dolphins often approach boats to bow-ride.

of ships, the animals that do it the most are the dolphins. Getting to stand just feet away from these bow-riding torpedoes is a special sight and an excellent opportunity to photograph them. For most cetacean photographers it's the one and only time that they can usefully employ a wide-angle lens. And even if your vantage point doesn't allow you to look straight down on their twisting, turning antics, their surfacings will be sufficiently predictable to get close-up pictures of them grabbing breaths of air.

While taking cetacean pictures above the surface may be a test of your reaction speeds, capturing them underwater requires both snorkeling competence and the appropriate equipment. There are a range of cameras specifically for underwater photography but there are also many waterproof housings made to fit land cameras (digital or film). Housings vary hugely in price and generally scale in proportion to the cost of the camera with the most inexpensive being acrylic housings for digital compacts. Throw-away underwater cameras may be appropriate if an unexpected opportunity comes up but generally give disappointing results. Low light conditions underwater mean that any wobbles on your part or movements of your quarry run the risk of blurry shots so consider using faster ISO settings than above water. It's also wise to meticulously follow the manufacturers advice on maintenance and cleaning of your housing as salt water and electronics have a love-hate relationship.

Though you may be a skilled photographer, don't be put off if your pictures at the end of your first or your tenth trip disappoint you. Books such as this may be crammed with excellent pictures but they never show the many thousands that were out of focus, poorly composed or simply of blank water. The chances are that you will come home with many more bad pictures than good ones. So when you're out there, striving for the best picture ever taken, don't forget to put the camera down every now and again and simply enjoy the animals through your own eyes.

Seasickness

It is impossible to talk about going on the water without saying a few words about seasickness. This is caused when the conflicting senses produced by the movement of the boat confuse the brain, resulting in very unpleasant and often debilitating nausea. Almost everyone succumbs to seasickness at one time or another and this should not deter you from going to sea and enjoying the spectacular wildlife. There are a number of simple steps you can take that will minimize problems and ensure that you have a great time. First, take a motion sickness tablet before you get on the boat. There are many brands available. Second, make sure you get a good night's sleep before your trip. Tiredness is a strong catalyst for seasickness. If you begin to feel a little queasy, it really helps to get out into the fresh air, especially if there is a nice breeze. Looking at the horizon helps your inner ear to regain its balance and, combined with the breeze, this simple remedy often works wonders.

The condition itself is caused by an excessive mismatch between what the eyes are seeing and what the balance organs (the semicircular canals in the inner ears) are detecting. The results confuse the brain and lead to what is probably an attempt by the brain to shut you down. Early symptoms range through cold sweats, headaches, a feeling of drowsiness, lethargy, and frequent yawning. People in this state become withdrawn as they concentrate intensely on the motion or the developing nausea. Their skin becomes pallid and the fairer skinned become the proverbial "green about the gills". As the condition worsens people begin to feel nauseous and eventually vomit. This may dampen down the nausea for a few minutes or, if you are lucky, entirely. People vary greatly in how badly they respond to a boat's motion; some are incapacitated the moment the boat leaves the harbor while others appear to be immune in the roughest conditions. If you are fortunate to have good "sea legs", quietly thank your lucky stars and help those that are feeling at their worst.

Though it might come as a surprise to the afflicted, motion sickness is not life threatening. Sufferers may wish that they were dead, but so long as they don't fall overboard this will not happen, nor will they suffer any lasting consequences. Most people adjust to the motion after a few hours or, at worst, days and can laugh about it later. There are, however, a very small number of hugely unlucky people who cannot shake off the symptoms and will continue to feel ill until returning to dry land. For them, dehydration and exhaustion are likely to be significant and those around them should pay special attention to these needs.

What can be done to lessen the chances of seasickness? If you know that you or members of your group are prone, try to pick a trip that is less likely to encounter rough seas or deep swells. Similarly, try a shorter trip or one that promises lots of things to look at rather than a long slog out to deep water with an uncertain chance of some rarely encountered species. Thankfully most commercial whale-watch operations rely on their passengers having a good time and so use boats that handle the swells well. Increasingly, multi-hulled boats, such as catamarans, are used with this in mind. Skilled captains design the route to minimize the time spent in rough water or working against the swell. That said, it is often necessary to travel through some lumpy seas and it is always best to be prepared. For trips lasting several days or more, there is simply no guarantee of good weather and you must be prepared for the unexpected. Most operators are happy to give you advice ahead of time and can often put your mind at rest right away. Their advice will likely be good because, after all, they're the ones that have to clean up after the passengers have disembarked. If you have a choice of boats, pick the larger or more modern-looking vessel, as it is likely to be the most stable. If seasickness is a significant concern, opt for a short trip or shore watching. You may not see everything that is out there but you will have a much more enjoyable time of it. If you don't have to book well in advance, make your decision on the day, based on the current and forecasted weather and advice from the operator.

Prepare ahead of time. Being well rested makes a huge difference so avoid a heavy night out on the town the night before. Prior to leaving the dock, visit the washroom and also sort out your things. Make sure the fresh batteries, blank memory card or new film are already in your camera, and organize your bag so that you can get at sun glasses, lotion, bottled water and so on without having to rummage around once the boat is in three-dimensional motion. When you board, pick a spot that's not going to make you ill. Sitting within sniffing distance of engine exhausts or cafeteria fans is a bad idea. Staying on deck in a position with a clear view of the sea is a great way to see whales and also one that will give you a chance to see the horizon, which often helps reduce symptoms. When the boat is underway, avoid reading, writing or involving yourself in fiddly things that take your attention away from the outside world. Likewise, going inside to use washrooms or using internal staircases can also accelerate the onset of seasickness. For larger boats the pitching motion (end to end) is usually least about half way down the vessel so if you have a choice this is a good position to base yourself. For a boat that rolls from side to side, the motion will be greater the higher you are from the water, so locating yourself near the waterline may be a good idea. For smaller, fast-moving boats the motion is often more comfortable towards the rear. If you're in doubt, ask the crew.

It's well known that a fried breakfast and choppy seas do not add up to poetry in motion but it's good to have something in your stomach, a light meal or sandwich for example. Hot drinks also help but avoid caffeine, alcohol or dairy products. Instead, herbal teas and especially drinks that contain ginger are worth targeting. In fact ginger of all kinds, crystallized, raw or cooked into things like gingersnaps appear to sooth queasy stomachs. Many people find that eating citrus fruits, sucking candies or chomping on saltines are good to do. One thing is for sure, worrying obsessively about getting sick or watching other people being ill is a surefire way to bring on the same feelings in you. It's best to simply relax, and occupy your mind with what you originally came along to experience. Actually seeing cetaceans cures many people instantly and probably results from the combination of having something other than your stomach to think about and the kick of adrenaline that comes with the sighting.

While there is no cure for motion sickness, there are a plethora of medications on the market to alleviate the symptoms. Both the British and US Navies tested several of these drugs and the researchers discovered which were most successful by filling ships with soldiers and taking them out to sea in bad weather. Before leaving port, some troops got real drugs while others got dummies (placebos). Bizarrely, some troops felt that the placebo was best while others believed that it was actually the tablets that made them ill. Today, most over-the-counter medications are antihistamines and include products such as Benadryl (diphenhydramine), Bonine (meclizine), Dramamine (dimenhydrinate), Marezine (cyclizine), and Stugeron (cinnarizine). These work by interrupting the nervous pathways between the balance organs and the appropriate brain control centers. The effects are associated with relief from both nausea and vomiting but may cause drowsiness as a side effect. It is not uncommon for whale-watching boats to be awash with snoozing clients on the ride back to port. There are also several prescription medications available. One of the most popular is the Transderm Scop® patch, an adhesive patch placed on the skin behind one of the ears allowing a slow release of the drug scopolamine (also known as hyoscine) through the skin. These drugs can be very effective but do have side effects, including dry mouth, drowsiness and blurred vision. It is worth talking to a physician or pharmacist before purchasing and using any of these motion-sickness medications, as some may have complications with certain medical conditions. While there are a variety of drugs, not all people benefit from the same ones, so if you discover one that works, stick with it. Most also require that you take them some hours before you are likely to be exposed to the motion. Having to take the pills in advance of discovering that your whale-watching trip has turned into a day on a bucking bronco is another good reason to talk to the trip organizers about sea conditions before you set out.

As with everything else in medicine, there are alternatives and one of the most common are wristbands that stimulate the P6 acupuncture point. The point lies on the underside of the forearm, about an inch towards the heart from the wrist. The wristbands have a button that presses against the skin, producing a steady pressure. More elaborate versions are battery powered and produce tingling sensations. Although anecdotal, people often report receiving relief from the devices even after they are already feeling unwell. They also don't yet have any reported side effects. As with conventional medications, believing in what you are using may be a large component of ensuring that they work. Some trial and error is needed to find the option that works best for you.

As we've said earlier, being in the fresh air often helps dispel seasickness, as does active participation in finding animals. If the symptoms continue to gain ground, the best thing to do is to find a quiet spot and lie down and if possible, sleep. The nausea usually subsides remarkably quickly once you are horizontal. If you're going to vomit, most (but not all) boat owners prefer you to do so outside and over the rail. You provide a little food for the gulls and may recover quicker in the fresh air. Choose the leeward side (downwind) and brace yourself against something solid to stop yourself falling overboard. If you are helping a friend who is feeling ill, try not to crowd them. Most victims would rather be left alone in their misery than be fussed over. But helping them find a quiet part of the boat, holding onto them, handing them a tissue and some water to rinse their mouths if they've been sick or making sure their children or things are safe will all be welcome.

The good news about seasickness is that the symptoms quickly subside once the motion stops. It is often only a few moments after a homebound boat has rounded the harbor wall when the boat's galley or cafeteria will refill with all those who felt too ill to eat something earlier on. But beware. If you've been at sea for a long time (days or weeks) and got used to the motion you can, ironically, get ill all over again on returning to shore! So-called "land-sickness" usually makes itself known when you sit or lie down for the first time ashore. The walls and furniture take on the sensation of being oddly squishy and the room may feel like it's gently swaying. Time is the ultimate cure, but there is also an instant solution and it's simple – get back on a boat, any kind of boat, even if it's just rocking gently in the harbor.

Getting Out and Watching Whales

HOW TO CHOOSE A TRIP

Selecting the Right Vessel for Whale Watching

Areas that are known for whale watching may offer a variety of organized trips. Which one to choose? Key considerations are the combination of people wishing to travel with you, the current and forecasted weather conditions, what types of whales or dolphins you hope to see and lastly whether you feel comfortable with the attitude of the operator towards the animals and their environment.

Before you book your trip or buy tickets for a certain boat, ask for an information leaflet, read display boards or ask questions at the booking office. Make sure that you are happy with what is on offer. Do they include a naturalist as part of the crew? Do they emphasize the fact that they adhere to official or voluntary guidelines for encounters? Is the boat well maintained and licensed to carry passengers? What is their refund policy if the trip is weathered out?

If you have young children or older folk in your party then you should ensure that you are on a vessel that offers shelter – trips out at sea can be chilly; or shelter from the sun may be important on a hot day. Larger vessels tend to offer the most shelter and comfort, with seating indoors as well as outside, toilet facilities and often will have hot drinks available. After three hours or more at sea every one of these things will be appreciated. Larger vessels generally offer more stability and will be more resistant to bobbing and rolling around than smaller ones, key issues if seasickness is a concern. Vessels with only limited outdoor access are never good – neither for viewing nor for escaping into the fresh air. As a general rule, whale-watching trips will not run when the sea conditions are forecast to be rough as the chance of finding whales and having an opportunity to observe them is significantly reduced.

There are two factors associated with getting a good view of whales, which you might consider when faced with a choice of whale-watch boats to go out on: height above the water and angle of view. Whales are generally at a distance when first spotted and most whale-watching regulations forbid boats approaching to within a certain distance. Therefore, unless the whale chooses to approach the stationary vessel (which many do), you may be looking at an animal that is a few hundred yards away. The higher up you are, the further you can see out across the water and the more you are likely to see if looking down at an angle towards the whale. However, if the whale does choose to approach the boat, you are going to see far more detail of its skin, its color, even the smell of its blow, if you are closer to the water.

Húsavík Harbor in Iceland: some whale-watching venues are hard to miss.

An all-round view is a valuable asset on a whale-watch trip. On large vessels, the ideal top deck has 360° vision so that your view is never obscured by a large chimney or cabin. Again, these vessels are likely to maneuver to ensure each area of deck faces the whales at some point; however, vessels that only have companionways that you have to walk around to see the far side of the boat, can be annoying. Small boats sometimes have a console or a small cabin for the skipper at the front of the vessel, which can be frustrating for the passengers on seats behind, especially when the whale is straight ahead and the vessel still moving in that direction. That said, the boat driver would be aware of this and usually position the craft appropriately. Once a boat has neared its intended distance to the whale it will stop and use its engine to turn the vessel so that everyone has a view of the whales. Your view will invariably be affected by the number of people on board, almost irrespective of the size of the vessel. Large vessels with high running costs may be more likely to wait until they have a full complement of passengers than smaller vessels, but with most whale-watch tours running to a published schedule this is unlikely to be the general situation.

Good elevation helps to reveal this Minke Whale.

If a whale does approach a boat, then a smaller vessel, or one where you can get down close to the water level on a lower deck, will give you the most intimate experience and a feeling of closeness to the animal. It may make it more difficult to take good photographs, as the boat will be less stable and the whale may actually be too close or at too acute an angle to the horizon (squashing the view of the sea into a small strip). A small boat will also, however, give you an intimate closeness to the sea itself, particularly as you will most likely be covered in spray on a breezy day! If you enjoy that wet and wild aspect of the experience, arriving back on shore encrusted in briny salt, then a small boat can offer a fun-filled trip in itself, and an absence of whales will not mean that the trip is a total loss.

Small Hard Boats: 15 to 30 ft (5 to 10 m) in Length

In many parts of the world, small fishing boats are used for whale and dolphin watching. On the smallest ones, the wheelhouse will tend to obscure the view forward and there is likely to be little protection from the elements for most of the passengers. Likewise there will be few or no facilities and these vessels are also likely to bob around in the swell. However, the experience with the whales can be wonderfully intimate, both in terms of having a small number of fellow passengers to deal with and being in close contact with the captain and crew. In eastern North America, so called "head-boats" are often used for whale watching. These are designed for "pay as you go" fishing trips, with access to the rail all the way round the vessel. Although they may carry a large number of passengers, there is usually enough space for everyone to get a good view and most captains are skilled at turning the vessel side-on to the animals. These boats are relatively fast and can get out to productive areas several to many miles off shore in a fairly short time. Indeed they may be fast enough to attract dolphins to the bow wave.

There is usually seating inside, possibly a snack bar, rest rooms and a second raised deck that can be used to look for animals. Dedicated whale-watching boats may employ a trained naturalist. A knowledgeable guide can add tremendously to the experience. Many will use a PA system that can be heard around the boat to alert you to any animals and provide information about the

One Humpback Whale, many eyes.

ecology of the cetaceans you are seeing as well as the habitat. On smaller boats, the skipper may act as a guide, often relying on his or her experience in local waters.

Large Vessels and Cruise Ships: 65 ft (20 m) or Over

Definitely the most comfortable option. They will have warm, dry seating indoors, toilet facilities and food and drink on offer. They generally offer good viewing opportunities, but make sure there is plenty of outdoor deck space: these boats can be crowded if they pile on the people to cover their costs, and may not have proportionally as much outdoor seating as smaller boats. They are generally faster than smaller boats so may offer more time in the best areas for whales but usually a less intimate view. Cruise ships are sometimes used for whale-watching excursions, or encounter whales in the course of a cruise. Certainly if you plan to visit Antarctic waters, choose a cruise ship!

Commercial Ferries

Cetaceans are often seen from ferries, especially if they cross productive feeding areas. One of the finest examples is the ferry that runs between Portsmouth, England and Bilbao in Spain. As the ferry crosses the Bay of Biscay, it skirts along the edge of the continental shelf and regularly encounters an impressive variety of whales and dolphins. There are many examples of ferries that provide excellent viewing platforms, in fact, it is surprising how often just keeping your eyes peeled while riding a ferry will result in a worthwhile sighting. Occasionally, the crew of the boat will let the passengers know if they've seen something of interest. However, one ferry is reported to have capsized when the crew called out a whale sighting on the Tannoy and the resulting rush of passengers to one side caused the illegally overloaded boat to flip over! Undoubtedly, the biggest drawback to whale-watching from ferries is that the boat will not stop or deviate from its course unless there is a risk of collision. A benefit is that large ferries are sufficiently stable that you can often use a telescope on a tripod to view distant animals.

Rigid Inflatables

Often referred to as RIBs, Zodiacs, pangas or NIADS, these flexible rubber craft can be good fun but can also be quite uncomfortable, offering little protection from rain or sea spray. They are capable of high speeds, offering a fast and furious ride even in moderately rough water. Bouncing up over the waves and slamming down

Small boats offer high exposure to both weather and whales.

into the troughs can be a lot of fun particularly at the front, but the jarring can become tiresome and is not recommended for people with back problems! The benefit is that these boats keep you very close to the water and, if you are lucky, close to the animals as well. Their speed allows the boats to cover a lot of water in a relatively short time, useful in locating mobile animals. When inflatables routinely cover a long distance to reach the whales, a transparent shell may be added, protecting passengers from the spray but limiting the view and flow of fresh air. Needless to say, inflatables lack bathroom facilities of any kind, so make sure you take care of things before you set foot aboard!

Vessels with Underwater Viewing Windows

These can offer a wonderful opportunity to see the whale or dolphin in its own world. However there are a number of issues associated with this type of viewing. Water clarity is a major factor affecting what can be seen – in murky water the visibility can be only a few yards. This means that, unless the dolphin or whale chooses to come up to the window (which is not common, unlike in captivity, when dolphins regularly approach viewing ports) you may not see a thing. Additionally, unscrupulous tour operators will tend to ride their vessels right up behind the animals to ensure the paying customer sees something. This can easily lead to a situation where the dolphins or whales are being pursued and is clearly a bad thing. Never choose a boat just for its underwater viewing potential – that potential is often not realized, and even when it is, it may come at a cost of disturbing the animals you are trying to enjoy. An underwater viewing window is more appropriate for observing fishes and other marine life in shallow water where the sea floor can be appreciated, perhaps as part of a more general marine wildlife trip.

Sea Kayaks

Bobbing around on the ocean with only a paddle and your arms for propulsion may not be everybody's cup of tea, but for the adventurous, sea kayaking can be one of the most rewarding and intimate ways to view whales. With care, you are able to move about so quietly and steadily that the whales or dolphins may be unaware of you altogether or may approach to take a look. Important limitations are that the whales or dolphins must be within easy reach of shore; you must have calm sea conditions and stable weather; and you must have people confident and fit enough to make the journey. With a favorable combination of all of these factors, whale watching "up close and personal" from a kayak can be one of the most memorable experiences of your life. Organized sea-kayak tours often use double kayaks, offering more stability and less of a requirement for exertion than single kayaks. Importantly, the kayak guides will understand local conditions – currents, tides and winds – all of which have significant effects on progress out or, more importantly, ease of return to shore, on a particular day. Being self-propelled and quiet, kayaks are also great platforms from which to use hydrophones to listen to the underwater sounds of the animals around you. Several hydrophones have been specifically manufactured for kayakers.

In summary, if it is your first trip to see whales, you may want to ensure that the day is a great experience, rather than a feat of survival. Choosing a boat that offers a degree of comfort and a generally good view of the whales is probably the best way to go. Always consider the most vulnerable member of your party and what they are going to have to withstand, particularly if it is a cold or very hot day or a particularly long trip.

The whale-watch experience can also include splendid scenery.

Swimming with Whales and Dolphins

In many parts of the world it is possible to get in the water with wild cetaceans. Because of the very real concerns about animal welfare, this remains a controversial practice and for many experts, the jury is still out on whether commercial "swim-with-dolphin" ventures should be permitted. On the positive side, the experience can be a remarkable and often life-changing event for the viewer. Few people can come away unmoved from a one-on-one encounter with a wild cetacean in its natural element – for once, you are a guest in the alien world of another intelligent species. On the negative side, these activities require boats and swimmers to get very close to the animals, literally dropping in uninvited.

Opportunities to swim with cetaceans are becoming increasingly common, most often with wild dolphins. For example, in New Zealand more than 30 coastal sites offer commercial "swim-with-dolphin" trips. Most often, these trips will involve the more social species like Bottlenose, Spinner or Dusky Dolphins. There are also rare opportunities to swim with more exotic species like the Boto. Many cetaceans have schedules that allow them time to indulge in activities that are not directly necessary for day-to-day survival and it is at these times that swimmers have their best chances for mutually interactive encounters. In many parts of their ranges, Spinner, Spotted and Dusky Dolphins, for example, feed nocturnally and in several areas, the local animals wait out the daylight hours in sheltered, shallow waters. These spots have yielded some of the most famous sites for "swim-with" programs.

For reasons not yet understood, individual dolphins along coastlines all around the world sometimes seek out the company of people. These "friendly" animals, as they are known, are most often Bottlenose Dolphins, but Killer Whales, Risso's and Common Dolphins, among others, have been known to take up the habit. These animals may be male or female, young or old. Usually, the animal will take up residence in a bay or coastline and begin to approach local boats. From there the animal will become well known to the boating community, and eventually someone may successfully swim with it. It's not known why the dolphins take up this solitary life style, but the human company is likely to be a replacement for their former associates. The animals may show interest in anyone who gets in the water and end up swimming with hundreds of people in a single day, or may keep its interest to particular individuals.

It's not only humans that are curious.

Several friendly dolphins have established themselves off the coasts of Europe in recent decades and each time they do, they attract a fanatical following. People will travel hundreds of miles to see the animal and in the process transform the fortunes of the nearest town offering accommodation, boat rides and trinkets.

The reasons why people want to swim with these animals vary. Many simply want the experience of an eye-to-eye encounter with a large, wild and beautiful animal; others seek something much more spiritual. There have been many claims that dolphins have the power to cure people of both physical and mental ailments. Unsubstantiated declarations on the powers of echolocation and the dolphin mind abound. It would be unscientific to dismiss these viewpoints out of hand and it is more than likely that simply being the focus of a large, powerful and mysterious animal's interest can have uplifting influences on a person's self-confidence and state of mind. Disentangling these psychological benefits from any of the more fantastic claims will be quite a challenge for an interested, quantitative health scientist. As a result of the thinking that dolphins have these powers, there are several companies that hold dolphins captive, then encourage debilitated people to swim with or pet them as part of a healing process. Whether you think these initiatives are positive missions of alternative medicine or misguided initiatives to extract money from the most vulnerable is up to you. One thing is for sure; the dolphins that are held captive don't gain much from the association.

It is often the young that approach swimmers.

If swimming with wild dolphins, it is important that swimmers do not interfere with the dolphin's normal activities. Slipping quietly into the water in small groups near the animals reduces the chances of frightening them and then a good way to minimize your impact is to let the animals come to investigate if they choose to, rather than the other way around. Your arms should be held near your body and you should not attempt to touch them. Grabbing dorsal fins and getting a free ride may be something you might see at an aquarium, but in the wild this could result in a severe bite or cuff. The way the animals are approached by the support boat is very important and studies have shown that drawing up to one side of a group and then letting people carefully enter the water is less disturbing than dumping them into the animals' path. Adult dolphins may show little interest in swimmers, and more often than not it is the adolescents that show the most curiosity. Often the dolphins will simply move in to investigate and then continue off into the blue when they lose interest, but occasionally they may display more overt signs of interaction. This might include close approaches with eye-to-eye contact, games that involve mimicking the swimmer's posture or occasionally the presentation of gifts like seaweed or fish. One must not forget that these are wild animals and powerful predators at that. In many ways, leaving the safety of a boat is equivalent to stepping out of your vehicle on an African safari. The chances are that you won't be harmed, but you have to be prepared to accept that your presence might not be welcome. Thankfully, unprovoked attacks are very rare and if they occur at all, are usually preceded by overt signs such as jaw snaps, forceful head nodding or bubble blowing. Keep your wits about you and treat the animals with the respect they deserve.

There are a few "swim-with-whale" operations, most often with Humpback Whales. Dive companies offer trips in the warm waters surrounding the Kingdom of Tonga in the central Pacific or to the waters of the Silver Bank in the Caribbean. Another swim-with-whales industry has developed on the northern section of the Great Barrier Reef in Australia, and focuses on Dwarf Minke Whales. The area is a marine park and has strict guidelines for the swimming-with-whales activity.

Whether swimming with cetaceans is an acceptable practice remains a topic for discussion at many levels and quality research on the matter is still in its infancy. A wide variety of short-term impacts have been documented but in the vast majority of cases it's just too early to know whether these add up to long-term changes in the status of the animals involved. As with guidelines for boats, most areas have codes of behavior that they expect the operators and swimmers to adhere to. These are usually derived from a combination of gut feelings, common sense and the

Swimming with whales can be very humbling.

small but growing number of research studies. It is not much use having guidelines if they are not followed and often the only police are, ironically, the passengers themselves. So if you feel that the operator or other passengers are breaking the rules, pushing their luck or disturbing the animals, don't be afraid to say so. Obviously being so close to a large, wild animal in its own domain is a powerful experience and such encounters have great potential to promote further efforts to preserve them and their habitats. Balanced against that, we have to be aware that our presence is likely to have an impact and there will be a threshold upon which our curiosity will become overpowering to them.

Finding Whales and Dolphins

One of the many pleasures of whale watching is the challenge of finding the animals in the first place. Because of the remarkable mobility of marine mammals and the immense size of the oceans, this can seem like a daunting task at first.

Although luck is important, there are a number of strategies that can significantly improve your chances.

The first thing to do is to figure out what you want to see. Perhaps you are already committed to going to a particular place, want to see animals in your local area or simply want to see a whale. If so, then your choices are relatively simple. However, if you want to see a particular species or event, then you'll probably want to put in some homework. To do this, focus your search for a whale-watching trip,

Seeing a rare Blue Whale means being in the right place, such as the Sea of Cortez, Mexico.

boat platform or shore-watching site in areas that are most likely to contain the species you are interested in seeing. Deep divers such as Sperm Whales are rarely found inshore of the continental shelf rim. This is because they feed almost exclusively on deep-water squid, and to a lesser extent fish, that simply do not occur in shallower shelf waters. Harbor Porpoises live almost exclusively inshore of the continental shelf break and then only in the temperate northern hemisphere. They're particularly abundant in coastal areas with strong tidal flows. More often than not, the crew of tour boats or local fisherman will have a good idea of where animals can be encountered. Don't be afraid to talk to them about the possibilities and let them know what you are interested in seeing.

When at sea, be patient! Don't expect to find your quarry within a few minutes of leaving the dock. It may take an hour or two of careful searching before you are rewarded. First-time watchers often stare fixedly into the far distance without a clear mental picture of what they are actually looking for. If you are on a big ship, for example, it's pointless looking off into the far distance if what you are looking for is as small as a Harbor Porpoise – you will only see it within a few hundred yards of the boat, so concentrate your efforts appropriately. It's notoriously difficult to judge distance and size at sea so use the size of seabirds or floating objects to help tune your eye.

Searching blank water is far harder than it might seem at first. If the water is mirror calm then you might have to contend with the reflections of clouds or distant shorelines, while if there are waves they'll obscure your view of intermittently appearing objects. They'll also introduce an infinite variety of moving shapes and splashes for you to sort through. Seeing a dark fin or a blow becomes quite a challenge. When you don't know exactly what you are looking for, it is tempting to try and look hard at all the waves and ask yourself if each one of them might be a whale or dolphin. Very soon you'll lose concentration or get disillusioned. A better strategy is simply to relax your gaze onto the seascape and let your eyes wander around at will. What you want your mind to flag up is anything out of the ordinary – a glint of light in an area where there aren't any others or a wave going backwards or a smudge on the horizon. When you notice one of these signs you can become more alert and focus your eyes or binoculars on that spot. Seabirds often give a clue to the presence of cetaceans and can usually be seen from a much greater distance. Larger, plunge-diving species such as gannets or boobies are often attracted to feeding cetaceans, which push fish or squid up towards the surface where they can be preyed upon by the birds. Likewise, smaller seabirds such as terns, auks, gulls and storm-petrels regularly feed over whales pushing fish, krill and other small food items to the surface where they can be snatched.

If you are the first person on board to see a cetacean, the easiest way to get everyone's attention is to shout out the sighting – the "Thar she blows" moment, if you like. But shouting "Whale over there" isn't particularly helpful. It's better to give specific information. By convention, angles away from the boat are usually described as if you were sitting in the middle of a clock face. Directly ahead of the bow (the front end) is 12 o'clock and directly astern (behind the boat) is considered 6 o'clock. Thus if you spy a whale on the right (starboard) side, it will be somewhere between 1 and 5 o'clock and if it is on the left (port) side, somewhere between 7 and 11 o'clock. This system works well, especially when combined with information on distance – "a hundred yards out" or "half way to the horizon" and so on. Spotters can also help the captain steer towards distant animals by holding an arm out in the right direction. This is particularly useful when the boat turns and the clock position changes. After calling attention to an animal you've spotted, it is helpful to describe in the simplest terms what it was doing. Blowing? Leaping clear of the water? Porpoising? If so, to the left or right? For example, "Whale blow at 3 o'clock, just below the horizon" or "Dolphins coming into the bow".

For newcomers, the first encounters with whales can be a little puzzling. The first trace of whale is often a distant puff of vapor that is almost instantly snatched away by the wind. Was this an illusion or just the splash of one wave against another? After a few seconds there may be another puff in the same area. Now you are in business! Closer sightings will give you a glimpse of the glistening back of the whale or maybe even a dorsal fin, giving you clues to the direction it is moving. If an animal makes a particularly long roll and then lifts its tail flukes clear of the water, this is a sign that it is making a deeper dive. In some species, such as Humpbacks, this dive may be only a few minutes but for others, notably Sperm Whales, you might have to wait for up to an hour! After spending time with one type of cetacean, operators will often move to another area in hopes of finding something different, or will respond to information from other boats passed over the radio. Even the ride back to port can be interrupted with an unexpected sighting, so don't stop looking until you are safely tied up in dock.

Watching Whales from Land

A variety of whales and dolphins inhabit inshore waters or river estuaries and in many parts of the world, excellent whale watching is possible from land. Viewing cetaceans this way has the great advantage of not disturbing the animals and does not require the complications, expense or time limitations of boats. In general, the best sites are headlands that offer unobstructed views over the water. Choosing an elevated vantage point allows you to see over the ocean's swell, making it much easier to see animals over greater distances as they break the surface. It is difficult to predict where cetaceans will occur on a given day but some areas will be better than others. Larger whales, for instance, often feed or loaf in the relative calm of large bays but will pass close to headlands as they move along the coast. The Pacific coast of North America offers literally hundreds of spots where you can see migrating Gray Whales as they travel between Mexico and Alaska. Humpbacks also often migrate within a few miles of shore and can be seen from land in many parts of the world. The Cape Town area of South Africa, Nullarbor Coast of Australia and Patagonia in Argentina, are all places in which you can easily see Southern Right Whales lolling just beyond the surfline, so close that they might easily be mistaken for partially submerged rocks.

In places where tourists and whales are common, dedicated whale-watching viewing platforms or lookouts may have been established. These may consist of purpose-built structures offering shelter from the elements, unobstructed viewing and interpretive material. Others may simply be viewing spots that offer parking for cars. Small telescopes, often called "spotting scopes", are superb for land-based observers. Again, the more powerful the optics the narrower your field of vision, so scanning the ocean with a scope can be hard work. Many enthusiasts prefer to scan the water with binoculars and then use a scope to focus on objects of interest. Don't forget to use your naked eyes as well. It's all very well spotting a blow on the

Whale sightings off headlands are often sufficiently predictable for lookouts to be established.

horizon with a telescope but that's probably all you are likely to see of that animal. However, if you look both far with binoculars and near with your unaided eyes you might spot an animal moving along nearer the breakers, and when you get your binoculars or telescope on the animal(s), you'll get a fantastic view.

Even if you are on a coastline that's not acknowledged as a whale-watching hot spot, there's no harm in keeping an eye on the sea. Whales, dolphins and porpoises sometimes turn up in the most unlikely places – a harbor, a river mouth or an isolated bay. If you seen an animal or a group of them in one of these sites, you're sure to get a good view, so it's well worth keeping your eyes peeled. Maybe the animals will be spotted on a regular basis once you know where to look.

Encountering Dead Whales

Perhaps the closest encounter that many of us will ever have with a wild whale, dolphin or porpoise will be when we come across one that has stranded on the beach. Much of what we know about the biology of cetaceans, especially the more timid species such as beaked whales, comes from beach-cast animals. From a whale-watching point of view, being up close and personal to a stranding is quite an event. It's an opportunity to gaze at their superb adaptations, to gauge in a meaningful way just how large they are and potentially it's an opportunity to improve the status of these animals' lives – through efforts to put the animal back in the water or to retrieve the carcass for scientific research.

Even dead whales are memorable sights.

Strandings occur on almost every stretch of coastline at some time or another and if you regularly walk a beach there is a chance that you will eventually come across a stranded whale, dolphin or porpoise. It might be a single individual or maybe a whole group of them. If you are one of the first on the scene, it is imperative to find out whether the animal(s) is alive or dead. If you are unsure then watch and listen for breathing though the blowhole on the top of the head. Many of the deep-diving cetaceans can hold their breath for long periods, so if you are unsure wait a little longer. While watching, keep your distance: a distressed animal may thrash around and could easily injure bystanders. If it is definitely dead, then try and work out what species it is, note any distinctive features, estimate its length and if possible take notes and photographs and remember the spot where it is. Organized strandings schemes, which collect and carry out post-mortem examinations, operate on many coastlines, so contact them as soon as possible. Don't assume that someone else will. If the animal is dead and likely to get washed away, then tie it to something at the top of the beach. Finally, as with any rotting body, take hygiene precautions. Try to avoid touching it, wash your hands as soon as possible if you did make physical contact and keep children and dogs at a safe distance. And beware, large rotting whales produce large quantities of gas and have been known to explode!

If the animal is alive, then swift action is appropriate if it is to be rescued or if its suffering is to be minimized. Don't panic however. The first thing to do is to get appropriate help. The local strandings scheme, if there is one, should be the first people you call; if there isn't one, then call the coastguard, local authority, veterinary surgeon, aquarium, marine park or animal welfare organization. While waiting for help, douse the animal with sea water to keep it cool and to prevent its skin from drying out, but also take care not to allow water to enter its blowhole or it will drown. If you have to move the animal, do so on a tarpaulin, and never drag it over the ground or pull it by the flukes, flippers or dorsal fin. Keep yourself clear of the mouth for your own safety and avoid breathing your germs over it or scaring it by talking loudly. Ask onlookers to stay at a safe distance or ask for their help if assistance is required. When rescue personnel arrive don't be too hopeful; the best decision may well be to put the animal down. Finally, if it is to be re-floated, remember your own safety as well. Life jackets, waterproofs, wetsuits and a lifeguard are all good measures to avoid further casualties.

Some rescues of live stranded cetaceans take only minutes and involve just a few people but others, particularly for bigger species or mass strandings, require huge efforts. Teams of people, earth-moving machinery, specialized flotation equipment, veterinary expertise, boats and helicopters may all become involved. However, the motivation that people have to carry out these labors is often very different. Many rescuers focus on animal welfare and aim purely to relieve the animal of its suffering. They accept that the euthanasia of injured or sick animals is just as valid an outcome as putting more healthy ones back into the sea. Other people feel that crowd control is most important and that the animals should be left alone to die with dignity, or that all animals should be put back into the water regardless of the outcome. Many, motivated by conservation concerns, feel that the efforts and resources would be better spent stopping the human activities that may lead to cetaceans becoming disorientated, injured or sick in the first place rather than focusing on the small proportion that wash ashore. To confuse the debate still further, surprisingly few animals have been followed with electronic tags or natural marks after they have been "rescued". Figuring out whether the cetaceans survive after returning to the sea, one might think, would be the first thing that would be done before major funds are spent on rescue infrastructure, but unfortunately this hasn't been the case. Imagine the scientific value of that photograph you took of the dorsal fin of that dolphin you found stranded on the beach just before the tide took it away, when those distinctive marks are later recognized by researchers or whale-watchers on an apparently healthy animal among its associates at sea!

Interpreting Cetacean Behavior

When you're looking at a group of wild whales, dolphins or porpoises, the question that's often on people's lips is, "What are they doing?" There appears to be one universal rule about people and whale behavior: the less someone knows about the animals in front of them, the more certain they will be about exactly what activity the animals are engaged in. It's an easy trap to fall into, so don't be a victim. The more that is found out about cetaceans, the more complicated their lives turn out to be.

It's common practice to put cetacean behavior, of any appearance whatsoever, into one of the following categories: feeding, traveling, resting, socializing and milling. You see a couple of animals thrashing at the surface and ask what they're doing, and one person will tell you that they're feeding, while another will be adamant that they're socializing. The truth is that everybody saw the splashing, there'll be little disagreement about that, but watchers are often keen to squeeze a function out of those fragments of observation. Even worse, they'll only consider a limited list of functions (feeding, socializing etc) from which to pick their guess. For sure, we know that cetaceans feed, they travel from one place to another, they probably need rest at some time or other and they are social. But they don't necessarily compartmentalize their lives to do these activities one at a time. Why shouldn't feeding and socializing occur at the same occasion? After all, we frequently mix these pursuits. What's more, there are a lot of other activities that animals could be engaged in besides. Animals may lie still at the surface for prolonged periods to rest, but they might also behave the same way when they are listening to the distant calls of their associates or the sounds made by their prey. A dolphin thrashing at the surface might be simply having fun, or you might be witnessing a female fighting off the unwanted attentions of males, or giving birth, or ridding herself of the parasites clinging to her skin. Or perhaps the dolphin is up to something that nobody has yet thought to consider.

There's a Bottlenose Dolphin behavior that is seen every now and again off the coast of Virginia. Originally it was called "calf tossing", and what dolphin watchers saw was several dolphins, adults and young, engaged in energetic activities at the surface. During these events the young dolphin was repeatedly seen flying out of the water. This activity was initially thought to be some sort of game, but when young dolphins with fatal internal injuries began turning up on nearby beaches, the activity took on a more sinister aspect. In fact, calf tossing is more likely to be extreme aggression directed by adults upon the young and resulting in infanticide. Exactly why this behavior goes on remains unknown but once the connection with the damaged beach-cast carcasses was made, people noticed that the activities at sea looked less like a game. Instead, on close inspection many of the "tosses" actually looked sufficiently violent to cause real damage.

The moral is, when you see animals behaving in a particular way, keep an open mind and consider what you actually saw rather than what you thought you saw. The world of cetacean behavior is still an excitingly mysterious one and there's plenty of potential for fresh and open minds to revolutionize the way we envisage the daily activities of these spectacular animals. Perhaps your observation will prove to be the key that unlocks one of the mysteries of cetacean behavior. Happy whale watching!

You no longer have to be an intrepid mariner to experience the pure majesty of whales.

Where to Watch Whales & Dolphins

This chapter gives an overview of the many hundreds, if not thousands, of whale-watching opportunities around the world. Often, whales and dolphins can be watched from the land, especially with the aid of binoculars or a telescope, but for many people, it is venturing out onto the water for close-up encounters that offers the greatest thrill.

The chapter is structured as a world-wide gazetteer and takes a geographical approach to watching opportunities. For the majority of the localities covered, there are boat operators who run scheduled trips or charters specifically aimed at observing wild whales and dolphins. Because whale-watch companies are continually changing we will for the most part only list the localities and their target species rather than the specific operators. Individual companies can then be found by searching the web with the place and species names given. For locations where commercial whale-watching operations are not available, it may be possible to charter a local fishing- or dive-boat to take you out. This is often an expensive option, so take care to negotiate the price and planned route before setting out. Also make sure there are adequate safety provisions onboard. This pioneering approach may be rewarding and sow the seeds of future local interest in whale watching and cetacean conservation.

Of course, taking boats close to wild cetaceans is not without risks. Most obvious is the risk that the boat and surfacing cetacean collide. More subtle but equally worrying are the effects of the simple presence of the boat itself. Engine noise may frighten the animals or mask the sounds that they are making and listening to. Alternatively, boats may get in the way over and over again, forcing the whales or dolphins to take avoiding action and so waste their time and energy. For these and other reasons, efforts have been made to come up with rules, recommendations, codes of best practice, guidelines and so on to reduce the potential impacts of whale-watching boats (or planes, or swimmers) on the target animals. There are literally hundreds of these codes (too many to list here), specifically tailored to the nature of the local whale-watch activity, the species being watched, the local sea conditions, the history of whale-watching in the area, the latest scientific research and existing legislation.

Most of the measures in these rules or recommendations concentrate on limiting the distances that boats can approach, the angle of approach relative to their trajectories as well as limiting marine pollution, feeding and petting.

Other common measures aim to limit erratic boat behavior, the practice of leapfrogging moving animals, the number of boats present at one time and the amount of time that a boat can remain with the cetaceans. Few places have 'whale police' so it is up to the operators and you – the sponsor of that trip – to make sure that the local guidelines are being followed. When looking for an operator or deciding between different companies to go out with it is worth asking about any rules or regulations. It is also worth asking the operator when you are onboard. This will bring it to their attention that you're interested in the welfare of animals and that you'll be there watching him or her maneuvering the vessel.

For convenience, we have divided the oceans and major rivers of the globe into seven major zoogeographic regions:

Sometimes a nation's boundaries fall into more than one region. For example, the Hawaiian Islands are politically part of the United States (treated under North America) yet lie in the central Pacific and share much greater affinity with other nations spread across the tropical Pacific. They are therefore included in Section 7 as part of the Pacific faunal region. Likewise, Antarctica is discussed in Sections 3 and 7, reflecting the proximity of the Antarctic Peninsula to the southern tip of South America and of the Ross Sea to Australia and New Zealand.

Organization: Each section begins with a brief review of the regional geography as it pertains to whale watching and then overviews the cetaceans that can be found in the region, focusing where appropriate on species that can be found nowhere else (endemics) or with difficulty elsewhere (specialties). Due to space restrictions and inevitable turnover, it is for the most part impractical to list individual operators; however, we do give addresses for organizations that can provide timely information. Many operators have their own websites and offer up-to-date information, schedules and pricings.

North America & Mexico

Top Spots

USA – Migrant Humpbacks and Northern Right Whales off Cape Cod.

USA – Bottlenose Dolphins in the lagoons on the Gulf coast of Florida.

USA – Summer Blue Whales and Gray Whale migration along California's coast.

USA – Feeding Humpbacks in the sheltered waters of southeast Alaska.

Canada / USA – Close encounters with Killer Whales off Vancouver Island and San Juan Islands.

Canada – Belugas off Quebec City and Blue Whales in the St Lawrence River Estuary.

Mexico – Gray Whales and Blue Whales in Baja California.

The United States, Canada and Mexico can proudly boast an unparalleled number and variety of whale- and dolphin-watching opportunities. Literally hundreds of operators are found along the Atlantic and Pacific coasts, with growing numbers in the Gulf of Mexico and Gulf of California (Baja). Whale watching is also available in scattered communities throughout the Arctic from Alaska in the west to Greenland in the east. While there are many different species to look out for, two – the Humpback Whale and Gray Whale – dominate the commercial scene. Twice a year, Humpback Whales migrate along the Atlantic and Pacific coasts, moving from their warm-water breeding grounds to more temperate feeding areas. Consequently, Humpbacks can be seen in many locations especially feeding areas such as the Stellwagen Bank in Massachusetts, Monterey Bay in California and Glacier Bay in southern Alaska. Along the Pacific coast, Gray Whales follow a similar annual migration between calving grounds in Baja, Mexico and the rich feeding areas off British Columbia and Alaska. Generally inshore migrants, Gray Whales can often be seen from land and almost any coastal headland between San Diego, California and Vancouver Island, British Columbia is suitable.

Elsewhere, there are a number of species that can be seen more easily in North America than say in Europe or Asia. These include Fin Whales (especially off New England and the New York Bite), Northern Bottlenose Whales (mainly Nova Scotia), Bowhead Whales and Narwhals (both in the Arctic) and Beluga (Canadian Arctic, Alaska and St Lawrence River, Quebec). A regional specialty is the North Atlantic Right Whale. Driven almost to extinction by commercial whaling, the species is slowly recovering. The Bay of Fundy is used as a summer nursery, whilst the waters around southern Nova Scotia are important for mating and feeding. In spring, the whales congregate to feed around Cape Cod (principally the Great South Channel and Massachusetts Bay) and calving occurs in the warm waters of Georgia and northern Florida.

United States of America

Gulf of Maine and New England

The Gulf of Maine extends from the Bay of Fundy in Canada south to Cape Cod Bay in the United States. Most whale watchers who come to this area visit the Stellwagen Bank, Jeffrey's Ledge, Great South Channel and Cashes Ledge. New England's Stellwagen Bank, located only a few miles from Boston, is one of the most important seasonal feeding areas for whales in the western North Atlantic. Indeed, the scientific name for the Humpback Whale, *Megaptera novaeangliae,* means "big-winged New Englander". In the spring, aggregations of North Atlantic Right Whales can be seen in the Great South Channel, east of Cape Cod, and sometimes in Massachusetts Bay, as they travel northwards to their summering grounds in the Bay of Fundy and along the continental shelf edge south of Nova Scotia (Browns and Banks). The Right Whales come to feed on copepods and juvenile *euphausiid* shrimps. Between May and October Long-Finned Pilot Whales occur along the shelf edge (328 to 3280 ft / 100 to 1000 m contour), often in the company of Bottlenose Dolphins, but are also seen on the George's Bank and in the Great South Channel. The Channel also attracts numbers of Humpback Whales and a few Minke, Fin and Sei Whales. Several other species are regularly encountered including Harbor Porpoises, Common, Risso's, Atlantic White-Sided and White-Beaked Dolphins. The "Coastal Research and Education Society of Long Island" (CRESLI) runs dedicated overnight whale-watching trips to the Great South Channel in mid summer departing from Montauk at the eastern end of Long Island. During the summer they also operate day-long tours to the Block and Hudson Canyons in search of Fin Whales.

Cape Cod, Massachusetts

The Stellwagen Bank is a shallow mound of sand and gravel rising just north of Cape Cod, a remnant of retreating glaciers from the last Ice Age. Nutrient-rich waters flowing from the deeper Stellwagen Basin and Gulf of Maine strike the bank and rise up over this underwater obstruction, causing a major upwelling of nutrients and creating a bloom of plankton. The complex ecosystem that grows around the abundant plankton provides food for Humpback, Fin and Northern Right Whales that visit the Bank, creating one of the oldest and most well-established centers for whale-watching. In 1996, the World Wildlife Fund named the Bank one of its ten top whale-watching sites in the world and each year close to a million people take commercial wildlife-viewing trips out onto Stellwagen Bank. Although a few Fins winter off Cape Cod they are most abundant on the Stellwagen Bank from April and October. Large schools of herring on Jeffrey's Ledge attract Fin Whales and hundreds of Atlantic White-Sided Dolphins. In late summer (mid July to September) Killer Whales follow schools of tuna onto Jeffrey's Ledge and occasionally the Stellwagen Bank.

During the summer numerous daily tours leave from Provincetown at the tip of the Cape as well as Boston Harbor, Plymouth and Gloucester. Whales are often seen from shore along Cape Cod, especially from Race Point near Provincetown at the north tip of the Cape. Tours are also available from Nantucket Island and Newburyport. Organized whale-watching excursions to the Great South Channel during July and August regularly encounter numbers of Humpback, Fin, Sei, Minke and Long-Finned Pilot Whales together with Common, Atlantic White-Sided and Risso's Dolphins. Some trips also find Sperm Whales, Northern Right Whales and White-Beaked Dolphins.

Main Species: Humpback Whales.

Other Species Seen: Northern Right, Fin, Minke, Killer, Sei, Sperm and Long-Finned Pilot Whales, Common, Atlantic White-Sided, Risso's and White-Beaked Dolphins and Harbor Porpoises.

Season: June–October.   **Code of Conduct:** All whales, dolphins and porpoises are federally protected under the Marine Mammal Protection Act (MMPA). Violation may result in fines or civil penalties. For further information on whale-watching guidelines in the US visit the National Marine Fisheries Service website: www.nmfs.noaa.gov/pr/education/viewing.htm

Information

Provincetown Center for Coastal Studies
PO Box 1036
Provincetown, MA 02657
Tel: 508 487-3622 ext. 101
Fax: 508 487-4495
ccs@coastalstudies.org
www.coastalstudies.org

The Whale Center of New England
24 Harbor Loop
Gloucester, MA 01930
Tel: + 978 281 6351
E-mail: info@whalecenter.org
www.whalecenter.org

Coastal Research and Education Society
of Long Island (CRESLI), Inc.
Division of Natural Sciences and Mathematics
Kramer Science Center, Dowling College
Oakdale, NY 11769-1999
Tel: + 631 244 3352
E-mail: information@cresli.org
www.cresli.org

Massachusetts Office of Travel and Tourism
100 Cambridge Street,13th Floor,
Boston, MA 02202.
Tel: + 617 973 8500; Toll free: 800 227-MASS
E-mail: vacationinfo@state.ma.us
www.mass-vacation.com

Florida

The state of Florida occupies the large peninsula that partly separates the Gulf of Mexico from the Atlantic Ocean. The climate is tempered by the proximity to water and most of the state enjoys a humid subtropical climate with the extreme tip of Florida and the chain of islands known as the Florida Keys becoming increasingly tropical. Bottlenose Dolphins can be found all year round (from Florida north to the Chesapeake Bay in Maryland), becoming more numerous in the winter months. Dolphins can be relatively easy to see from land on both sides of the peninsula as they frequently swim close inshore entering mangrove forests in search of food. Sheltered bays (e.g. Sarasota Bay, Biscayne Bay, Apalachicola Bay and Choctawatchee Bay) or bridges and causeways linking islands or crossing inland waterways (Indian River) are particularly good. Dolphin-watching tours set out from Key West, Jupiter, Fort Lauderdale, Indialantic and Miami Beach. The weather is generally calm and warm to hot, although this can change during hurricane season (June – October). The Biminis (see under Bahama section) are close to the coast of southeastern Florida and are a popular destination for tour operators. Bottlenose Dolphins are regularly sighted from the Caladesi Island ferry and can be seen (along with West Indian manatees) along the edges of the flooded mangrove forests on the eastern side of Caladesi Island.

Main Species: Bottlenose Dolphins.

Other Species Seen: Atlantic Spotted Dolphins, and Short-Finned Pilot Whales.

Season: May–September.   **Code of Conduct:** National Marine Fisheries Service regulations in place. Swimming with captive dolphins only permitted under controlled conditions.

Information

Florida Division of Tourism
126 Van Buren Street
Tallahassee, FL 32399
www.visitflorida.com

Mote Marine Laboratory and Aquarium
1600 Ken Thompson Parkway,
Sarasota, Florida 34236
(941) 388-4441 - (800) 691-MOTE
www.mote.org

Cook Inlet, Alaska

The Cook Inlet population of Belugas is estimated to number 400 to 500 animals but is thought to be declining. During the warmer months, animals can be seen from the roadside only a short distance south of Anchorage along the Turnagain Arm of the inlet. Aptly named Beluga Point has ample parking spaces.

In early May they gather off the mouth of the Kenai River, feeding on young salmon leaving the river and smelt entering the river to spawn. The whales may travel as much as 5 miles (8 km) up the river on incoming high tides. At the Kenai Beach, the river mouth can be watched from the Coast Guard light tower or from parking areas on bluffs overlooking the river. Whales may even appear at the Kenai City Dock. At the Warren Ames Memorial Bridge crossing, a parking lot is provided for viewing the Kenai Flats wetlands and Belugas can often be seen downstream from this location. Another good area is the beach at Captain Cook State Park at the end of the North Kenai Road.

Main Species: Belugas

Other Species Seen: Killer, Gray and Humpback Whales.

Season: June–September.   **Code of Conduct:** National Marine Fisheries Service regulations in place.

Information

Alaska Travel Industry Association
PO Box 196710,
Anchorage, AK 99519
Tel: 800 862 5275   www.travelalaska.com

Prince William Sound and Kenai Fjords, Alaska

Prince William Sound located in the northeast corner of the Gulf of Alaska has the densest concentration of tidewater glaciers in the world. Pods of both resident and transient Killer Whales (Orcas) are found in the Sound mainly in the waters around Kenai Fjords, feeding on the salmon and marine mammals that are abundant there. Gray and Humpback Whales can be seen on their annual migration to and from the rich feeding grounds of the Bering Sea. Whale-watching trips operate from Seward on the Kenai Peninsula, Valdez which is the central point for most trips and Whittier on the western shores. A car ferry runs from Whittier to Valdez across Prince William Sound.

Main Species: Humpback, Gray, Killer Whales (Orcas) and Dall's and Harbor Porpoises.
Other Species Seen: Beluga, Fin and Minke Whales.

Season: Mid March–November.   **Code of Conduct:** National Marine Fisheries Service regulations in place.

Information

Valdez Visitor Information Center
200 Fairbanks Street
Valdez, AK 99686
Tel: + 907 835 4636
E-mail: info@valdezalaska.org
www.valdezalaska.org

Seward Visitors Bureau
2001 Seward Hwy
Seward, AK 99664
Tel: + 907 224 8051
E-mail: visitseward@seward.net
www.sewardak.org

Southeast Alaska & the Inside Passage

An expanse of sheltered fjords intermingled with mountain ranges and glaciers, the area combines excellent whale watching with magnificent backdrops and the pervasive ambience of true wilderness. Although the most frequently traveled routes are in Alaska, the region also extends to coastal British Columbia in Canada. The main attractions are Humpback and Killer Whales with Dall's Porpoises and Pacific White-Sided Dolphins as the supporting cast. Humpback Whales spend the summer feeding in this area and feed by blowing 'nets' of bubbles to concentrate their prey. The best areas to witness this spectacle are in Fredrick Sound and Chatham Strait, which are world famous for their synchronous bubble-netting groups and their haunting underwater feeding calls. Humpback watching is primarily a summer activity but many whales continue feeding in the area (especially Lynn Canal, Seymour Canal and Sitka Sound) until mid January. Both transient- and resident-type Killer Whales are seen throughout the region. Lucky observers may see transients stalking seals and sea lions at one of the many haul-outs in the area. One can explore the possibilities by joining an organized excursion or on a do-it-yourself basis. Many people visit southeast Alaska on board a cruise ship and often see whales as they travel up or down the Inside Passage and at spectacular locations like Glacier Bay. Day trips on smaller vessels are available from coastal towns (Auke Bay, Sitka, Petersburg among others) or from the many fishing or adventure holiday lodges. High-quality live-aboard charters specializing in wildlife range throughout the region, offering prolonged views, access to remote sites and customized experiences tailored to the wishes of those aboard. For the adventurous and bear-aware, kayak rental offers access to hundreds of miles of unspoilt coastline. As a whole, southeast Alaska is relatively remote and direct road access from the North American road network is limited to the towns of Haines and Skagway. The ferries of the Alaska Marine Highway System connect with the road system and convey passengers with or without vehicles to the other major towns. Scheduled flights connect the major towns with each other and the rest of the mainland US. Seaplanes and water taxis provide access to all other areas.

Main Species: Humpback and Killer Whales.

Other Species Seen: Dall's Porpoises, Harbor Porpoises, Pacific White-Sided Dolphins, Gray Whales.

Season: June–September. **Code of Conduct:** National Marine Fisheries Service regulations in place.

Information

Alaska Travel Industry Association
PO Box 196710
Anchorage
AK 99519
Tel: 800 862-5275
www.travelalaska.com

Juneau Convention & Visitors Bureau
One Sealaska Plaza, Suite 305
Juneau, AK 99801
Tel: 800 587-2201
or 907 586-1737
www.traveljuneau.com

Petersburg Visitor Information Center
PO Box 649
Petersburg
AK 99833
Tel: 907 772 4636
www.fs.fed.us/r10/tongass/districts/petersburg vic.shtml

Sitka Annual WhaleFest
PO Box 6004
Sitka, AK 99835
Tel: 907 747 7964
www.sitkawhalefest.org

Puget Sound, Straits of Juan de Fuca and the San Juan Islands, Washington State, USA, and British Columbia, Canada

Located in the northwest corner of Washington State, north of Puget Sound proper, the San Juan Islands are remnants of a mountain range that once connected Vancouver Island to the mainland (see also p 195). Eighty-three of the islands are protected as part of the San Juan Islands National Wildlife Refuge. Approximately 80 to 90 Killer Whales, comprising three major pods, use the area, sustained by migrant salmon and other fish. Pods can often be seen from shore or from sea kayaks, sometimes blessing patient watchers with spectacular displays of breaching or other aerial behaviors. In addition to the resident pods, groups of so-called 'transient' Killer Whales also pass through the area. Other cetaceans include Humpback, Minke and Gray Whales, and Dall's and Harbor Porpoises. In Washington State, a number of scheduled and private boat tours operate from Friday Harbor, Snug Harbor, and Roche Harbor. The Whale Watch Operator's Association Northwest (WWOANW) brings together a number of local tour companies dedicated to responsible wildlife viewing and protection of the declining 'southern resident' population of Killer Whales. Most operators provide their services during the peak whale-watching season, typically from May through September. These sightseeing excursions range from one hour to a half-day. Organized kayaking trips offer a unique way to explore these picturesque islands and encounter Killer Whales and other wildlife at close hand with minimal disturbance. Trips are usually multi-day and include camping on remote and otherwise inaccessible coastlines. Prior kayaking experience is not always necessary and the trips generally proceed at a leisurely pace suitable for most levels of fitness.

Main Species: Killer Whales.

Other Species Seen: Gray, Humpback and Minke Whales, Dall's and Harbor Porpoises.

Season: April–October.   **Code of Conduct:** Recommended Best Practice Guidelines issued by the Whale Watch Operators Association North West in place, alongside the National Marine Fisheries Service regulations.

Information

The Whale Museum
62 First Street North
Friday Harbor, WA 98250
Tel: + 360 378 4710
www.whalemuseum.org

Whale Watch Operators Association Northwest
PO Box 2404, Friday Harbor,
WA 98250
E-mail: info@nwwhalewatchers.org
www.nwwhalewatchers.org

San Juan Islands Visitor Bureau
PO Box 1330, Friday Harbor, WA 98250
Tel: + 888 468 3701
www.guidetosanjuan.com

Washington State Tourism
PO Box 42525
Olympia,
WA 98504
Tel: + 360 725 4028;
Toll-free: 800 544 1800
E-mail: tourism@cted.wa.gov
www.experiencewashington.com

Tourism British Columbia
802-865 Hornby Street
Vancouver,
BC V6Z 2GB
Tel: + 604 435 5622
Toll Free 1 800 4355 5622
www.hellobc.com

California, Oregon and Washington Coastline

Along the Pacific coast there are numerous signposted whale-watch lookouts, with more than 50 in California alone. The first public lookout was created in 1950 on a former US Army artillery battery at the Cabrillo National Monument at Point Loma in San Diego. Although a few Gray Whales can be seen at almost any time of year, the winter months are by far the best. From late December to February, close to 30 whales per hour can be seen from principal watch points. Using binoculars or a telescope, it's possible to see the 15 ft (5 m) blows as much as 5 miles (8 km) offshore but many animals pass significantly closer to land and many are visible to the naked eye. As a rule, calm conditions make it much easier to spot the animals. In Oregon, the Whale

Watching Spoken Here program organizes a series of "watchweeks" with trained volunteers stationed at 28 lookouts, and these are timed to coincide with peak migration times during winter and spring holidays. Other popular lookouts are at the Point Reyes Lighthouse north of San Francisco; Yaquina Head Interpretive Center, Oregon; Depoe Bay Sea Wall, Oregon; Spanish Head near Lincoln City, Oregon; and the Lewis and Clark Interpretive Center, Ilwaco, Washington.

Main Species: Gray and Humpback Whales, Pacific White-Sided Dolphins.
Other Species Seen: Blue, Minke and Killer Whales, Harbor Porpoises and Bottlenose Dolphins.

Season: Year-round, (Dec–Feb peak Gray Whale migration).
Code of Conduct: National Marine Fisheries Service regulations in place.

Information

Whale Watching Spoken Here
Oregon Parks and Recreation Department
Depoe Bay Whale Center, Depoe Bay, OR 97341
Tel: + 541 765 3407
E-mail: morris.grover@state.or.us
www.whalespoken.org

Center for Whale Research
PO Box 1577
Friday Harbor, WA98250
Tel: 360 378 5835
E-mail: orcasurv@rockisland.com
www.whaleresearch.com

Monterey Bay, California

This large bay on the coast of central California is bisected by a very deep submarine canyon that works its way into shore close to the small fishing port of Moss Landing. The combination of very deep water and prevailing currents gives rise to a major upwelling system and explosion of marine life. Many whales and dolphins are attracted to Monterey Bay by the abundance of small fish, notably sardines, and the area is justifiably considered one of the premier whale-watching spots in North America, if not the world. The Monterey Submarine Canyon begins within a few miles of the shore and then quickly plummets to depths of 10,363 ft (3250 m) or approximately 2 miles (3 km) – considerably deeper than the Grand Canyon. In 1992, some 5300 square miles (13,700 sq km) of the bay and neighboring offshore waters were incorporated into the Monterey Bay National Marine Sanctuary (MBNMS), forming the largest federally protected marine sanctuary in the United States.

During the summer and autumn (May to mid December), Humpback and Blue Whales migrate into Monterey to feed on anchovies and krill and together with the annual migration of Gray Whales have given rise to a thriving whale-watching industry. Almost the entire eastern Pacific population of Gray Whales passes through the Bay during the winter and spring (mid December to mid May) en route between Alaska and Baja California. Gray Whale calves are sometimes preyed upon by pods of Killer Whales, which become more common in the Bay when calf numbers are high. Whale-watching boats occasionally witness active hunts, providing an unquestionably memorable experience for both crew and participants alike. More commonly, however, Killer Whales are seen in pursuit of northern elephant seals. Mature bull Sperm Whales are encountered along the walls and main body of the Canyon during late summer and autumn. Occasionally, beaked whales, principally Baird's with a few Cuvier's, are seen in deep water most often during late summer and autumn. Humpback, Gray and Blue Whales can be seen from shore, although Blues are more likely further out into the Bay. Large whales become less common in the Bay from late November to mid December but Pacific White-Sided, Risso's, Long-Beaked, Common and Northern Right Whale Dolphins can be encountered year round. These are often found in large mixed species groups, sometimes numbering in the hundreds to thousands of animals concentrating over the deep water of the Monterey Canyon where they feed on squid. Bottlenose Dolphins, Dall's and Harbor Porpoises are also present year round. A small number of Minke Whales appear in the winter to feed on "among other things" immature rockfish, and it is still unclear where these animals spend the remaining months of the year. California sea lions and harbor seals are abundant, especially around the harbors, and fluffy sea otters can be found easily in the kelp beds along the shore where they hunt abalone and urchins. Northern fur and northern elephant seals also occur in smaller numbers, the former sometimes hauling out on the main jetty.

Several whale-watching companies operate from the end of Monterey's Fisherman's Wharf (Wharf No.1). Parking is available in several large lots near the harbor or along Cannery Row. Walk along the pier past the seafood restaurants and souvenir shops to a large red sign that says 'Monterey Bay Whale Watch Center'. Usually there are multiple trips per day lasting between 3 and 5 hours. Additional departure points are the marina at Moss Landing and in the north of the bay at Santa Cruz. Trips can be popular and it is wise to book in advance. Reservations can be made online, where recent sightings, schedules and local weather conditions are posted on a daily basis. In Santa Cruz, whale-watching charters are available from the Municipal Wharf and from Santa Cruz Yacht Harbor. Good land-based viewing spots include the pull-offs along Route 1 in Pacific Grove, Big Sur and Marina. Between boat trips, it is worth a visit to the outstanding Monterey Bay Aquarium (www.mbayaq.org) on Cannery Row.

Main Species: Gray, Humpback and Blue Whales, Risso's, Pacific White-sided, Common and Northern Right Whale Dolphins, Dall's Porpoises.

Other Species Seen: Killer, Sperm, Fin and Minke Whales, Harbor Porpoises, Bottlenose Dolphins, Baird's Beaked Whales, Cuvier's Beaked Whales.

Season: Year-round.   **Code of Conduct:** National Marine Fisheries Service regulations in place.

Information

Monterey Bay National Marine Sanctuary
299 Foam Street
Monterey, CA 93940
Tel: + 831 647 4201
www.montereybay.noaa.gov

Chris' Whale Watching Tours
48 Fisherman's Wharf No. 1
Monterey,
CA 93940

Tel: + 831 375 5951
www.chriswhalewatching.com

Monterey Bay Aquarium
886 Cannery Row
Monterey,
CA 93940
Tel: + 831 648 4888 (English);
+ 1 800 555 3656 (Spanish)
www.mbayaq.org

Sanctuary Cruises
'A' Dock,
Moss Landing Harbor
Moss Landing
Tel: + 831 643 0128
E-mail: sanctuarycruises@sbcglobal.net
www.sanctuarycruises.com

Monterey County Convention & Visitors Bureau
PO Box 1770
Monterey, CA 93942

Tel: + 888 221 1010
E-mail: info@mccvb.org
www.montereyinfo.org/page/whale_watching/

Monterey Bay Whale Watch
84 Fisherman's Wharf
PO Box 52001
Monterey, CA 93940
Tel: + 831 375 4658
E-mail: trips@montereybaywhalewatch.com
www.montereybaywhalewatch.com/

Central and Southern California

Located northwest of Los Angeles, the Santa Barbara Channel provides one of the best places in the world to see Blue Whales. The Channel is a deep basin formed by the mainland and a line of eight arid islands that lie approximately 20 miles (32 km) offshore. Cool nutrient-rich water sweeps in from the north near Point Conception giving rise to an abundance of marine life when it mixes with warmer water from the south. Several hundred Blue Whales visit the Channel each summer to feed off krill (*Thysanoessa spinifera*) and there may be as many as 100 animals in a 30 by 5 mile (38 by 8 km) area. Krill tend to concentrate at the western end of the Channel and this is also the best area for Blue Whales, which arrive in June and remain common until August when they travel south to the Gulf of California and a seamount known as the Costa Rican Dome. A few linger as late as November. Between December and mid February 20,000 Gray Whales pass through on their southward migration, returning northward again between mid February and the end of April. The northward movement tends to the hug the coast whereas the southbound route is more spread out; however, the majority pass through the 4 mile (6 km) wide channel separating Santa Rosa from Santa Cruz. Excursions into the Channel may also encounter Killer Whales, Humpback (summer and autumn), Fin (summer) and Minke Whales (summer), Common, Bottlenose, Pacific White-Sided, Risso's and Northern Right Whale Dolphins, and Dall's Porpoises. Although most Killer Whales appear to be migrants, a few are present all year preying on the numerous sea lions, fur and elephant seals. Half-day tours leave from Santa Barbara Harbor ('SEA' landing and Stearns Wharf), The Channel Islands Harbor in Oxnard and from Ventura Harbor. The Channel Islands National Park and Channel Islands National Marine Sanctuary incorporate the islands of San Miguel, Santa Rosa, Santa Cruz, Anacapa, and Santa Barbara. Further south around San Diego, Gray Whales can be seen from numerous headlands (e.g. Point Loma, on the west side of San Diego Bay) and there are boat- and kayak-based viewing tours from Dana Point, La Jolla and San Diego Harbor. Common, Risso's and Pacific White-Sided Dolphins are also regularly encountered.

Main Species: Gray (Dec–April), Humpback (May–Nov) and Blue Whales (May–Nov), Bottlenose (year-round) and Pacific White-Sided Dolphins (May–Sept).

Other Species Seen: Killer Whales (Jan–May), Fin (June–Aug) and Minke Whales, Risso's

Dolphins (May–Sept), Common and Northern Right Whale Dolphins (year-round), Dall's Porpoises (year-round).

Season: Year-round.   **Code of Conduct:** National Marine Fisheries Service regulations in place.

Information

Channel Islands National Park

1901 Spinnaker Drive, Ventura, CA 93001

Tel: + 805 658 5730

Canada

Gulf of St Lawrence

During the summer and autumn (June to November), the broad St Lawrence Gulf near the mouth of the Saguenay River plays host to both Fin and Minke Whales, with smaller numbers of Beluga and Harbor Porpoises. The same species occur elsewhere along the north shore of the Gulf of St Lawrence and around the Mingan Islands between June and November with occasional sightings of Killer Whales and Atlantic White-Sided Dolphins. Blue Whales visit between August and November. Half-day, full-day and some extended multi-day tours are available; try the towns of Tadoussac, Baie-Ste-Catherine, Grandes-Bergeronnes, Les Escoumins, Godbout, Baie-Comeau, Baie-Trinite or Pointes-des-Monts (St Lawrence River); Longue-Pointe-de-Mingan or Havre-Saint-Pierre (Gulf of St Lawrence); Gaspe or Riviere-du-Renard (Gaspe Peninsula). Between July and September it is cool to cold on the water, with fog common and some heavy summer rains. By October/November snow is common.

Tadoussac, Quebec

Situated at the confluence of the St Lawrence and the Saguenay River, this is a picturesque area with its steep cliffs and the mighty St Lawrence River – at this point 15 miles (24 km) across. This junction of the river and estuary creates a special microclimate favoring marine life and the whale watching can be spectacular. In addition to the city of Tadoussac, boats leave from Baie-Sainte-Catherine on the western side of the Saguenay Fjord and provide opportunities to observe Minke Whales, Fin Whales, and Blue Whales.

Main Species: Fin, Minke and Blue Whales.

Other Species Seen: Beluga, Minke and Killer Whales, Atlantic White-Sided Dolphins and Harbor Porpoises.

Season: June–November.   **Code of Conduct:** Voluntary guidelines.

Information

Mingan Island Cetacean Study
Research Station
378 Bord de la Mer
Longue-Pointe-de-Mingan, Quebec G0G 1V0

Canada
Tel: + 418 949 2845
E-mail: mics@globetrotter.net
www.rorqual.com

Tourism Quebec
PO Box 979
Montreal,
Quebec H3C 2W3, Canada

Tel: + 514 864-3838;
Toll free: 1 877 266 5687
E-mail: info@bonjourquebec.com
www.bonjourquebec.com

A useful website with information on the whales of the Gulf of St Lawrence, Whales on-line, can be found at: www.whales-online.net.

Maritimes and Newfoundland

Between June and October, visitors are likely to encounter Fin, Humpback and Minke Whales, plus Atlantic White-Sided Dolphins and Harbor Porpoises. Between August and early November, endangered Northern Right Whales congregate off Nova Scotia and in the Bay of Fundy. Blue Whales have been seen regularly during summer around southern and northern Newfoundland. Between June and August the weather is often cool and foggy, and it gets even colder but clearer in September/October. Half-day, full-day and some extended multi-day tours are available from a number of harbors; try Grand Manan, Leonardville or Fredericton (New Brunswick); Halifax, Tiverton, Cheticamp or Capstick (Nova Scotia); Westport (Brier Island); St Johns's, Bay Bulls, Trinity or Twillingate (Newfoundland).

Main Species: Fin, Minke and Humpback Whales.

Other Species Seen: Blue and Northern Right Whales, Atlantic White-Sided Dolphins and Harbor Porpoises.

Season: June–October.   **Code of Conduct:** Voluntary guidelines.

Information

Tourism New Brunswick
Box 6000
Fredericton, New Brunswick E3B 5HI
Canada
Tel: Toll free: 1 888 840 7555
www.tourismnewbrunswick.ca

Tourism Newfoundland
Box 8700
St John's, Newfoundland A1B 4J6
Canada

Tel: Toll free: 1 800 563 6353
www.gov.nf.ca

Nova Scotia Department of Tourism, Culture and Heritage
PO Box 456
Halifax, Nova Scotia B3J 2R5
Canada
Tel: + 902-425-5781; Toll free: 1 800 565 0000
E-mail: explore@gov.ns.ca
www.novascotia.com

British Columbia and Puget Sound

The Pacific Northwest has become nearly synonymous with Killer Whales. Largest of the dolphins, pods of these fantastic animals can be seen almost anywhere in the region. The best areas are around the southern tip of Vancouver Island and in Johnstone Strait at the northern tip of Vancouver Island. Victoria is one of the main departure points in the south of Vancouver Island.

More than ten separate pods of Killer Whales reside in Johnstone Strait and one or more of these family groups can usually be located during half and full-day whale-watching excursions. Plenty of other wildlife will also be in evidence including Dall's and Harbor Porpoises, Pacific White-Sided Dolphins and California and Steller's sea lions, harbor seals and occasionally elephant seals. Whales and other wildlife are regularly sighted from the numerous passenger ferries that ply these waters.

Tofino, Vancouver Island, British Columbia

From March through to October 20,000 Gray Whales migrate along the western shores of Vancouver Island traveling between Alaska and Mexico. During the summer months, a few may remain in the area. Visitors may encounter Steller's sea lions that haul-out on the outer islands during this period. Tofino is a small community on the western side of Vancouver Island experiencing the full force and majesty of the North Pacific. Several local whale-watching ventures run small craft from the town dock. Tours also depart from Ucluelet to the south. The area can be reached by car from the ferry terminal at Nanaimo which connects to Vancouver.

Main Species: Gray and Killer Whales.

Other Species Seen: Humpback Whales, Pacific White-Sided Dolphins, Dall's and Harbor Porpoises.

Season: March–October.   **Code of Conduct:** Voluntary guidelines.

Information

Vancouver Aquarium
PO Box 3232
Vancouver, BC V6B 3X8
Tel: + 604 659 3474
E-mail: information@vanaqua.org
www.vanaqua.org

Vancouver, Coast & Mountains Tourism Region
250-1508 West 2nd Avenue
Vancouver, BC V6J 1H2
Tel: + 604 739 9011
E-mail: info@vcmbc.com
www.vcmbc.com

Tourism Vancouver Island
203-335 Wesley Street
Nanaimo, BC V9R 2T5
Tel: + 250 754 3500
E-mail: info@islands.bc.ca
www.islands.bc.ca

Tofino-Long Beach Chamber of Commerce
PO Box 249
Tofino, BC V0R 2Z0
Tel: + 250 725 3414
E-mail: tofino@island.net
www.islands.net/~tofino

Tourism Victoria
812 Wharf Street
Victoria, BC V8W 1T3
Tel: + 250 953 2033;
Toll-Free: 800 663 3883
E-mail: info@tourismvictoria.com
www.tourismvictoria.com

Ucluelet Chamber of Commerce
Box 428,
100 Main Street
Ucluelet, BC V0R 3A0
Tel: + 250 726 4600
E-mail: pacificrimvisitorcentre@telus.net
www.uclueletinfo.com

Telegraph Cove, Vancouver Island, British Columbia

The protected waters of Johnstone Strait and the Blackfish Archipelago on the northeast coast of Vancouver Island are acknowledged as the most accessible and predictable location to see Killer Whales in the world. One of the most popular starting points is the tiny hamlet of Telegraph Cove at the northern end of Vancouver Island. Here Stubbs Island Whale-Watching, the first commercial venture in British Columbia, began a long-standing and successful operation. Their boats have hydrophones connected to speakers so that the vocalizations can be heard anywhere on the boat. Besides Killer Whales, Minke, Humpback and Gray Whales are regularly encountered together with Dall's Porpoises, Harbor Porpoises and Pacific White-Sided Dolphins. Convenient accommodation can be found in Telegraph Cove itself or in Port McNeill (30 min drive). Whale-watching boats are not permitted in the Robson Bight (Michael Biggs) Ecological Reserve, famous for the gravel beds used as 'scratching posts'.

Main Species: Killer Whales.

Other Species Seen: Minke, Humpback and Gray Whales, Pacific White-Sided Dolphins, Dall's and Harbor Porpoises.

Season: May–October.   **Code of Conduct:** Voluntary guidelines.

Information

Orca Lab
PO Box 510
Alert Bay, British Columbia V0N 1A0
Tel: + 250 974 8068
E-mail: orcalab@island.net   www.orcalab.org

For further tourist information contact:
Vancouver Island North Visitors Association
PO Box 1755
Port McNeill, British Columbia V0N 2R0
Tel: + 250 949-9094; Toll Free: 1 800 903 6660
E-mail: tourism@vinva.bc.ca
www.vinva.bc.ca

Useful websites:

Stubbs Island Whale-Watching
www.stubbs-island.com

Tourism British Columbia
Tel: + 250 387 1642;
Toll free: 1 800 HELLO-BC
www.hellobc.com

www.britishcolumbia.com

www.vancouverisland.com

Churchill, Manitoba

Over 3000 Belugas spend the summer in the estuary of the Churchill River, making it the world's largest readily accessible population. Although the timing varies from year to year, the river ice begins to break up in early to mid June. The Belugas often swim within a few feet of boats, turning on their sides to examine the humans looking down upon them. For the hardy, it is even possible to get into the water during July and August and snorkel with them!

Main Species: Belugas.

Season: Mid June–August.   **Code of Conduct:** Voluntary guidelines.

Information

Churchill Chamber of Commerce
PO Box 176
Churchill, Manitoba R0B 0E0
E-mail: cccomm@churchillmb.net
www.churchillmb.net

Churchill Arctic Travel
140 Kelsey Blvd
Churchill, Manitoba R0B 0E0
Tel: + 204 675 2811
E-mail: churchillarctictvl@churchillmb.net

Churchill Wild
PO Box 425
Thompson, Manitoba R8N 1N2
Tel: + 204 778-3700;

Toll free: 1 866-UGO-WILD
E-mail: info@churchillwild.com
www.churchillwild.com

Sea North Tours
PO Box 222
Churchill, Manitoba R0B 0E0
Tel: + 204 675-2195
E-mail: seamprtj@mts.net
www.seanorth.com

Travel Manitoba
7th Floor, 155 Carlton Street
Winnipeg, Manitoba R3C 3H8
Tel: Toll free: 1 800 665 0040
www.travelmanitoba.com

Pond Inlet, Nunavut

The small Inuit community of Pond Inlet lies at the northern tip of Baffin Island. The adjacent waters around Baffin Island and Bylot Island are very rich in marine mammals, including important concentrations of Narwhal, Bowhead and Beluga along with many Harp, Bearded and Ringed Seals, wandering polar bears and walrus. Unfortunately, Narwhal and seals are hunted aggressively during the short period of open water and the former are consequently extremely shy. A small number of cruise ships now visit the region including some of the narrower channels in search of local wildlife including Narwhals and Bowhead Whales. Scanning the water with binoculars or a telescope may be rewarding. The adventurous can join guided camping trips using snowmobiles or Inuit sledges (*komatik*) to travel out onto the ice floes where Narwhal can be relatively common. These are not always successful but when they are, the views of tusks emerging from narrow cracks in the ice are unforgettable.

Main Species: Beluga and Bowhead Whales.

Other Species Seen: Narwhals, Killer Whales.

Season: August.   **Code of Conduct:** Voluntary guidelines.

Information

Canadian Tourism
55 Metcalfe Street
Ottawa, Ontario K1P 6L5
Canada
Tel: + 613 946 1000

E-mail: trdc@ctc-ctc.ca
www.canadatourism.com

Baffin Island Visitors Guide
www.baffinisland.ca

North Winds Polar Expeditions
Tel: + 867 979 0551
Fax: + 867 979-0573
Email: north@northwinds-arctic.com
www.northwinds-arctic.com

Black Feather
The Wilderness Adventure Company

250 McNaughts Road
RR#3,
Parry Sound
Ontario P2A 2W9
Tel: + 705 746 1372;
Toll free: 1 888 849 7668
E-mail: info@wildernessadventure.com
www.blackfeather.com

Greenland

Greenland is the largest island in the world, with 90 percent of the land covered by glaciers, and a human population of less than 100,000. The surrounding waters are home to more than eight species of whales as well as other high-latitude specialities such as Walrus, Polar Bears, Reindeer and Musk Oxen. Most locations can be reached by air from the settlement of Kangerlussuaqa at the head of Søndre Stromfjord with connecting flights to Copenhagen, Denmark, Reykjavík, Iceland and Ottawa, Canada.

Aasiaat

Located within the Arctic Circle, Aasiaat Kommune is a small community on the western coast of Greenland in the southern part of Disko Bay. The presence of a large prawn and crab factory ensures year-round access. There is an airport at the nearby town of Ilulissat. From the middle of June until the end of September, there are many whales around the Aasiaat coastline. You do not have to go out in a boat to see the whales as they come very close to the shore. If you do want to get up close to the whales, you have to sail out to sea. Fin Whales, Killer Whales, Minke Whales, Harbor Porpoises, Humpback and Bowhead Whales (sometimes referred to as Greenland Whales) are especially numerous in the Aasiaat waters. Narwhal and Beluga (October to May) are present only during winter when the water freezes over. Whale-watching tours are available from July to the end of September.

Nuuk

Whale-watching tours are available from this the capital of Greenland (June to October), primarily in search of Humpback and Minke Whales.

Uummannaq

Uummannaq is situated 370 miles (590 km) north of the Arctic Circle at 70° 40′ N and 58° 08′ W, in one of the most beautiful areas of Greenland. Whales are often encountered on boat trips to the little settlement Qaarsut.

Main Species: Fin, Minke, Killer, Humpback and Bowhead Whales.
Other Species Seen: Beluga, Narwhals and Harbor Porpoises.
Season: June–November.   **Code of Conduct:** Please check with local operators.

Information

Greenland Tourism

The National Tourist Board of Greenland

PO Box 1615

Hans Egedesvej 29

3900 Nuuk

Greenland

Tel: + 299 34 28 20

E-mail: info@greenland.com

www.greenland.com

Greenland Tourism

P.O. Box 1139

Strandgade 91

1010 København K

Denmark

Tel: + 45 32 83 38 80

E-mail: info@greenland.com

www.greenland.com

Aasiaat Tourist Service

Post Box 241

3950 Aasiaat

Greenland

Tel: + 299 89 25 40

E-mail: aasiaat.tourist@greennet.gl

www.greenland-guide.dk

Mexico

Mexico is a superb destination for cetacean enthusiasts. Best known for the shallow lagoons that serve as a nursery for Gray Whales, Mexico can offer a very diverse whale-watching experience. Blue Whales, together with several other whale and dolphin species, are relatively common in the Sea of Cortez (also known as the Gulf of California). A very rarely encountered endemic to the northern end of the Gulf of California is the Vaquita (*Phocoena sinus*), or "little cow" in Spanish. This tiny and poorly known porpoise is found only in the shallow lagoons at the mouth of the Colorado River. Known locally as "cochito", this mysterious porpoise hovers on the brink of extinction. Despite its extremely small and well-defined range, the exact size of the population has been very hard to gauge. Vaquita are believed to roam in small groups of five or less, and are extremely shy of boats. They are equally difficult to spot from shore in the murky and silt-laden waters. When surfacing to breathe, they barely disturb the water and may remain submerged for relatively long periods. Moreover, they have never been observed breaching. There is general agreement, however, that only a few hundred remain. In 1993, the Mexican government established the Upper Gulf of Mexico Biosphere Reserve specifically to protect this species and its habitat.

Despite these measures, animals are still killed on a regular basis by entrapment in legal gillnets set to catch totoabas, a large fish which spawns in the Colorado River delta, and by shrimp dredgers. Damming and removal of water from the Colorado River as it passes through the southern United States has almost certainly altered the marine ecosystem and presents yet another threat. To date, most live sightings have come from shallow water (less than 120 ft or 40 m) and within 16 miles (25 km) of the shore. It is thought that the species has specialized to eat fish and squid attracted to the river mouth. No reliable viewing sites are known but careful and prolonged searches in likely habitats might be successful. The shallow coastal waters of San Felipe (Baja California Norte) and El Golfo de Santa Clara (Sonora) are good places to start.

Baja California

Many regard the west coast of the long Baja California peninsula as one of the best whale-watching venues in the world and more than 20 species of cetaceans are encountered on a regular basis. From December to March, the Pacific (west) coast serves as the principal breeding ground for several thousand California Gray Whales, which come to mate and give birth in the warm lagoons and protected waters of the region. Gray Whales can often be seen from shore, but by taking a whale-watching cruise you can observe the animals up close. Three lagoons are particularly good. Scammon's Lagoon (Laguna Ojo de Liebre), located about 430 miles (692 km) south of the US-Mexico border; San Ignacio Lagoon, located about 525 miles (845 km) south of the border; and Magdalena Bay, located about 800 miles (1287 km) from the border. These lagoons are government-protected marine parks and whale watching is only allowed in small boats (called pangas) operated by trained guides. A short ride out into the lagoon allows visitors the chance to view Gray Whales at arm's length. Magdalena Bay has become increasingly popular as a whale-watching destination because of the proximity to international airports in La Paz and Loreto. It is also possible to drive from San Diego, just across the US border from Baja. It is worth remembering that away from the main tourist resort areas (e.g. Cabo San Lucas and Ensenada), the roads tend to be unpaved and bumpy, and distances between main attractions can be considerable. Although there are no large lagoons, smaller numbers of Gray Whales travel as far south as Cabo San Lucas and the East Cape where they are often spotted from shore or from sport-fishing boats. Humpbacks and Blue Whales breed in the Sea of Cortez (Bahia de los Angeles). In addition to whales, the waters surrounding the Baja Peninsula are outstandingly rich and beautiful: indeed Jacques Cousteau once labeled this "the world's aquarium" in recognition of the extraordinary diversity of marine life.

Scammon's Lagoon (Laguna Ojo de Liebre)

Destination for the largest number of Gray Whales, approximately 1500 (including newborn calves) every year. Present from mid December to March. Public access to the lagoon and the Gray Whale Natural Park can be reached by dirt road from the town of Guerrero Negro. The park is open only during whale-watching season and use of kayaks and private boats is prohibited at all times. Instead, several licensed tours operate from Guerrero Negro (season December 15 to April 15). The lagoon is named after Captain Charles M. Scammon, one of the founders of the Pacific coastal whaling industry which brought the Gray Whale to near-extinction in only 20 years. Thankfully those days are behind us and these critically important breeding lagoons are protected.

San Ignacio Lagoon

Located 90 miles (145 km) south of Guerrero Negro and some 45 miles (72 km) by dirt road off Highway 1, this remote lagoon is part of the Vizcaino Desert Reserve (UN Biosphere Reserve Program). Females with young calves prefer the shallower waters of the eastern side (average 15 ft / 5 m deep) but in the spring move to the western side frequented by non-breeding adults in anticipation of the migration north. Adult males leave in March and this is a good time of year to visit if you hope to interact with the inquisitive calves. The mothers are less protective of the calves and tolerate close approach by small pangas better. Private tours of the lagoon can be arranged with local fishermen or through the Baja Adventure Company based in La Paz, Mexico. Peak times to see Gray Whales in the lagoon are February to early April.

Magdalena Bay

Whale-watching excursions leave from a number of ports dotted along the coast of this 100 mile (160 km) long lagoon. Two of the most popular are Puerto Lopez Mateos and San Carlos, sleepy Mexican fishing villages less than two hours from Loreto (see below). The water is deeper off San Carlos and the whales tend to be more aerobatic. Excellent land-based viewing is possible from Punta Entrada, at the southern tip of Isla Magdelena, which forms the north end of the wide channel between Bahia Magdelena and the Pacific.

Sea of Cortez (Bahia de los Angeles)

The Sea of Cortez separates the Baja Peninsula from mainland Mexico and ranges from warm and temperate in the north, to tropical in the south This rich and diverse ecosystem is an ideal breeding ground, particularly for Blue and Fin Whales. Just east of La Unica lies the Canal de Los Baenes or Whale Canal. An impressive 23 species of cetaceans have been recorded here. Fin Whales are relatively numerous and are probably resident. These large and fast-moving whales can often be seen in the Canal de Ballenas and the Canal de Salsipuedes, as well as near Puerto Peñasco, Puerto Libertad, San Pedro Mártir, Turner Islands, Tiburón Island (southern tip), between San Pedro Nolasco Island and Guaymas and between La Paz Bay and Carmen Island. The colonial town of La Paz, on the southwest coast, is a main starting point for whale-watching trips to the Sea of Cortez.

Loreto Bay National Park (Parque Nacional Bahia De Loreto)

Located in the Gulf of California on the eastern side of the Baja California Peninsula. Three uninhabited and arid islands, Danzante, Carmen, and Monserrate, form the corners of the so-called "Blue Triangle", an important wintering and calving area for Blue Whales. Other species include Minke, Fin, Bryde's, Humpback and Sperm Whales. There are daily flights to the town of Loreto. The area is popular with sport fisherman, divers, kayakers and cruise ships and there is a rapidly growing whale-watching industry. The regulation of these activities have sparked a debate about the future prospects for the park and its wildlife. Guided camping and kayaking tours through the islands are available and often encounter Blue Whales.

Main Species: Gray, Fin and Blue Whales.

Other Species Seen: Humpback, Sperm, Bryde's, Minke and Killer Whales.

Season: December–April.   **Code of Conduct:** Guidelines in place. Swimming not permitted with whales.

Information

For information on cetacean research
in the Sea of Cortez contact:
Baja Adventure Company – Mexico Office
La Paz,
Baja California Sur
Mexico
Tel: + 52 612 124 6629
E-mail: diverdown@bajaecotours.com
www.bajaecotours.com

An informative website on Baja-California
can be found at www.baja-web.com

Baja Adventure Company – US Office
603 Seagaze Drive #732
Oceanside,
CA 92054
USA
Tel: + 1 760 721 8433;
Toll free: 877 560 2252
E-mail: info@bajaecotours.com
www.bajaecotours.com

Sea Quest Kayak Expeditions
PO Box 2424 Friday Harbor,
WA 98250
USA
Tel: + 1 360 378 5767
E-mail: orca@sea-quest-kayak.com
www.sea-quest-kayak.com

Mingan Island Cetacean Study
Research Station
378 Bord de la Mer
Longue-Pointe-de-Mingan,
Québec G0G 1V0
Canada
Tel: + 1 418 949-2845
E-mail: mics@globetrotter.net
www.rorqual.com

For information on traveling to Mexico:
Mexican Government Tourism Office
375 Park Avenue
Floor 19, Suite 1905
New York,
NY 10152
USA
Tel: + 212 308 2110;
Toll free: 1 800 44 63942
E-mail: newyork@visitmexico.com
www.visitmexico.com
Offices also in: Chicago, Coral Gables (Miami),
Houston and Los Angeles

Mexican Tourism Promotion Board
Wakefield House
41 Trinity Square,
London EC3N 4DJ
UK
Tel: + 0207 488 9392
E-mail: uk@visitmexico.com
www.visitmexico.com

Embassy of Mexico
1911 Pennsylvania Ave,
Washington, DC 20006
USA
Tel: + 1 202 728 1600
http://portal.sre.gob.mx/usa/

Mexican Embassy
to the United Kingdom
16 St George Street
Mayfair
London W1S 1LX
UK
tel +44 (0) 20 7499 8586
fax +44 (0) 20 7495 4035
email: mexuk@easynet.co.uk
http://www.embamex.co.uk/

Central America & the Caribbean

Top Spots

Bahamas – Atlantic Spotted Dolphins over the Great & Little Banks.

Dominican Republic – Swimming with Humpback Whales on the Silver Bank.

Dominica – Resident Sperm Whales and tropical dolphins feeding close to shore.

In terms of geography and politics, the Caribbean is a particularly fascinating region. The Greater Caribbean Sea is encircled by a ring of more than 7000 islands, reefs and keys belonging to 25 nations and territories. A long chain of islands, known collectively as the West Indies, runs from Bermuda in the north down to Trinidad & Tobago and separates the Caribbean from the North Atlantic. For convenience, the coast of Florida bordering the Gulf of Mexico is treated under the North American section. At least 30 species of cetaceans have been recorded in the Caribbean, reflecting a tremendous diversity of marine habitats. In addition to numerous shallow banks, coral reefs, mangrove swamps and so on, there are also deep oceanic valleys such as the Puerto Rico Trench (reaches a depth of 28,230 ft or 8600 m) and the Cayman Trench (25,220 ft or 7690 m) and these attract deep divers such as Dwarf Sperm Whales. As of 1999, commercial whale watching was available in 14 Caribbean countries and this number continues to grow. The Silver Bank in the Dominican Republic is perhaps the most famous whale-watching spot in the region, where the courageous can get in the crystal-clear water with Humpback Whales. Many other countries are beginning to develop their whale-watching and dolphin-swimming potentials.

Costa Rica and Panama

Both countries have extensive coastlines with both the Pacific Ocean and Caribbean Sea and are newly emerging as ecotourist destinations. One of the main areas for seeing breeding Humpback Whales off Panama is in the warm waters of the Coiba Island Marine Park on Panama's Pacific west coast. Another place is in the Gulf of Panama, 40 miles (65 km) west of Panama City. Costa Rica, to the north of Panama, enjoys one of the most biologically diverse ocean ecosystems in the world. Shallow warm waters lie on top of oxygen-rich cold water, creating the perfect ecosystem for a variety of marine life. The Marino Ballena is a National Park on Costa Rica's Pacific coast, where Humpbacks migrate from both the northern and southern hemispheres to breed.

Main Species: Humpback Whales, Bottlenose Dolphins, Spinner Dolphins, Spotted Dolphins, Short-Finned Pilot Whales, and in Panama: Sperm Whales.

Other Species Seen: Bryde's Whales, Sperm Whales, and tropical dolphins.

Season: All year.   **Code of Conduct:** Enforced regulations. Swimming not permitted.

Information

For further information on research in
Costa Rica contact:
Vidamarina Foundation
Postal address:
Interlink 827
7801 NW 37th Street
Miami, Florida 33166
Tel: Costa Rica: + 506 282-9284
E-mail: sierrra@vidamarian.org
www.vidamarina.org or
www.divinedolphin.com

For information on travel to Costa Rica
contact:
Instituto Costarricense de Turismo (ICT)
Apartado 777

1000 San José
Costa Rica
Tel: + 506 299 5800; Toll-free: 1-866 Costa Rica
E-mail: info@tourism-costarica.com
www.visitcostarica.com:

For information on travel to Panama contact:
Instituto Panameño de Turismo (Institute of
Tourism)
Apartado 4421, Zone 5
Centro de Convenciones ATLAPA
Vía Israel
Republic of Panamá
Tel: + 507 226 7000
E-mail: infotur@ns.ipat.gob.pa
www.visitpanama.com

The Bahamas

The Bahamas comprise an archipelago of more than 700 low-lying islands and cays located in the Atlantic Ocean just east of Florida and northwest of Cuba, of which only 24 are inhabited. The subtropical/tropical climate is maintained year-round by the proximity of the Gulf Stream. In the 1970s a friendly and accessible group of Atlantic Spotted Dolphins was discovered on Little Bahama Bank, which lies north of Grand Bahama Island, and prompted the first commercial whale-watching venture in the Caribbean region. The Atlantic Spotted Dolphins found in the Bahamas and along the southeastern coast of the United States are particularly large and heavily spotted. Today, several operators offer multi-day "swim-with-dolphins" excursions. One of the most popular areas for dolphin watching and swimming are the Bimini Islands (only 50 miles / 80 km from Miami, Florida). Here both Spotted and Bottlenose Dolphins are found closer to shore, making trips more attractive to visitors. Growth of this site has relieved some of the pressure on the dolphins around Grand Bahama. Both Atlantic Spotted Dolphins and Bottlenose Dolphins are essentially resident in the Bahamas but few trips are offered outside of summer (May-Sept) due to uncertain weather conditions. Hurricanes do occur on a regular basis between June and October and the associated windy conditions and swells can disrupt dolphin-watching schedules. Recent research has discovered a resident population of Dense-Beaked Whales in deep water to the north of the islands. Whale-watching boats operate from West End, Port Lucaya or Freeport on Grand Bahama Island, and from Alice Town, Bimini. Tourism provides a major part of the local economy and there is plenty of accommodation for visitors and regular flights from Miami and Fort Lauderdale.

Main Species: Atlantic Spotted Dolphins, Bottlenose Dolphins and Dense-Beaked Whales.

Other Species Seen: Humpback Whales, Sperm Whales and False Killer Whales.

Season: May–September.   **Code of Conduct:** Voluntary guidelines. Swimming with dolphins permitted.

Information

Bahamas Ministry of Tourism
PO Box N-3701, Nassau Bahamas
Tel: + 242 302 2000
E-mail: tourism@bahamas.com
www.bahamas.com

Wild Dolphin Project
PO Box 8436
Jupiter, FL 33468 USA
Tel: 561 575 5660   E-mail: wdp@igc.org
www.WildDolphinProject.com

Dominican Republic

The Silver Bank and surrounding waters are thought to be the most important breeding and calving area for Humpback Whales in the North Atlantic, with between 3000 and 5000 animals passing over the bank each season (December to the middle of April). Photo-identification studies have shown that these Humpbacks come from the Gulf of Maine, Newfoundland, Labrador, the Gulf of St Lawrence, Greenland and even Iceland, passing through key whale-watching sites such as Stellwagen Bank en route. Designated a marine sanctuary, the Silver Bank lies 62 miles (100 km) north of the Dominican Republic, a journey of 5–12 hours depending on your boat. The bank is in fact a limestone platform approximately 47 miles (75 km) across, and belongs to a series of reefs that extend from the Bahamas in the east, to the Navidad Bank closer to the main island of the Dominican Republic. The reefs and coral heads that fringe the bank provide the whales with some protection from the ocean swells. Humpbacks also winter in Samana Bay, which is more easily reached by visitors. Tours, especially those traveling as far out as the Silver Bank, often encounter other whale species including Sperm Whales, Pygmy Sperm Whales, False Killer Whales, Short-Finned Pilot Whales, Spinner Dolphins, Spotted Dolphins and Risso's Dolphins. The Dominican Republic is a 90-minute flight from Miami and there are several tour companies that offer day trips into Samana Bay (no swimming with the whales permitted in this part of the sanctuary), or multi–day cruises to the offshore banks departing from Puerto Plata. Offshore operators offer snorkeling encounters with the Humpback Whales from small inflatables, when the activity of the whales permits.

Main Species: Humpback Whales, Spinner Dolphins, Spotted Dolphins.

Other Species Seen: Sperm Whales, Pygmy Sperm Whales, False Killer Whales and Short-Finned Pilot Whales; Spinner, Spotted and Risso's Dolphins.

Season: December–mid April.   **Code of Conduct:** Enforced guidelines. Swimming not permitted in Samana Bay. Swimming permitted at Silver Bank with licensed operators.

Information

Ministry of Tourism
Apdo 497, Santo Domingo, Dominican Republic
Tel: + 806 221 4660   www.dominicana.com.do

Puerto Rico

From January to April it is possible to see Humpback Whales from headlands on the western side of the island, most notably the Punta Higuera Lighthouse near Rincón. Built on the top of a cliff, the lighthouse offers stunning views over the Mona Passage, which connects the Atlantic with the Caribbean. Sometimes Humpback Whales and Bottlenose Dolphins come right into the surf zone or just beyond it and are visible to the naked eye. Boat excursions in the passage regularly encounter Spinner Dolphins as well as Bottlenose Dolphins and Humpbacks. Sperm Whales and False Killer Whales have also been sighted.

Main Species: Humpback Whales and Bottlenose and Spinner Dolphins.

Other Species Seen: Sperm and False Killer Whale.

Season: January–April.   **Code of Conduct:** Marine Mammal Code of Conduct in place. Swimming not permitted.

Information

Puerto Rico Tourism

PO Box 902-3960, San Juan, Puerto Rico

Tel: + 787 721 2400: Toll free: 1800 866 7827   www.gotopuertorico.com

Dominica

The isle of Dominica (not to be confused with the Dominican Republic) is part of the Lesser Antilles and lies between the French islands of Guadeloupe and Martinique. This is considered one of the less touristy of the so-called Windward Islands in part because it lacks sandy beaches. The volcanic nature of the island, with steep drop-offs and crystal-clear water, has made Dominica very popular with sport divers. This is also a superb location for viewing Sperm Whales and a number of animals are present year round. Those with calves favor the protected western (lee) side of the island. The proximity to extremely deep water means that a number of toothed whales are also a possibility including Short-Finned Pilot Whales, Pygmy Sperm Whales, False Killer Whales, Dwarf Sperm Whales and Melon-Headed Whales. Mixed groups of Pantropical Spotted and Spinner Dolphins, sometimes numbering in the hundreds, are frequently encountered on whale-watching or dive trips. Migrant Humpback Whales pass the island in January and February. Organized excursions are run by the Anchorage Hotel & Dive Center in Roseau with scheduled trips (approx. 3.5 hours) every Wednesday and Sunday afternoon. Alternative days or times may be possible by prior arrangement. Typically the boats range up and down the western coast between the town of Salisbury and Scotts Head at the southern tip. Hydrophones are used to locate the Sperm Whales and offer visitors the chance to enjoy their fascinating vocalizations. Resident female Sperm Whales and attendant calves are joined by adult males between late November and the end of March, and this is generally considered the best season for whale watching. The southwestern tip of the island between Scotts Head and Pointe Michel has been designated a marine reserve. There are no direct international flights into Dominica, so you must travel to a gateway island (Antigua, Barbados, Guadeloupe, Martinique, Puerto Rico, St Lucia and St Martin) and then take a local carrier. It is also possible to travel by inter-island ferry.

Main Species: Sperm Whales, Short-Finned Pilot Whales, Pantropical Spotted Dolphins and Spinner Dolphins.

Other Species Seen: Humpback Whales, Bryde's Whales, Pygmy Sperm Whales, False Killer Whales, Dwarf Sperm Whales, Melon-Headed Whales, Killer Whales, Cuvier's Beaked Whales, Fraser's Dolphins, Bottlenose Dolphins and Risso's Dolphins.

Season: December–March.   **Code of Conduct:** Voluntary code of conduct. Swimming with dolphins permitted under controlled conditions.

Information

Anchorage Dive Center
PO Box 34
Roseau
The Commonwealth of Dominica
Tel: (767) 448-2638
FAX: (767) 448-5680
E-MAIL: anchorage@cwdom.dm

Division of Tourism
National Development Corporation
PO Box 293, Roseau
The Commonwealth of Dominica
Tel: (767)-448-2045   Fax: (767)-448-5840
E-mail: ndctourism@cwdom.dm
Web: http://www.dominica.dm

Other Caribbean Islands

The tropical waters surrounding many other Caribbean Islands host an excellent variety of whales and dolphins, both resident and migratory. Some of the best are Bermuda, the Turks and Caicos Islands, Guadeloupe, Martinique, St Lucia, St Vincent and the Grenadines, and Grenada. For the most part, whale-watching opportunities are limited. It is worth enquiring with local dive operators or checking out local boat owners to see what is on offer. Because many of the islands lie in very deep water it may be possible to find exciting deep-water species such as Sperm Whales within reach of shore by chartered fishing boat. Sperm and Humpback Whales often consist of mother-calf pairs. Commercial whale-watching is taking hold in Soufrière, a picturesque rural town on the southwest coast of St Lucia. Spinner and Pantropical Spotted Dolphins occur close to shore in Soufrière Bay with Sperm Whales, Short-Finned Pilot Whales and sometimes False Killer Whales occurring further out. Comparatively sheltered waters between St Lucia and Martinique are also productive and accessible as half-day trips (3–5 hours). Cetaceans are often seen from land, particularly lookouts along the coast between Castries and Gros Islet, including Pigeon Pointe. Anse Chastanet near Soufrière is worth trying.

Main Species: Sperm Whales, Humpback Whales (Dec–April), Spotted Dolphins, Spinner Dolphins, Risso's Dolphins.

Other Species Seen: Bryde's Whales, Pygmy Sperm Whales, False Killer Whales, Killer Whales, Short-Finned Pilot Whales, Fraser's Dolphins, Striped Dolphins, Bottlenose Dolphins.

Season: Year-round.   **Code of Conduct:** Please check with local operators. Bermuda allows swimming with dolphins under controlled conditions. The Turks and Caicos Islands has enforced regulations and swimming is not permitted. St Lucia has enforced regulations and swimming is not permitted. St Vincent has a voluntary code of conduct. Grenada has a voluntary code of conduct, which does not permit swimming.

Information

Bermuda Department of Tourism
PO Box HM465
Hamilton HM BX   Bermuda
Tel: + 441 292 0023
E-mail: travel@bermudatourism.com
www.bermudatourism.com

Turks & Caicos Islands Tourist Board
PO Box 128, Front Street, Grand Turk
Turks & Caicos Islands   British West Indies
Tel: + 649 946 2321
E-mail: tci.tourism@tciway.tc
www.turksandcaicostourism.com

Office du Tourisme
5 square de la Banque, 97166 Pointe-à-Pitre
Guadeloupe
Tel: + (590) 820930
E-mail: info@lesilesdeguadeloupe.com
www.lesilesdeguadeloupe.com

Martinique Tourist Office
Immeuble le Beaupré,
Pointe de Jaham
97233 Schoelcher
Martinique
Tel: + 596 616177
www.touristmartinique.com

St Lucia Tourist Board
PO Box 221, Sureline Building
Vide Boutielle, Castries
St Lucia
Tel: + 758 452 4094
E-mail: slutour@candw.lc   www.stlucia.org

St Lucia Whale & Dolphin Watching
Association (SLWDWA) can be found at
www.geocities.com/RainForest/Vines/1106/

Soufriere Marine Management
Association Inc.
3 Bay Street, P.O. Box 305
Soufriere
Saint Lucia
Tel: + 758 459 5500
Fax: + 758 459 7799
E-mail: smma@candw.lc   www.smma.org.lc

Ministry of Tourism and Culture (St Vincent)
PO Box 834, Kingstown
St Vincent
Tel: + 457 1502. Fax: 451 2425.
E-mail: tourism@caribsurf.com
www.svgtourism.com

Grenada Board of Tourism
PO Box 293, St George's
Grenada
Tel: + 473 440 2279
E-mail: gbt@caribsurf.com
www.grenadagrenadines.com

British Virgin Islands Tourist Board
PO Box 134, 2nd Floor
Akara Building, De Castro Street
Road Town, Tortola
British Virgin Islands
Tel: + 284 494 3134; Toll free: 800 835 8530
E-mail: bvitourb@surfbvi.com
www.bvitouristboard.com

South America & Antarctica

Top Spots

Amazonia – Freshwater dolphins in forested rivers of Peru and Brazil.

Argentina – Southern Right Whales and playful Dusky Dolphins off Península Valdés.

Chile – Blue Whales around Chiloé Island and Chilean Dolphins in the fjords and channels.

Antarctic Peninsula – Humpbacks and Antarctic Minke Whales feeding in a true wilderness.

Running almost directly north to south, the continent of South America encompasses a myriad of marine habitats, ranging from the warm waters of the equatorial tropics to the iceberg-strewn seas of Antarctica. With thousands of miles of coastal waters and the several giant river systems, South America is superb for marine mammals and boasts an unprecedented number of endemic or near-endemic porpoises and dolphins. Whale watchers visiting the region can also enjoy a large number of more widespread species, especially those typical of the tropics and southern oceans. Península Valdés in Patagonia is probably the top spot on the continent, and known throughout the world for the superb viewing of Southern Right Whales and Dusky Dolphins. Elsewhere in South America, organized whale watching is generally in its infancy but this is likely to change as numerous coastal communities realize the tourism potential and build on it. Several tourist lodges on the tributaries of the Amazon and Orinoco Rivers cater for people wanting to see freshwater dolphins amid the abundance of other rainforest wildlife. The southern cities of Ushuaia in Argentina and Puntas Arenas in Chile serve as embarkation points for most ship-based cruises to the Antarctic Peninsula and South Georgia. Whales and dolphins are regularly encountered on the crossings, especially in the convergence zones where waters of different temperatures meet. For the adventurous whale watcher, the rivers and fjords of some South American countries offer a unique challenge of seeing several, often secretive, dolphins and porpoises that are found nowhere else in the world.

The coastal waters and large rivers of South America are notable for the diversity of dolphins and porpoises. Several species are found nowhere else (endemic), whilst others are most easily seen in this region.

Peale's Dolphin (*Lagenorhynchus australis*): Restricted to cool inshore waters of southern South America, including the Falkland Islands. Traveling in small groups, they enter bays and canals and are often found around kelp beds.

Boto or **Amazon River Dolphin** (*Inia geoffrensis*): Found throughout the immense Amazon and Orinoco River basins in Brazil, Peru, Bolivia, and Venezuela, this is without doubt the most numerous and easily seen of the world's four species of "river dolphin". Expansion of blood vessels close to the surface of the skin gives older animals an appealing pinkish blush that tends to be strongest when animals have been energetic. There are three geographically isolated subspecies divided between the Orinoco (*I. g. humboldtiana*), Amazon (*I. g. geoffrensis*) and Madeira (*I. g. boliviensis*) river systems.

Franciscana (*Pontoporia blainvillei*): Also known as La Plata Dolphin, this is one of the rarest dolphins in South America and ranges from the Doce River in Brazil south to Península Valdés in Argentina. Franciscana are regularly seen in the Bay of San Blas near Buenos Aires, Argentina.

Tucuxi (*Sotalia fluviatilis*): Pronounced "toó-koo-shee", this medium-sized dolphin resembles a Bottlenose Dolphin and is found in major river systems (such as the Amazon and Orinoco) and coastal waters from Brazil north to Nicaragua in Central America.

Commerson's Dolphin (*Cephalorhynchus commersonii*): This spectacular black-and-white dolphin is found in shallow waters and river mouths around the tip of southern South America, including the Falkland Islands. Oddly, the only other known location for this species is the remote island of Kerguelen many thousands of miles away in the Indian Ocean. Within their range, Commerson's are often seen from shore.

Chilean or **Black Dolphin** (*Cephalorhynchus eutropia*): Poorly known, this species occurs along the coast of Chile (Valparaiso to Tierra del Fuego) preferring shallow and enclosed waters, such as rivers or bays.

Burmeister's Porpoise (*Phocoena spinipinnis*): Another poorly known species that inhabits shallow and temperate waters along the Pacific coasts from Paita Bay in Peru to Tierra del Fuego and then along the Atlantic coast to Sao Paulo, Brazil. These small, dark-grey porpoises are shy and generally difficult to observe, preferring to swim quickly away without disturbing the water's surface.

Spectacled Porpoise (*Phocoena dioptrica*): Although circumpolar in distribution, this distinctive but very poorly known porpoise appears to be most numerous around the southern tip of South America, especially in oceanic waters off Patagonia.

Colombia

Bordered by the Pacific and Caribbean, Colombia has considerable potential as a whale-watching destination. Bottlenose, Pantropical Spotted and Spinner Dolphins can be seen all year round as can Killer Whales, Sperm Whales and Bryde's Whales. On the Pacific Coast near Isla Gorgona, Humpback Whales (August to October) and occasionally Sperm Whales can be seen. Both Humpback Whales and Bottlenose Dolphins (June to November) occur in the Parque Nacional Natural Ensendada de Utria (Departmento de Chocó). Tours may be available from Cali, Buenaventura, Bahia, Juanchaco, Ladrilleros, Bahia Solano, El Valle or Chocó. Unfortunately, the Republic of Colombia has been plagued with bloody conflict brought on by the illegal drug trade and guerrilla insurgents. This has made tourism to remote parts of the country very dangerous for foreigners and presently many countries strongly advise against their citizens visiting the country, particularly the Chocó Region, the only Colombian department to have coastlines on both the Pacific and Caribbean sides of the country.

Main Species: Humpback Whales, Bottlenose, Pantropical Spotted, and Spinner Dolphins.

Other Species Seen: Bryde's Whales, Sperm Whales, Killer Whales.

Season: Year-round.　　**Code of Conduct:** Enforced regulations.

Information

Please contact the Embassy of Columbia:　www.colombiaemb.org

Brazil

The equatorial coastline of Brazil is influenced by the westward-flowing South Equatorial Current, which sweeps water across the Atlantic and then deflects southwards along the coastline of South America as the Brazil Current. Brazil offers a surprising range of whale- and dolphin-watching possibilities, with some 39 species recorded in Brazilian waters and river systems. In the austral winter and spring, Humpback Whales can be seen off Salvador in Bahia State and at the Abrolhos National Marine Park. During the same season, Southern Right Whales come close to shore along the coast of Santa Catarina State. Interest in whale watching has bolstered the economies of several coastal communities and the township of Imbituba, Santa Catarina, is generally recognized as Brazil's "Whale Capital". The Brazilian coastline has a long history of commercial whaling and records suggest upwards of 15,000 animals were taken in the years between 1770 and 1950. The industry effectively self-destructed when Southern Right Whales all but vanished from the Brazilian coast. Thankfully, with the end of whaling, they have returned in increasing numbers.

Abrolhos National Marine Park (Bahia State)

Not to be confused with the Australian islands of the same name, the Abrolhos archipelago and Abrolhos Bank are recognized as an important breeding and calving area for Humpback Whales. The bank itself represents an extension of the continental shelf and includes the southernmost coral reef in the western South Atlantic Ocean. The shelter provided by the Abrolhos archipelago is particularly important for mother-calf pairs. The Brazilian Humpback Whale Project (established in 1988) operates whale monitoring programs for ecovolunteers from Praia do Forte, an attractive fishing community about 50 miles (80 km) north of Salvador.

Imbituba and Garopaba (Santa Catarina State)

The southern state of Santa Catarina has a growing whale-watching industry based around the population of Southern Right Whales that arrive each June to escape the Antarctic winter. A whale sanctuary was created in 2000 and visitors can get superb views of the whales from tours using 33 ft (10 m) long inflatables.

Amazon River System

Tourist cruises along the Amazon River or its tributaries often report dolphins, either Boto (Amazon River Dolphin) or Tucuxi. A population of at least 140 Botos resides in the Mamiraua Wildlife Reserve situated on the Japura River. Boto favor turbid waters that attract fish. Schooner cruises of the Bay of Dolphins and Environmental Protection Area of Anhatomirim leaving from Florianopolis often sight Tucuxi.

National Marine Park of Fernando de Noronha

The Fernando de Noronha Archipelago and Rocas Atoll are the peaks of a large submarine volcano system that rises from the ocean floor some 13,000 ft (4000 m) below. The bay is closed to boat traffic and local Spinner Dolphins (total population around 1200 animals) can be watched from clifftop lookouts. Laguna – cooperative relationship between Bottlenose Dolphins and local fishermen can be watched from shore.

Main Species: Humpback Whales (July–Nov), Southern Right Whale, Boto, Tucuxi.

Other Species Seen: Bottlenose Dolphins.

Season: April–October.   **Code of Conduct:** Enforced regulations. Swimming not permitted.

Information

EMBRATUR – Instituto Brasileiro do Turismo
(Brazilian Tourist Institute)
SCN, Quadra 02, Bloco 'G',
70712-907 Brasília DF, Brazil
Tel: + 61 429 7704
E-mail: presedencia@embratur.org.br
www.embratur.gov.br

Brazilian Humpback Whale Project
National Marine Park of Abrolhos
Praia do Kitongo s/n, 45900-000
Caravelas, Bahia
Tel: + 55 73 2971320
ibj.caravelas@baleiajubarte.com.br
www.baleiajubarte.com.br

Argentina

Península Valdés, Patagonia (Chubut Province)

Jutting seawards from the rugged coastline of Patagonia, Península Valdés is rightly considered one of the world's top whale-watching spots. Southern Right Whales visit the shallow water from mid July through to November, with the best viewing in September and October. They are easiest to see in the sheltered water of the Golfó Nuevo on the southern side of the peninsula and Golfo San José on the northern side. Dusky Dolphins occur year round. Later in the season (December to March), the striking black-and-white Commerson's Dolphins congregate around Puerto Deseado along with smaller numbers of Peale's Dolphins. Killer Whales can be seen year-round, especially off Punta Norte on the northern side of the Peninsula, and are notorious for their habit of deliberately beaching themselves to catch unwary South American Sea Lion pups. In the austral winter the weather is often cold and remains so during the peak dolphin-watching season (December to March). Most of the peninsula itself is barren land with a few saltwater lakes. Day tours are available locally but many people take advantage of extended multi-day expeditions that begin in Buenos Aires or smaller towns such as Puerto Piramide, Puerto Madryn, Rawson or Trelew (all in Chubut province) or Puerto San Julián and Puerto Deseado (in Santa Cruz province) – see below. The Golfo San José marine park was created in 1974.

San Julián (Santa Cruz Province)

The small town of Puerto San Julián is located on a spit extending into the bay formed by Cabo Curioso (Curious Cape) and Punta Desengaño (Deception Point). This is a possible departure point for seeing Southern Right Whales and Killer Whales, Peale's, Commerson's, Franciscana and Dusky Dolphins and Burmeister's Porpoises.

Puerto Deseado (Santa Cruz Province)

This busy deep-sea fishing port is located 190 miles (300 km) south of the city of Comodoro Rivadavia and sits at the mouth of the Deseado River (Ria Deseado). The tiny Commerson's Dolphin is a local speciality and local operators run tours into the estuary mouth specifically to see this species. Kayak tours are also possible. The dolphins are curious and often closely approach small boats. The much larger Peale's Dolphin, another regional endemic, is also found in the area. The warmer summer months (December to March) are the best time to visit. Other pods of Commerson's Dolphins can be found near Río Gallegos and Puerto Santa Cruz. Rarely seen away from the coast, Commerson's Dolphins favor shallow waters of river mouths, bays, fjords, and estuaries. The entire area is superb for wildlife and organized Península Valdés tours often include a side trip down to Puerto Deseado.

Main Species: Southern Right Whales, Killer Whales, Dusky, Commerson's and Peale's Dolphins.

Other Species Seen: Franciscana Dolphins and Burmeister's Porpoises.

Season: Dolphins: December–March; Southern Right Whales: July–November; Killer Whales: All year.   **Code of Conduct:** Enforced regulations. Swimming not permitted.

Information

Fundación Cethus
Juan de Garay 2861 - Dpto. 3
(B1636AGK) Olivos Pcia. de Buenos Aires
Argentina
Tel: + 54 11 4799 3698
E-mail: cethus@warehouse.com.ar
www.cethus.org

Secretariat of Tourism
Tourist Information Center
Av. Santa Fe 883
(C1059ABC) Buenos Aires

Argentina
Tel: Toll free: 0800 555 0016
E-mail: info@turismo.gov.ar
www.turismo.gov.ar

Patagonia Wildlife
La Tierra, como solía ser S.A.
956 Libertad St. Local 15B
(C1012AAT) Buenos Aires
Argentina
Tel: + 54 (11) 5236 4164 / 65
www.patagonia-argentina.com

Falkland Islands

The Falkland Islands (a British Dependent Territory) lie in the southwestern Atlantic approximately 280 miles (450 km) from Tierra del Fuego, and are perched on the edge of the Patagonian continental shelf. The archipelago is made up of two main islands, East and West Falkland, with several hundred smaller islets. The oceanic climate is cool and dominated by westerly winds. To the south lies the Antarctic Convergence, where cool surface waters meet warmer surface waters from the north, creating an abundance of marine life including Antarctic

(*Euphausia sp.*) and lobster krill (*Munida gregaria*), which in turn attract an exciting selection of whales and dolphins including several of the South American specialities, notably Commerson's, Peale's, Spectacled, Dusky and Southern Right Whale Dolphins. Many cruise ships visit the islands on their way to or from South Georgia and the Antarctic Peninsula.

Main Species: Killer Whales, Commerson's Dolphins, Peale's Dolphins, and Dusky Dolphins.

Other Species Seen: Long-Finned Pilot Whales, Spectacled Porpoises, Southern Right Whale Dolphins.

Season: All year.   **Code of Conduct:** Please check with local operators.

Information

Falkland Islands Tourist Board
Shackleton House, Stanley,
Falkland Islands FIQQ 1ZZ

Tel: + (500) 22215
E-mail: tourism@horizon.co.fk
www.falklands.com

Chile

Both Chilean and Peale's Dolphins are caught for use as bait in the commercial swordfish and crab fisheries and this has had a severe impact on their populations. Fortunately, stiffer protection laws and changes in the fishing industry have reduced this unnecessary slaughter, although accidental by-catch in gillnets remains a major problem. The Gulf of Corcovado and the western coast of Chiloé Island are particularly good for cetaceans. Both Chilean and Peale's Dolphins occur in coastal waters but are generally very shy of boats. In 2003, researchers discovered that this area is also a major feeding and nursing ground for Blue Whales, possibly the distinct but poorly known "Pygmy" subspecies (*Balaenoptera musculus brevicauda*).
On Choros Island, there are on-going efforts to establish dolphin-watching out of the small community at Caleta Punta de Choros using local boat owners. This area is home to resident Bottlenose Dolphins with frequent sightings of Dusky Dolphins and 14 other species of cetacean occur in the general area.

Main Species: Sperm Whales, Pygmy Blue Whales, Dusky Dolphins, Peale's Dolphins, Chilean Dolphins.

Other Species Seen: Humpback Whales, Sei Whales, Killer Whales, Cuvier's Beaked Whales, Southern Right Whale Dolphins, Bottlenose Dolphins, Burmeister's Porpoises.

Season: Year-round.   **Code of Conduct:** Please check with local operators.

Information

Centre for Marine Mammals Research
Leviathan   www.leviathanchile.org

Chilean Tourism Promotion Corporation
Av. 11 de Septiembre 2353

Floor 15, Office 1501
Providencia, Santiago, Chile
Tel: + (56-2) 4310530
E-mail: cpt@cptchile.cl
www.visit-chile.org

Peru

The coastline of Peru is influenced by the Humboldt Current and the nutrient-rich water supports one of the largest anchovy, sardine and squid fisheries in the world. On the other side of the Andes, the major rivers host two species of river dolphin, the Boto or Amazon River Dolphin and the smaller Tucuxi. Both can be encountered on river cruises through some of the major national parks. More than 30 species of whales and dolphins have been recorded in the rich offshore waters of Peru, primarily because of the upwellings associated with the cold Humboldt Current. The variety is similar to neighbors Ecuador and Chile, and Peru has great but as yet untapped potential as a whale-watching destination. Unfortunately, in some coastal areas (Cerro Azul and Pucusana), dolphins continue to be hunted by fishermen for human consumption.

Amazon Region

Located in northern Peru, the Pacaya-Samiria National Reserve (Department of Loreto) is an excellent place to view both Boto (Amazon River Dolphin) and Tucuxi. Boto are distinctively colored, varying from a rosy blush to almost flamingo pink with a bulbous forehead and long, flexible snout. It is estimated that there are at least 700 within the reserve, making this one of the largest accessible populations. Mating occurs between late October and early November and the calves are born between May and July, coinciding with highest water levels. This allows the dolphins to access a greater area of flooded lowland, thus ensuring better feeding. The smaller and faster-moving Tucuxis are harder to spot but are often seen near Botos. Amazonian Manatees and Giant River Otters also occur in the rivers. The reserve is located 115 miles (180 km) from the Amazonian city of Iquitos near the juncture of the Marañón and Ucayali Rivers. There are a number of tourist lodges close to the reserve that organize tours in wooden riverboats. Most visitors choose the "dry season" between May and October when it rains less heavily and the flood waters subside, forcing the dolphins back into the more accessible channels.

Main Species: Boto (Amazon River Dolphin), Tucuxi.

Other Species Seen: Blue Whales, Long-Finned Pilot Whales, Bottlenose Dolphins, Dusky Dolphins.

Season: All year.   **Code of Conduct:** Please check with local operators.

Information

Comercializadora Electrónica de Turismo -
COMELTUR
Av. Casimiro Ulloa 333
San Antonio
Miraflores, Lima 18, Peru
Tel: + (511) 446 6981;
Toll free: 1 (305) GO2PERU (462-7378)
E-mail: info@go2peru.com www.go2peru.com

Mundo Azul,
Manuel A Fuentes 884 C,
Lima – San Isidro,
Peru
Tel: 0051-1-421 66 85
E-mail: mundoazul@terra.com.pe
www.peru.com/mundoazul

Ecuador

This welcoming country straddles the equator and combines the rarified air of the Andes, the rainforests of the Amazon basin and of course the unique wildlife of the Galapagos archipelago. Less often visited, the coast of the mainland offers excellent whale-watching prospects. Bottlenose, Pantropical Spotted and Spinner Dolphins can be seen all year round, with chances of Killer Whales, Sperm Whales and Bryde's Whales. Humpback Whales migrate along the coasts between June and September. Tours are available from the major cities of Guayaquil or Quito, or more locally in Machalilla National Park, Puerto Lopez and Salango.

Mainland

Local operators in the beach resort of Salinas offer offshore trips in traditional fishing boats known as pangas to view migrant Humpback Whales (June to September).

Galapagos Islands

The Galapagos archipelago consists of 19 islands and lies in the central Pacific around 600 miles (960 km) west of mainland Ecuador. Positioned at the confluence of five ocean currents, the individual islands experience subtly different water temperatures and weather conditions. The cold Humboldt (Peruvian) Current sweeping up the coast of South America from the Antarctic provides a strong cooling influence and this explains the abundance of marine life including true coldwater species such as penguins and fur seals. Strong upwellings bring nutrients to the surface, driving the marine food chain. At least 24 species of cetaceans have been recorded in and around the islands, some of which are likely to be seen from the small armada of boats that carry tourists between the different islands. Bottlenose Dolphins are the most likely but other possibilities include Humpback Whales, Bryde's Whales, Blue Whales, Sperm Whales, Cuvier's Beaked Whales, False Killer Whales, Killer Whales, Short-Finned Pilot Whales, Common Dolphins, Risso's Dolphins, Spotted Dolphins and Striped Dolphins.

Main Species: Bottlenose, Pantropical and Spinner Dolphins.

Other Species Seen: Killer Whales, Bryde's, Humpback and Sperm Whales.

Season: Dolphins, all year. Whales, June–September.   **Code of Conduct:** Voluntary code.

Information

For further information contact:
FEMM, Fundacion Ecuatoriana para el Estudio
Mamiferos Marinos
Velez 911 y 6 de Marzo
Ed Forum
5to. piso, Of. 5-16
PO Box 09 01 11905
Guayaquil
Ecuador

For information on traveling to Ecuador
contact
Ecuador Travel
Eloy Alfaro N32-300 Carlos Tobar
Quito
Ecuador
Tel: + (593 2) 2507 559
E-mail: info@vivecuador.com
www.vivecuador.com

Antarctica

The great frozen continent of Antarctica needs little introduction. The surrounding waters remain relatively pristine with an abundance of marine life. Massive upwellings of nutrient-rich water occur along the Antarctic Divergence (approximately 65° S), the southern boundary of the Atlantic Convergence Zone, and the resulting bloom of phytoplankton provides sustenance for immense numbers of Antarctic krill (*Euphausia superba*), which in turn feed millions of predatory fish, seabirds and of course cetaceans. Larger whales are relatively common during the summer months, ranging from Killer Whales and Antarctic Minke Whales to Humpbacks and Blue Whales. Southern Bottlenose and other beaked whales (Arnoux's, Gray's, Shepard's and Cuvier's) also occur along the edge of the shelf break as well as in deeper pelagic waters.

One of the highlights of sailing south of the Antarctic Convergence to either the Antarctic Peninsula or sub-Antarctic Islands such as South Georgia or South Shetland Islands is an encounter with the spectacular Hourglass Dolphin. With its harlequin-like black and white markings, this is one of the most spectacular cetaceans in the world. They often come in to play in the pressure waves produced by fast-moving ships, giving superb views. Well adapted for cold water, this is the only species of small dolphin to occur in the Antarctic waters from 45° S to 65° S on a regular basis.

The entire area around the continent of Antarctica has been declared an international whale sanctuary, but some nations continue to hunt Minke Whales under the guise of scientific investigation. Not surprisingly, most tourist visits occur during the Antarctic summer (late November to March). Although unlikely, there is always the possibility of glimpsing the hard-to-find Spectacled Porpoise or one of several beaked whales from a cruise or expedition ship sailing between Ushuaia and the Falkland Islands or Antarctic Peninsula.

The Peninsula, South Orkney and South Shetland Islands

For most of us the only way to witness the splendor of Antarctica and associated island groups is by joining a commercial cruise. During the short Antarctic summer (November–February), a small armada of ships makes the relatively short crossing from the southern tip of South America to the Antarctic Peninsula, often by way of South Georgia and/or the Falkland Islands. The trips range from the very comfortable to the super luxurious and needless to say, prices vary accordingly.

One of the most frequently visited spots is Andvord Bay, a sheltered and very scenic bay off the eastern edge of the Gerlache Strait. Framed by icy peaks and rimmed with a succession of glaciers, the bay provides feeding for Minke and Humpback Whales. Perhaps the best area is on the west side of the Antarctic Peninsula, along the route followed by most of the cruise ships.

Arriving from the north, via the South Shetlands, the cruise track usually crosses the Bransfield Strait (productive for whales on each side but fewer in the middle); Gerlache Strait (probably the best area, especially in shallower water on each side); and then in a series of channels and straits down as far as Lemaire Channel and Petermann Island, the southernmost point reached by most of the regular ships. Recommended areas are Andvord Bay and Neko Harbour; Paradise Harbour; Errera Channel and Cuverville Island; Neumayer Channel and Port Lockroy; and finally Lemaire Channel and to the south of it, Penola Strait as far as the Argentine Islands. Species to be seen (late November-late February) are mostly Humpback Whales and Antarctic Minke Whales, with less regular Killer Whales. One remarkable early January trip logged 202 cetaceans (128 Humpbacks, 58 Antarctic Minkes and 16 Killer Whales) in 8 hours sailing between Port Lockroy and the Bransfield Strait. The waters around the South Shetland Islands can be good for Humpbacks and Antarctic Minke Whales, with occasional Fin Whales and small pods of Killer Whales. Humpbacks and Minke Whales are seen regularly at popular cruise ship destinations such as outside Deception Island, around Snow and Smith Islands and along the southern side of Livingstone and King George Islands. The channels and islands between these spots can also be productive – Aitcho Islands, Half Moon Island, and Nelson Island.

At the northern end of the Peninsula, the Antarctic Sound, which connects the Bransfield Strait and the Weddell Sea, is often good for Humpbacks and Minkes, with regular sightings of Killer Whales. Fewer ships go through here as it often contains a lot of ice. A small number of ships (including the *Professor Molchanov,* on its annual repositioning trip from Ushuaia back to its base in Holland, and the *Clipper Adventurer*) – enter the Weddell Sea and travel as far south as Vega Island through the Erebus and Terror Gulf. This can be very good with plenty of Minke Whales, Humpback Whales and Killer Whales, and occasionally Fins, between Vega Island and Paulet Island, with more to the north around the (aptly named) Danger Islands.

Main Species: Humpback Whales, Blue Whales, Minke Whales, Killer Whales, Long-Finned Pilot Whales and Hourglass Dolphins.

Other Species Seen: Fin Whales, Sei Whales, Southern Bottlenose Whales, Cuvier's Beaked Whales, Gray's Beaked Whales.

Season: Late November–March.   **Code of Conduct:** Enforced regulations.

Information

For information on companies organizing tours to Antarctica contact:

International Association of Antarctica Tour Operators
PO Box 2178
Basalt
CO 81621
USA
Tel: + (970) 704 1047
E-mail: iaato@iaato.org
www.iaato.org:8181/iaato/directory/

British Antarctic Survey
High Cross, Madingley Road
Cambridge
CB3 0ET
United Kingdom
Tel: +44 (0)1223 221400
Fax: +44 (0)1223 362616
www.antarctica.ac.uk/

A website with news and information on Antarctica is located at:
www.70south.com

Europe & Scandinavia

Top Spots

Iceland – A wide range of species at Húsavík in the northeast;
Blue Whales and White-Beaked Dolphins in the west.

Norway – Sperm Whales in summer and feeding Killer Whales in winter.

Scotland – Feeding Minke Whales in the Inner Hebrides and Bottlenose
Dolphins in the Moray Firth.

Bay of Biscay – Beaked Whales along the continental shelf edge.

Azores – Pilot Whales, Sperm Whales and a wide variety of dolphins
all year round.

Italy – Fin Whales and Striped Dolphins and more in the Ligurian Sea.

Northwestern Europe is warmed by the remnants of the Gulf Stream, a great current
that sweeps across the North Atlantic from the Caribbean. The constant mixing of warm water
from the Atlantic and cold water traveling south from the polar region supports a diverse and
abundant marine fauna and this of course includes a host of whales and dolphins. The most
familiar are Bottlenose Dolphins and Harbor Porpoises, which occur along many coasts with
notable concentrations in sheltered bays and large estuaries. Often both can be seen from
shore, but it is generally more fun to see them up close from a small boat and this is offered
in tens, if not hundreds, of harbor towns from Iceland to Greece. As elsewhere in the world,
the edge of the continental shelf, just where it begins to drop to the abyssal plain, is especially
good for whales and open ocean (pelagic) dolphins, with a wide variety of species possible.

For many enthusiasts, their first exposure to the mysterious world of beaked whales and
pelagic dolphins comes from a trip on the large commercial ferry that crosses the Bay of Biscay
en route between Portsmouth, England and Bilbao, Spain. These trips are so successful from
a whale-watching standpoint that a miniature industry of guided tours has sprung up and the
best viewpoints on the ship can be crowded with anxious whale and seabird enthusiasts armed
with binoculars and telescopes. The waters off southwest Ireland are less well explored than the
Bay of Biscay but offer similar potential. The adventurous may consider a winter trip to northern
Norway, where groups of Killer Whales congregate to feed on spawning herring, or travel in
summer to the west coast of Iceland, arguably the most reliable place in Europe to see Blue
Whales.

For those preferring warmer climes, the mid-Atlantic islands, notably the Azores and the
Canary Islands, and the azure-blue waters of the Mediterranean make for superb destinations.
Recent surveys have shown that significant populations of Fin, Sperm and Cuvier's Beaked
Whales occur in several regions of the Mediterranean, especially around a permanent upwelling
zone in the Ligurian Sea; a triangular deepwater area between Sardinia and the coasts of
mainland France, Monaco and Italy. The tremendous whale-watching potential of this heavily

traveled stretch of ocean is recognized by all three countries with the creation of the Pelagos Sanctuary for Mediterranean Marine Mammals. The Strait of Gibraltar, the meeting point of the North Atlantic and Mediterranean, also enjoys a well-deserved reputation for superb whale-watching opportunities, in particular large numbers of dolphins.

Iceland

Situated in the North Atlantic close to the Arctic Circle but warmed by the Gulf Stream, Iceland offers some of the best whale and dolphin watching in Europe. A variety of species can be seen from May to September, although June to August is the most optimal period in terms of weather and numbers of species. White-Beaked Dolphins are a regional specialty and are seen on most of the day trips out of Kéflavík and other harbors on the Reykjanes Peninsula. Occasionally, large groups of White-Beaked Dolphins are seen in the fjords and bays, but more often this fast-moving dolphin is found in small groups. Humpbacks and Fin Whales occur in early summer. An astonishing number of Killer Whales occur in Icelandic waters and are seen most frequently in the rich herring grounds off the East Fjords, and along the southern and western coasts. During the summer they enter inlets and bays but move further offshore during the winter. Equally impressive are the 700 to 1000 Blue Whales that migrate into Icelandic waters during the summer, particularly off the Snæfellsnes Peninsula in western Iceland, making this the most reliable place in Europe to see these magnificent creatures. Visits to deeper water off western Iceland may also produce Sei Whales and bull Sperm Whales. In coastal waters, Minke Whales and Harbor Porpoises occur year round. Further offshore, Northern Bottlenose Whales and large groups of Atlantic White-Sided Dolphins are regularly encountered.

Despite the Icelandic government's continuing interest in commercial whaling, watching whales has become extremely popular with the public. By 2002, more than 62,000 people took whale-watching trips from Icelandic ports, including many tourists from outside the country. In keeping with the northerly latitude, the climate is often cold and damp with intermittent rain and rough seas. Tours are available from Húsavík, Hofn, Dalvík, Hauganes, Stykkishólmur, Kéflavík, Grindavík, Arnarstapi or Olafsvík. The waters around the Westman Islands (Vestmannaeyjar) off southwest Iceland hold a large population of Killer Whales and various dolphins, which are often encountered by boat tours visiting the enormous seabird colonies, dramatic coastlines and sea caves that make these islands famous.

Húsavík

This northerly fishing village is located on the shores of Skjálfandi Bay, about an hour's drive from Akureyri, the principal town in northern Iceland. One of the main attractions is the highly acclaimed Húsavík Whale Centre, Iceland's only dedicated whale museum and one of the best of its kind. Situated only 25 miles (40 km) from the Arctic Circle, Húsavík enjoys 24 hours of daylight during the summer and midnight whale-watching cruises are offered in mid July. A number of guided whale-watching tours operate from the harbor, many using traditional oak fishing-boats. Whale-watching cruises depart within steps of the harbor-front center. Tours are also available from Dalvík and Hauganes.

Snæfellsnes Peninsula

The towns of Stykkísholmur and Ólafsvík offer the best Blue Whale watching in Europe, plus chances of seeing Humpback and Minke Whales, White-Beaked Dolphins and Harbor Porpoises. In clear weather visitors will be rewarded with spectacular views of the Snæfellsjökull glacier. Inshore species such as Minke and occasionally Killer Whales can be seen from shore at various spots along the Snæfellsnes Peninsula.

Keflavík Area

Kéflavík Harbor is located 30 miles (50 km) west of Reykjavík and close to the main international airport. Most half- and full-day trips encounter White-Beaked Dolphins, particularly in August and September, as well as Minke Whales. Tours are also available from Reykjavík harbor or Grindavik on the southern side of the Reykjanes Peninsula.

Main Species: Blue, Fin, Humpback, Minke, Pilot and Killer Whales, White-Beaked Dolphins.

Other Species Seen: Atlantic White-Sided Dolphins, Harbor Porpoises, Northern Bottlenose Whales, Sei and Sperm Whales.

Season: April–October.   **Code of Conduct:** Voluntary guidelines issued by the Húsavík Whale Center.

Information

Húsavík Whale Center
PO Box 172
640 Húsavík, Iceland
Tel: +354 464-2522 or +354 464-2520
E-mail: icewhale@centrum.is
www.icewhale.is

Icelandic Tourist Board
Lækjargata 3
101 Reykjavík, Iceland
Tel.: +354-535-5500
E-mail: info@icetourist.is
www.visiticeland.com

Faroe Islands

Warmed by the Gulf Stream, the Faroe Islands lie northwest of Scotland and halfway between Iceland and Norway. Considering the high latitude, the winter temperatures are very moderate and the harbors never freeze. Local mixing of cold Arctic currents with the warmer Gulf Stream results in a particularly rich marine environment, which attracts cetaceans including Minke Whales, Long-Finned Pilot Whales, Atlantic White-Sided Dolphins and White-Beaked Dolphins. June through to August seem to be the best months. Cruise ships sailing between the British Isles and Svalbard or Iceland pass through Faroese waters and have logged Sperm, Fin, Blue and Northern Bottlenose Whales. The attractiveness of the islands for viewing wildlife is marred by the continuing "grind" or Pilot Whale hunt, in which hundreds of Long-Finned Pilot Whales and small numbers of Bottlenose and Atlantic White-Sided Dolphins and occasionally Northern Bottlenose Whales are herded to shore and slaughtered. Some whale-watchers prefer not to visit the islands for this reason while others believe that increased revenue from watching whales will eventually lead to an end of the hunt.

Main Species: Fin, Minke and Long-Finned Pilot Whales, Atlantic White-Sided Dolphins & White-Beaked Dolphins.

Other Species Seen: Sperm, Fin, Blue and Northern Bottlenose Whales.

Season: Late June–August.   **Code of Conduct:** Please check with local operators.

Information

For further information on travel to the Faroe Islands contact:

Faroe Islands Tourist Board
undir Bryggiubakka 17
PO Box 118 FO-110 Tórshavn, Faroe Islands
Tel: + 298 355 800
E-mail: tourist@tourist.fo
www.visit-faroeisland.com

Prime Minister's Office
Tinganes
PO Box 64
FO-110 Torshavn
Faroe Islands
www.tinganes.fo

Norway

Norway's rugged coastline, indented with many deepwater fjords, offers superb opportunities to see Sperm Whales and Killer Whales relatively close to shore. An estimated 5000 Sperm Whales spend all or part of the year in Norwegian waters, and are most easily found during the summer months (late May to September). In the autumn (October and November), large numbers of Killer Whales move into sheltered inlets, such as Tysfjord, to feast on the immense shoals of Atlantic herring (*Clupea harengus*). Whale-watching tours are available from the towns of Andenes, Nysund, Myre, Sto and Storjord.

Andenes and the Lofoten Islands

This harbor town lies at the tip of Andøya Island in northern Norway, 190 miles (300 km) north of the Arctic Circle, and is well known for its nearby population of Sperm Whales. The majority are mature males, which feed along a submarine canyon that cuts into the continental shelf. The canyon comes within a few miles of shore and is within easy reach by boats. Limited by the weather and sea conditions, the whale-watching season lasts from May to September. The Andenes Whale Center is located in an old fish-processing building, near the lighthouse. Accessible by bus and train, Andenes also has an airport (Andø) with daily flights to Tromsø, Bodø and Narvík.

Tysfjord

Every October immense shoals of Atlantic herring migrate into Vestfjord and adjoining fjords in the Lofoten area to spend the winter and are followed by an estimated 600–700 Killer Whales. The small town of Tysfjord serves as the main base for visitors wanting to encounter these spectacular animals at close hand. Although the Killer Whales can be seen from land, most visitors take an invigorating 1 to 2 hour boat ride onto the relatively placid waters of the open fjord. The Killer Whales are generally encountered in small groups ranging from 10–12 individuals but occasionally there are larger gatherings of 100–150 animals – a spectacular sight when you are in a tiny Zodiac. The Killer Whales often feed by rounding up the schools of herring into tight balls, which are then stunned by underwater swipes with their powerful tails. Snow-capped mountains tower over the fjords, and on clear nights visitors may be treated to a display of the Northern Lights. Tysfjord is an hour and a half from Narvík. Many visitors stay at the Tysfjord Turistsenter, an attractive hotel complex from which several tour operators offer pick-ups for clients.

Svalbard

Despite the proximity to the North Pole, the Svalbard (or Spitzbergen) archipelago has a relatively mild climate compared to other areas at the same latitude. During the summer several species of whales and dolphins can be encountered in ice-free water, mainly around the southern and western islands. Belugas are one of the most numerous cetaceans and can be seen from shore. In addition to cetaceans, visitors will encounter ringed, bearded and harbor seals and with luck may also find walrus (Moffen Island) and polar bears. Several specialist companies offer wildlife tours through the islands on expedition ships, using inflatable Zodiacs to explore near-shore waters and make landings. Visitors to the administrative capital Longyearbyen can look for Belugas at the mouth of the Adventdalen River or if ice conditions permit, along the coast near the airport. Likewise on Sveagruva, Belugas sometimes feed off the spit south of the airport. The archipelago can be reached by plane from Oslo (3 hours) and Tromsø (1.5 hours).

Main Species: Sperm, Beluga and Killer Whales.

Other Species Seen: Harbor Porpoises, Minke Whales.

Season: May–January. **Code of Conduct:** Voluntary code of conduct. Swimming with Killer Whales permitted in controlled conditions.

Information

The Andenes Whale Centre
PO Box 58,
8483 Andenes,
Norway
Tel: + 47 76 11 56 00
E-mail: post@whalesafari.no
www.whalesafari.no

Lofot-Akvariet
Storvågan, 8310 Kabelvåg,
Norway
Tel: + 47 76 07 86 65
E-mail: post@lofotakvariet.no
www.lofotakvariet.no

Andøy Touristinformation
Hamnegata 1c, Fyrvika
N-8483 Andenes,
Norway
Tel: + 47 76 14 18 10
E-mail: post@andoyturist.no
www.andoyturist.no

Innovation Norway
Postboks 448, Sentrum 0104
Oslo, Norway
Tel: + 47 22 00 25 00
E-mail: post@invanor.no
www.visitnorway.com

Russia

A number of expedition companies offer tours to the remote archipelagos and peninsulas of northern Russia (Franz Josef Land, Novaya Zemlya, Serenya Zemlya and the Taimyr Peninsula) using icebreakers. A variety of marine mammals can be seen during these trips including the occasional Narwhal, Beluga and Bowhead Whales.

Solovetskiy Islands

Located in the White Sea, the islands are known for a monastery that was used as a prison during the Soviet era. The islands have become a reliable place to see Belugas during the summer when mothers bring their calves close to shore. A joint Finnish-Russian venture runs a number of tours to search for Belugas.

Main Species: Narwhal, Beluga and Bowhead Whales.

Season: May–September.　　**Code of Conduct:** Please check with local operators.

Information

For more information on trips to the Solovetskiy Islands contact:

Kon-Tiki Tours
Riitankuja 1-3 G 58
00840 Helsinki
Finland
Tel: + 358 (0) 9621 2525
E-mail: kontiki@kontiki.fi
www.kontiki.fi

Lukomorie Travel Company
Petrozavodsk 185030
Republic of Karelia
Russia
Tel: + 7 (8142) 5724 29, 7850 33
E-mail: lukomorie@onego.ru
www.lukomorie.ru/english

For further information on traveling to the Russian Federation contact:

Intourist Ltd.
7 Wellington Terrace, Notting Hill
London W2 4LW

United Kingdom
Tel: + 44 (0)20 7727 4100
E-mail: info@intourist.co.uk
www.intouristuk.com

Russian National Tourist Office
130 West 42nd Street
Suite 1804, New York, NY 10036
USA
Tel: (877) 221-7120
or (212) 575-3431
E-mail: info@rnto.org
www.russia-travel.com

For information on volunteer programmes to the White Sea (Belugas) contact:

Ecovolunteer Program
Meyersweg 29,
7553 AX Hengelo
Netherlands
Tel: + 31 74 2508250
Fax: + 31 74 2506572
E-mail: info@ecovolunteer.com
www.ecovolunteer.org.uk

Denmark / Germany

The shallow waters of the southern North Sea (referred to as the Wadden Sea) were inundated following the retreat of the glaciers at the end of the last Ice Age. A number of sandy islands emerge from the shallow water and areas of rocky bottom with boulders provide excellent habitat for fish. Unfortunately, continuous land reclamation efforts including draining of coastal marshes has led to significant declines in the local herring population, which once attracted numbers of Bottlenose Dolphins. The area remains a very important calving and nursery area for Harbor Porpoises and the population is estimated to comprise more than 4500 animals. In 1999, the North German state of Schleswig-Holstein designated the waters around the islands of Sylt and Amrum as a cetacean sanctuary to limit disturbance. Porpoises are often seen from shore (particularly on the rising tide) or from the inter-island ferries. The largest numbers occur between the Amrum Bank and Horns Reef. Good viewing locations are from beaches on the islands of Sylt (Germany), Amrum (Germany) and Rømø (Denmark). The sandy islands also attract gray and harbor seals. Increasing numbers of Porpoises, Bottlenose and Common Dolphins have been reported from the Southern North Sea, perhaps reflecting rising sea temperatures.

Main Species: Harbor Porpoise.
Other Species Seen: Minke Whale, Bottlenose Dolphins.

Season: May–September. **Code of Conduct:** Please check with local operators.

Information

Danish Tourist Board
Islands Brygge 43, 3. sal
DK-2300 Copenhagen S
Denmark
Tel: + 45 3288 9900.
E-mail: dt@dt.dk
www.visitdenmark.com

German National Tourist Board
Beethovenstrasse 69
60325 Frankfurt am Main
Germany
Tel: + 49 69 974 640
E-mail: info@d-z-t.com
www.germany-tourism.de

Scotland

The west coast of Scotland is deeply indented with sea lochs, reminiscent of the Norwegian fjords, and sheltered from the full force of the open Atlantic by numerous islands including the wild and very beautiful Outer and Inner Hebrides. Some 22 species of whales and dolphins have been sighted off the coast, with Minke Whales and Harbor Porpoises the most regular. In the spring, Minke Whales return from more southerly breeding grounds to spend the summer feeding in Scottish waters, notably off the west coast in the waters of the Inner Hebrides. They are often seen lunging at the water surface with mouth open to scoop up shoals of fish. Harbor Porpoises are abundant year round off the west coast and can often be seen from land or inter-island ferries. Bottlenose Dolphins tend to appear in summer and may be repeatedly seen around one island or another for a week or two before moving to another spot. In some areas, like the Sound of Barra, sightings are more predictable. The north coast of Scotland is more rugged and the sea less sheltered. Boat-based tours from Scarfskerry near Thurso and John O' Groats near Wick, regularly encounter White-Beaked Dolphins, Minke Whales and Harbor Porpoises. Headlands and other lookouts can often be excellent for land-based viewing. The Scottish east coast is less convoluted than the west, but includes some excellent places to see cetaceans.

While there are a variety of companies offering day or week long whale- / wildlife-watching trips, there are also many places to watch from land. These include: Chanonry Lighthouse and North Kessock in the Moray Firth (for Bottlenose Dolphins); Ardnamurchan Lighthouse (Harbor Porpoises and Minke Whales), Greenstone Point, Ross-shire (April to Dec, Harbor Porpoises, dolphins and Minke Whales); Eye Peninsula, Isle of Lewis (Risso's and White-Beaked Dolphins, Harbor Porpoises and Minke Whales); Loch Indaal, Islay (Bottlenose Dolphins); Sumburgh Head, Shetland (Harbor Porpoises, Risso's and White-Beaked Dolphins, Minke Whales, Killer Whales and very occasionally Humpback Whales).

Moray Firth and East Coast

One of the most important areas in Scotland for viewing whales, dolphins and porpoises. Bottlenose Dolphins are the highlight with a local population of 130 individuals being relatively easy to see in most months of the year and particularly summer. It's the most northerly known resident population in the world and the only remaining population in the North Sea. Risso's and White-Beaked Dolphins are also occasionally spotted from headlands. Minke Whales appear in the Firth during the late summer and autumn. A number of locations provide excellent shore-based viewing of the dolphins, including Chanonry Point and Fort George in the Moray Firth and the headlands at the mouth of the Cromarty Firth. Headlands along the southern shores of the Moray Firth between Burghead and Fraserburgh also offer opportunities to watch Bottlenose Dolphins and Harbor Porpoises. Dolphins are often visible from the Dolphin and Seal Centre at North Kessock near Inverness at the mouth of the Beauly Firth (best late May to September). The Whale and Dolphin Conservation Society's (WDCS) Wildlife Centre is located in Spey Bay and hosts regular exhibitions and initiatives to promote awareness of the Moray Firth dolphins and their habitat. During the summer, short dolphin-watching tours are available from a number of ports and harbors along the coast including Portmahomack, Cromarty, Inverness, Nairn, Lossiemouth and Buckie. In recent years, the Bottlenose Dolphins appear to have expanded their range and can now be seen along the coast of eastern Scotland as far south as the Firth of Forth. Aberdeen Harbour mouth and nearby headlands can be good shore watching spots for Bottlenose Dolphins and occasionally White-Beaked Dolphins.

Inner and Outer Hebrides

An area to the west of the Isle of Mull, including the Treshnish Isles, the Islands of Coll and Tiree, and the Ardnamurchan Peninsula on the mainland, is one of the most reliable spots for Minke Whales in Britain. Whale-watching trips go out daily from the towns of Oban and Tobermory, on the Isle of Mull. Trips from Gairloch mainly see Harbor Porpoises, but Minke

Whales, Common and White-Beaked Dolphins are occasionally sighted. Whales and dolphins are often seen from ferries crossing the Minch (Hebridean Sea) to the Outer Hebrides. Highlights include sightings of White-Beaked and Risso's Dolphins, the latter favoring waters off the Eye Peninsula just north of Stornoway Harbor on Lewis. Regularly occurring species include Minke Whales, Bottlenose Dolphins, Risso's Dolphins and Harbor Porpoises. Longer trips that reach deeper water have the potential to encounter Humpback Whales, Northern Bottlenose Whales, Pilot Whales, Sei Whales, Sperm Whales, Atlantic White-Sided Dolphins, Common Dolphins, Striped Dolphins and Killer Whales. Trips are also available out of Stornoway and Uig on the Isle of Lewis in the summer months.

Firth of Clyde

The Firth of Clyde just west of Glasgow supports a reasonably large population of Harbor Porpoises. A good spot to look for them is the Cloch Lighthouse at Gourock. Harbor Porpoises are also sighted almost daily from the ferry between McInroy's Point in Gourock and Hunter's Quay in Dunoon.

Main Species: Bottlenose, Risso's and White-Beaked Dolphins, Minke Whales and Harbor Porpoises.

Other Species Seen: Humpback Whales, Northern Bottlenose Whales, Pilot Whales, Sei Whales, Sperm Whales; Atlantic White-Sided Dolphins, Common Dolphins, Striped Dolphins and Killer Whales.

Season: Moray Firth: all year. West Coast: May–September.

Code of Conduct: Voluntary guidelines. Swimming not permitted.

Information

WDCS –
The Whale and Dolphin Conservation Society
Brookfield House, 38 St Paul Street
Chippenham, Wiltshire SN15 1LY
United Kingdom
Tel: + 44 (0)1249 449500
E-mail: info@wdcs.org   www.wdcs.org

Sea Watch Foundation
11 Jersey Road, Oxford 0X4 4RT
United Kingdom
Tel: + 44 (0)1865 717276
E-mail: info@seawatchfoundation.org.uk
www.seawatchfoundation.org.uk

HWDT – Hebridean Whale and Dolphin Trust
28 Main Street
Tobermory, Isle of Mull PA75 6NU

United Kingdom
Tel: + 44 (0)1688 302620
E-mail: info@hwdt.org
www.hwdt.org

Friends of the Moray Firth Dolphins
4 Craigview, Findochty, Banffshire AB56 4QF.
United Kingdom
Tel: + 44 (0)1542 833867
E-mail: dolphinpete@tiscali.co.uk
www.loupers.com

SMWOA – Scottish Marine Wildlife
Operators Association
Kylerhea, Isle of Skye IV42 8NH
United Kingdom
E-mail: info@merger.demon.co.uk/smwoa
www.merger.demon.co.uk/smwoa

Dolphins and Seals of the Moray Firth
Tourist Information Centre Grounds
North Kessock,
Ross & Cromarty IV1 1XB
United Kingdom
Tel: + 44 (0)1463 731866
www.highland.gov.uk/educ/publicservices/
visitorcentres/dolphins.htm

For tourist information contact:
VisitScotland
23 Ravelston Terrace, Edinburgh EH4 3EU
United Kingdom
Tel: UK 0845 22 55 121;
from outside the UK + 44 (0) 1506 832121
E-mail: info@visitscotland.com
www.visitscotland.com

Wales

The Welsh coast offers opportunities to watch whales and dolphins from both the shore and on boat trips. Bottlenose Dolphins are resident in Cardigan Bay and offer the most reliable whale watching. Shore sightings are perfectly possible and boat trips leave from coastal ports, notably New Quay (Cei Newydd). These are short trips of half a day or so. Harbor Porpoises are also frequently seen, particularly off headlands with strong tidal flows. It's also possible to see other species including Common and Risso's Dolphins and occasionally Minke Whales.

Cardigan Bay

It is estimated that upwards of 130 Bottlenose Dolphins regularly use Cardigan Bay (Ceredigion's Bay) and this is also an important area for Harbor Porpoises. The dolphins can be seen from almost anywhere along the length of the bay between Cardigan to the mouth of the Dyfi Estuary (e.g. Penbryn Beach, Mwnt, Ynys Lochtyn near Llangrannog and Aberporth). One of the most popular viewpoints is New Quay. A crowd of people gathered on the quayside is often a sign that the dolphins are feeding around a reef not far from the harbor wall. The New Quay lookout, a renovated coastguard's hut overlooking Bird Rock, is also a good spot to try. Spring and summer (April to September) offer the calmest sea conditions and the animals are easier to spot. Organized boat trips depart from a number of coastal towns, including New Quay, Aberaeron and Aberystwyth. Harbor Porpoise are most likely around Strumble Head, Skomer, Ramsey, Skokholm, St Davids Head and Bardsey Island. Deeper water attracts other cetaceans including Risso's Dolphins, Common Dolphins and Minke Whales.

Main Species: Bottlenose Dolphins, Harbor Porpoises.
Other Species Seen: Common Dolphins, Risso's Dolphins and Minke Whales.
Season: April–October.　　**Code of Conduct:** Voluntary guidelines. Swimming not permitted.

Information

The Whale and Dolphin Conservation Society
Brookfield House, 38 St Paul Street,
Chippenham, Wiltshire SN15 1LY
United Kingdom
Tel: + 44 (0)1249 449500

E-mail: info@wdcs.org
www.wdcs.org

Cardiganshire Coast and Country:
www.cardiganshirecoastandcountry.com

Sea Watch Foundation Cymru
Paragon House, Wellington Place
New Quay, Ceredigion SA45 9NR
United Kingdom
Tel: + 44 (0)1545 561227
E-mail: info@seawatchfoundation.org.uk
www.seawatchfoundation.org.uk

Official Tourism Site:
Visit Wales
Tel: + 44 (0) 8708 300 306
Fax: +44 (0) 8701 211259
email: info@visitwales.co.uk
www.visitwales.co.uk

England

Southwest Coast

The southwest corner of England juts out into the Atlantic and is less disturbed by confined shipping traffic than the southeast coast. Thirteen species of dolphins and whales inhabit these waters and can be sighted from numerous spots in Cornwall, Devon and Dorset. The best time of year is August to March. Bottlenose Dolphins and Harbor Porpoises range along the shoreline region-wide and Short-Beaked Common Dolphins may be abundant offshore. Small groups of Bottlenose Dolphins visit the tidal rips close to shore at Durlston near Swanage on the Dorset coast and are probably part of a larger population that ranges along the southeast coast from Cornwall to the Isle of Wight. Other good spots include St Agnes Head in Cornwall and Prawle Point in Devon.

Northeast Coast

Harbor Porpoises, Minke Whales and occasionally White-Beaked Dolphins can be seen from headlands along this coast between Skegness and Berwick-upon-Tweed. Minke Whales are most likely to be seen in late summer. White-Beaked Dolphins are far more abundant a short distance offshore and particularly between June and October, so if there is a chance of a boat trip this species may be encountered. With sightings of Bottlenose Dolphins from the Scottish east coast gradually spreading southwards, their distribution may soon encompass this coastline too.

Main Species: Bottlenose Dolphins, Harbor Porpoises.

Other Species Seen: Common Dolphins, Risso's Dolphins & Minke Whales.

Season: Year-round.   **Code of Conduct:** Voluntary guidelines. Swimming not permitted.

Information

For further information on the Dorset Marine Mammal Research Programme contact:

Durlston Marine Project
Durlston Country Park
Lighthouse Road
Swanage,

Dorset BH19 2JL
United Kingdom
Tel: + 44 (0) 1929 421111
E-mail:
dolphinsightings@durlestonemarineproject
.co.uk
www.durlstonmarineproject.co.uk

The Whale and Dolphin Conservation Society
Brookfield House,
38 St Paul Street,
Chippenham, Wiltshire
SN15 1LY
United Kingdom
Tel: + 44 (0)1249 449500
E-mail: info@wdcs.org
www.wdcs.org

Silver Dolphin Marine Conservation
The Silver Dolphin Centre, Trinity House,
Wharf Road, Penzance, Cornwall TR18 4BN
United Kingdom
Tel: + 44 (0)1736 364860
E-mail:
conservation@silverdolphin.freeserve.co.uk
www.silverdolphinmarineconservationand
diving.co.uk

Ireland

Dolphins and porpoises can be seen off the coasts of County Cork all year round, although whales are more typically encountered from June to January. Huge inshore aggregations of Common Dolphins, associated with migrating herring, occur off the south coast between November and February. Deep-water trips to the continental shelf edge may encounter Cuvier's Beaked Whales, White-Beaked Dolphins (northwest coast) and Atlantic White-Sided Dolphins. Small numbers of Blue Whales pass through Irish waters each year and appear to be increasing. Seven of the ten strandings of True's Beaked Whales in northern Europe have occurred on the west coast of Ireland, suggesting the species might be relatively common in the under-explored deep-water canyons beyond the shelf edge.

Land-based whale and dolphin watching is possible from many headlands on the south and west coast. Popular spots include Old Head Kinsale and Dursey Island, Co. Cork; Saltees Islands, Co. Wexford and the Blasket Islands in Co. Kerry. Harbor Porpoises, Common Dolphins, Fin and Minke Whales are often sighted from the Dublin–Holyhead and Rosslare–Pembroke ferries. Dolphin-watching in Dingle, County Kerry started in 1984 when a solitary dolphin named "Fungi" started frequenting the mouth of the harbor.

West Cork

The southwest corner of Ireland projects into the Gulf Stream, giving it a relatively mild climate. Small harbors and historic villages dot a very picturesque coastline, which is rapidly becoming a top location for whale watching in Europe. Land-based viewing is possible from several headlands including Old Head of Kinsale, Sevens Head, Galley Head, Cape Clear Island, Mizen Head, and Dursey Island. Organized boat tours run from Castletownshend and Reen Pier in Union Hall. A variety of species are possible including Common Dolphins (summer), Harbor Porpoises (resident), Minke Whales (April to December), Fin Whales (June to February), Humpback Whales (August to January). In addition, Blue Whales, Sei Whales (winter), Sperm Whales, Killer Whales, Bottlenose Dolphins, Risso's Dolphins, Striped Dolphins and Long-Finned Pilot Whales are seen occasionally.

Shannon Estuary, County Clare / County Kerry

The 30 mile (50 km) long estuary of the Shannon River has been designated Ireland's first marine Special Area of Conservation (SAC) and is home to resident groups of Bottlenose Dolphins. More than 100 animals are present in the area year round. Calves are born between May and August and are often seen shadowing their mothers. The dolphins can be seen on ferry crossings between Tarbert, Co. Kerry and Killimer, Co. Clare. Land-based whale watching is possible from a number of headlands including Blasket Island as well as Loop and Black Heads. Minke Whales occur off Loop Head in the autumn. Dolphin-watching tours run from the villages of Carrigaholt and Kilrush (Kilrush Creek Marina).

Main Species: Fin and Minke Whales, Common, Bottlenose, White-Beaked and Atlantic White-Sided Dolphins, Harbor Porpoises.

Other Species Seen: Blue, Sei, Sperm, Long-Finned Pilot, Killer and Cuvier's Beaked Whales, Risso's and Striped Dolphins.

Season: April–October.   **Code of Conduct:** Enforced code of conduct. Swimming not permitted from commercial tour boats.

Information

Shannon Dolphin and Wildlife Foundation
Merchants Quay
Kilrush, County Clare, Ireland
Tel: + 35 365 905 2326
E-mail: info@shannondolphins.ie
Website:www.shannondolphins.ie

Irish Whale & Dolphin Group (IWDG):
Gortagrenane, Castlefreke
Clonakilty, Co. Cork,
Ireland
Tel: + 35 323 31911

E-mail: enquiries@iwdg.ie
www.iwdg.ie

For general information on Ireland contact;

Fáilte, Ireland
Baggot Street Bridge
Baggot Street,
Dublin 2, Ireland
Tel: + 35 31 602 4000
E-mail: info@failteireland.ie
www.tourismireland.com

France

During the 1980s, survey work in the central Mediterranean revealed an unexpected abundance of large whales, including Fin Whales, Sperm Whales and Cuvier's Beaked Whales. Fin and other baleen whales are attracted by the abundance of krill (*Meganyctiphanes norvegica*) but a variety of toothed whales and dolphins also occur and prey on the fish and squid associated with the krill schools.

A diamond-shaped sliver of ocean bounded by the French Riviera, island of Corsica, Monaco and Italian Riviera has been designated as the "Pelagos Sanctuary for Mediterranean Marine Mammals". This new sanctuary includes the deep and cetacean-rich waters of the Corso-Ligurian Basin and Gulf of Lion and represents both the biggest protected marine area in the Mediterranean and the first to include international waters. A number of organizations run multi-day tours into the sanctuary.

Brittany Coast

Resident populations of Bottlenose Dolphins live year round along the coast of Brittany and they are often seen around Ile de Sein and Molène Archipelago. Offshore excursions may also encounter Long-Finned Pilot Whales, Common Dolphins, Risso's Dolphins, Striped Dolphins and Harbor Porpoises.

Riviera Coast and Corsica

During the summer (April to September), Baleines et Dauphins Sans Frontières (Whales and Dolphins Without Frontiers) run multi-day (3–14 days) whale-watching excursions from Bandol near Toulon, exploring the Ligurian Sea and island of Corsica. Regularly encountered species include Fin Whales, Sperm Whales, Long-Finned Pilot Whales, Risso's Dolphins, Bottlenose Dolphins, Short-Beaked Common Dolphins and Striped Dolphins.

Main Species: Bottlenose, Common and Striped Dolphins.

Other Species Seen: Humpback, Sperm, False Killer, Minke, Long-Finned Pilot and Killer Whales.

Season: Year-round, but best June–September.   **Code of Conduct:** Please check with local operators. There are currently no guidelines at national level. Local areas operate a voluntary code of conduct.

Information

Baleines et Dauphins Sans Frontières (BDSF)
1173 Les Escans
83330 Le Beausset, France
Tel: + 33 (0) 4 94 98 70 51
E-mail: info@bdsf.net
www.bdsf.net

For information on travel to France, contact the French Tourist Office at www.franceguide.com and follow the links to your country's website.

Bay of Biscay (France / Spain)

The unique combination of warm water and full range of water depths and bottom types makes the Bay of Biscay one of the most exciting areas in Europe for keen whale watchers. Indeed, diligent observers crossing and re-crossing the Bay of Biscay on commercial ferries have logged almost every species of whale and dolphin recorded in the North Atlantic.

The premier whale-watching venue is aboard the *Pride of Bilbao*, a luxurious ferry that sails between Portsmouth, England and Bilbao in Spain. The route follows the shelf edge for part of this journey and also crosses some very deep water, home to some of the rarer species. The ship's size offers a very stable viewing platform and observers often use telescopes mounted on tripods to get superb views of breaching animals. Fin, Minke, Sperm, Long-Finned Pilot and Cuvier's Beaked Whales are recorded on many trips. Numbers vary considerably but up to 100 Fin Whales have been recorded on a single crossing. Sightings of Cuvier's Beaked Whales are most frequent along the Cap Breton Canyon, on the northern edge of the Spanish portion of the continental shelf, making this one of the best places in Europe to see this attractive species.

Other rarities include Killer Whales, Northern Bottlenose Whales, False Killer Whales, Sowerby's and True's Beaked Whales. The ferry often encounters groups of Common, Striped and Bottlenose Dolphins, sometimes in large numbers and the dolphins may come in to ride on the pressure wave produced by the enormous vessel. Sightings of Risso's and Atlantic White-Sided Dolphins are less frequent but still regular. The trips have become so popular that there can be real competition for a place at the rail in the best sections of the ship. Several wildlife tour companies now offer mini-tours accompanied by expert guides who can help spot and identify animals.

Main Species: Fin, Minke, Long-Finned, Pilot & Cuvier's Beaked Whales, Common Dolphins.

Other Species Seen: Killer Whales, Northern Bottlenose, False Killer, Sowerby's and True's Beaked Whales. Striped, Bottlenose, Risso's & Atlantic White-Sided Dolphins.

Season: Late June–late September.   **Code of Conduct:** Please check with local operators.

Information

The Company of Whales
Longhill
Maywick,
Shetland
ZE2 9JF
United Kingdom
Tel: + 44 (0) 1950 422483
E-mail: info@companyofwhales,co.uk
www.companyofwhales.co.uk

Biscay Dolphin Research Programme
Tel: + 44 (0) 1202 827957
www.biscay-dolphin.org.uk

P&O Ferries
Tel: UK 08705 980 333
From outside the UK:
P & O Switchboard + 44 (0) 1304 86300
www.poferries.com

Portugal, Spain and Gibraltar

The Iberian Peninsula is bounded by the Atlantic Ocean, Bay of Biscay and the Mediterranean. Portugal and Spain have rich associations with the sea, as does the tiny British dependency of Gibraltar, which overlooks the narrow strait separating the Mediterranean from the Atlantic. All three are popular tourist destinations and offer many whale-watching opportunities. The two best areas, the Azores Islands (Portugal) in the central North Atlantic and the Bay of Biscay (France and Spain) are treated separately.

Setúbal, Portugal

The city of Setúbal, approximately 31 miles (50 km) south of Lisbon, sits on the north bank of the Sado River where it enters the Atlantic. This was once an important part of Portugal's sardine industry but now is sustained by tourism. The estuary provides habitat for some 30 Bottlenose Dolphins, the best group in the country. The animals can often be seen feeding in the estuary on cuttlefish which they break into pieces at the surface. Unfortunately, industrial pollution presents a serious threat to the survival of these animals. Local boat owners offer trips out to the mile-wide river mouth to view the dolphins, which are well acclimatized to visitors.

Land-based viewing of the estuary mouth is good from the northern tip of Peninsula de Tróia near the ferry dock on the beach.

Madeira, Portugal

This volcanic island is closer to Morocco than Portugal. Bottlenose Dolphins and Harbor Porpoises are found around the islands (try the marine nature reserves at Ilhas Desertas, Ponta de S. Lourenço, and Ilhéu da Viúva) and a variety of whales are found offshore including Sperm Whales and Short-Finned Pilot Whales.

Northern Coast, Spain

The deepwater section of the Bay of Biscay is covered in its own section. From land, Bottlenose, Common and Striped Dolphins are often encountered along the coast between Gijón and San Sebastián. Offshore excursions may encounter Risso's Dolphins and various small whales. Similar species including Bottlenose Dolphins are found off Galicia.

Straits of Gibraltar, Spain / Gibraltar

The British outpost of Gibraltar overlooks the narrow strait of 8.7 miles (14 km) that separates the Iberian Peninsula from North Africa. Boat-based excursions (2–3 hours) from Gibraltar or neighboring Spanish ports of Tarifa and Sevilla regularly encounter herds of dolphins, principally Common and Striped Dolphins, as well as encounters with Long-Finned Pilot Whales and Bottlenose Dolphins. Killer Whales, Fin and Sperm Whales are fairly regular. Common and Striped Dolphins are often seen from the ferry (80 min) that runs across the Strait to Tangier in Morocco. Unfortunately, thousands of dolphins are caught illegally in fishing nets each year. Sufficient numbers of Sperm Whales once migrated through the Straits of Gibraltar to sustain a small local hunting industry and sightings are more occasional now. Land-based viewing can be good from Punta del Carnero, at the western end of the Bahía de Algeciras and from the Castle in Tarifa. Several species of dolphins are regularly seen from here along with Fin and Sperm Whales.

Mediterranean Coast, Spain

Although the coastline from the Costa del Sol to the Costa Blanca swarms with beachgoers year round, it can be remarkably good for dolphins, principally Bottlenose, Striped, Short-Beaked Common and Risso's. Further offshore it may be possible to find Sperm Whales and Long-Finned Pilot Whales. Similar species are found around the Balearic Islands and along the Costa Brava on the mainland.

Main Species: Bottlenose, Common, and Striped Dolphins.

Other Species Seen: Humpback, Sperm, False Killer, Minke, Long-Finned Pilot and Killer Whales.

Season: Year round but best June–September.

Code of Conduct: All three countries operate a voluntary code of conduct.

Information

The Original Dolphin Safari
Marina Bay Complex
Gibraltar
Tel: (0034) 9567 71914
E-mail:dolphin@gibnet.gi
www.dolphinsafari.gi

Coordinadora para o Estudo dos Mamíferos
Mariños (CEMMA)
PO Box 165
36380 Gondomar

(PONTEVEDRA)
Tel: + 34 686 989 008
E-mail: cemma@arrakis.es
www.arrakis.es/~cemma

Vertigem Azul
Av. Luisa Todi, nº375-305
2901-876 Setúbal
Tel: + 351 265 238000
E-mail: vertigemazul@mail.telepac.pt
www.vertigemazul.com

Canary Islands

Formed by the tops of submarine volcanoes, the Canary Islands consist of seven main islands and six smaller islets. Situated in the mid Atlantic some 60 miles (100 km) off the coast of Morocco, the islands are cooled by the Canary Current which sweeps down from the north. These nutrient-rich cool waters and sharp drop of the ocean floor to depths of more than 8000 feet (2500 m) provide superb habitat for cetaceans. At least 26 species of whales and dolphins have been recorded in the surrounding waters. Atlantic Spotted and Short-Beaked Common and Bottlenose Dolphins are particularly numerous and are present year-round. The waters between Tenerife and La Gomera are also very productive with a local population of more than 500 Short-Finned Pilot Whales. The extraordinary diversity of cetaceans around the islands is demonstrated by recent strandings of several species of beaked whales including Cuvier's, Blainville's and Gervais' Beaked Whales. These stranding have coincided with naval sonar exercises and raise serious concerns about the impacts of these activities on the conservation of deep diving marine mammals.

Commercial whale-watching tours are available from La Gomera, Lanzarote, Tenerife and Gran Canaria. More than 40 boats operate from Tenerife alone, sailing from Los Cristianos, Los Gigantes and Puerto Colon, near Playa de las Americas.

The Canary Islands have long been a popular holiday destination, notably during the winter months. There is excellent tourist infrastructure with inexpensive flights to the main islands from many European cities and numerous apartment and hotel room rentals. This is a perfect location to combine whale watching with more traditional beach getaways. On the southern side of Gran Canaria, the holiday resorts of Puerto Rico and Puerto de Mogán provide a good base with several local operators offering short (2 to 6 hour) whale-watching excursions. Groups (4 to 8 people) might also consider chartering local sport-fishing boats. There are numerous package holidays to the Canary Islands on offer with whale watching a major emphasis, some are land-based with transport to and from the dock included, others provide accommodation aboard a sailing ship offering an escape from the crowds and more time with the animals.

Main Species: Short-Finned Pilot Whales, Atlantic Spotted, Bottlenose and Common Dolphins.

Other Species Seen: Bryde's, Blue, Minke, Fin, Sei, Sperm, and Killer Whales, Rough-Toothed, Risso's and Striped Dolphins.

Season: All year.   **Code of Conduct:** Regulations in place.

Information

Further information on the Canary Islands:
Dirección General de Turespaña
Jose Lázaro 6,
28071 Madrid,
Spain
Tel: + (91) 343 3500
E-mail: info@spain.info
www.okspain.org/communidades/canaries.asp

For information on the European Whale Festival held in Tenerife contact:
Atlantic Whale Foundation
St Martins House, 59 St Martins Lane
Covent Garden, London WC2N 4JS UK
Tel: + 44 (0)1162 404566
E-mail: edb@whalenation.org
www.whalefoundation.org.uk

The Azores

The nine islands of the Portuguese Azores (Açores) belong to a small archipelago located in the subtropical North Atlantic, about 900 miles (1400 km) from mainland Portugal and on the same latitude as New York and Lisbon. The steep-sided and mountainous islands are actually the summits of underwater volcanoes and the surrounding waters are therefore very deep.

Consequently this is an ideal place to encounter deep-water species such Sperm and Short-Finned Pilot Whales, which are found relatively close to shore. Bottlenose, Common, Striped, Spotted and Risso's Dolphins are also encountered regularly. Other species found in recent years include Blue, Fin, Sei, Minke, Pygmy Sperm and False Killer Whales. The baleen whales are migrants to the archipelago, occurring primarily in May and June. Rarities such as Northern Bottlenose Whales, Cuvier's and Sowerby's Beaked Whales are found occasionally and there have been credible reports in recent years of the enigmatic True's Beaked Whale.

Because of the abundance of cetaceans close to land, the islands were used as a base for the Yankee whaling fleet during the 1700s and local whaling using traditional open boats and hand-held harpoons continued until 1985. Fortunately the islands' long relationship with whales now continues in the form of excellent whale watching.

Although Sperm Whales are resident, the best time to look for them is between May and October when the sea conditions are likely to be optimal. Tours are available from the harbors at Capelas and Ponta Delgada on the main island São Miguel, as well as Horta on the island of Faial, Lajes and Madalena on Pico. Whale-watch permits are issued by the Department of Tourism and regulations have been developed but full enforcement is difficult.

Many tours employ former whalers and spotters who use lookout towers called "vegia". These white towers are situated on land high above the water and were formerly used to locate whales for the whaling industry. In general these are only accessible to the companies that maintain them, however, Vigia da Queimada near the town of Lajes on Pico has been restored and is open to the public.

A number of wildlife travel companies offer package tours to the islands with whale watching as the primary focus. Some are land-based taking half or full-day boat excursions, others (such as Whale Watch Azores) provide accommodation aboard a catamaran or yacht and weave through the islands visiting as many productive spots as possible. Another company, Pico Sport, runs a "dolphin school for kids" during the summer holiday period. This educational program staffed by marine biologists involves a two-week camping program.

Main Species: Sperm and Short-Finned Pilot Whales, Bottlenose, Common, Striped, Spotted and Risso's Dolphins.

Other Species Seen: Blue, Fin, Sei, Minke, Pygmy Sperm and False Killer Whales. Cuvier's Beaked Whales, Sowerby's Beaked Whales, True's Beaked Whales & Northern Bottlenose Whales.

Season: April–October.   **Code of Conduct:** Enforced regulations. Swimming with dolphins permitted.

Information

Whale Watch Azores
5 Old Parr Close
Banbury, Oxfordshire OX16 5HY
United Kingdom
Tel: UK + 44 (0)1295 267652;
Azores: + 351 96 527 4312
E-mail: info@whalewatchazores.com
www.whalewatchazores.com

Pico Sport
(Blue Ocean Whale Watching Azores)
Pico Sport Lda., Frank Wirth,
9950 Madalena, Pico Island, Azores
Portugal
Tel: + 49 162 183 6064
E-mail: whales@gmx.net
www.whales-dolphins.net

Azores Tourism Office
Direcção Regional do Turismo dos Açores
Rua Ernesto Rebelo 14
P 9900-112
Horta-Acores
Azores
Portugal
Tel: + 351 292 200 500
www.drtacores.pt

Futurismo Azores Whale Watching
Estrada da Ribeira Grande 1001-A
9500 Ponta Delgada
Azores
Tel: + 351 296 628522
E-mail: futurismo@mail.telepac.pt
www.azoreswhales.com

Italy

Our awareness of cetaceans in the Ligurian Sea has a long history. The Roman name for what is now the Italian Riviera was *Costa Balenae,* meaning "Whale Coast" and likewise the glamorous resort of Portofino is derived from the Roman name *Portus Delphinii* meaning "Dolphin's Port". Arrangements for visiting the best areas of Pelagos Marine Sanctuary are somewhat limited but this may change with time. Five to six hour excursions operated by "Whale Watch – bluWest" and "Whale-watching in San Remo" to the Pelagos Marine Sanctuary leave from the ports at Imperia (tourist quay at Porto Maurizio), Sanremo and Andora (eastern quay). Regularly encountered species include Fin Whales, Cuvier's Beaked Whales, Striped Dolphins. Other possibilities include Sperm Whales, Long-Finned Pilot Whales, Risso's Dolphins and Short-Beaked Common Dolphins. Some trips follow the coast towards Portofino, others visit the waters off Finale Ligure between Capo Noli and the Rock of Caprazoppa. The Tethys Research Institute runs a series of multi-day research cruises searching for Fin Whales or deepwater species such as Sperm and various beaked whales. Participants take part in scientific studies, learning photo-identification techniques, suction cup tagging and so on. On the Adriatic, Bottlenose Dolphins occur along the northern coast, including the Venice lagoon, with Striped and Risso's Dolphin further south. A variety of dolphins occur in the Gulf of Napoli, especially over the Cuma submarine canyon.

Main Species: Fin Whales, Bottlenose Dolphins, Common Dolphins and Striped Dolphins.

Other Species Seen: Humpback Whales, Sperm Whales, False Killer Whales, Minke Whales, Long-Finned Pilot Whales and Killer Whales.

Season: Year-round, but best June–September.   **Code of Conduct:** Voluntary code of conduct.

Information

Tethys Research Institute
c/o Acquario Civico
Via Pompeo Leoni 2
20141 Milano, Italy
Tel: +39 0258314889
Fax +39 0258315345
Email: tethys@tethys.org
www.tethys.org/

Whale Watch – bluWest
Via Scarncio 12
18100 Imperia (IM), Italy
Tel: +39 (0)183 769 364
Fax: +39 (0)183 765 954
Email: bluwest@uno.it
www.whalewatch.it

Whale-watching in San Remo
Sanremo Navigazione s. r. l.
Molo di Levante 35
18038 Sanremo (IM)

Italy
Tel: +39 (0)184-505055
Fax: +39 (0)184-506444
Email: info@sanremonavigazione.it
www.rivieraline.it

Tethys Research Institute –
Venice Dolphin Project
c/o Museo Civico di Storia Naturale
Santa Croce 1730
30135 Venezia
Italy
Tel: +39 (0)412750206
Fax: +39 (0)417210000

Fondazione Cetacea Onlus. – Italian only
via Ascoli Piceno
47838 Riccione (RN)
Tel + 39 0541 691557
E-mail: informazione@fondazionecetacea.org
www.fondazionecetacea.org

Croatia

The Adriatic coast of Croatia is beautiful and is once again a popular tourist destination. A resident population of around 200 Bottlenose Dolphins frequent the inshore waters, and are often seen around the islands of Cres and Lošinj. Striped and Risso's Dolphins may occur further offshore.

Main Species: Bottlenose and Striped Dolphins.

Other Species Seen: Risso's Dolphins.

Season: Year-round, but best June–September.

Code of Conduct: Voluntary guidelines.

Information

Lošinj Marine Education Centre
Kaštel 24
51551 Veli Lošinj
Croatia
Tel: + 385 51 604666
E-mail: info@plavi-svijet.org
Web site: www.blue-world.org

Croatian National Tourist Board
Iblerov Trg 10/4
10000 Zagreb
Croatia
Tel: + 385 1 469 9333
E-mail: info@htz.hr
www.croatia.hr

Greece

The eastern Ionian Sea is one of the few areas in the central Mediterranean where Common Dolphins are regularly encountered. Recent survey work has focused on waters around the island of Kalamos, which also holds a population of Bottlenose Dolphins. During the summer, the Ionian Dolphin Project maintains a field station in the small town of Episkopi and runs a residential program for volunteers who wish to participate in the research. In Crete, there is a resident population of Sperm Whales along the southwestern coast, associated with a steep drop-off, and is among the more reliable locations for the species in the Mediterranean. Striped and Risso's Dolphins also occur and there are regular sightings of Cuvier's Beaked Whales.

Main Species: Bottlenose and Striped Dolphins.

Other Species Seen: Sperm Whales, Cuvier's Beaked Whales, Risso's Dolphins, Short-Beaked Common Dolphins.

Season: Year-round, but best June–September.

Code of Conduct: Voluntary code of conduct.

Information

Pelagos Cetacean Research Institute
Terpsichoris 21,
GR 16671 Vouliagmeni,
Greece
www.pelagosinstitute.gr/en/
homepage/index.html

Tethys Research Institute -
Ionian Dolphin Project
c/o Museo Civico di Storia Naturale
Santa Croce 1730, 30135 Venezia, Italy
Tel: + 39 0412750206
E-mail: tethys@tethys.org
www.tethys.org

Asia & the Indian Subcontinent

Top Spots

Hong Kong – 'Pink' Humpback Dolphins off Lantau Island.

India – River Dolphins in the Ganges and major tributaries.

Japan – Humpback Whales and several species of dolphins around the Ogasawara Islands.

Maldives – Spectacular mix of tropical dolphins and other toothed whales.

Seychelles – Melon-Headed Whales and other tropical specialities.

Although there is a wide variety of whales and dolphins in Asia, including several fantastic endemics, the opportunities to go out on organized whale-watching excursions are still limited. Hopefully this will change soon as coastal communities realize the potential. Japan is clearly the most advanced nation in the region in terms of whale watching. To many this seems at odds with the government's continued zeal for commercial whaling and one may be surprised to find an extensive network of commercial operators (often former whalers) and a very enthusiastic public base of support. Taiwan follows with a growing whale-watching industry operating from a number of ports along the eastern coast of the island. A dazzling array of Asiatic specialties should be enough to attract the traveling whale watcher. Along the coasts of southern China, Hong Kong, Singapore, Thailand and Vietnam the ghostly Sousa or "Pink" Humpbacked Dolphin can be locally common. The Chinese River Dolphin or Baiji on the other hand, is found only in China's Lower Yangtze River and is now critically endangered. The Susu or Ganges River Dolphin occurs in the large river systems of India, Bhutan, Bangladesh and Nepal and there is also the endangered Bhulan or Indus River Dolphin, which is restricted to the Indus River system of Pakistan. Also notable is the Irrawaddy Dolphin, which occurs most commonly in the coastal waters of northern Borneo, Papua New Guinea and northeastern Australia. Populations in large rivers such as the Irrawaddy, Mekong and Mahakam are under serious threat from human activities such as dams and habitat degradation. The waters around the Philippines, particularly the Camotes Sea and southern end of Bohol Strait, are one of the more reliable areas to encounter Fraser's Dolphin, an attractive deepwater tropical species.

Japan

Despite its reputation for hunting and consuming whales, Japan is fast emerging as a nation of vigorous whale-watching fanatics. Although there are no endemics, the rich area of upwelling and variety of water temperatures result in a superb selection of species. Humpback Whales from the western Pacific stock breed and calve off Japan during the winter and spring. The best areas to see them are the Ogasawara and Kerama Islands, both of which lie south of the larger islands. Bryde's Whales are relatively common residents in Tosa Bay, Kochi Prefecture on the Pacific coast of Shikoku Island. Some 19,000 Finless Porpoise reside in coastal waters off central and southern Japan, including the Inland Sea, Ise, Mikawa and Omura Bays.

Kochi Prefecture

The waters of Tosa Bay (peak season March to December) are particularly productive with Bryde's Whales, Sperm Whales, Humpback Whales (spring and autumn migrants), Northern Right Whales (extremely rare migrants in spring and early summer), Short-Finned Pilot Whales, Common Dolphins, Bottlenose Dolphins and Risso's Dolphins. Ogata on the southwestern edge of Tosa Bay is one of the best places in the world to see Bryde's Whales (peak numbers from May to September). On the northeastern side of the bay, Sperm Whales are regular in the deep water, 3280 ft (1000 m), that lies to the southwest of Cape Muroto. Land-based viewing is possible from Cape Muroto and Cape Ashizuri. Organized whale watching began in 1989 and is thriving. Boats can be chartered at the Irino Fishing Port in Ogata Town as well as the towns of Saga and Toshashimizu.

Visit between May and September for Bryde's Whales off Ogata, Saga and other communities in Kochi Prefecture; Short-Finned Pilot Whales, Sperm Whales and dolphins can be seen year round but best between March and December off Cape Muroto. The weather varies from cool to warm at sea, dependant on local currents, but be aware that the typhoon season is August to early October. Half-day and full-day tours are available; try Ogata, Saga, Shimonokae, Tosashimizu, Kochi City or Cape Muroto.

Main Species: Bryde's, Sperm and Humpback Whales.

Other Species Seen: Northern Right Whales and Short-Finned Pilot Whales; Common, Bottlenose and Risso's Dolphins.

Season: All year.   **Code of Conduct:** Voluntary code of practice.

Information

For information on Kochi Prefecture contact:
Kochi Prefecture Information Center
JR Kochi Station 2-7-1
Kitahonmachi

Kochi City
Japan
Tel: + 088-882-7777
www.attaka.or.jp/foreign/english

Ogasawara Islands

Located in warm subtropical waters 600 miles (970 km) south of Tokyo, the islands can only be reached by ferry from Tokyo. There are two inhabited islands, Chichi-jima and Haha-jima, 30 miles (50 km) farther south. Above the main town of Futami Port on Chichi-jima, there is a whale-watching platform with magnificent views across the waters to the west. Principal species: Humpback Whales (February to April); Spinner and Indo-Pacific Bottlenose Dolphins (all year but June to October best); Sperm Whales (late August to October). Spotted Dolphins and Short-Finned Pilot Whales also occur. Upwards of 20 different companies offer scheduled whale-watching trips and charters throughout the year, three-quarters of which are based on the more populated island of Chichi-jima. Many whale-watching trips also offer snorkeling amid the coral reefs that surround the islands and when conditions permit, swimming with dolphins and Manta Rays. Most operators belong to the Ogasawara Whale Watching Association (OWA). In addition to an intensive research program, the OWA sets guidelines for approaching the animals with minimal disturbance. The OWA has an office near Futami Port on Chichi-jima and can arrange bookings.

Visit between February and April for Humpback Whales around Ogasawara, the Kermana Islands and Okinawa; various dolphins can be seen year-round. It can be warm to very hot during the season but much cooler and windier at sea. Half-day tours are available from a number of towns, notably Chichi-jima and Haha-jima in the Ogasawara Islands; Zamami and Tokashiki in the Kerama Islands or Naha or Okinawa.

Main Species: Humpback and Sperm Whales, Spinner and Indo-Pacific Bottlenose Dolphins.

Other Species Seen: Short-Finned Pilot Whales and Spotted Dolphins.

Season: All year – see above.   **Code of Conduct:** Voluntary code of practice.

Information

For further information contact:
Ogasawara Whale Watching Association
Chichi-jima
Ogasawara-mura
Tokyo
100-2101
Japan
Tel: + 81 4998 2 3215
www.h2.dion.ne.jp/~owa/english

For further information on the Ogasawara Islands contact:
Ogasawara Tourist Association
Chichi-jima
Ogasawara-mura
Tokyo
100-2101
Japan
Tel: + 81 4998 2 2587

A website with information on Ogasawara (Bonin) Islands can be found at:
www.bonin-islands.com

Okinawa and the Kerama Islands

A number of whale-watching tours operate from January to March, principally from the Kerama Islands. In addition to Humpback Whales (peak January to April), possibilities include Blainville's Beaked Whales, Melon-Headed Whales, Pygmy Killer Whales, False Killer Whales, Rough-Toothed Dolphins, Risso's Dolphins and Spotted Dolphins. Sperm Whales are regular slightly further offshore. Whale watching is available from Zamami and Tokashiki.

Main Species: Humpback and Sperm Whales.

Other Species Seen: Blainville's Beaked, Melon-Headed, Pygmy Killer, False Killer Whales; Rough-Toothed, Risso's Dolphins and Spotted Dolphins.

Season: All year – see above.   **Code of Conduct:** Voluntary code of practice.

Information

Tokashiki Village Office
183 Tokashiki
Tokashiki-son
Shimajiri-gun
Okinawa
Japan
Tel: + 098-987-2321
www.vill.tokashiki.okinawa.jp/en/

Okinawa Convention & Visitors Bureau
1831-1 Oroku
Naha City
Okinawa 901-0152
Japan
Tel: + 098-857-6884
www.ocvb.or.jp/en/

Shibetsu, Hokkaido

The harbor town of Muroran is located in the southwest corner of Hokkaido, facing the eastern coast of the Oshima Peninsula and its port is on a small peninsula jutting out into the sea at the entrance of the Uchiura Bay. Volcano Bay is a popular dolphin and whale area. Boat excursions are available from the end of April to the middle of August.

Main Species: Minke Whales, Pacific White-Sided Dolphins.

Other Species Seen: Bryde's Whales, Baird's Beaked Whales, Killer Whales and Dall's Porpoises.

Season: April–August.   **Code of Conduct:** Voluntary code of practice.

Information

IKAN – Iruka (Dolphins) & Kujira (Whales)
Action Network,
#205 Kiyo Bldg, 2-5-5 Hyakunin-cho
Shinjuku-ku, Tokyo 169-0073
Japan
Tel: + 81 3 3366-8122
E-mail: QWP06555@nifty.ne.jp
www.homepage1.nifty.com/IKAN/
eng/index.html

Japan National Tourist Organisation (JNTO)
Tokyo Kotsu Kaikan Building
10th Floor,
2-10-1 Yuraku-Cho,
Chiyodaku
Tokyo 100-0006
Japan
Tel: + 81 (3) 3201 3331
www.jnto.go.jp

Taiwan

Since the first whale-watching venture opened in Hualien in 1997, the number of whale-watching boats has increased to more than 30 and in the following two years, an astonishing 30,000 people went whale-watching! The peak season is between July and October, with commercial tours available from several different ports in Taipei, Ilan, Hualien and Taitung Counties, located on the eastern coast.

At least 27 species of cetacean have been recorded in Taiwanese waters. Rough-Toothed Dolphins are relatively common. Boats from Hualien regularly encounter Melon-Headed Whales. The port of Houpihu near Kenting was once the main base for commercial whaling but now hosts a whale-watching company. Other regularly encountered species include

Bottlenose Dolphins, Risso's Dolphins and False Killer Whales. Sperm and Humpback Whales are seen occasionally.

Main Species: False Killer and Melon-Headed Whales, Rough-Toothed, Bottlenose and Risso's Dolphins.

Other Species Seen: Sperm and Humpback Whales.

Season: July–October.   **Code of Conduct:** Please check with local operators, who are being encouraged by the Taiwan Cetacean Society to form a self-regulating alliance to protect the local cetaceans.

Information

Taiwan Cetacean Society (TCS)
3F-3, No.184
Section 3
Tingjhou Road
Taipei 100,
Taiwan
Tel: + 886-2-23661331
E-mail: tcs@whale.org.tw
www.whale.org.tw

Taiwan Visitors' Association
5th Floor, 9F-2
9 Minchuan East Road
Section 2
Taipei 104
Taiwan
Tel: + (2) 2594 3261 (information hotline).
E-mail: gtva@ms26.hinet.net
www.tva.org.tw

Philippines

The Philippines has long been a base for whale hunting. Happily the industry is essentially defunct and many of the former whale and dolphin hunters ply their skills as whale-watching guides and spotters. The best season is from March to June, but resident dolphins and small whales can be found all year. Key species include Bryde's Whales (March–June), Sperm Whales (March–June) and Pantropical Spotted Dolphins. Other regularly encountered species include Short-Finned Pilot Whales, Spinner Dolphins, Fraser's Dolphins, Bottlenose Dolphins, Melon-Headed Whales and Risso's Dolphins.

The best area for whale watching is Pamilacan Island off Bohol, which is situated just north of Mindanao in the Visaya group. Organized trips from Pamilacan use refitted whale-hunting boats called canters. The Tañon Strait between the islands of Negros and Cebu connects the Visayas and Bohol Seas and is an outstanding area for finding Dwarf Sperm Whales, Melon-Headed Whales and other tropical species. Manta Rays and Whale Sharks are also regularly encountered in these waters and whale-watching trips often provide opportunities for snorkeling and land-based exploration.

Main Species: Bryde's and Sperm Whales.

Other Species Seen: Short-Finned Pilot, Dwarf Sperm and Melon-Headed Whales, Spinner, Fraser's, Bottlenose and Risso's Dolphins.

Season: March–June.   **Code of Conduct:** Voluntary code of practice.

Information

The Pamilacan Island Dolphin and Whale
Watching Tours (PIDWWT)
Public Market
Poblacion, Baclayon
Bohol
Philippines 6301
Tel: + 63 38 5409279
E-mail: pamilacan@yahoo.com
http://whales.bohol.ph/index.php

Philippines Convention & Visitors Corp
4th Flr, Legaspi Towers 300
Roxas Blvd
PO Box EA-459
Metro Manila
Philippines
Tel: + 63 2 525-9318
E-mail: pcvcnet@dotpcvc.gov.ph
www.wowphilippines.com.ph

A website with local information for Bohol can be found at www.bohol.ph.

Indonesia

Key species to see in the waters surrounding Indonesia include Sperm Whales, Common
Dolphins and Spinner Dolphins. Also the Irrawaddy Dolphin occurs in the Mahakam River
and Lakes in East Kalimantan, Indonesia. A commercial whale- and dolphin-watching industry
is not well developed; however, on the spectacular island of Bali, whale watching is available
off Lovina Beach. Contact the Tourist Information Centres in Jalan, Leguan, Kuta, Denpasar
and Bali.

Main Species: Sperm Whales, Common Dolphins, Spinner Dolphins.

Other Species Seen: Irrawaddy Dolphins.

Seasons: Year round   **Code of Conduct:** Please check with local operators.

Information

Indonesia Tourism Promotion Board (ITPB)
Wisma Nugra Santana Building
9th Floor, Jalan Jend Sudirman Kav 7-8
Jakarta 10220
Indonesia
Tel: + (21) 570 4879
www.tourismindonesia.com

Bali Tourism Authority
Jl. S. Parman Niti Mandala
Denpasar
Bali
Indonesia
Tel: + (62-361) 222387
www.balitourismauthority.net

Malaysia

At present, whale and dolphin watching is not well developed in Malaysia, however Irrawaddy,
Indo-Pacific Humpback and Spotted Dolphins as well as the enigmatic Finless Porpoise occur in
coastal waters and river estuaries of northern Sarawak (Borneo), particularly the Rejang and
Saribas river systems. These areas are becoming increasingly accessible to ecotourism and offer
the possibility of some very exotic whale watching.

Main Species: Indo-Pacific Humpback Dolphins, Spotted Dolphins.

Other Species Seen: Irrawaddy Dolphins, Finless Porpoises.

Season: Year-round.   **Code of Conduct:** Please check with local operators.

Information

Malaysia Tourism Centre (MTC)
109, Jalan Ampang
50450 Kuala Lumpur
Malaysia
Tel: + 03 2163 3664/2164 3929
E-mail: enquiries@tourism.gov.my
www.mtc.gov.my

Tourism Malaysia
120 East 56th Street
Suite 810
New York, NY 10022
Tel: 212 754 1114
E-mail: mtpb.ny@tourism.gov.my
www.tourism.gov.my

China

The immense Yangtze River hosts the endemic Baiji or Chinese River Dolphin as well as Finless Porpoises. The Chinese River Dolphin is critically endangered and may now be the world's most endangered cetacean. In the last few years, the population has undergone a catastrophic decline from 6000 in the 1950s to 400 in 1984. Only a handful now remain. The future looks very bleak. Chinese River Dolphins are well adapted to life in turbid, silty water. Shy animals, Chinese River Dolphins are wary of boats and less easily seen than Finless Porpoises. Typically encountered in pairs but in the past would occasionally occur in small groups. The tragic decline was a result of a barrage of threats, including extensive damming of the Yangtze River, boat traffic, entrapment in fishing gear, and continued degradation of the habitat. The Chinese River Dolphin is protected in China and concerted efforts are being made towards its preservation, including the establishment of reserves. A lone male, Qi Qi, lived in captivity at the Chinese Academy of Sciences Institute of Hydrobiology in Wuhan for 22 years until his death in 2002. Finless Porpoises are regularly seen from ferries traveling along the Yangtze River, especially during the winter.

Hong Kong

The murky waters of the Pearl River spill into the South China Sea between Hong Kong and Macau. The delta has a population of 1000 or so 'Pink Sousa' or Indo-Pacific Humpback Dolphins (*Sousa chinensis*) and also a number of Finless Porpoises. In contrast to populations off Africa and Australia, most Humpback Dolphins found along the Chinese coast are bright pink rather than gray. These animals also lack a pronounced humpback and have a larger dorsal fin, more reminiscent of the Bottlenose Dolphin. Between 120 and 200 Sousa occur in the waters off Hong Kong's Lantau Island and are routinely encountered on trips run by Hong Kong Dolphin Watch Ltd, a non-profit organization that helps to promote preservation of this spectacular animal. Most sightings occur in the vicinity of the Brother Islands, the airport, Castle Peak Power Station, and the Sha Chau and Long Kwu Chau Marine Park. The summer months are optimal in terms of weather and numbers of animals. Unfortunately, the Pearl River passes through a large region of China and is heavily polluted. The delta itself is threatened with massive development for industry and it is unclear what effect this will have on the population. Construction and continued expansion of Hong Kong's new airport at Chek Lap Kok, northwest of Lantau Island, resulted in substantial habitat loss and documented disturbance of local dolphins. Hong Kong Dolphin Watch offers half-day "Sousa" viewing trips that leave from Lantau island.

Main Species: Indo-Pacific Humpback Dolphins and Finless Porpoises.

Other Species Seen: Baiji (Chinese River Dolphins – not Hong Kong).

Season: Summer.   **Code of Conduct:** Please check with local operators. Voluntary code of practice in Hong Kong.

Information

Hong Kong Dolphin Watch Ltd
1528A Star House
Tsimshatsui, Kowloon,
Hong Kong
Tel: + (852) 2984-1414
E-mail: info@hkdolphinwatch.com
www.hkdolphinwatch.com

China National Tourism Administration (CNTA)
9A Jianguomennei Avenue
Beijing 100740
People's Republic of China
Tel: + (10) 6520 1114
E-mail: webmaster@cnta.gov.cn
www.cnta.com

Discover Hong Kong
9-11/F Citicorp Centre
18 Whitfield Road, North Point
Hong Kong
Tel: + (852) 2807 6543
E-mail: info@www.hktb.com
www.discoverhongkong.com

China International Travel Service (CITS)
CITS Building, No.1 Dongdanbei Avenue
Beijing 100800
People's Republic of China
Tel: + (10) 6255 2991 or 8522 7930
E-mail: shuyu@cits.com.cn
www.cits.net

Kampuchea

The geography of Kampuchea (also known as Cambodia) is dominated by the immense Mekong River, which flows through the country on its long journey from Tibet to its great delta in neighboring Vietnam. The Mekong River is notable for its small but declining population of Irrawaddy Dolphins, a small and oddly blunt-nosed dolphin resembling a miniature Beluga Whale. Only 100 or so Irrawaddy Dolphins remain in the entire Mekong River, with 40 or so along a 125 mile (200 km) stretch between the town of Kratie and the border with Laos. Kratie is halfway between Phnom Penh and Ratanakiri and can be reached by bus. Local boats can be rented in Kratie to go out on the river to see the dolphins. Across the border in Laos, a group of 10 or so dolphins are found in the "4000 islands" region or Si Phan Don near Don Khon. Again local boatmen can be hired to escort visitors. Considered sacred by the local fishing communities, industrial pollution and entanglement in fishing nets pose a serious threat to the survival of this dwindling population. There are plans to dam several tributaries upstream of this region and this is likely to have a significant effect on the ecology of the lower reaches of the river.

Main Species: Irrawaddy Dolphin.

Seasons: Year round.   **Code of Conduct:** Please check with local operators.

Information

Cambodian Mekong Dolphin Conservation Project (CMDCP)
E-mail: wcs.ps@everyday.com.kh

Ministry of Tourism
#3 Monivong Blvd.
Phnom Penh 12258
Cambodia
E-mail: info@mot.gov.kh
www.mot.gov.kh

Royal Embassy of Cambodia
4530 16th Street NW
Washington, DC 20011, USA
Tel: 202 726 7742
E-mail: cambodia@embassy.org
www.embassy.org/cambodia

Vietnam

Irrawaddy Dolphins inhabit the coast and rivers of the Mekong Delta, and are considered sacred by fisherman in Vietnam, and if one dies, it is cremated in a religious ceremony. The dolphins are known to herd schools of fish into the nets of the villagers and in return are fed a share of the catch. Searching out the Irrawaddy Dolphins is for the determined dolphin watcher, as the areas they inhabit along the Mekong River on the border between Cambodia and Vietnam are generally not visited by tourists.

Information

Tourist Information:
VNAT - Vietnam National Administration of Tourism
80 Quan Su Street, Hoan Kiem District, Hanoi
Tel: +84 4 942 3760   www.vietnamtourism.com

Thailand

Whale watching is available on the island of Phuket in the Andaman Sea off southeast Thailand. This is already a well-known spot for sport diving, and local operators have begun to realize the additional potential for dolphin watching. Occasionally, an immense but harmless Whale Shark is encountered, adding extra spice to an offshore trip.

Main Species: Bottlenose Dolphins.

Other Species Seen: Bryde's Whales, Killer Whales, Indo-Pacific Humpback Dolphins.

Season: Year round.

Code of Conduct: Voluntary guidelines. Swimming not advised.

Information

Tourism Authority of Thailand
1600 New Phetchaburi Road,
Makkasan
Ratchathewi
Bangkok 10400
Thailand
Tel: + 6602 250 5500
E-mail: center@tat.or.th
www.tourismthailand.org

Phuket Tourist Association
Baan Sukhothai Hotel
Patong Beach
Phuket
Thailand
E-mail: pta@phukettourist.com
www.phukettourist.com

Bangladesh

Some of the best areas for seeing the extremely rare Ganges River Dolphin are the Karnaphuli and Sangu Rivers in southern Bangladesh. Ganges River Dolphins have very poor eyesight and use echolocation to find their prey, which is caught in their long beak which contains many small, sharp teeth. Surveys conducted in January-April 1999 revealed a population of about 125 animals, a perilously small number. There are a few organized tours that specifically seek out these fascinating animals. Bangladesh is one of the world's most densely populated areas and the rivers are being dammed for electricity and irrigation. Other threats such as boat traffic, fishing and chemical pollution are also increasing. Most cetacean authorities consider the Ganges and Indus River Dolphins as a single species, *Platanista gangetica*. This of course increases the population size but does little to ensure the future survival of either population.

Information

Bangladesh Parjatan Corporation (National
Tourism Organisation)
233 Airport Road
Tejgaon, Dhaka-1215

Bangladesh
Tel: + (2) 811 7855-9 or 9192
E-mail: bpcho@bangla.net
www.bangladeshtourism.org

Nepal

Although this landlocked and very mountainous country would seem a most unlikely venue for whale watching, the large rivers of Nepal offer some of the best opportunities to see the endangered but fascinating Ganges River Dolphin. Small numbers are regularly encountered on trekking or rafting tours. The Karnali River in western Nepal is one of the more reliable spots and might be reached by joining an organized rafting tour or through the Dolphin Manor resort in Bardiya National Park.

Main Species: Ganges River Dolphin.
Season: Year round.   **Code of Conduct:** Please check with local operators.

Information

Nepal Tourism Board
Bhrikuti Mandap
PO Box 11018
Kathmandu, Nepal
Tel: + 977 1 4256909, 4256229
E-mail: info@ntb.org.np
www.welcomenepal.com

Royal Nepalese Embassy
2131 Leroy Place NW
Washington
DC 20008, USA
Tel: 202 667 4550
E-mail: info@nepalembassyusa.org
www.nepalembassyusa.org

India

Ganges River Dolphins survive in the relatively unpolluted waters of the Chambal River (Uttar Pradesh), especially within the National Chambal (Gharial) Sanctuary located 37 miles (65 km) south of Agra. Originally conceived to protect the Gharial alligator, this well-maintained park supports a population of 10-20 Ganges River Dolphins as well as a host of other wildlife. It is possible to stay at the Sanctuary and explore the river with park rangers. In neighboring Bihar State, a 50 km (30 mile) stretch of the Ganges between Sultanganj and Kahalgaon has been designated the Vikramshila Gangetic Dolphin Sanctuary and supports the largest population of river dolphins in India, with a count of 115 animals in 2000. Unfortunately, the protection offered by the Sanctuary is not adequately enforced and dolphins still drown in gill nets or fall prey to poachers. Another large population of Ganges River Dolphins occurs along the Kosi River, between the Kosi Barrage on the border with Nepal and where the river merges with the Ganges at Kursela. Many holiday-makers visit the tiny state of Goa on the Arabian coast. Bottlenose and Indo-Pacific Humpback Dolphins are often seen along the coastline. Other species such as Striped Dolphins and Finless Porpoises occur on an irregular basis. Similar species occur near Kozhikode in Kerala.

Main Species: Bottlenose Dolphins, Striped Dolphins, Ganges River Dolphins.

Other Species Seen: Irrawaddy Dolphins, Common Dolphins, Indo-Pacific Humpback Dolphins, Finless Porpoises.

Seasons: Year round.   **Code of Conduct:** Please check with local operators.

Information

Incredible India (Ministry of Tourism)
Transport Bhavan
Parliament Street, New Delhi 110 001
India
Tel: + (11) 2371 5084
E-mail: contactus@incredibleindia.org
www.TourismOfIndia.com

Incredible India in the USA
1270 Avenue of the Americas
Suite 1808
New York, NY 10020-1700
Tel: 212 586 4901
E-mail: contactus@incredibleindia.org
www.incredibleindia.org

The official tourism website for Goa can be found at www.goatourism.org

Sri Lanka

In the early 1980s, the tropical island of Sri Lanka seemed set to become a prime international destination for whale watchers. The waters off the capital city of Trincomalee on the northeastern coast were found to contain very impressive numbers of large whales, particularly during the months of January to April. Researchers found this to be one of the best areas in the world to study female Sperm Whales with calves. The proximity of deep water close to land even makes it possible to observe large whales from shore, such as from the Swami Rock near Fort Frederick or from Nilaveli near Trincomalee. Unfortunately, tourism to this area has slumped because of the on-going ethnic conflict and the promise of a booming whale-watching industry has yet to materialize. Fortunately the western and southern coasts are trouble free and offer excellent whale-watching opportunities. Sperm Whales occur along the edges of a submarine canyon that cuts close to shore off the Yala National Park, 180 miles (300 km) southeast of Colombo and the canyon also features Blue and Bryde's Whales, Risso's, Spinner, Fraser's and Bottlenose Dolphins.

For Sri Lanka as a whole, December represents the best month for seeing whales but dolphins can be seen at any time of year. Key species include Blue, Bryde's, Sperm, False Killer, Dwarf Sperm, Melon-Headed and Cuvier's Beaked Whales as well as Killer Whales. Dolphins include Spotted, Spinner, Fraser's, Risso's, Common and Bottlenose. The Blue Whales probably belong to the distinct northern Indian Ocean subspecies (*Balaenoptera musculus indica*). Nature Quest Expeditions offers dolphin- and whale-watching tours off the western and southern coast.

Main Species: Blue Whales, Bryde's Whales, Sperm Whales, False Killer Whales, Dwarf Sperm Whales, Melon-Headed Whales, Cuvier's Beaked Whales, Spotted Dolphins, Spinner Dolphins, Risso's Dolphins, Common Dolphins and Bottlenose Dolphins.

Other Species Seen: Killer Whales, Fraser's Dolphins.

Season: December–February; dolphins all year.   **Code of Conduct:** Voluntary code of conduct.

Information

Nature Quest Expeditions
c/o Noel Narendranath Daniels
79/2-A, Polhengoda Road

00500 Colombo, Sri Lanka
Tel: + 94 (75 336 839
E-mail: seaquestexpeditions@yahoo.com

Pakistan

The endangered Indus River Dolphin or Bhulan (*Platanista minor*) occurs only in the Indus River and its tributaries, all of which lie within Pakistan. This remarkable dolphin is virtually sightless. It is estimated that fewer than 600 Indus River Dolphins remain, divided into several now isolated populations, and the future for the species looks bleak. The largest population (approximately 400) is found in the Sindh Province along a 100 mile (160 km) stretch of river between the Sukkur and Guddu barrages. Smaller populations occur further upstream in Punjab Province, between the Guddu-Taunsa and Taunsa-Chasma barrages. Drought and increasing disturbance threaten the Indus River Dolphin. There are no organized dolphin-watching tours, however, expeditions to suitable stretches of the river may be rewarding.

Main Species: Indus River Dolphin.

Season: Year round.   **Code of Conduct:** Please check with local operators.

Information

WWF-Pakistan
Ferozepur Road
PO Box 5180
Lahore 54600
Pakistan
Tel: + 92-42 5862360 / 5869429
E-mail: info@wwf.org.pk
www.wwfpak.org

Ecotourism Project for the Conservation of the Indus Dolphin
c/o Adventure Foundation Pakistan
Garden Avenue
National Park Area
PO Box 1807
Islamabad 44000

Tel: + 92-51 2825805
E-mail: afopak@yahoo.com
www.adventurefoundation.org.pk

For information on travel to Pakistan contact:
Pakistan Tourism Development Corporation (PTDC)
Information Service
PO Box 1465
Agha Khan Road
Markaz F-6 (Super Market)
Islamabad 44000
Pakistan
Tel: + 92-51 9212760, 9202766
E-mail: info@tourism.gov.pk
www.tourism.gov.pk

Maldives

The Republic of Maldives is a collection of 1200 tiny islands in the central Indian Ocean. Formed from the exposed tops of a series of coral atolls, many are true "picture postcard" islands with swaying palm trees, pristine white sandy beaches and turquoise lagoons. In recent years, the Maldives has been considered as one of the most outstanding whale-watching locations in the world, with a remarkable diversity of species in beautiful surroundings. The main whale-watching season is between February and May with good chances of Blue Whales, Sperm Whales, Dwarf Sperm Whales, Cuvier's Beaked Whales, Killer Whales, Short-Finned Pilot Whales (common), Spinner Dolphins (common), Risso's Dolphins, Striped Dolphins and Pantropical Spotted Dolphins. Melon-Headed Whales are commonest around the southern atolls, where they can occur in enormous schools (500 or more) and will regularly bow-ride faster-moving craft. Fraser's Dolphins, Bottlenose Dolphins and Rough-Toothed Dolphins are also encountered regularly. The Blue Whales are thought to belong to the distinctive northern Indian Ocean or "pygmy" subspecies (*Balaenoptera musculus indica*) and genetic studies are underway to clarify this. In recent years, several species of beaked whales (including Dense-Beaked and Ginkgo-Toothed Whales) have been recorded. Interestingly there have been a number of sightings of a mysterious "tropical bottlenose whale" and a stranding finally revealed this to be the very poorly known Longman's Beaked Whale. As a bonus, immense Whale Sharks are also sighted regularly. From March to May, the Whale and Dolphin Company runs multi-day whale- and dolphin-watching cruises to some of the most remote atolls aboard its 150 ft (45 m) ship M.V. *Pollux*.

Main Species: Blue, Sperm, Dwarf Sperm, Cuvier's Beaked, Short-Finned Pilot, Melon-Headed Whales and Killer Whales; Spinner, Risso's, Striped and Pantropical Spotted Dolphins.

Other Species Seen: Dense-Beaked and Ginkgo-Toothed Whales; Fraser's, Bottlenose and Rough-Toothed Dolphins.

Season: February–May.   **Code of Conduct:** Code of conduct under discussion.

Information

The Whale and Dolphin Company
PO Box 2074
Malé
Republic of Maldives
Tel: + 960 327024
E-mail: Anderson@dhivehinet.net.mv

Maldives Tourism Promotion Board (MTPB)
3rd Floor, H. Aage 12, Boduthakurufaanu Magu
Malé
Republic of Maldives
Tel: + 960 323228
E-mail: mtpb@visitmaldives.com
www.visitmaldives.com.mv

Seychelles

A widely dispersed archipelago of 115 islands (33 inhabited) situated off the coast of East Africa, the Seychelles are bathed by the warm waters of the tropical Indian Ocean. Strong upwelling between Denis and Bird Islands north of Mahé attract numbers of Sperm Whales and other deepwater species. Large numbers of Melon-Headed Whales are a major attraction and often mixed with Risso's Dolphins and other species. A number of companies market whale-watching holidays to the Seychelles.

Main Species: Humpback Whales, Sperm Whales, Melon-Headed Whales, Risso's Dolphins, Pantropical Spotted Dolphins, Fraser's Dolphins.

Other Species Seen: Fin Whales, Sei Whales, Bryde's Whales, Antarctic Minke Whales, Killer Whales, False Killer Whales, Dwarf Sperm Whales, Cuvier's Beaked Whales, Blainville's Beaked Whales, Dense-Beaked Whales, Rough-Toothed Dolphins.

Season: Year round.   **Code of Conduct:** Guidelines under discussion.

Information

Marine Conservation Society Seychelles
PO Box 1299
Victoria, Mahé, Seychelles
Tel: + 248 26 15 11
E-mail: info@mcss.sc
www.mcss.sc

Seychelles Tourism
Independence House
PO Box 1262, Victoria, Mahé, Seychelles
Tel: + 248 61 08 00
E-mail: info@seychelles.net
www.aspureasitgets.com

Africa & the Middle East

Top Spots

Namibia – Haviside's Dolphins in the surf of Walvis Bay.

South Africa – Wintering Southern Right Whales at Hermanus, Walker Bay.

Madagascar – Humpback Whales off Masoala Park.

United Arab Emirates – Inshore Indo-Pacific Humpback & Bottlenose Dolphins.

With the exception of the Canary Islands, near-shore waters of South Africa and Namibia and most recently Masoala Park in Madagascar, the many opportunities for whale and dolphin watching in Africa remain virtually untapped. Two species of dolphins, Haviside's (often misspelled Heaviside's) and Atlantic Hump-backed, are found only in Africa, as are a large percentage of the world's Pygmy Right Whales. Five major ocean currents swirl around the edges of the continent, creating several major upwelling zones with a super-abundance of fish and invertebrate food. These support large populations of whales and dolphins.

Atlantic Humpback Dolphins probably occur widely in West Africa, from Dakhla Bay in southern Morocco south to the coasts of Cameroon and Guinea-Bissau. The West African nations of The Gambia and Senegal are popular holiday destinations. Bottlenose, Atlantic Humpback and Common Dolphins occur along the coasts, especially in and around the mouths of the Casamance, Sénégal and Gambia Rivers. Bryde's Whales are seen offshore.

The east coast of Africa offers several excellent locations for Humpback Whales as well as Indo-Pacific Bottlenose and Indo-Pacific Hump-Backed Dolphins, two inshore species of special interest to many traveling whale watchers. In the Republic of South Africa, the Cape Town area, especially the holiday resort town of Hermanus, represents one of the world's premier whale-watching destinations. Southern Right Whales occur all along the coastline and can easily be seen from land and numerous other species are found in the surrounding waters.

Egypt

Many dive companies on the Red Sea coast of Marsa Alam offer opportunities to view and swim with dolphins. The Shaab Samadai Reef, often referred to as the Dolphin House Reef, is one of the most popular areas. The large horseshoe-shaped reef encloses a shallow natural lagoon. Sheltered from the ocean currents, the lagoon is a traditional site used by groups of adult female Spinner Dolphins with calves. Unfortunately, the sheer volume of tourists and unscrupulous practices of some boat operators resulted in unacceptable reef damage caused by illegal use of anchors and uncontrolled pollution and put so much pressure on the local Spinner Dolphins that they deserted the site. The Egyptian Government stepped in and has established strict regulations including setting aside areas where the dolphins cannot be disturbed. The Dolphin House Reef is now a National Park. Trips run weekly from Hurghada and Soma Bay and daily from Marsa Alam.

Main Species: Spinner and Long-Beaked Common Dolphins.

Season: Year round.   **Code of Conduct:** Voluntary guidelines. Swimming permitted.

Information

Egyptian Tourist Board
Misr Travel Tower
Abassia Square
Abassia, Cairo, Egypt
Tel: + (2) 285 4509 or 284 1970
E-mail: contact@touregypt.net
www.touregypt.net

Egyptian Tourist Authority
630 Fifth Avenue
Suite 2305
New York, NY 10111 USA
Tel: 212 332 2570
E-mail: info@egypttourism.org
www.egypttourism.org

Kenya

Malindi Marine National Park

Located on the coast north of Mombasa, the town of Malindi is a well-known centre for big-game fishing, drawing the writer and fisherman Ernest Hemingway in the 1930s. The Malindi and Watamu marine reserves are administered by the Kenya Wildlife Service, primarily for the impressive coral reefs, but provide important habitat for inshore dolphins, notably the tidal mangrove swamps. Many sport diving companies offer dolphin-watching excursions or impromptu opportunities to swim with dolphins when encountered. A few operators use traditional sailing vessels known as dhows, providing a more tranquil way to get out on the water. Humpback Whales, Spinner and Spotted Dolphins are usually found in deeper water beyond the reefs, while Indo-Pacific Bottlenose Dolphins are more likely to be encountered in the surf zone or in clear water at the mouths of rivers. Indo-Pacific Hump-Backed Dolphins are found in similar habitat but also over reefs and in turbid channels with mangrove forests and between sandbanks.

Kisite – Mpunguti Marine National Park

Some 75 miles (120 km) south of Mombasa, the marine park and in particular the Wasini Channel, is a good spot for Indo-Pacific Humpbacks. Many consider the coral reefs here some of the best in Kenya and a few days visiting this beautiful tropical coastline with its reefs and mangroves makes a nice end-of-trip extension to a Kenyan Safari.

Main Species: Humpback Whales, Indo-Pacific Hump-Backed, Indo-Pacific Bottlenose, Spinner and Spotted Dolphins

Season: September–March.   **Code of Conduct:** Please check with local operators.

Information

Kenya Tourist Board
PO Box 30630, Nairobi, 00100 Kenya
Tel: + (202) 711 262
E-mail: info@kenyatourism.org
www.magicalkenya.com

Embassy of Kenya
2249 R Street NW
Washington, DC 20008 USA
Tel: 202 387 6101
www.kenyaembassy.com

Madagascar

The newly established Masoala National Park (840 square miles / 2176 sq km) is an expanse of tropical wilderness on the roadless edge of Antongil Bay. Cetaceans are found in the bay all year, with breeding Humpback Whales the main attraction. The whale-watching industry here is new and now regulated, so please be conscientious in choosing an operator. The following species are encountered with regularity: Humpback Whales and Bottlenose, Spinner and Indo-Pacific Humpbacked Dolphins. Whale watching is possible year round.

Main Species: Humpback Whales.

Other Species Seen: Bottlenose (Indo-Pacific), Spinner and Indo-Pacific Humpback Dolphins.

Season: All year (peak: July–Sept).   **Code of Conduct:** Guidelines in place.
Swimming not permitted.

Information

Ministère de la Culture et du Tourisme de Madagascar (Ministry of Culture & Tourism)

BP 610 rue Fernand , Kasanga Tsimbazaza

Antananarivo 101, Madagascar

Tel: + (2022) 66805

E-mail: mct@tourisme.gov.mg   www.tourisme.gov.mg

Another website with information on Madagascar can be found at www.madagascar-guide.com

South Africa

This is certainly the most accessible and popular whale-watching destination in Africa and one of the top spots in the world. This is in part due to a concerted effort to promote whale-orientated tourism, culminating in the establishment of the award-winning Cape Whale Route. South Africa boasts a diverse cetacean fauna including several species that are difficult to see elsewhere. At least 37 species of whales and dolphins can be found in the waters off South Africa. The diminutive but immensely attractive Haviside's Dolphin is endemic to the cold waters of the Benguela Current that runs along the Atlantic coast from Cape Point up towards southern Angola. They prefer coastal waters of less than 500 ft (150 m) deep and can be seen from land or on short boat trips. The coast around Cape Town is perhaps most famous for Southern Right Whales, and it is estimated that 3000 or more visit South African waters each winter to breed. The population was reduced to only 100 or so animals until the cessation of hunting but now grows at the rate of 7 percent per year. Mating and calving occur in different parts of the coast, the latter concentrated in the sheltered waters of St Sebastian Bay and De Hoop Bay. The "Whale Route" covers 1200 miles (1930 km) of coastline, starting near Cape Town and running eastwards to Durban. Humpback Whales are seen off both Atlantic and Indian Ocean coasts in May to November as they migrate to and from breeding grounds off Mozambique and Angola. Indo-Pacific Humpback Dolphins are a feature of the warmer eastern coast, often found in small groups just beyond the surf zone.

Lambert's Bay

Lambert's Bay is a small coastal fishing port 180 miles (290 km) north of Cape Town, and is an excellent place to find Haviside's Dolphins (year round). They often occur just beyond the surfline, or even within the surf itself, and can be seen from a car park near the harbor mouth, the dunes in front of the Lambert's Bay caravan park or from the Cape gannet colony on Bird Island. Southern Right Whales (July-Nov), Humpback Whales (July-September), Killer Whales, Dusky Dolphins (year round) and Common Dolphins also occur along the coast. There are local short boat trips (2-3 hours) from the harbor to see the dolphins. Morning trips are generally the best. There are several hotels and guesthouses in or near the town. The weather is generally mild to warm. A similar mix of species can be found at Eland's Bay, about 15 miles (25 km) south of Lambert's Bay, and is part of the Cape Whale Route (signposted). Southern Right Whales and other species are often sighted just beyond the breaking surf. The cliffs at Baboon Point on the south side of the Verlorenvlei River estuary offer an ideal vantage point.

Hermanus

Known as the "Heart of the Whale Coast", Hermanus is one of the best whale-watching sites in Africa. The town sprawls along the shore of Walker Bay near the southernmost tip of the African continent. The climate is generally mild, even during the winter rainy season, and summer heat is usually tempered by sea breezes. The peak whale-watching season runs from July to November, with late July and August being the best time to visit. Between 60 and 100 Southern Right Whales visit the bay off Hermanus every year and often come within yards of the shore. If you are lucky, the whales can be seen from your guesthouse or hotel room! Other regular species include Bryde's Whales, Short-Beaked Common Dolphins and Bottlenose Dolphins. Land-based whale watching is popular from Gearings Point near the Old Harbor, at Die Gang to the northeast of Hermanus along Main Road, at Kwaaiwater and from the Voelklip and Grotto beaches. Boat-based trips are also available. The World Wide Fund for Nature (WWF) acknowledges Hermanus and Walker Bay as one of the 12 best whale-viewing sites in the world, especially from shore.

False Bay, Cape Town

This large bay is bordered by Cape Town's most southerly suburbs and extends along the western side of the Cape Peninsula past the naval harbor at Simonstown. The metropolitan train line runs from the city, terminating in Simonstown, offering a scenic trip through seaside villages like Muizenberg, Kalk Bay and Fish Hoek. Good whale-watching lookouts include the watchway between Muizenburg and St James, Boyes Drive (False Bay) and overlooks between Kalk Bay and Lakeside. The species mix is similar to Hermanus with Southern Right Whales, Humpback Whales and Dusky Dolphins the most common. Cetaceans are also frequently seen in Hout Bay on the other side of the peninsula, particularly from various rest spots along Chapman's Peak Road, a meandering cliffside drive about 2000 feet (600 m) above the sea. Besides Southern Right Whales, there is a chance of seeing Haviside's Dolphins, Dusky Dolphins or Killer Whales. Similar species occur in Table Bay. Viewing is possible from vantage points along Victoria Drive which winds between Camps Bay and Llandudno, Sea Point Esplanade, Mouille Point Lighthouse and Blouberg Beach.

Plettenberg Bay

The town of Plett is 5 1/2 hours' drive from Cape Town and provides an excellent base from which to explore the Knysna coast. Plettenberg Bay is best known for its Indo-Pacific Humpback Dolphins, which also occur in bays west to Knysna. Small groups of Humpback Dolphins are often found just beyond the surfline. Kerboom Strand north of Plettenberg and Lookout Beach are excellent land-based viewing spots, sometimes with groups of as many as 100 animals. In addition to resident Bottlenose Dolphins (Indo-Pacific type), Long-Beaked Common Dolphins come into the bay during April and May. Bryde's Whales (year round), Southern Right Whales (July-December) and Humpback Whales (May–July and October-December) are also common. Killer Whales occur on occasion, with May the peak month for sightings.

Durban and KwaZulu-Natal Coast

The eastern coastline of South Africa from Port Elizabeth to the border with Mozambique is very different from that of Cape Town and the west coast. The warm Mozambique-Agulhas Current sweeps down from the tropics providing a strong warming influence. Cetaceans can be seen from numerous lookouts along the length of the coast and include Humpback Whales, Bryde's Whales, Minke Whales, Southern Right Whales, Humpback Dolphins and Bottlenose Dolphins. Large numbers of Short-Beaked Common Dolphins are attracted by schooling sardines during July and August.

Main Species: Southern Right Whales, Bryde's Whales, Haviside's Dolphins and Dusky Dolphins.

Other Species Seen: Killer Whales, Humpback Whales (Apr–July, Sept–Dec), Short-Beaked Common Dolphins.

Season: July–December.   **Code of Conduct:** Enforced regulations. Swimming not permitted.

Information

Cape Town Tourism
103 Louis Building
4 Regent Road,
Sea Point, Cape Town
South Africa
Tel: + 27-21-434-1750
E-mail: info@cape-town.org
www.cape-town.org

Centre for Dolphin Studies
1 Hopwood Street
Central Beach, Plettenberg Bay
Mail to: PO Box 1856
Plettenberg Bay, 6600 South Africa
Tel: + 27 (044) 533 6185

E-mail: cdswhale@worldonline.co.za
www.dolphinstudies.co.za

Lambert's Bay Tourism
28 Church Street
PO Box 245
8130 Lambert's Bay
Western Cape, South Africa
Tel: + 027 432 1000
E-mail: lambertsinfo@mweb.co.za
www.tourismcapetown.co.za

Lambert's Bay Boat Charter
Tel: 027 432 1230
Email: ronselley@kingsley.co.za

For information on Hermanus & Whale Route:
Hermanus Tourism Bureau
Tel: + 27 (0) 28 312 2629
E-mail: infoburo@hermanus.co.za
www.hermanus.co.za

Another website with information on the
Whale Route is www.hermanus.com

South Africa Tourism
Private Bag X10012
Sandton, 2146
South Africa
Tel: + 27 (0) 11 895 3000
Fax: +27 (0) 11 895 3001
E-mail: info@southafrica.net
www.southafrica.net

Namibia

There are strong similarities between the coast of Namibia and the northwestern coast of South Africa. Bathed by the cold Benguela Current from the Antarctic, the coast is cool and often fog-bound and yet juxtaposed with extremely arid desert. Compared to South Africa, Namibia is still relatively under-populated and the so-called Skeleton Coast Park makes for a wonderfully exotic holiday destination. Between June and December (peak in September), Southern Right Whales congregate in sheltered bays to calve and mate. The most accessible of these sites are Lüderitz and Walvis Bays. Walvis Bay's huge natural lagoon is also worth visiting for the hundreds of thousands of seabirds found there. The delightful Haviside's Dolphin occurs close to shore in these same areas.

Lüderitz

The quaint town of Lüderitz is perched on a rocky peninsula between the cold Atlantic Ocean and the arid Namib Desert. This is a reliable site for the semi-endemic Haviside's Dolphin and there have been deep water sightings of the much sought after Southern Right Whale Dolphin.

Main Species: Southern Right Whales.

Other Species Seen: Haviside's Dolphins.

Season: June–December.   **Code of Conduct:** Please check with local operators.

Information

Namibia Tourism Board
Ground Floor Sanlam Centre
Independence Avenue
Private Bag 13244
Windhoek
Namibia
Tel: + 264 61 2906000
FAx: + 264 61 254848
E-mail info@namibiatourism.com. na
www.namibiatourism.com.na

Embassy of the Republic of Namibia
1605 New Hampshire Avenue NW
Washington
DC 20009
USA
Tel: 202 986 0540
Fax: 202-986-0443
E-mail: info@namibianembassyusa.org
www.namibianembassyusa.org

Cape Verde Islands

The Cape Verde Islands are in the Atlantic Ocean, 385 miles (620 km) west of West Africa's coast at Mauritania. The archipelago is volcanic in origin and rises from the deep abyssal plain beyond the African continental shelf. There are 10 major islands and five islets, all of volcanic origin and grouped into the Barlavento (Windward) group (Santo Antão, São Vicente, Santa Luzia, Ilheu Branco, Ilheu Raso, São Nicolau, Sal and Boa Vista) to the north and the Sotavento (Leeward) group (Maio, São Tiago, Fogo and Brava) to the south. Waters are cooler than along the West African coast.

Humpback Whales occur around the islands during the winter months and based on photo-IDs are thought to be animals that spend the summer in waters off Iceland and Norway. Pilot Whales and Rough-Toothed Dolphins are also commonly encountered. The Cape Verde Islands are also an important nesting site for loggerhead sea turtles. International flights arrive on Sal and there are local flights or ferries between the islands. Whale watching is most popular off the western and southern coasts of Boa Vista.

Main Species: Humpback Whales.

Other Species Seen: Pilot Whales and Rough-Toothed Dolphins.

Season: Year round.   **Code of Conduct:** Please check with local operators.

Information

CI: Agência Cabo-verdiana de Promoção do Investimentos (Promotion of Investments, Tourism and Exports in Cape Verde) Rotundo do Cruz do Papa Achada Santo António, PO Box 89C, Praia, Santiago Cape Verde Tel: + 260 4111/0 E-mail: cvinvestment@cvtelecom.cv www.virtualcapeverde.net

Embassy of the Republic of Cape Verde 3415 Massachusetts Avenue NW Washington, DC 20007 USA Tel: 202 965 6820

Cape Verde Consul in England 18-20 Stanley Street Liverpool L1 6AF UK Joao.Roberto@capeverdeconsul.com www.capeverdeconsul.com

The Persian Gulf and Gulf of Oman

Comprising a federation of seven independent states or emirates, the United Arab Emirates (UAE) is located on the Arabian Peninsula at the mouth of the Persian Gulf where it connects into the Gulf of Oman and Arabian Sea (Indian Ocean). The "Gulf" is also bordered by Iran, Saudi Arabia, Qatar, Bahrain, Kuwait and Iraq.

The generally shallow waters exhibit strong tidal movements and are rich in marine wildlife including several species of dolphins and whales. Indo-Pacific Humpback Dolphins and Indo-Pacific Common Dolphins are relatively common in shallower inshore waters and can be seen in many places around the Persian Gulf.

The Bahrain Yacht Club in Sitra organizes twice-daily dolphin-watching trips. Indo-Pacific Humpback Dolphins are often seen in and around a deep-water channel running out from the Bahrain Yacht Club and along past the Al Dar Islands. There have been a number of Killer Whale sightings in this area. Several dolphin species are possible on crossings to the Hawar Islands from the Ad Dur Jetty. Finless Porpoises are rare but possible in coastal shallows with sandy bottoms. Additional survey work is urgently needed to establish the true status of Finless Porpoises in the region.

In the Gulf of Oman, off Al Fujairah and Muscat, the water becomes much deeper and attracts Sperm Whales, Long-Beaked Common Dolphins (*tropicalis* form) and Risso's Dolphins along the continental shelf edge and associated canyons. Circular motion of the surface waters, especially during the monsoon season, causes continuous upwelling of cooler and nutrient-rich waters, promoting plankton blooms that attract several species of baleen whales. The Oman Dive Centre in Bandar Jissah (25 minutes from Muscat) runs daily dolphin-watching trips, typically encountering several species of dolphin and occasional Sperm or Humpback Whales.

The weather in the region is usually warm to very hot, but during the winter (Dec to Feb) northerly winter winds (*shamal*) can sweep down the Gulf, making boat-based viewing more difficult. Shallow areas with large beds of seagrass may also hold dugongs, which were once very numerous in the Gulf but have declined due to hunting and pollution. It is estimated that 7500 remain, with the majority in the UAE, Bahrain, Qatar, and Saudi Arabia.

Main Species: Indo-Pacific Humpback Dolphins, Long-Beaked Common Dolphins, Indo-Pacific Bottlenose Dolphins.

Other Species Seen: Humpback Whales, Blue Whales, Fin Whales, Sei Whales, Bryde's Whales, Minke Whales, Sperm Whales, False Killer Whales, Spinner Dolphins, Risso's Dolphins, and Finless Porpoises.

Season: All year (best late March to July).
Code of Conduct: Check with local operators. Oman operates under voluntary guidelines.

Information

Bahrain Yacht Club,
PO Box 5390, Manama-Bahrain
Arabian Gulf, Bahrain
Tel: 1770 0677
www.bahrainyachtclub.com.bh/

Bahrain Tourism Company
PO Box 5831
Manama, Bahrain
Tel: + 7 530 530
E-mail: btc@alseyaha.com
www.alseyaha.com

Environment Society of Oman
Office Location:
Office number: 103
Mezzanine floor, Building number: 87
Building name: Al-Aali House
Way number: 3501, Al-Khuwair
Postal Address
PO Box. 3955, P.C. 112, Ruwi
Sultanate of Oman
Tel: 24482121
Fax: 24486876
www.environment.org.om/

United Arab Emirates
Department of Information & Culture
PO Box 17
Abu Dhabi
UAE
www.uaeinteract.com

Oman Ministry of Tourism
PO Box 200
Postal Code 115
Muscat,
Sultanate of Oman
Tel: + 968 245 88700
www.omantourism.gov.org

Oman Dive Centre
PO Box 199,
Madinat Al Sultan Qaboos P. C 115,
Sultanate of Oman
Tel: +(968) 24824240
Fax: +(968) 24824241
Email: info@omandivecenter.com
www.diveoman.com.om/

Oman Whale and Dolphin Research Group
Tel: + 968 246 96912
www.whalecoastoman.com

Kerguelen

This extremely remote volcanic archipelago lies in the southern Indian Ocean and is part of the French Southern and Antarctic Territories. Because of their remoteness, very few people have the opportunity to visit the islands. The population rarely tops 100, almost all scientists working out of the main research base at Port-Aux-Français. Occasionally the more adventurous expedition cruise ships will visit the islands en route across the Indian Ocean. In terms of whale watching, the Kerguelen Islands are notable for an isolated population of Commerson's Dolphins, a species that is otherwise endemic to the southern tip of South America and nearby Falkland Islands, some 5000 miles (8000 km) to the west. There are differences between the two populations and it is not inconceivable they will be treated as separate species at some time in the future. Commerson's Dolphins are most commonly sighted in the Golfe du Morbihan on the eastern side of the island near the scientific base.

Main Species: Commerson's Dolphins, Dusky Dolphins.

Other Species Seen: Blue Whales, Fin Whales, Sei Whales, Antarctic Minke Whales, Humpback Whales, Southern Right Whales, Pygmy Right Whales, Arnoux's Beaked Whales, Killer Whales, Long-Finned Pilot Whales, Hourglass Dolphins.

Seasons: November to March.   **Code of Conduct:** Please check with local operators.

Information

Territoire des Terres Australes et Antarctique Françaises
Rue Gabriel Dejean, 97410 Saint Pierre,
France
Tel: +33 (0)262967802   Fax: +33 (0)262967806
E-mail: taaf.com@wanadoo.fr   www.taaf.fr/

Mer et Voyage (Travel Operator)
9, Rue Notre Dames des Victoires
75002 Paris, France
Tel: +33 (0)149269333   Fax: +33 (0)142962939
E-mail: info@mer-et-voyages.com
www.meretvoyages.com/

Australasia, Oceania & Antarctica

Top Spots

Australia – Migrant Humpbacks and Southern Right Whales along the New South Wales coast.

Australia – People-friendly dolphins of Monkey Mia in the extreme west.

New Zealand – Close encounters with Sperm Whales and Dusky Dolphins off Kaikoura.

New Zealand – Hector's Dolphins in the shelter of Akaroa Harbour near Christchurch.

Tonga – Swimming with Humpback Whales.

The Pacific is the largest of all the oceans, encompassing a full third of the earth's surface or nearly 70 million square miles (180 million sq km). Extending from pole to pole and incorporating more than 25,000 islands, the Pacific contains an extraordinary diversity of habitats and is home to a substantial proportion of the world's marine mammals. This section focuses on the whale-watching possibilities in several of the more accessible Pacific island groups such as Hawaii, Tonga and New Zealand. Collectively these island groups are referred to as "Oceania". Australia is also included here, primarily because its most populated coastlines are influenced more by the Pacific than the Indian Ocean. Most of the Pacific islands and atolls are formed from the tops of submarine volcanoes or coral reefs. Sometimes they are a mixture of both. Several enormous trenches (including the Tonga, Kermadec and Marianas Trenches) plunge to extraordinary depths.

Following the lead taken by the Cook Islands, a number of South Pacific nations have created whale sanctuaries, which also protect resident populations of dolphins. The focus is on Humpback Whales, which migrate northwards from Antarctica in order to breed in the warm waters of the tropical Pacific. A number of the archipelagos, especially those with large lagoons, provide shelter for Humpback Whales during the austral winter and in many, there is a growing whale-watching industry offering both land- and boat-based viewing. Arguably, Vava'u in the Tonga Group is one of the most popular locations, in part because visitors are allowed to snorkel (but not scuba or free-dive) with the whales. Inshore dolphins, principally Dusky, Spinner and Bottlenose Dolphins, are also found in many of the whale sanctuaries. Deep-water species such as False Killer Whales, Pygmy Killer Whales, Melon-Headed Whales, Pygmy Sperm Whales, Dwarf Sperm Whales, Fraser's Dolphins and Striped Dolphins occur between the island groups. To see some of these, the adventurous might try one of the freight ships that run from Tahiti through the Tuamotu Archipelago and Marquesas Islands. In terms of whale and dolphin watching, the tropical Pacific represents one of the least-explored frontiers and we can look forward to many new developments as more scientists and whale watchers explore this immense area.

Papua New Guinea

Papua New Guinea (PNG) lies north of Australia, just south of the equator. The country is made up of some 600 islands and has some 800 indigenous languages. Heralded as the new "cetacean hotspot", PNG offers tremendous potential for superb whale watching in a fascinating part of the world. One of the best-known spots, Kimbe Bay, on the northern side of New Britain Island, is visited by Killer Whales, which apparently feast on large fish including hammerhead sharks! Spinner, Risso's and Bottlenose Dolphins, False Killer and Melon-Headed Whales also occur. Dugongs can be found over seagrass beds. The area is popular with divers and dive-boats can be rented by whale watchers. In May 2002, Papua New Guinea designated its entire Exclusive Economic Zone, roughly 200 miles, as a whale sanctuary.

Kimbe Bay (West New Britain Province)

Straddling the Bismark and Solomon Seas, this popular dive spot on the north side of New Britain Island supports a remarkable diversity of marine life. In addition to Killer Whales, recent surveys have found Sperm, Melon-Headed, False Killer, Pygmy Killer and Short-Finned Pilot Whales, Risso's, Bottlenose, Indo-Pacific Bottlenose, Spinner and Rough-Toothed Dolphins. Sightings have been concentrated around Stettin Bay, with Spinner and Indo-Pacific Bottlenose being the most numerous. The area is also internationally famous for its extraordinary coral reefs. Accommodation is available at several dive lodges. There are regular flights from the capital Port Moresby to Hoskins.

Milne Bay (Milne Bay Province)

Located on the southeastern tip of the main island, Milne Bay is the site of an important World War II battle. The full whale-watching potential of the area has yet to be fully explored but is likely to be comparable to Kimbe Bay. There are a number of lodges and village guest-houses and the main town of Alotau (Gurney Airport) can be reached by daily flights from Port Moresby.

Main Species: Sperm Whales, Killer Whales, Spinner and Indo-Pacific Bottlenose Dolphins.

Other Species Seen: False Killer and Melon-Headed Whales, Risso's and Bottlenose Dolphins.

Season: Year round.　　**Code of Conduct:** Please check with local operators.

Information

Papua New Guinea Tourism
Promotion Authority
PO Box 1291
Port Moresby
Papua New Guinea
Tel: + 675 3200 211
E-mail : info@pngtourism.org.pg
www.pngtourism.org.pg

Embassy of Papua New Guinea
to the Americas
1779 Massachusetts Avenue NW
Suite 805,
Washington, DC 20036 USA
Tel: 202 745 3680
E-mail: info@pngembassy.org
www.pngembassy.org

Australia

With a coastline of 44,000 miles (70,000 km) (including nearby islands), Australia is the smallest continent, but combines a wide variety of landscapes with a rich ocean environment that includes all five of the world's ocean temperature zones: tropical, subtropical, temperate, subpolar and polar. The East Australian Current runs along the east coast of Australia and the Leeuwin Current runs along the west. In Queensland, Dwarf Minke Whales visit the Great Barrier Reef during the austral winter (May–Aug) and often approach boats, sometimes even allowing swimmers in the water with them. The Great Barrier Reef Marine Park Authority oversees a strict code of conduct for swimmers in the Ribbon Reefs and Offshore Port Douglas Sectors of the marine park.

Hervey Bay

This is a traditional calving area for Humpback Whales, which are present between late July and early November. Whale watching in Hervey Bay began in 1987 and shortly afterwards, the area was designated a Marine Park, with the Queensland National Parks and Wildlife Service controlling the number of commercial operators, enforcing whale-watch regulations and monitoring the effects of whale watching. Bottlenose and the Indo-Pacific Humpback Dolphins are relatively common in the bay and are often seen from shore points such as the Urangan Pier. The Indo-Pacific Humpbacks favor shallow areas with mangroves or the estuarine habitat and it is not uncommon to encounter dugongs in the same areas.

Main Species: Humpback Whales, Bottlenose Dolphins, Indo-Pacific Humpback Dolphins.

Other Species Seen: Risso's Dolphins, Common Dolphins.

Season: July–November.   **Code of Conduct:** Enforced regulations. Swimming with dolphins permitted under controlled conditions.

Information

Try 'Discover Hervey Bay' for whale-watching information: www.hervey.com.au

Tourism Queensland
Level 10, Queensland House,

30 Makerston Street
Brisbane, QLD 4000, Australia
Tel: + 61 7 3535 3535
E-mail: info@tq.com.au
www.queenslandholidays.com.au

New South Wales Coast

Cape Solander near Sydney and other headlands along the New South Wales (NSW) coast from Cape Byron in the north to Red Point in the south provide ideal whale-watching spots during the austral winter. The main attraction are migrant Humpback Whales; up to 1000 animals in a season swim past the key watch points as they travel between their Antarctic feeding grounds and calving grounds in the warm Coral Sea off the Queensland coast. The northwards migration along the NSW coast begins in May and continues to the end of July, with the same animals returning southwards between September and November. Inshore migration is so impressive that this stretch of coastline has been described as a "whale superhighway".

Southern Right Whales pass through in smaller numbers later in winter and are often seen in very shallow water, including estuaries and bays. Bottlenose Dolphins also feature from many of the lookouts or enter river mouths. The New South Wales National Parks and Wildlife Service has established a whale-watching platform at Cape Solander at the end of the Kurnell Peninsula. Sheer cliffs and an open horizon create an ideal vantage point for viewing migrating whales, which often come within yards of the shore. Other popular land-based viewing sites include Iluka Bluff (Bundjalung National Park), Angourie Point (Yuraygir National Park), Smoky Head (Hat Head National Park), Tomaree Head (Tomaree National Park), Crac
neck Lookout (Wyrrabalong National Park), Barrenjoey Headland (Ku-ring-gai Chase National Park), North Head (Sydney Harbour National Park), Cape Banks (Botany Bay National Park), NSW Jervis Bay National Park, Moruya Head (Eurobodalla National Park), and Red Point (Red Ben Boyd National Park).

Boat trips will encounter plenty of Humpback and Southern Right Whales as well but also give visitors the chance to find several additional species including Blue Whales, Bryde's Whales, False Killer Whales, Killer Whales, and Common Dolphins. Organized whale-watching cruises are available from Coffs Harbor, Sawtell, Port Stephens, Jervis Bay, Eden, Sapphire Coast and Bermagui/Montague Island. In Port Macquarie the harbor cruises often encounter Bottlenose Dolphins in the mouth of the Hastings River and there are conventional offshore whale-watching excursions as well.

Main Species: Humpback Whales, Southern Right Whales and Bottlenose Dolphins.

Other Species Seen: Blue Whales, Bryde's Whales, False Killer Whales, Killer Whales, Indo-Pacific Humpbacked Dolphins, and Common Dolphins.

Season: May–November.   **Code of Conduct:** Enforced regulations. Swimming with dolphins permitted under controlled conditions.

Information

Tourism New South Wales
GPO Box 7050, Sydney, NSW 2001, Australia
Tel: + 61 2 9931 1427
E-mail: visitor.callcentre@tourism.nsw.gov.au
www.sydneyaustralia.com

Sapphire Coast Tourism
Office 2, 163 Auckland Street
PO Box 424, Bega, NSW 2550
E-mail: info@saffhirecoast.com.au
www.sapphirecoast.com.au/whales

Monkey Mia and Shark Bay, Western Australia

Shark Bay is located near the most westerly point of Australia, around 500 miles (800 km) north of Perth. The area is considered of international significance and was listed as a World Heritage Site in 1991. The Monkey Mia Dolphin Resort is located on a section of World Heritage coastline 17 miles (27 km) from the town of Denham. Most mornings (07.00 – 12.00), three females (bottlenose dolphins) and their offspring visit the beach to receive fish from the Department of Conservation and Land Management (CALM) rangers. Visitors are permitted to enter the shallows and assist in the feeding under the supervision of the rangers. Humpback Whales use Shark Bay as a staging post on migration and Killer Whales and Southern Right Whales are seen occasionally. Besides the cetaceans, Shark Bay has one of the largest populations of dugongs in the world (approx. 16,000) and these fantastic animals are often encountered in and around the seagrass beds.

Main Species: Bottlenose Dolphins.

Other Species Seen: Humpback and Southern Right Whales.

Season: All year (peak June–Nov). **Code of Conduct:** Enforced regulations. Swimming with dolphins permitted under controlled conditions.

Information

Monkey Mia Dolphin Research Foundation (Australia), PO Box 140, Claremont Western Australia, 6010, Australia
E-mail: akc24@georgetown.edu
www.monkeymiadolphins.org

Monkey Mia Dolphin Research Foundation (United States), c/o David and Kayo Burman, 21 Colchester Rd, Weston,
MA 02493,
United States

Fremantle, Western Australia

The Perth Canyon cuts a deep trough into the continental shelf and runs west before plunging down to the abyssal plain. Blue Whales, probably the so-called "Pygmy" form of Blue Whale, migrate south into the Canyon, arriving as early as November but with peak numbers in March, to May. By late June most have left. The whales use the canyon to feed on krill (*Euphasia recurva*) which are particularly abundant at the eastern end. Blue Whales are also seen off Exmouth, Cape Leeuwin and in Geographe Bay. A strong upwelling along the "Bonney" coast of Victoria also attracts Blue Whales in spring. Between May and June, numbers of Southern Right Whales arrive on the southern coast of Australia (from Apollo Bay to Portland) to give birth, raise their calves and mate before returning to the Antarctic for the summer. The lookout platform at Logan's Beach in Warrnambool is perhaps the best spot in Victoria to view Southern Right Whales, with occasional sightings of Humpback (June–Nov) and Blue Whales. Boat charters are available from the Breakwater Jetty in Warrnambool. Stops along the Great Ocean Road that connects to Melbourne may also yield Southern Right Whales.

Port Hedland, Western Australia

Humpback Whales occur from July to October as they migrate to the warmer waters to breed.

Main Species: Humpback Whales, Blue Whales, Southern Right Whales.

Other Species Seen: Common Dolphins.

Season: March–October, dolphins year round. **Code of Conduct:** Enforced regulations. Swimming with dolphins permitted under controlled conditions.

Information

Port Hedland Tourist Bureau
13 Wedge St , PO Box 664
Port Hedland
WA 6721
Australia
Tel: + 61 8 9173 1711
Email: phtbinfo@norcom.net.au

Western Australian Visitor Centre
Forrest Place
Perth,
WA 6000
Australia
Tel: + 61 8 9483 1111
www.westernaustralia.com

Tasmania

From May to late July Humpback and Southern Right Whales migrate along the coasts en route to warmer breeding areas and return in August, September and October on their way to Antarctica. A few Southern Right Whales will calve in Tasmanian waters. Sei Whales occur in summer, and dolphins, porpoises and Killer Whales are fairly common. Whale-watching tours are available from Hobart, Orford, Pirates Bay, Storm Bay, Port Dalrymple, St Helens and Tamar River.

Main Species: Humpback and Southern Right Whales.

Other Species Seen: Sei Whales and Killer Whales, Bottlenose Dolphins and porpoises.

Season: May–October.　**Code of Conduct:** Enforced regulations. Swimming with dolphins permitted under controlled conditions.

Information

Tourism Tasmania
GPO Box 399, Hobart, Tasmania
7000, Australia
Tel: + 61 3 6230 8235
E-mail: reception@tourism.tas.gov.au
www.discovertasmania.com.au

Parks & Wildlife Service
GPO 1751, Hobart,
Tasmania
7001 Australia
www.parks.tas.gov.au/wildlife/
mammals/whales.html

New Zealand

The mountainous islands of New Zealand lie in extraordinarily rich seas, a product of several different oceanic currents that bathe the islands in both warm and cold water. The North Island and many small associated islets receive the warming influence of the East Cape and East Australian Currents resulting in subtropical sea conditions. The South Island is more influenced by the cold West Wind Drift. Consequently, the Subtropical Convergence bisects New Zealand, with the Antarctic Convergence that forms a relatively short distance to the south. There are large areas of relatively shallow shelf waters such as the Chatham Rise and Challenger Plateau as well as deep trenches, including the Hikurangi Trench, which comes very close to shore at Kaikoura.

With thousands of miles of unspoiled coastline bathed in nutrient-rich seas, New Zealand can boast a stunning variety of marine wildlife that includes a number of species of whales and dolphins. These can be viewed from shore and on boat excursions. Almost half the world's cetacean species have been sighted in New Zealand's waters. Specialities include the endemic Hector's Dolphin, which has a total population of fewer than 4000 animals and is listed as endangered on the International Red List of Species. Hector's Dolphin numbers are rapidly dwindling and genetic studies have shown that the species consists of only three or four distinct populations that do not interbreed. All are affected by entrapment in gillnets. Commercial tours in search of Hector's Dolphins are available at Akaroa, Greymouth, Waikawa (near Picton) and elsewhere.

Other inshore dolphins such as Dusky, Bottlenose and Common can be seen in many places around the coast. Commercial whale and dolphin watching ventures, including swim-with-dolphin options, are available in many coastal towns and the New Zealand Department of Conservation (DOC) administers Marine Mammals Protection Regulations, developed to manage the rapidly growing whale- and dolphin-watching industry. There are two marine mammal sanctuaries, one around the Banks Peninsula near Christchurch designed to protect Hector's Dolphins and the other around the Auckland Islands, which is a major breeding area for Southern Right Whales and New Zealand sea lions.

North Island

There are a number of coastal harbors scattered across the North Island that offer trips to swim with Common and Bottlenose Dolphins. These include several towns on the Bay of Islands (Paihia); Whangamata on the Bay of Plenty, Whitianga on the Coromandel Peninsula 125 miles (200 km) east of Auckland.

Greymouth, South Island

The largest town on the west coast of the South Island is situated appropriately enough at the mouth of the Grey River where it empties into the Tasman Sea. The river mouth is a favored spot for Hector's Dolphins. Swimming with dolphins is not allowed.

Milford and Doubtful Sounds, South Island

A popular tourist destination, Milford Sound has a resident pod of 40-60 Bottlenose Dolphins with even larger numbers in Doubtful Sound.

Kaikoura, South Island

There is little doubt that Kaikoura, on the northeastern coast of the South Island, is one of the top locations. Here the end of the deep Hikurangi submarine trench comes very close to shore and the combination of deep water and towering, often snow-capped, mountains makes for a very memorable experience. More than 100 male Sperm Whales are present in these waters year round and Dusky Dolphins are also very abundant, especially on the deeper southern side of the peninsula. Sometimes the dolphins are gathered into huge herds numbering hundreds, if not thousands, of animals. Although present all year, the Dusky Dolphins tend to come closer to shore during the summer months (Oct–April) when it is not unusual for whale-watching tours to encounter pods of 200-300 animals. Visitors can witness the spectacular aerobatics that are very characteristic of this species as well as other aspects of their highly social lives. Calves are born in the spring (Sept–Dec). Other regularly encountered species include Humpback Whales (June–July), Killer Whales (Oct–April), Long-Finned Pilot Whales, Common Dolphins and the endemic Hector's Dolphins.

Kaikoura lies within the Southern Hemisphere Whale Sanctuary. The town of Kaikoura is situated on the northern side of a small rocky peninsula and can be reached easily from Christchurch or Picton by air, rail or road (2-2.5 hours). There are plenty of bed & breakfasts, motels, hotels and campsites in and around the town. Several local families run commercial whale-watching and swim-with-dolphins ventures. Sometimes the weather can make it too rough to go out and it is well worth planning several days in the area to ensure success. It is also advisable to book in advance, especially during summer and/or school holidays, as the trips can be very popular. When the dolphins are close to shore, they are only 10 minutes away from the dock, other times it can take an hour of searching. The water can be chilly (11° C in the winter months climbing to 18° C in summer) but fortunately wetsuits are provided. Alternatively, you can view the larger whales from the air by taking a helicopter ride. This is a little unusual but does provide a unique perspective on these immense animals. The DOC is undertaking a research program to assess the impact of tourist vessels on the behavior of Sperm Whales and Dusky Dolphins at Kaikoura.

Akaroa, Christchurch and Lyttelton Harbours, South Island

This small fishing town on the Banks Peninsula lies close to Christchurch on South Island (80-90 minute drive). Akaroa is the only French settlement in New Zealand and many streets and local families still bear French names. Hector's Dolphins are resident in the narrow harbor inlet from September to May but can be encountered at any time of year. Tours run daily. The best months are from November to April. Cruises last for three hours or so and it may be possible to snorkel with the dolphins using a wetsuit for buoyancy and warmth. Visitors to Christchurch can cruise the scenic Lyttelton Harbour, which hosts Hector's Dolphins and other marine wildlife.

Chatham and Subantarctic Islands

Fin Whales and Gray's Beaked Whales are sometimes encountered by ships crossing the Chatham Rise en route to Dunedin or Lyttelton Harbour.

Main Species: Hector's and Dusky Dolphins.

Other Species Seen: Humpback Whales, Sperm Whales, Killer Whales and Bottlenose Dolphins.

Season: September–May.   **Code of Conduct:** Enforced regulations. Swimming with dolphins permitted under controlled conditions.

Information

New Zealand Whale and Dolphin Trust
PO Box 56, Dunedin
New Zealand
Tel: + 64 3 479 7980
Fax: + 64 3 479 8336
E-mail: nzwdtrust@hotmail.com
www.nzwhaledolphintrust.tripod.com

Tourism New Zealand
PO Box 95, Wellington
New Zealand
Tel: + 64 4 917 5400
www.newzealand.com

Kaikoura Information & Tourism Inc.
West End
Kaikoura
New Zealand
Tel: +64 3 319 5641
Fax: +64 3 319 6819
Email: info@kaikoura.co.nz
www.kaikoura.co.nz

Whale Watch® Kaikoura Ltd
Tel: + 64 3 319 6767
Email: res@whalewatch.co.nz
www.whalewatch.co.nz/a

New Caledonia

New Caledonia is the third-largest island in the Pacific and is located about 900 miles (1500 km) east of Australia and 620 miles (1000 km) northeast of New Zealand. A genuine tropical paradise with unique wildlife, New Caledonia comprises Grande Terre (the mainland), the Isle of Pines, the Loyalty Islands, Belep archipelago and numerous smaller islets. The main island, Grande Terre, is encircled by an immense reef enclosing the largest coral lagoon in the world. More than 100 Humpback Whales use the southern end of the lagoon and waters around Lifou (Loyalty Islands) as a breeding area. In August 2003, New Caledonian Exclusive Economic Zone (EEZ) waters were declared a whale sanctuary. From July to September, organized whale-watching excursions operate from the capital city, Nouméa, as well as other harbors along the southern side of the main island. Spinner and Bottlenose Dolphins can be viewed at the Ténia marine reserve, a popular diving area 60 miles (97 km) north of Nouméa. Dugongs (sea cows) also occur in the lagoon and might be encountered on whale-watching excursions.

Main Species: Humpback Whales, Bottlenose and Spinner Dolphins.

Season: July–September.   **Code of Conduct:** Voluntary code of practice.

Information

Opération Cétacés (Cetacean Project)
BO 12872
998802 Nouméa, New Caledonia
Tel: + 687 241 634
E-mail: op.cetaces@offratel.nc
www.offratel.nc/op.cetaces

New Caledonia Tourism South
BP 688
98845 Nouméa Cédex, New Caledonia
Tel: + 687 242 080
E-mail: info@nctps.com
www.nctps.com

Vanuatu (New Hebrides)

This group of 83 islands lies northeast of New Caledonia and northwest of Fiji. In addition to Humpbacks, Sperm Whales, Spinner Dolphins, Short-Finned Pilot Whales and Pan-Tropical Spotted Dolphins have all been observed.

Main Species: Humpback Whales, Sperm Whales, Spinner Dolphins, Pan-Tropical Spotted Dolphins.

Other Species Seen: Short-Finned Pilot Whales.

Season: Year round.   **Code of Conduct:** Please check with local operators.

Information

Vanuatu Tourism
Promocom Ltd, PO Box 1163, Port Vila
Vanuatu
Tel: +678 267 18
E-mail: info@vanuatu.com.vu   www.vanuatutourism.com

Fiji

The Republic of the Fiji Islands comprises an archipelago of several hundred islands, with Viti Levu and Vanua Levu being the largest. The islands are a very popular destination for tourists seeking tropical beaches or superb diving. The best time to visit is during the dry season (May to Oct) when rainfall and humidity are lower. The international airport at Nadi is located on the western side of Viti Levu and is the primary entry point for most visitors; many of whom then take ferries or local flights to other islands, notably the Mamanuca Islands. Spinner Dolphins are relatively common year-round throughout the archipelago and often come in to bow-ride. Two groups of Spinners live in Natewa Bay near the Lomalagi Resort on Savusavu (daily flights from Nadi). Other resident pods are found near Namotu, Waya, Yasawa, Taveuni and Nukurauvula Passage, a popular dive site. Organized dolphin-watching excursions are available on the western coast of Viti Levu or may be arranged through local dive-boat operators.

Small numbers of Humpback Whales (peak July and Aug), Sperm Whales (year round), Killer Whales, Short-Finned Pilot Whales and Bottlenose Dolphins occur as seasonal migrants. In 2003, the Fiji government declared the Exclusive Economic Zone of 486,500 sq miles (1.26 million sq km) a whale sanctuary. Tagging studies in the 1950s showed that the Humpback Whales migrated to New Zealand and eastern Australia.

Main Species: Spinner Dolphins.

Other Species Seen: Humpback Whales, Sperm Whales, False Killer Whales, Killer Whales, Short-Finned Pilot Whales, Fraser's Dolphins and Bottlenose Dolphins.

Season: May–Oct.   **Code of Conduct:** Please check with local operators.

Information

Fiji Visitors Bureau,
Suite 107 Colonial Plaza,
Namaka, Nadi, Fiji Islands
Tel: + 679 6722 433
Email: infodesk@bulafiji.com
www.BulaFiji.com

The Americas Fiji Visitors Bureau
5777 West Century Blvd, Suite 220
Los Angeles, CA 90045 USA
Tel: 310 568 1616; Toll Free 800 932 3454
E-mail: infodesk@bulafiji-americas.com
www.fijifvb.gov.fj

Tonga

This large archipelago lies directly south of Western Samoa and is composed of 96 inhabited islands, subdivided into three main groups: Vava'u, Ha'apai, and Tongatapu. The capital city, Nuku'alofa, is on the largest island, Tongatapu. With a royal decree, the King of Tonga banned all whaling within Tongan waters in 1978. Whale watching in Tonga is centered mainly on the Humpbacks, which migrate to the islands in June to breed. This is one of only a few locations in the world that offers the thrilling opportunity to get in the water with Humpbacks. However, other exciting species such as False Killer Whales, Short-Finned Pilot Whales, Spinner and Bottlenose Dolphins are also often encountered.

Vava'u

Located in northern Tonga, the small island group of Vava'u is a Mecca for whale enthusiasts. From July to November, Humpback Whales migrate from Antarctica to the sheltered and shallow waters throughout the island group to calve and mate. Getting in the water with these immense animals, armed with only a snorkel and perhaps an underwater camera, is becoming very popular. Tours run from Neiafu, capital of the Vava'u Island Group, and from Mounu beach resort. Average water temperatures at this time of the year are a very comfortable 24 to 28° C. Visits can be arranged privately or as organized tours including those focusing on photography. Some tours spend the mornings with the whales, with the afternoons devoted to the more leisurely pursuits typical of a tropical paradise, including snorkeling on the reefs.

Main Species: Humpback Whales.

Other Species Seen: Short-Finned Pilot and False Killer Whales, Spinner and Bottlenose Dolphins.

Season: July–November.   **Code of Conduct:** Guidelines in place. Swimming permitted.

Information

Tonga Visitors Bureau
PO Box 37
Vuna Road,
Nuku'alafa
Kingdom of Tonga
Tel: + 676 25334
E-mail: info@tvb.gov.to
www.tongaholiday.com

WhaleSwim Adventures
PO Bag #49
Neiafu, Vava'u
Kingdom of Tonga
Tel: (676) 71266
Fax: (676) 70024
Email: whales@kalianetvav.to
www.whaleswim.com

Niue

The island of Niue is one of the world's largest coral islands and sits atop an undersea mountain with pristine clear water that is sometimes hundreds of feet deep right at the shore. There are no significant rivers or streams on the entire island and rainwater simply filters through the coral structure, entering the ocean devoid of any silt run-off and thus crystal clear.

Like Tonga, Niue has become a popular destination for people wishing to snorkel with Humpback Whales (Aug to Oct). In addition to mothers with calves, visitors may occasionally encounter playful groups of males. Scuba and free-diving is not permitted. Local diving operators can be chartered for whale and dolphin watching. There are twice-weekly flights from New Zealand (3 hours).

Main Species: Humpback Whales.

Other Species Seen: Spinner Dolphins.

Season: June–October.

Code of Conduct: Voluntary guidelines in place.

Information

da Talagi-Hekesi
Niue Tourism Office
PO Box 42
Alofi
Niue Island
Tel: + 683 4224
Email: niuetourism@mail.gov.nu
www.niueisland.com

The South Pacific Tourism Organisation (SPTO) promotes tourism throughout the South Pacific, including Niue:
PO Box 13119, Suva,
Fiji Islands
Telephone: (679) 330 4177
Fax: (679) 330 1995
www.spto.org

Cook Islands

The Cook Island archipelago lies about 2000 miles (3220 km) south of Hawaii in the South Pacific. There are 15 principal islands which are clustered into two main groups and spread over some 850,000 square miles (2.2 million sq km) of tropical ocean. The majority of the human population lives on the so-called "High Islands" that form the southern group and are most easily visited by tourists. In 2001 the Cook Islands government declared 772,000 sq miles (2 million sq km) of the South Pacific Ocean within the country's Exclusive Economic Zone as the Cook Island Whale Sanctuary. Their intention is to combat the devastation of commercial whaling and provide a positive example to other Pacific nations who might similarly establish protected areas. Besides banning scientific or commercial whaling, the sanctuary forbids harassment or accidental capture (by-catch) of whales and dolphins.

Humpback Whales migrate to the waters surrounding the Cook Islands in July to mate and calve, remaining until October when they return to Antarctic waters. They are most numerous off the largest islands, Rarotonga (north and west coasts) and Atiu, and are often visible from shore. Humpbacks can also be seen around Aitutaki, Palmerston and Penrhyn. A number of other species occur within the CIWS, including Short-Finned Pilot Whales and Spinner Dolphins. These are all regularly encountered by chartered sport-fishing and diving boats. Away from the islands, the seabed drops very steeply, providing excellent habitat for deep-diving species such as Sperm Whales, which appear to be resident and can be seen breaching, as well as some of the more elusive beaked whales.

In recent years, small family groups of Dense-Beaked Whales have approached small boats off Aitutaki and Roratonga, allowing absolutely spectacular views in the clear water. An unidentified whale which was photographed off Rarotonga in September 2000 may be one of the first live sightings of the newly described Omura's Whale (*Balaenoptera omurai*). Rarotonga is the entry point for the Cook Islands by air, with internal flights to most of the other inhabited islands. There is a new Whale Center in Avarua on Rarotonga.

Main Species: Humpback Whales, Short-Finned Pilot Whales, Dense-Beaked Whales, Spinner Dolphins.

Other Species Seen: Killer Whales, Cuvier's and Blainville's Beaked Whales.

Season: July–October.   **Code of Conduct:** Voluntary guidelines.

Information

Cook Islands Whale Research (CCRC)
Box 3069
Avarua Rarotonga
Cook Islands,
South Pacific
Tel: + 682 21 666
E-mail: info@whaleresearch.org
www.whaleresearch.org

Cook Islands Tourism
PO Box 14
Rarotonga
Cook Islands,
South Pacific
Tel: + 682 29 435
E-mail: headoffice@cook-islands.com
www.cook-islands.com

American Samoa

This is a good place to see Humpback Whales between August and October. By December most have migrated south past New Zealand to spend the austral summer feeding in the rich waters around Antarctica. The eroded volcanic crater of Fagatele Bay has been designated a National Marine Sanctuary and extensive coral reef provides a haven for Humpback Whales and several species of dolphin.

Main Species: Humpback Whales, Spinner Dolphins.
Other Species Seen: Bottlenose Dolphins.

Season: August–October.
Code of Conduct: Please check with local operators.

Information

Office of Tourism
Department of Commerce
American Samoa Government
PO Box 1147
Pago Pago
American Samoa 96799
Tel: + 684 633 1091
E-mail: samoa@samoatelco.com
www.amsamoa.com

National Park of American Samoa
(Part of the US National Park Service)
C/O The Superintendent
Pago Pago,
American Samoa 96799 USA
tel: 011-684-633-7082
fax: 011-684-633-7085
e-mail NPSA_Administration@nps.gov
www.nps.gov/npsa/

Hawaiian Islands (USA)

The spectacular volcanic islands of the Hawaiian chain rise dramatically out of the North Pacific, thrusting up from the abyssal plain some 18,000 feet (5486 m) below. This is the world's most isolated archipelago, situated more than 1800 miles (2900 km) from the nearest landmass. The main attractions for the whale watcher are Humpback Whales and Spinner Dolphins. In 1997, the Hawaiian Islands Humpback Whale National Marine Sanctuary was established to protect this important mating and calving ground for Humpbacks (mid December to end of April). Two-thirds of the entire North Pacific population (approximately 4000-5000 whales) migrate into the comparatively warm and shallow waters around the main Hawaiian Islands of Kauai, Oahu, Hawaii, Maui, Molokai, Lanai and Kaho'olawe to breed, calve and nurse their young.

More than 40 companies operate whale-watching boats in the archipelago. Many of these excursions leave from the marina on Wharf Street in Lahaina (Maui) or At Kihei (Maui) and Kewalo Basin (Oahu). Although the peak season for Humpbacks is from January to March, boats from the main islands may operate year-round, focusing on toothed whales and dolphins. There are also plenty of opportunities to see Humpback Whales and dolphins from land-based watch points. On the southwest coast of Kauai, try Highway 50 between Kekaha and Hanapepe, on Hawaii Hwy 270 between Lapakahi State Park to Upolu Point and along the lee (Kona) coast from Kiholo Bay to Kealakekua Bay. Although the weather is invariably warm, it is often windy, making it impossible to go offshore and even difficult to look for whales and dolphins from land. Under these conditions try some of the more sheltered bays or inter-island channels.

Main Species: Humpback Whales and Spinner Dolphins.

Other Species Seen: Bottlenose Dolphins, Pygmy Killer Whales, Short-Finned Pilot Whales.

Season: Mid December–April.

Code of Conduct: National Marine Fisheries Service regulations in place. Swimming with captive dolphins permitted under controlled conditions.

Information

Hawaiian Islands Humpback Whale
National Marine Sanctuary,
726 South Kihei Road
Kihei, HI 96753
USA
Tel: + 808 879-2818
E-mail: hihumpbackwhale@noaa.gov.
www.hawaiihumpbackwhale.noaa.gov

Hawaii Whale Research Foundation
PO Box 1296
Lahaina, HI 96767, USA
www.hwrf.org

Island Marine Institute
658 Front Street, #101
Lahaina, Maui, Hi 96761
email: info@whalewatchmaui.com
Toll Free 1 866 410 6284

Hawaii Visitors Bureau
2270 Kalakaua Avenue
Suite 801, Honolulu, HI 96815, USA
Tel: + 808 923 1811
E-mail: info@hvcb.org   www.gohawaii.com

Activity and Attractions Association of Hawaii
355 Hukilike Street
Kahului, Hi 96732, USA
Telephone: 808-871-7947   Fax 808- 877- 3104
Email: info@hawaiifun.org
www.hawaiifun.org

Ocean Sports – Waikoloa
PO Box 383699, 69-275 Waikoloa Beach Drive,
Waikoloa, Hi, USA 96738
Tel: +1 808 886 6666   Fax: +1 808 886-9407
information@hawaiioceansports.com
www.hawaiioceansports.com

Ross Sea / Antarctica

The Ross Sea is an immense bay that cuts into the Antarctic Continent and covers an area the size of southern Europe. The name itself has special significance to anyone with an interest in the history of Antarctic exploration, as this was the starting point for many of the grueling overland journeys to the heart of the continent. A complex system of frontal zones, moving water masses and currents contribute to the circulation of water throughout the Southern Ocean.

The Ross Sea is also special in terms of its wildlife and remains one of the biologically richest areas in Antarctica. Large areas of open water mixed with thin ice known as *polynyas* are prominent features and play an important role in phytoplankton production and in heat transfer from the ocean to the atmosphere. Several species of baleen whales are attracted by the abundance of crystal krill (*Euphausia crystallorophias*) that feast on the phytoplankton bloom. Antarctic Minke and Blue Whales are relatively common along the ice edge and even within it. Killer Whales and Sei Whales are also numerous. Several beaked whales have been reported by survey ships including Southern Bottlenose, Arnoux's, Gray's and Strap-Toothed. Whaling logs confirm that Southern Right Whales occurred in the Ross Sea in numbers before they were exterminated by relentless harvesting. Hopefully they will return as the population slowly recovers.

A number of expedition-style cruises visit the Ross Sea during the summer months. Most sail from Australia (Hobart) or New Zealand (Invercargill, Lyttelton), visiting one or two of the sub-Antarctic islands (usually Macquarie, Campbell or Auckland Island) en route. Sightings of several species of cetaceans are likely during the voyage south, including the spectacular black-and-white Hourglass Dolphin that favors the nutrient-rich waters around the Antarctic Convergence. Other abundant wildlife within the Ross Sea includes crabeater, Weddell, and Ross seals.

Main Species: Blue Whales, Antarctic Minke Whales, Killer Whales, Hourglass Dolphins.

Other Species Seen: Humpback Whales, Fin Whales, Sei Whales, Long-Finned Pilot Whales, Strap-Toothed Whales, Gray's Beaked Whales.

Seasons: December to February.   **Code of Conduct:** Enforced regulations.

Information

The following companies offer superb expedition-style cruises to the Ross Sea:

Heritage Expeditions (NZ)
53 B Montreal Street
Christchurch
New Zealand
Phone: 03 365 3500
Fax: 03 365 1300
E-mail: info@heritage-expeditions.co.nz
www.heritage-expeditions.com

Quark Expeditions
1019 Boston Post Road
Darien, CT 06820
USA
Tel: +1 (203) 656 0499
Fax: +1 (203) 655 6623
E-mail: enquiries@quarkexpeditions.com
www.quarkexpeditions.com

Resource Directory
Further Reading

Cetacean Societies: Field Studies of Dolphins and Whales, by Janet Mann, Richard Connor, Peter Tyack & Hal Whitehead, University of Chicago Press (2000). ISBN 0226503410. A detailed account of cetacean social behavior.

Encyclopedia of Marine Mammals, edited by William Perrrin, Bernd Wursig & JGM Thewissen, Academic Press (2002). ISBN 0125513402. A comprehensive, authoritative and fascinating survey of everything to do with marine mammals.

A Field Guide to the Marine Mammals of the World: Whales, Dolphins and Seals, by Hadoram Shirihai & Brett Jarrett (illustrator), A & C Black, London (2006). ISBN 0713670371. Excellent for accurate field identification.

A Guide to Whales, Dolphins and Porpoises, by Mark Carwardine, Erich Hoyt, R Ewan Fordyce & Peter Gill, Fog City Press, San Francisco (1998). ISBN 1877019496. A richly illustrated overview.

Killer Whales of Southern Alaska by C Matkin, G Ellis, E Saulitis, L Barrett-Lennard, D Matkin, North Gulf Oceanic Society (1999). ISBN 0963346792. A long-term Killer Whale study.

Killer Whales: The Natural History and Genealogy of Orcinus orca in British Columbia and Washington State, by John K B. Ford, G M. Ellis, K C. Balcom, UBC/UWP (2003). ISBN 0295979585. Contains over 300 identification photographs from this study area.

Transients: Mammal-Hunting Killer Whales of British Columbia, Washington, and Southeastern Alaska, by John K B. Ford, G M. Ellis, UBC/UWP (1999). ISBN 0295978171. A natural history describing over 200 Killer Whales in this long-term study area.

National Audubon Society Guide to Marine Marine Mammals of the World, by P. Folkens, (illustrator); R. R. Reeves, B. S. Stewart, P. J. Clapham, J. A. Powell (contributors), Alfred A. Knopf, New York (2002). ISBN 0375411410. A superbly illustrated and detailed identification guide suitable to take in the field.

Whale Nation, by Heathcote Williams, WDCS (1988). ISBN 0517569329.

The Oceanic Society Field Guide to the Gray Whale, by The Oceanic Society (1989). ISBN 0912365250. Gray Whale natural history and whale watching.

On the Trail of the Whale, by Mark Carwardine, Thunder Bay Publishing Co (1994). ISBN 1899074007. Entertaining whale-watching experiences from around the world.

Voyage to the Whales, by Hal Whitehead, Chelsea Green Pub Co (1990). ISBN 0930031253. A pioneering book on whale studies.

Whales & Dolphins: Cetacean World Guide by R Kiefner, Conch Books (2002). ISBN 3925919589.

Whales, Dolphins and Porpoises, by James D. Darling, Flip Nicklin, Kenneth S. Norris, Hal Whitehead and Bernd Würsig, National Geographic Society (1995). ISBN 0792229525.

Whales Dolphins and Porpoises by Mark Carwardine, illustrated by Martin Camm. Dorling Kindersley (2000). ISBN 0751327816. A detailed illustrated guide to cetaceans.

Whales & Dolphins of the World, by M Simmonds, The MIT Press (2004). ISBN 0262195194. A comprehensive overview, richly illustrated.

WorldLife Library

Accessible and superbly illustrated natural history portraits written by internationally recognized experts in the field. Published by Colin Baxter Photography and Voyageur Press.

Beluga Whales, by Tony Martin (2002). ISBN 1841070823.

Blue Whales, by John Calambokidis & Gretchen Steiger (1997). ISBN 1900455218.

Bottlenose Dolphins, by Paul Thompson & Ben Wilson (2001). ISBN 1841071161.

Discovering Whales, Dolphins & Porpoises, by Tony Martin (2003). ISBN 1841071730.

Dolphins, by Ben Wilson (2002). ISBN 1841071633.

Gray Whales, by Jim Darling (1999). ISBN 1900455625.

Humpback Whales, by Phil Clapham (2004). ISBN 1841072567.

Killer Whales, by Sarah Heimlich & Jim Boran (2001). ISBN 1841070785.

Killer Whales, by Robin Baird (2002). ISBN 184107103X.

Minke Whales, by Rus Hoelzel & Jonathan Stern (2000). ISBN 1900455757.

Porpoises, by Andrew Read (1999). ISBN 1900455609.

Right Whales, by Phil Clapham (2004). ISBN 1841072559.

Sperm Whales, by Jonathan Gordon (1998). ISBN 1900455528.

Whales, by Phil Clapham (2001). ISBN 1841070955.

Regional Whale-Watching Guides

The Complete Guide to Antarctic Wildlife, Birds and Marine Mammals of the Antarctic Continent and Southern Ocean, by Hadoram Shirihai and Brett Jarrett (Illustrator), Princeton University Press (2002). ISBN 0691114145.
A ground breaking, illustrated field guide.

Guide to Marine Mammals of Alaska, by Kate Wynne and illustrated by Pieter Folkens, Alaska Sea Grant College Program, University of Alaska, Fairbanks (1993). ISBN 1566120098.
A handy guide to Alaska and the Bering Sea.

Guide to Marine Mammals and Turtles of the U.S. Atlantic & Gulf of Mexico, by Kate Wynne and Malia Schwartz, illustrated by Garth Mix. Rhode Island Sea Grant, University of Rhode Island (1999). ISBN 0938412434.
A convenient and well-designed guide.

Guide to Whale Watching: Britain & Europe by Mark Carwardine, New Holland Publishers (UK) Ltd (2003). ISBN 1843300591.
Recently updated whale-watching guide.

Marine Protected Areas for Whales Dolphins and Porpoises, by Erich Hoyt, Earthscan, London (2005). ISBN 1844070646.
A comprehensive and fascinating catalogue.

Whales, Dolphins, and Porpoises of the Eastern North Pacific and adjacent Arctic Waters: A Guide to Their Identification, by Stephen Leatherwood, Randall R. Reeves, William F. Perrin and William E. Evans, Dover Publications, New York (1988). ISBN 0486256510.
An old, but still excellent publication.

Whale Watching, by Nicky Leach, Insight Discovery Guides (1999). ISBN 1563318369. An illustrated whale-watching guide to the USA and the Caribbean.

Whale Watch: A Guide to Whales and Other Marine Mammals of South Africa, by Vic Cockcroft and Peter Joyce, Struik Publishers, Cape Town (1998). ISBN 1868721639.
An introduction to South African cetaceans.

The Whale Watcher's Guide: Whale-Watching Trips in North America, by Patricia Corrigan, NorthWord Press (1999). ISBN 1559716835.

Whale Watching in Australian & New Zealand Waters, by Peter Gill and Cecilia Burke, New Holland Publishers Ltd (1999). ISBN 1864364726. Very useful descriptions of a large number of whale-watching sites, accompanied by helpful maps.

Whale Watching in Iceland, by Asbjorn Bjorgvinsson & Helmut Lugmayr, JPV Publishers (2002). ISBN 9979761555. An unusual and attractive publication describing Icelandic species and locations.

Web Sites & Electronic Media

The growth of the Internet has revolutionized the dissemination of information and is an extremely useful resource for whale watchers. To prevent this book becoming as thick and dense as a telephone directory, we have deliberately chosen to limit individual companies or boats offering whale- or dolphin-watching opportunities. There are literally far too many nowadays and businesses change from year to year. We strongly recommend that readers use the gazetteer section of this book to pick localities of interest and then search the web to find companies that operate in or visit those places. For many of the top whale-watching destinations, local operators maintain informative web sites in English and other languages that provide accurate schedules, details of the boats and prices. It is often possible to make reservations on-line or at least find a telephone number so that you can call ahead to check on conditions and make sure they have a place for you. Operators often provide news of recent sightings, driving directions to get you to the dock and details of local accommodation.

Whale-Watching Database www.wdcs.org and follow the "Whale Watching" links to the database. This site is run by the Whale and Dolphin Conservation Society and includes a useful search tool that allows the selection of species, location, time of year, type of platform and the presence of guides.

Whale-Watching-Web. Useful collection of links. www.physics.helsinki.fi/whale/

WhaleGuide.com A large collection of links to whale- and dolphin-watching trips around the world. www.whaleguide.com/directory/index.htm

Of course the web can be used for more than finding places to go and watch whales. It is also possible to watch whales directly over the net! There are several sites with web cams overlooking hotspots and one of leaders has been the Orca-Live site: www.orca-live.net. In addition to being able to see Killer Whales in the waters off northern Vancouver Island via the webcam, the site also streams live underwater sound from a network of hydrophones. This allows you to listen – in real time – to their haunting calls.

Organizations

There are many charities and societies that cater for the entire range of interests from enthusiasts to advocacy groups to professional societies.

ANTARCTIC

International Association of Antarctica Tour Operators (IAATO): *Aims to advocate, promote and practice environmentally responsible private-sector travel to the Antarctic.* www.iaato.org

AUSTRALIA

The Oceania Project: PO Box 646, Byron Bay, New South Wales 2481. Tel: + 61 2 6685 8128   www.oceania.org.au

WDCS Australia: PO Box 720, Port Adelaide Business Centre, South Australia 5015. info@wdcs.org.au   www.wdcs.org.au

BAHAMAS

Wild Dolphin Project: PO Box 8436, Jupiter, FL 33468, USA. Tel: + 1 561 575 5660 wdp@igc.org   www.wilddolphinproject.com

CANADA

GREMM (Group for Research and Education on Marine Mammals): C.P. 223, 108, de la cale sèche, Tadoussac, Québec, Canada G0T 2A0. Tel: + 1 418 235 4701   www.gremm.org

International Marine Mammal Association Inc.: 1474 Gordon St.,Guelph, Ontario, Canada N1L 1C8. Tel: + 1 519 767 1948   www.imma.org

EUROPE

ACCOBAMS – *Agreement on the Conservation of Cetaceans in the Black and Mediterranean Seas.* Permanent Sectariat: Jardins de l'UNESCO, La Terrasses de Fontvieille, MC 98000, Monaco. Tel: + 377 93 15 81 10 mcvanklaveren@accobams.mc www.accobams.mc

ASCOBANS – *Agreement on the Conservation of Small Cetaceans of the Baltic and North Seas* Secretariat can be reached at United Nations Premises in Bonn: Martin-Luther-King-Str. 8, 53175 Bonn, Federal Republic of Germany. Tel: + 49 228 815 2416   www.ascobans.org

European Cetacean Society (ECS): *promotes and coordinates the scientific study and conservation of marine mammals.* www.broekemaweb.nl/ecs/

IUCN: The World Conservation Union Rue Mauverney 28, Gland 1196 Switzerland Tel: + 41 (22) 999-0000   www.iucn.org

ICELAND

Húsavík Whale Center: PO Box 172, 640 Húsavík, Iceland. Tel: + 354 464 2522 icewhale@centrum.is   www.icewhale.is

IRELAND

Irish Whale & Dolphin Group (IWDG): Gortagrenane, Castlefreke, Clonakilty, Co. Cork, Ireland. Tel: + 353 23 31911 enquiries@iwdg.ie   www.iwdg.ie

ITALY

Delphis – Mediterranean Dolphin Conservation: Island of Ischia, via Zaro 22, 80075 Forio, Naples, Italy. Tel: + 39 081 989578 info@delphismdc.org   www.delphismdc.org

Tethys Research Institute: c/o Acquario Civico, Via Pompeo Leoni 2, 20141 Milano I, Italy. Tel: + 39 0258 314889 tethys@tethys.org   www.tethys.org

JAPAN

Ogasawara Whale Watching Association (OWA): *Helps manage, educate and regulate whale watching in the tropical Ogasawara Islands.* Chichi-jima, Ogasawara-mura, Tokyo, 100-2101, Japan.
Tel: + 81 4998 2 3215
www.h2.dion.ne.jp/~owa/english

NEW ZEALAND

New Zealand Whale and Dolphin Trust:
PO Box 56, Dunedin, New Zealand.
Tel: + 64 3 479 7980   Fax: + 64 3 479 8336
nzwdtrust@hotmail.com
www.nzwhaledolphintrust.tripod.com

NORWAY

The Andenes Whale Centre:
PO Box 58, 8483 Andenes, Norway
Tel: + 47 76 11 5600
post@whalesafari.no   www.whalesafari.no

NORCA – Norwegian Killer Whale Project:
www.killerwhale.no

SEYCHELLES

Marine Conservation Society Seychelles:
PO Box 1299, Victoria, Mahé, Seychelles
Tel: + 248 26 15 11
info@mcss.sc   www.mcss.sc

SOUTH AFRICA

Centre for Dolphin Studies: PO Box 1856, Plettenberg Bay, 6600, South Africa.
Tel: + 27 44 533 6185
cdswhale@worldonline.co.za
www.dolphinstudies.co

TONGA

Whale Quest Foundation:
PO Bag 49, Vava'u, Tonga
info@whalequest.com   www.whalequest.com

UNITED KINGDOM

International Fund for Animal Welfare (IFAW): 87-90 Albert Embankment,
London, SE1 9UD, United Kingdom.
Tel: + 44 (0)20 7587 6700
Info-uk@ifaw.org   www.ifaw.org

International Whaling Commission (IWC): *Is perhaps, at first sight, an unlikely listing, but the IWC performs a range of work to promote cetacean conservation and whale-watching guidelines.*
The Red House, 135 Station Road, Impington, Cambridge, CB4 9NP, UK.
Tel: + 44 (0)1223 233 971
secretariat@iwcoffice.org   www.iwcoffice.org

Organization Cetacea (ORCA): 7 Ermin Close, Baydon, Marlborough, Wiltshire SN8 2JQ.
Tel/Fax: + 44 (0)191 548 1850
www.orcaweb.org.uk

Sea Watch Foundation:
11 Jersey Road, Oxford, 0X4 4RT, UK.
Tel: + 44 (0)1865 717276
info@seawatchfoundation.org.uk
www.seawatchfoundation.org.uk

Whale and Dolphin Conservation Society (WDCS): *An international organization dedicated to the protection and conservation of cetaceans and their environment through funding of research and awareness campaigns.*
WDCS – The Whale and Dolphin Conservation Society:
Brookfield House, 38 St Paul Street, Chippenham, Wiltshire, SN15 1LY, UK.
Tel: + 44 (0)1249 449500
info@wdcs.org   www.wdcs.org

World Wildlife Fund (WWF) – UK:
Panda House, Weyside Park,
Godalming, Surrey, UK
Tel: 01483 426444   www.wwf.org.uk

UNITED STATES OF AMERICA

American Cetacean Society (ACS): *California-based organization that promotes education.* PO Box 1391, San Pedro, CA 90733-1391, USA. Tel: + 1 310 548 6279 info@ACSonline.org   www.acsonline.org

Center for Cetacean Research & Conservation: 800 Mere Point Road, Brunswick, Maine 04011, USA. Tel: + 1 207 729 1543 www.whaleresearch.org

Earthwatch Institute: *Engages people with scientific field research and education to promote better ecological understanding.* International Headquarters: 3 Clock Tower Place, Suite 100, Box 75, Maynard, MA 01754, USA. Tel: + 1 800 776 0188   www.earthwatch.org

Hawaii Whale Research Foundation: PO Box 1296, Lahaina, HI 96767, USA   www.hwrf.org

International Fund for Animal Welfare (IFAW): *Works to improve animal welfare, prevent cruelty and protect wildlife worldwide.* International Headquarters: 411 Main Street, PO Box 193, Yarmouth Port, MA 02675, USA. Tel: + 1 508 744 2000   Fax: + 508 744 2009 info@ifaw.org   www.ifaw.org

National Oceanic & Atmospheric Administration: 14th Street & Constitution Avenue, NW, Room 6217, Washington, DC 20230, USA. Tel: + 1 202 482 6090   www.noaa.gov

Ocean Alliance & The Whale Conservation Institute: 191 Weston Road, Lincoln, MA 01773, USA. Tel: + 1 781 259 0423 www.oceanalliance.org

Oceanic Society: Fort Mason Center, San Francisco, CA 94123, USA. Tel: + 1 800 326 7491   www.oceanic-society.org

Provincetown Center for Coastal Studies: 115 Bradford Street, PO Box 1036, Provincetown, MA 02657, USA. Tel: + 1 508 487 3622 Fax: + 1 508 487 4495 www.coastalstudies.org/

Sierra Club: *With over a quarter of a million members this grassroots America-based organization works to protect communities and the wider environment.* National Headquarters: 85 Second Street, 2nd Floor, San Francisco, CA 94105, USA. Tel: 415 977 5500   www.sierraclub.org

Society for Marine Mammalogy (SMM): *A non-profit organization based in North America but with a global membership.* PO Box 692042, Orlando, FL, 32869-2042, USA. Fax: + 1 407 352 3459 www.marinemammalogy.org

Whale and Dolphin Conservation Society (North America): 70 East Falmouth Highway, East Falmouth, MA 02536, USA. Tel: + 1 508 548 8328 contact@whales.org   www.whales.org

Wildlife Conservation Society (WCS): *Saves wildlife and wild lands through science, international conservation, education, and management.* 2300 Southern Boulevard, Bronx, NY 10460, USA.   www.wcs.org

World Wildlife Fund (WWF): *The world's largest privately financed conservation organization that aims to protect endangered species, their habitats and address global threats. Active in more than 100 countries.* WWF – US: 1250 Twenty-Fourth Street, N.W., PO Box 97180, Washington, DC 20090-7180. Tel: + 1 202 293 4800   www.worldwildlife.org

Index

*Entries in **bold** indicate pictures.*

UNITED KINGDOM ORGANIZATIONS

British Divers Marine Life Rescue:
Lime House, Regency Close,
Uckfield TN22 1DS.
Tel: 01825 765546
www.bdmlr.org.uk

Cetacean Research & Rescue Unit
(CRRU): PO Box 11307, Banff,
AB45 3WB. Tel: 0845 1081422
(local rate, UK only) 01261 851696
www.crru.org.uk

Cornwall Wildlife Trust:
Five Acres, Allet, Truro TR4 9DJ.
Tel: 01872 273939
www.cornwallwildlifetrust.org.uk

Dolphins and Seals of the Moray
Firth: Tourist Information Centre
Grounds, North Kessock,
Ross & Cromarty IV1 1XB.
Tel: 01463 731866
www.highland.gov.uk/educ/publicser
vices/visitorcentres/dolphins.htm

Dorset Marine Mammal Research:
Durlston Country Park, Lighthouse
Road, Swanage BH19 2JL.
Tel: 01929 421111
www.durlstonmarineproject.co.uk

Friends of the Moray Firth Dolphins:
4 Craigview, Findochty, Banffshire
AB56 4QF. Tel: 01542 833867
www.loupers.com

Hebridean Whale & Dolphin Trust:
28 Main Street, Tobermory,
Isle of Mull PA75 6NU.
Tel: 01688 302620   www.hwdt.org

The Irish Whale & Dolphin Group
(IWDG): Gortagrenane, Castlefreke,
Clonakilty, Co. Cork, Ireland
Tel: + 35 323 31911   www.iwdg.ie

Sea Watch Foundation: 11 Jersey Rd,
Oxford OX4 4RT. Tel: 01865 717276
www.seawatchfoundation.org.uk

Sea Trust (South & West Wales):
Tynewydd, Goodwick,
Pembrokeshire, SA64 0JY.
Tel: 01348 875639
info@seatrust.org.uk
www.seatrust.org.uk

Shannon Dolphin and Wildlife
Foundation: Merchants Quay,
Kilrush, County Clare, Ireland
Tel: + 35 365 905 2326
www.shannondolphins.ie

Shetland Sea Mammal Group:
www.nature-shetland.co.uk/
seamammal/index

WDCS – The Whale and Dolphin
Conservation Society:
Brookfield House,
38 St Paul Street,
Chippenham, SN15 1LY.
Tel: 01249 449500
www.wdcs.org

First published in Great Britain in 2006 by
Colin Baxter Photography Limited, Grantown–on–Spey, PH26 3NA, Scotland

www.worldlifelibrary.co.uk

Copyright © Colin Baxter Photography Ltd 2006. Text © 2006 Ben Wilson & Angus Wilson.
Illustrations © 2006 Keith Brockie. Maps © 2006 Colin Baxter Photography based on mapping supplied
by Map Resources. Essays on pages 126-149 © 2006 authors noted.

ISBN 1-84107-329-6   978-1-84107-329-3   Printed in China

Photography © 2006 by:
Colin Baxter: pages: 1, 2, 6, 10, 12, 13, 15, 20, 21,
    26, 30, 36, 54, 139, 150, 164, 170, 172, 177
Chris Beer: page 159
Mark Carwardine: page: 4
Mark Carwardine/NHPA: page 19
Brandon Cole/naturepl.com: Front Cover
Phillip Colla/SeaPics.com: page 42
Sue Flood: pages 18, 58
Danny Frank/SplashdownDirect: page 178
Francois Gohier: pages 16, 37, 41, 44, 45, 49, 50,
    61, 126, 141, 146, 154, 156, 157, 167, 174
Francois Gohier/ardea.com: pages 28, 134
Heimir Hardar/SplashdownDirect.com: page 166
Hiroto Kawaguchi/SeaPics.com: page 145
Ralf Kiefner/SeaPics.com: page 129

T Kitchin & V Hurst/NHPA: page 142
George McCallum/SeaPics.com: page 25, 168
Hiroya Minakuchi/SeaPics.com: pages 8, 29
Flip Nicklin/Minden Pictures/FLPA: pages 38,137
Michael S Nolan/SeaPics.com: pages 57, 132
Doug Perrine/SeaPics.com: page 171
Charlie Phillips Images: pages 148, 149
Robert L Pitman/SeaPics.com: pages 55,131
Todd Pusser: page 9
Todd Pusser/SeaPics.com: page130
Douglas David Seifert/ardea.com: page 135
Paul A Sutherland/SeaPics.com: page 24
Masa Ushioda/SeaPics.com: page 63
Ingrid Visser/SeaPics.com: pages 33, 173, 181
Doc White/SeaPics.com: page 140
Stephen Wong/SeaPics.com: pages 53, 133

Front Cover Photograph: *Humpback Whale, Frederick Sound, Alaska.* Back Cover Illustration: *Gray Whale & Spinner Dolphin.*